Preventive and Curative Intervention in Mental Retardation

Preventive and Curative Intervention in Mental Retardation

Edited by
Frank J. Menolascino, M.D.
Chairman
Department of Psychiatry
University of Nebraska Medical Center
Omaha
and
Jack A. Stark, Ph.D.
Department of Psychiatry
University of Nebraska Medical Center
Omaha

·P A U L·H·
BROOKES
PUBLISHING CO

Baltimore • London • Toronto • Sydney

Paul H. Brookes Publishing Co.
Post Office Box 10624
Baltimore, Maryland 21285-0624

Typeset by The Composing Room, Grand Rapids, Michigan.
Manufactured in the United States of America by
The Maple Press Company, York, Pennsylvania.

Library of Congress Cataloging-in-Publication Data

Preventive and curative intervention in mental retardation.

   Includes bibliographies and index.
   1. Mental retardation—Prevention.   2. Mental retardation—
Treatment.   I. Menolascino, Frank J., 1930–   II. Stark,
Jack A., 1946–   . [DNLM: 1. Mental Retardation—
prevention & control.
WM 300 P9445]
RC570.P695   1988   616.85′88   87-26832
ISBN 0-933716-81-8

Contents

Contributors

Carol R. Angle, M.D.
Department of Pediatrics
University of Nebraska
College of Medicine
42nd & Dewey Avenue
Omaha, NE 68105

Colleen Azen, M.S.
Maternal PKU Collaborative Study
Division of Medical Genetics
Children's Hospital of Los Angeles
Los Angeles, CA 90054-0700

Penelope H. Brooks, Ph.D.
The John F. Kennedy Center
Box 512
George Peabody College
Vanderbilt University
Nashville, TN 37203

David L. Coulter, M.D.
Associate Professor of Pediatrics and
  Neurology
Boston University School of Medicine
Director of Pediatric Neurology
Boston City Hospital
Boston, MA 02118

Allen C. Crocker, M.D.
Boston Children's Hospital
300 Longwood Avenue
Boston, MA 02115

Donald R. Davis, Ph.D.
Clayton Foundation Biochemical
  Institute
University of Texas
Austin, TX 78712

Robert B. Edgerton, Ph.D.
Neuropsychiatric Institute
Center for the Health Sciences
University of California-Los Angeles
760 Westwood Plaza
Los Angeles, CA 90024

Charles J. Epstein, M.D.
Department of Pediatrics, M-650
School of Medicine
University of California, San Francisco
San Francisco, CA 94143-0106

Karol Fishler, Ph.D.
University of Southern California
  School of Medicine
and
Division of Medical Genetics
Children's Hospital of Los Angeles
Los Angeles, CA 90054-0700

Eva Gross Friedman, B.A.
Maternal PKU Collaborative Study
Division of Medical Genetics
Children's Hospital of Los Angeles
Los Angeles, CA 90054-0700

Tammi L. Goldsbury, M.A.
Department of Psychiatry
University of Nebraska Medical Center
42nd & Dewey Avenue
Omaha, NE 68105

Calvin J. Hobel, M.D.
Professor of Obstetrics, Gynecology,
   and Pediatrics
UCLA School of Medicine
Director, Department of Maternal/Fetal
   Medicine
Cedars-Sinai Medical Center
Suite 3210
8700 Beverly Boulevard
Los Angeles, CA 90048

Peter R. Huttenlocher, M.D.
J.P. Kennedy, Jr. Mental Retardation
   Center
Department of Pediatrics
Box 228
University of Chicago
Chicago, IL 60637

Richard Koch, M.D.
Professor of Clinical Pediatrics
University of Southern California
School of Medicine, and Division of
   Medical Genetics
Children's Hospital of Los Angeles
P.O. Box 54700
Los Angeles, CA 90054-0700

Xuanto Leduc, M.D.
Division of Medical Genetics
Children's Hospital of Los Angeles
Los Angeles, CA 90054-0700

Charley M. McCauley, Ph.D.
The John F. Kennedy Center
Box 512
George Peabody College
Vanderbilt University
Nashville, TN 37203

Matilda S. McIntire, M.D.
Creighton University
School of Medicine
Department of Pediatrics
California at 24th Streets
Omaha, NE 68178

Frank J. Menolascino, M.D.
Chairman, Department of Psychiatry
University of Nebraska Medical Center
42nd & Dewey Avenue
Omaha, NE 68105

Edward C. Merrill, Ph.D.
The John F. Kennedy Center
Box 512
George Peabody College
Vanderbilt University
Nashville, TN 37203

Patricia Parton, M.D.
Division of Medical Genetics
Children's Hospital of Los Angeles
Los Angeles, CA 90054-0700

Oscar Resnick, Ph.D.
Senior Scientist
The Worcester Foundation for
   Experimental Biology, Inc.
Shrewsbury, MA 01545

Louis Rowitz, Ph.D.
University of Illinois at Chicago
2035 W. Taylor
Chicago, IL 60645

**Michael Rutter, M.D., C.B.E.,
   F.R.S.**
University of London
Institute of Psychiatry
De Crespigny Park
Denmark Hill
London, SE5 8AF

Jack A. Stark, Ph.D.
Department of Psychiatry
University of Nebraska Medical Center
42nd & Dewey Avenue
Omaha, NE 68105

Elizabeth Wenz, R.D., M.S.
Maternal PKU Collaborative Study
Division of Medical Genetics
Children's Hospital of Los Angeles
Los Angeles, CA 90054-0700

About the Senior Authors

Carol R. Angle is Director of the Toxicology Program, University of Nebraska Medical Center and Professor of Pediatrics in the College of Medicine. She also holds a courtesy appointment in Developmental Psychology, University of Nebraska, Omaha. Prior to her interdisciplinary appointment in Toxicology, she was Chairman of the Department of Pediatrics, College of Medicine, University of Nebraska Medical Center. She has served as President of the American Association of Poison Control Centers. She has served on numerous federal advisory committees in toxicology and is currently a member of the Advisory Council, National Institute of Environmental Health Sciences and the National Academy of Sciences, National Research Council, Subcommittee on Toxicology. She is associate editor of *Clinical Toxicology* and an editor of the *Journal of Toxicology and Environmental Health*.

Penelope H. Brooks is a Professor of Psychology at the George Peabody College for Teachers of the Vanderbilt University. She is also the Director of the Mental Retardation Research Training Program at Vanderbilt, and Coordinator of Research, Experimental School, at the John F. Kennedy Center for Research on Education and Human Development. She is coauthor of the recent book, *Cognitive Aspects of Mental Retardation*. She has also coauthored several articles in such journals as *Developmental Psychology* and the *American Journal of Mental Deficiency*.

David L. Coulter is an Associate Professor of Pediatrics and Neurology and Director of Pediatric Neurology at the Boston University School of Medicine and Boston City Hospital. He also serves as a consultant to the Child Psychiatry Program at the New England Memorial Hospital, Stoneham, MA. Dr. Coulter has served on numerous local, state, and national committees. He is currently serving on the Board of Directors of the Greater Boston Association for Retarded Citizens, serves on the Advisory Board of the Epilepsy Association of Greater Boston, as well as the Prevention Committee of the American Association on Mental Deficiency. He has published extensively in the area of pediatric and child neurology in journals such as *Lancet, JAMA,* and the *New England Journal of Medicine*.

Allen Crocker is Director of the Developmental Evaluation Clinic, located at the Children's Hospital, in Boston, MA. He is Associate Professor of Pediatrics at Harvard Medical School and lecturer in Maternal and Child Health at Harvard School of Public Health. He is currently a member of the New England Pediatric Society, the American Academy of Pediatrics, and the American Association of University Affiliated Programs for Persons with Developmental Disabilities. He has coauthored several books such as *Current and Future Needs for Genetic Services* and *Developmental-Behavioral Pediatrics*. He has authored and coauthored over 36 journal articles and book chapters during his professional career.

Donald R. Davis is a research scientist in nutrition at the Clayton Foundation Biochemical Institute. His research interests include the nutritional assessment of western foods and diets, individuality of nutritional requirements, and nutrition in relation to mental retardation. He is the editor-in-chief of the *Journal of Applied Nutrition* and is a member of the International Academy of Preventive Medicine, American College of Nutrition, and International College of Applied Nutrition. In addition to research, he devotes considerable time to fostering public and professional awareness of nutritional science.

Robert B. Edgerton is Professor-in-Residence in the Department of Psychiatry and Anthropology, and Coordinator of Socio-Behavioral Studies, Mental Retardation Research Center, at the University of California at Los Angeles, CA. He has received research awards from American Association on Mental Deficiency and Association for Retarded Citizens. His authored books include, *Environments and Behavior: The Adaptation of Mentally Retarded Persons,* and *Lives in Process: Mildly Retarded Adults in a Large City.* His numerous articles include contributions to *Mental Retardation, Normalization, Anthropology,* and *Mental Illness.* He has served as President of the Society for Psychological Anthropology, and elected Fellow of the American Association for the Advancement of Science.

Charles J. Epstein is Professor of Pediatrics and Biochemistry at the School of Medicine of the University of California, San Francisco, CA. As a leading authority on research in Down syndrome and aneuploidy, he has numerous publications in such journals as *Trends in Genetics* and *Journal of Experimental Medicine.* He is currently on the editorial board of the *American Journal of Medical Genetics, Human Genetics, Journal of Embryology and Experimental Morphology, Developmental Genetics,* and *Trisomy 21.*

Calvin J. Hobel is the Director of Maternal-Fetal Medicine, Co-Director of the Department of Obstetrics and Gynecology at Cedars-Sinai Medical Center, and Professor of Obstetrics, Gynecology, and Pediatrics at the UCLA School of Medicine. He also holds the Miriam Jacobs Chair in Maternal-Fetal Medicine and is board certified in both obstetrics and gynecology and in maternal-fetal medicine. In 1966, he was the recipient of a Bank of American Giannini Foundation Research Fellowship to train with Sir William Liley in fetal physiology at the National Womens Hospital, Auckland, New Zealand. As Director of the Cedars-Sinai/Harbor-UCLA Maternal-Fetal Medicine Training Program, he coordinates the clinical and research activities of obstetricians/gynecologists who are working toward their subspecialty boards in maternal-fetal medicine with careers planned in academic obstetrics. Dr. Hobel is a Fellow of the American College of Obstetricians and Gynecologists and of the American Gynecological and Obstetrical Society. In 1985, he coauthored the *Institute of Medicine's Report on Preventing Low Birthweight* and the *NIH Report on Prenatal and Perinatal Factors Associated with Brain Disorders.* He is currently the principal investigator of the West Los Angeles Premature Prevention Program, which has shown a significant impact on lowering preterm birth rates. He is the author of over 90 scientific papers and 15 chapters in books related to perinatal medicine.

Peter R. Huttenlocher is Professor of Pediatrics and Neurology and a member of the Committee on Neurobiology at the University of Chicago. He is Chief of the Pediatric Neurology section and attending physician at Wyler Children's Hospital. His research interests include the development of cerebral cortex and the reaction of immature brain to injury. In 1984, he received the Hower Award of the Child Neurology Society in recognition of this work. His clinical writings include the sections on the nervous system and neuromuscular diseases in Nelson's *Textbook of Pediatrics*. He has been a trustee of the Easter Seal Research Foundation and is a member of the medical advisory board of the National Tuberous Sclerosis Association and a member of the editorial boards of *Neuropediatrics* and *Pediatric Neurology*.

Richard Koch is a Professor of Pediatrics at the University of Southern California School of Medicine. He has been involved in many aspects of child development and genetic disorders, having served as the Director of the Child Development Division at Children's Hospital of Los Angeles and as the first Director of the Lanterman Regional Center for the Developmentally Disabled. He was the principal investigator of the Collaborative PKU Study, funded by the National Institute of Child Health and Human Development (NICHD) and he is currently the principal investigator of the Maternal PKU Study, also funded by NICHD. He has authored over 100 scientific articles chiefly dealing with mental retardation and has coauthored several books, including *The Mentally Retarded Child and His Family* and *Understanding the Mentally Retarded Child*. He has also contributed chapters to a number of books. In 1974, Dr. Koch received the Distinguished Service Award from Children's Hospital of Los Angeles in recognition of his services to retarded children and adults.

Frank J. Menolascino is Chairman of the Department of Psychiatry and a Professor in Psychiatry and Pediatrics at the University of Nebraska Medical Center. He has been actively involved in research, training, and advocacy efforts with persons with mental retardation, both nationally and internationally. He is the author of 10 books and 146 articles; he has received numerous national and international awards for his work with mental retardation. He has served on the President's Committee on Mental Retardation and as National President of the Association for Retarded Citizens of the United States. He was recognized by the American Psychiatric Association with the Strecker Award as the nation's outstanding young psychiatrist for his work on behalf of persons with mental retardation. Recently, he was elected Chairperson of the Mental Retardation Committee of the World Psychiatric Association. Dr. Menolascino served as a major architect and advocate of the development and growth of the Eastern Nebraska Community Office of Mental Retardation as well as consultant to other community-based programs for individuals with mental retardation at the national and international levels.

Oscar Resnick is the Senior Scientist at the Worcester Foundation for Experimental Biology and Chair of the Nutrition Section on Nutrition Teratology and Developmental Pharmacology of the National Institute of Child Health and Human Development. He has had numerous publications in journals such as *Developmental Psychobiology, Brain Research,* and *Experimental Neurology*. He is a member of the American Association for the Advancement of Science, the New York Academy of

Science, and the American Psychopathological Society. He has also been listed in the *World Who's Who in Science*.

Louis Rowitz is a Professor of Community Health Sciences and Associate Dean for Academic Affairs at the School of Public Health at the University of Illinois at Chicago. He is also editor of the journal, *Mental Retardation*. He is the author or coauthor of over 40 articles and book chapters in the fields of mental retardation and mental health. His research work has run the gamut from social epidemiological studies on service utilization in mental health and mental retardation, family research, factors in the prevention of teenage pregnancy, and issues related to the developmentally disabled elderly. He has also been involved in work on program evaluation in the human services field.

Michael Rutter is a Professor of Child Psychiatry and Head of the Department of Child and Adolescent Psychiatry and Honorary Director of the British Medical Research Council Child Psychiatry Unit at the University of London Institute of Psychiatry. He is a Fellow of the British Royal College of Physicians and the Royal College of Psychiatrists, and Honorary Fellow of the British Psychological Society and the American Academy of Pediatrics, and an Honorary Member of the American Academy of Child Psychiatry, reflecting his strong interdisciplinary interests. In 1961/1962, he spent a year as Nuffield Research Fellow at the Department of Pediatrics, Albert Einstein College of Medicine, New York and in 1979/1980 he was a Fellow at the Center for Advanced Study in the Behavioral Sciences, Stanford, California. He is European Editor of the *Journal of Autism and Developmental Disorders* and is on the editorial board of another 10 journals. His many research activities include stress resistance in children, developmental links between childhood and adult life, schools as social institutions, reading difficulties, interviewing skills, developmental neuropsychiatry, infantile autism, and psychiatric epidemiology. He has published 23 books including the coediting of *Autism: A Reappraisal of Concepts and Treatment, Child Psychiatry: Modern Approaches* (2nd edition), and *Depression in Young People: Developmental and Clinical Perspectives*. He has also authored 65 chapters and over 175 scientific papers.

Jack A. Stark is currently an Associate Professor of Medical Psychology in the Department of Psychiatry at the University of Nebraska Medical Center. He has 15 years experience of providing direct clinical services to persons with developmental disabilities and their families. In addition to his extensive teaching responsibilities, he has authored or coauthored numerous books, chapters, and articles, and presented hundreds of scientific papers. His more recent books include: *Handbook of Mental Illness in the Mentally Retarded, International Handbook of Community Services for the Mentally Retarded,* and *Pathways to Employment for Adults with Developmental Disabilities*. Dr. Stark also serves on the Board of Directors of the American Association of Mental Deficiency, American Academy of Mental Retardation, and the American Psychological Association's Division 33.

Preface

In 1977, the authors of this book were proud to be a part of the movement in which the Association for Retarded Citizens adopted, as their third major goal, the secondary prevention or reversibility (''cure'') of mental retardation. The acceptance of this bold step led to the convening of a national conference in 1981 that brought together leading scientists from throughout the country to address the latest research findings on the prevention and reversal of the symptom of mental retardation. As a result of this conference and additional research, the book, *Curative Aspects of Mental Retardation: Biomedical and Behavioral Advances,* was published in 1983. The response to this book from parents, and particularly from among our research colleagues who can be quite critical, has been extremely gratifying. This book continues to gain acceptance, and it is our hope that with the publication of this second volume our efforts and dedication to this goal will continue to be advanced by all of those who touch the lives of mentally retarded citizens.

It is estimated that every 5 to 10 years knowledge in a new scientific field doubles. Certainly, the biomedical and behavioral advances in the field of mental retardation have had a significant impact on our understanding of the many causes of this complex phenomenon. We are gratified by the in-depth treatment of these new areas by the many contributors of this volume. Our knowledge of the biomedical aspects of mental retardation has been enhanced by the significant improvement of diagnostic tools and techniques, ranging from nuclear magnetic resonance (NMR) and positron emission tomographic (PET) scans to recombinant DNA procedures. The behavioral aspects of mental retardation have been systematically and heuristically advanced by research in a broad number of areas that have also reciprocally enhanced the biomedical areas.

The editors of this volume realize that we have not adequately covered all areas, such as infectious diseases and other new research areas that are rapidly emerging as entities of hope and concern. We are also aware of awesome responsibility that goes along with publishing a book that purports to hold promise for the millions of families affected by mental retardation. We continue to believe that *hope* is essential for human existence—both physiologically and emotionally. It is interesting to note the changes in the last 5 years as they relate to the use of the word "cure" and "reversibility" in such areas as multiple sclerosis, muscular dystrophy, and spinal cord injury or paralysis to name just a few. Perhaps the reader can best understand our relentless pursuit of this goal through the following quotation:

> If a writer is so cautious that he never writes anything that cannot be criticized, he will never write anything that can be read. If you want to help other people you have got to make up your mind to write things that some men will condemn. (Thomas Merton, *New Seeds of Contemplation*)

Acknowledgments

We would like to acknowledge the generous contribution by the Clipped Wings Association for the complete funding of the second national conference and costs of preparing the manuscript. The Clipped Wings Association is the United Airlines flight attendant alumnae organization founded in 1953, which has donated money each year to fund mental retardation projects as their primary philanthropic focus. It is through their generous support that we hope to advance knowledge in the biomedical and behavioral fields that will improve the quality of life for persons with mental retardation. We would particularly like to thank Marilyn Hovorka-Schaefer and Chloe Ann Brown, past presidents of Clipped Wings, and Judy Hall, Chairman of the Research Committee, for their support and assistance throughout this project.

In addition, we deeply appreciate the assistance in the preparation of this volume provided by Vicki Morrison and particularly Tammi Goldsbury, who provided valuable contributions that enhanced the quality of the manuscript. We would also like to acknowledge the contribution of Dr. Jean Elder (former Commissioner of the Administration on Developmental Disabilities and Assistant Secretary for the Office of Human Development) and her staff who supported our efforts through a national grant.

Finally, we would like to thank each of the contributors to this volume who have dedicated their entire professional careers to serving this population. We all share in the dream that, with ongoing efforts of these contributors and many others, this volume will in some small way help to extend the knowledge and hope that we are truly on our way to finding ways to significantly reduce both the prevalence and severity of mental retardation.

John Stark

This book is dedicated to John and all the other developmentally disabled children of the world. The cause of John's severe disability is now totally preventable, but we have a long way to go before we can reverse his complex and multiple symptoms. Yet, it is our wish that this book will in some small way encourage researchers and provide *hope* for other families that progress is being made that can lead to significantly improving the meaningfulness of their children's lives.

John's contribution can perhaps best be summarized in the words of Nietzsche, ''He who has a *why* to live for can bear almost any *how*'' (Victor Frankl, *Man's Search for Meaning*).

Preventive and Curative Intervention in Mental Retardation

THEMES
AND OVERVIEWS

Chapter 1

An Updated Search for the Prevention of Mental Retardation

Jack A. Stark, Frank J. Menolascino, and Tammi L. Goldsbury

Longitudinal research that focuses on outcome studies of people who are most satisfied with life reveals three main findings: A person needs to have someone to love, something to work for, and something for which they can hope. Certainly, if you are the parent of a child with mental retardation, you already have someone to love, someone to work for, and someone to inspire your hope. The hope of all parents who have children with developmental disabilities is that their son or daughter will be able to improve so significantly that they need no longer retain the label of mental retardation. Such hope has always been considered too idealistic and, therefore, parents were admonished not to have such high expectations—the very expectations (hope) that often provided some purpose and direction in their lives.

The editors of this book have observed with great emotion the contributions that are made by each state toward the funding of research projects and are presented at the annual research luncheon of the Association of Retarded Citizens–U.S. Each year, contributions totaling more than $100,000 are donated for research efforts geared toward providing some aspect of hope for these parents of children with mental retardation. In small communities across the country, bake sales, car washes, and many other types of money-raising efforts also take place to fund these projects. We are frequently touched by the enormous amount of energy that goes into such efforts, but more symbolically, it represents the fact that parents want to do their part in the hope that there could be some new advancement that would directly help their son or daughter.

The purpose of this chapter is to focus on those new areas of research that provide us with an optimistic view that progress is continuing to be made toward the prevention of mental retardation. Although much has already been accomplished in the primary and tertiary prevention areas, we feel it necessary that new findings, not mentioned in other chapters of this book, be addressed. This chapter discusses the progress being made toward the secondary prevention or "cure" not for just a few, but for many of the millions of mentally retarded citizens in this country. It provides the reader with an understanding of why we remain committed to the goal of secondary prevention or "cure." We address the gaps that have not been discussed in the various chapters of this book (such as infectious diseases) and also briefly review other areas that should enhance the development of additional research areas in a given field (i.e., other advances in genetic development in addition to new findings in Down syndrome and the inborn errors of metabolism as discussed in Section II).

DIAGNOSTICS

It would appear that the major impetus for newfound optimism in significant breakthroughs in research, particularly in the biomedical sciences, has been directly related to significant advancements in our diagnostic instrumentation. In this section, we list a number of diagnostic instruments or processes that directly or indirectly impact upon the lives of persons with mental retardation and contain major implications for improving their overall quality of life.

A quiet revolution is taking place in neuroanatomy. Today's neuroanatomists are able to use fluorescent dyes and specifically tagged enzymes that are selectively taken up by nerve cells and that will mark a single nerve cell and, in turn, specifically identify its multiple array of intercellular (i.e., cell-to-cell) connections. As a result, we have been able to identify new major systems or pathways in the central nervous system as well as to develop a deeper understanding of how an individual neuron develops, changes, matures, and dies.

Neuroimaging

Diverse developments in microimaging utilizing ultrasound, computed tomography (CT), positron emission tomography (PET), nuclear magnetic resonance (NMR), digital radiography, and intervention radiology are being introduced at incredibly fast rates. These developments will have a major impact on our efforts to understand basic neuroanatomical systems and will provide rationales for treatment that can ultimately reduce the manifestations of mental retardation. The neuroimaging tools (which are eloquently delineated in Dr. Coulter's chapter, Chapter 5) will have a significant impact on the biomedical sciences. The PET scan, for example, allows one to exam the specific brain metabolism events in individuals with epilepsy, both during and between seizures. During a seizure, the brain area affected literally lights up with intense activity, but between seizures the affected brain area often shows up with a lower-than-normal level of metabolic activity. This finding and other observations have prompted many to speculate that epilepsy and other brain disorders, such as schizophrenia, may result from specific types of derangement and control over the underlying electrical-biochemical rhythms of the brain.

Positron Emission Tomography   PET uses an injection of short-lived chemical substances containing radioactive atoms that emit positrons. Following absorption by the organ (e.g., the brain) to be evaluated, these radioactive substances emit positrons that then directly encounter electrons. The two particles together produce gamma rays, which are then recorded on multiple X -ray films, and they, in turn, are converted by a sophisticated computer into images of the multiple metabolic events that are occurring in the organ. This PET technology gives us remarkable information about organ function and organ anatomy. It is believed by the neurosciences community that PET will do for the behavioral sciences what the CT scanners have done for physical medicine. It will not only help to record objectively the brain's chemistry, but will also allow examination of the interaction of other neurochemical factors (i.e., ligands) within the brain—and changes secondary to external psychological factors. In a sense, PET will be providing a "scientific window" into cognitive and emotional states.

Nuclear Magnetic Resonance (or Magnetic Resonance Imaging)   NMR uses magnetic fields of radiofrequency waves rather than ionizing radiation to give high-resolution images, particularly of soft tissues. It is a noninvasive and an essentially harmless procedure that is providing us an unparalleled look at the living anatomical state of the brain and other major organ systems. This diagnostic technique has provided very clear anatomical detail of organ systems—a look that had previously been available only after death. Since diagnostic clarity remains as the first stage to any rationale treatment intervention, the NMR permits us to know more clearly "what is wrong" as a prelude to "what can we do to help."

Intervention Radiology   Intervention radiology is a precise, clear, anatomical imaging technique to localize lesions and thus permit nonsurgical intervention procedures (such as insertion of catheters, needles, etc.) to correct physiological dysfunctioning. This is particularly helpful with the medically fragile, mentally retarded individual. Ultrasound technology is the process by which sound waves can be used to avoid high-level radiation and view the fetus in utero or guide a diagnostic or treatment needle in regards to intrauterine intervention.

Magnetic Resonance Spectroscopy   Magnetic resonance spectroscopy (MRS) uses powerful magnetic fields to detect abnormalities in the amniotic fluid chemical composition. This is a process that evaluates amniotic fluid samples and reveals not only genetic abnormalities, but other fetal abnormalities associated with prenatal exposure to pesticides, toxic chemicals, drugs, and physiological malfunctioning. In the near future, such tests will be done rather inexpensively and on a routine basis as a preventive test.

Tandem Scanning Reflective Light Microscope Developed by a Czech scientist, the tandem scanning reflective light microscope (TSRLM) is a new microscope that allows scientists to do something that has not been possible before. It allows them to look directly into the interior of living tissue in a nondestructive manner, enables a high resolution of the observed images, and obtains a picture that is recorded stereoscopically. The device does not make use of lasers or modern electronics imaging processes. This system, although developed 20 years ago, has not been put into practice until recently. Its focus will be to look into living brain tissue with reflected light. In essence, looking at and taking stereo pictures will be invaluable to neurobiology with the reconstruction of the three-dimensional relationship between neurons and their interactive processes. This instrument will be unique in making this possible. It will replace the tedious process of studying destroyed tissue from specimen tissue cells that are sectioned, stained, and preserved for analysis.

DNA Sequencer Researchers for the National Science Foundation announced the commercial availability of the DNA sequencer, which uses laser-enhanced colored dyes and a microcomputer that can speed identification of defects that cause genetic diseases. Many people feel that this will play a central role in biomedical science in the future. Defective genes or segments of the DNA molecule chain cause about 2,500 inherited diseases. The sequence is able to pinpoint the exact gene defect far more quickly and cheaply than existing manual methods.

Scanning Acoustical Microscopy Scanning acoustical microscopy (SAM) allows scientists to use sound waves to peek at the microscopic world. The use of SAM is a process whereby a synthesizer generates a stream of high-frequency sound waves, which are channeled through a focusing lens, producing sound waves that are picked up by a receiver, processed by a computer, and reproduced visually via a television screen.

Computer Chips and Computer Technology

Tremendous breakthroughs are occurring in the computer chip industry. Within the next 5 years, computers that now cost $10–20 million and take up a large amount of space will be condensed to fit on a scientist's desk for approximately $10,000 and will be able to process 10 million bits of data per second. Research is being conducted on the static random access memory (SRAM) chip, which is so fast that it can read an entire 75-volume encyclopedia in 1 second. These new 32- and 64-kilobyte memory chips can process a signal in 1–3 billionths of a second. Optic disks are also making their debut with computers and will continue to play a large role as their technology advances. For example, these optic disks and their technology will allow researchers to develop a wallet-sized card for $1.50 that can store a 1,000-page novel. Computer breakthroughs will someday be able to simplify many of the learning and training techniques for individuals with mental retardation. In addition, there has even been discussion of the possibility of developing computers that can see, touch, taste, and smell. Researchers are developing biological inputs for digital computers. Thick molecular layers of genetically laced protein may replace computer chips in this process.

Dr. Peter Davies, a biochemist at the Albert Einstein College of Medicine, has developed a routine test that can accurately diagnose an indicator of Alzheimer disease in people. He has found an abnormal protein in the spinal fluid of patients suspected of having Alzheimer disease. It is not known whether this protein, called A-68, is an effect or cause, but it seems to be quite unique to this disorder. The process that produces neurofibrillary tangles in plaques may be related to this abnormal accumulation of protein. Using monoclonal antibodies, which bind to specific proteins and thus act like biological markers, researchers are able to isolate and identify this A-68 protein. This research could have significant implications for individuals with mental retardation, particularly persons with Down syndrome.

Geneticists at UCLA Medical School have also found another protein, HLA-A2, on the surface of white blood cells in 100% of individuals with early Alzheimer disease (i.e., before age 60) as compared to 30% of normal individuals under the age of 60. Research is also underway to identify other proteins that could be implicated in this debilitating process. In effect, this research indicates that we may be able to develop effective proteins that can be used to provide early diagnosis and thereby prevent or reverse cognitive impairment.

Another promising diagnostic process is the development of radioactive gene probes. This new diagnostic evaluation will permit physicians to detect a person's potential for developing hereditary illnesses without any knowledge of their family history. This search for defective genes begins with sample cells such as white blood cells taken from an individual. The DNA is then extracted from the cells, broken into pieces, and grouped by size. Next, the fragments are unwound and divided into single strands and exposed to the radioactive probe. This probe is actually a small piece of synthetic DNA that has a genetic code corresponding to the suspected mutant. If the abnormal DNA is present in a sample, the probe will bind to it. The bound probe—and thus the mutant gene—can then be detected because it is radioactive. As we continue to develop better knowledge of the sequence of the normal and mutant gene in genetic codes, this process will become even more useful and will open the door to diagnosing a wider range of diseases. The pinpointing of these genetic abnormalities will allow us to provide early treatment of diseases through total prevention or reversal before such abnormalities become fully manifest.

GENETICS

No other area of biomedical research has received as much attention or, perhaps, holds as much promise for the primary and secondary prevention of mental retardation as the field of genetics and its potential intervention strategies. Genetically influenced conditions continue to rank among the leading causes of organically based mental retardation. Research has focused on location, organization, and regulation of genetic materials from the chromosomes and the genetic aberrations associated with the structure, morphology, and numeric abnormalities of these structures. Today, researchers have been able to map more than 800 of an estimated 50,000–100,000 individual genes that determine an individual's total makeup. In addition, we have been able to diagnose more than 200 of the roughly 3,000 disorders caused by single-gene defects.

Researchers have demonstrated for the first time that a psychiatric illness can be inherited. This is the result of a 10-year study of manic-depression found in three generations of an older-order Amish family in Pennsylvania. Researchers at the National Institute of Mental Health found in their study that 85% of those diagnosed as having the gene for manic-depressive illness developed this syndrome at some time during a 10-year period. At the same time that this finding was announced, other researchers found different genes that have also been highly predictive of manic-depressive illness, indicating that there may be up to five different genes responsible for this bipolar affective disorder.

Researchers have also found a consistent abnormality in chromosome 21 that appears to be highly predictive and related to Alzheimer disease. Scientists from Harvard Medical School and Massachusetts General Hospital, along with other colleagues, have indicated that this is the first definitive lead to the actual cause of Alzheimer disease and, perhaps, may be the gene responsible for rapid cognitive decline in individuals with Down syndrome at a later stage of their life. Most persons with Down syndrome who live past the age of 30 will develop neurological signs similar to those in Alzheimer disease; thus, the genetic markers on chromosome 21 are suspected of containing these abnormal proteins directly related to impaired functioning. Figure 1 shows a specific site on chromosome 21 that indicates the genetic marker for Alzheimer disease. Now that this marker has been discovered, researchers may be able to develop a diagnostic test that can lead to ways to prevent, and perhaps to cure, Down syndrome.

Until recently, inherited disorders have been perceived by many as essentially untreatable. The advent of gene therapy holds great promise for the treatment of genetic disorders, much as the introduction of antibiotics and immunization has revolutionized the treatment and prevention of many infectious diseases.

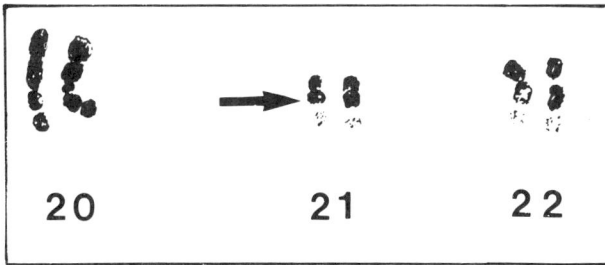

Figure 1. Genetic marker for Alzheimer disease.

It has been suggested (Editorial, 1987) that genetic disorders are amenable to treatment, and somatic gene therapy is not the only possible therapeutic approach, if one defines "therapy" as maneuvers that require continued administration of therapeutic agents that can result in amelioration as well as total cure. For example, this editorial indicated that, "scurvy (a universal human inborn error) Cretinism, and adrenogenital syndrome have been amenable to curative, albeit continuous, therapy for many decades. Severe combined immune deficiency disease can be permanently and reproducibly cured (essentially without hazard) by intravenous injection of bone marrow from a histocompatible sibling and (with some hazards and less reproducibly) by transmutation from haploidentical patient. Ameliorative therapy has been developed for phenylketonuria, galactosemia, hemophilia, and diabetes mellitus." These editors indicate that hereditary disorders can be prevented by either preventive therapy, metabolic manipulation, or replacement therapy. The editors postulate that the search into the investigation of replacement therapy—such as the immunodeficiency disease, adenosine deaminase (ADA)—indicates very promising early results of this therapeutic maneuver, which are important not only in terms of relieving this rare disease of ADA deficiency, but also in terms of the potential application of this therapy to a wide range of inherited as well as noninherited disorders.

SURGERY

There is hardly a part of the body that surgeons cannot repair or replace as a result of new developments in surgical tools, such as laser scalpels, a vast array of new diagnostic techniques, and a breakthrough in transplant surgery with the introduction of cyclosporin (a potent drug introduced in the early 1980s that suppresses the body's immune system and prevents organ rejection). Each year approximately 10,000 organs are transplanted. We are now on the brink of developing artificial organs, blood tissue, bone, and skin, along with such innovative devices as a polyurethane "skin button" (which provides an opening to the body) and body zippers (which permit the opening of cavities for direct surgical intervention). Obviously, these new discoveries have both direct and indirect implications for individuals with mental retardation, particularly those who also have other health conditions that complicate their developmental disability. Another promising area is "in utero fetal surgery," because of the development of a technology of high-resolution, gray-scale ultrasound equipment that has progressed in its ability to recognize fetal abnormalities with great precision. Even more astonishing is the possibility of correcting these anatomical malformations in utero via fetoscopy or hysterotomy (Council on Scientific Affairs, 1983). Fetal surgery has focused on the correction of anatomical malformations that interfere with fetal organ development. These malformations include congenital diaphragmatic hernia, congenital hydronephrosis, obstructive hydrocephalus, as well as various neurotubular defects. There have been a number of successful term pregnancies in which early decompression and diversion of the urine flow to the amniotic fluid have been accomplished in congenital hydronephrosis, secondary to urethra obstruction. This attempt has involved both in utero surgery and partial removal of the fetus from the uterus with a subsequent return and full-term pregnancy.

Correction of congenital diaphragmatic hernia in utero allows the lung to develop normally before delivery and prevents hypoplasticity. Obstructive hydrocephalus can be treated by shunting the spinal fluid from the lateral ventricles to the abdominal cavity in utero. Over a dozen in utero diverting procedures have been done in human fetuses as demonstrated in Figure 2 (Clewel, Johnson, & Meier, 1982). The world literature in this area would indicate that ardent optimism is guarded at the present. But it would appear that research will continue into in utero fetal surgery since: 1) early correction and defect may preclude irreversible damage, 2) early allografts are less likely to be rejected by a still undeveloped immune system, and 3) rapid postoperative healing is promoted in the in utero environment (Harrison, Globus, & Filly, 1981).

TISSUE TRANSPLANTS/NERVE REGENERATION OR REPAIR

Until recently, it has been accepted that once brain cells have been destroyed or injured, there is no way to repair the damage and that the brain cannot regenerate lost cells, nor repair itself, as do cells in other organs of the body. Now new research has taken a hopeful approach in attempting to heal damaged brain cells by replacement with new cells that can take over new functions. A controversial new technique involving fetal cell implants received a great deal of attention during the Chernobyl nuclear disaster. Severely irradiated patients received fetal cell implants surgically and although efforts were in vain, it raised the hope that such an approach could become an important medical tool in the future. Researchers in the Peoples Republic of

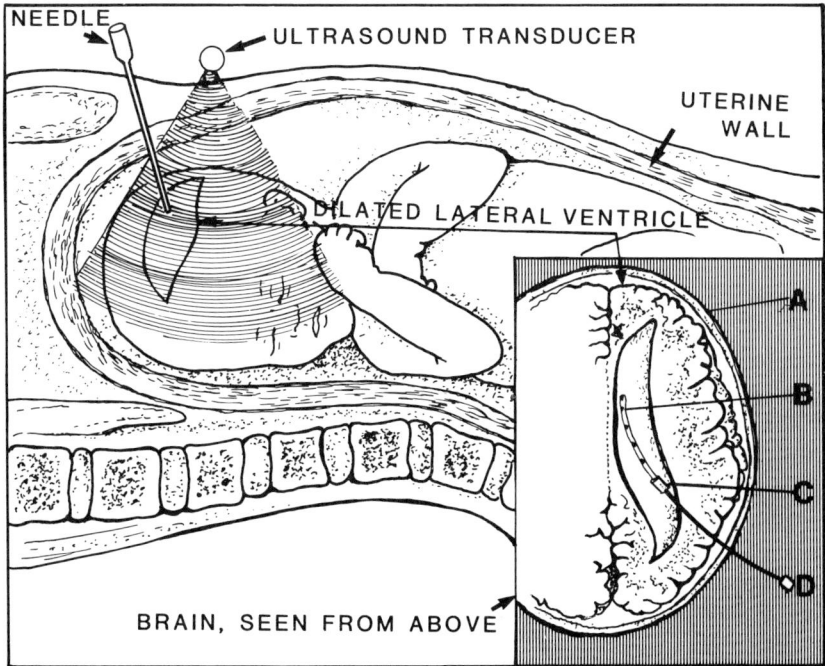

Figure 2. The technique uses a shunt inserted through the back of the soft skull of a fetus (A) via a hollow needle that is removed. When brain pressure mounts, the shunt's valve (C) opens to drain fluid from a tube with tiny holes (B) into the amniotic fluid around the fetus. The shunt's collar (D) holds it in place until the cesarean delivery.

China have been utilizing fetal tissue transplants since 1980 in treating diabetics. Similar research has taken place in the last few years in the United States.

Researchers at the National Institutes of Health and in Sweden are among the leading neuroscientists working on brain repair. For the last 15 years, these scientists have been working on the possibility of transplanting new brain tissue into humans. This field seems to be exploding in terms of research potential. The reason is that fetal cells are immunologically naive, particularly during the early stages of pregnancy, since they have not yet developed all the antigens or distinctive surface proteins that allow the recipient's immune system to identify and reject them. Another advantage of fetal cells is that they are generally not mature enough to cause graft versus host disease, which can occur when the tissues of a transplant recipient are attacked by implanted adult cells. Fetal cells are able to regenerate and, thus, have the potential to repair brain or spinal cord injuries. Research animals have been used in experiments. Small segments of the brain containing supraoptic nuclei, rich in vasopressin cells, have been injected into rat brains; this transplanted tissue seems to survive and establish healthy vasopressin cells in 90%

of the transplanted rats. This finding provides hope that Parkinson disease, diabetes, epilepsy, paralyses, spinal cord injury, and, perhaps, blindness or deafness attributed to brain damage would possibly be remediated by utilizing this approach. In Parkinson disease, grafted nerve cells seem to grow and send their long fibers (axons) to synapses with their normal target in the brain, as well as the caudate nucleus, the midbrain structure important for modulating motor movements. It is known that death of certain nerve cells in the central nervous system that operate with the neurotransmitter dopamine cuts off stimulation to the caudate, disturbing its function, which is a process that presumably accounts for the tremors and difficulties in originating movements that are the hallmarks of Parkinson disease. The grafted tissue in rats showed improved movement behavior under microscopic examination of brain tissue, and confirmed that the grafted cells had grown and established contacts within the body. There have also been promising results in working with monkeys with other drafted material, such as adrenogland tissue.

Nerve cell regeneration is a fertile field of current research and holds great promise for individuals who are mentally retarded (e.g., why certain injured nerve cell fibers regenerate while others do not). It is known that nerve fibers in the peripheral nervous system (which carry messages from the brain and spinal cord to the extremities) can elongate, reconnect, and regain normal function if severed. Investigators believe that the ability to regenerate may have less to do with the nerve cells, or neurons, than with their immediate environment. They think that chemical or physical properties of the cells that ensheathe peripheral nerves may encourage these central nerves to grow. One such approach has been conducted at McGill University in Montreal with the stimulation of nerve fibers in the central nervous systems of rats—especially growth of peripheral nerves. In these studies, when a small segment of peripheral nerve sheath was removed and attached by one end to the brain stem and by the other to the spinal cord, the axons near the two graft sites grew more than 1 inch (i.e., into and through the entire peripheral graft). It is now known that the central nervous system axon can elongate if the conditions are right and it would appear that something in the peripheral nerve environment may switch on this potential. It has now been shown that the functional capacity of axons to elongate over large distances is possible, especially within the individual nerve cells. Neurologist Albert Aguayo demonstrated this hypothesis by utilizing a piece of the sciatic nerve transplanted into a damaged portion of the optic nerve; it produced "pioneer axons," or exploratory fibers, which grew directly through the tube-like structure taken from the leg. This tube-like structure is exhibited in Figure 3, which shows a grafting of the brain stem of the spinal cord indicating that newly grown fibers can transmit electrical signals normally, and that they can grow through this tube structure to connect in the brain, as in this case, where vision is produced via a visual response. A critical question now facing researchers is: If growing nerve fibers make the correct connection(s), can they restore function?

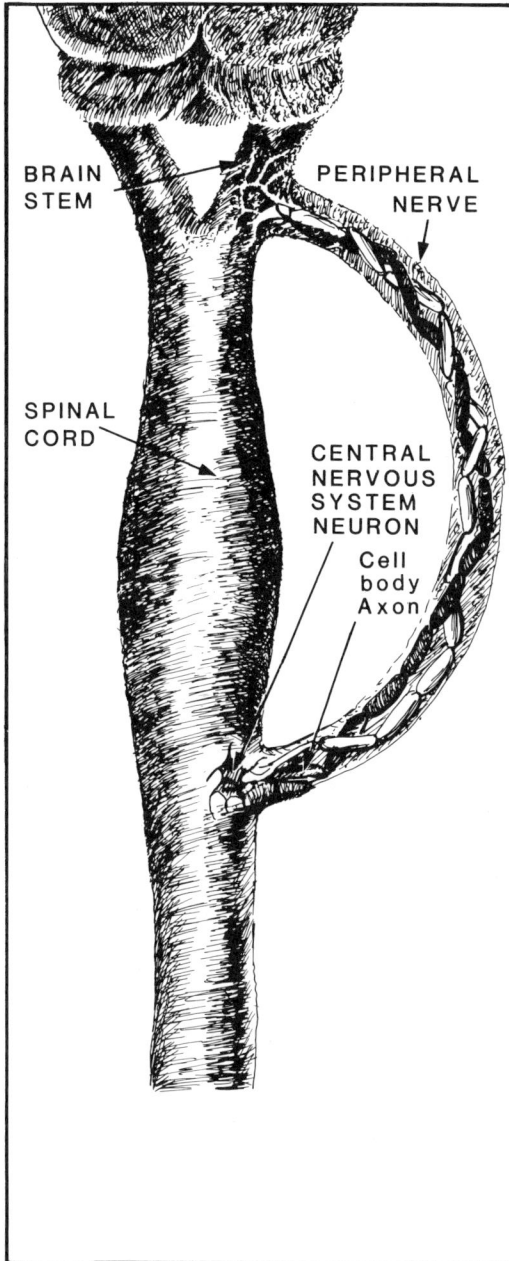

Figure 3. Scientists are trying to make axons in the central nervous system (CNS) elongate, which they don't usually do. From a sheath around peripheral nerves, which do not elongate, a tube is formed through which CNS nerves can grow.

A specific corollary to the above hypothesis was postulated by neurobiologist Eric Schooter of Stanford University School of Medicine. He and his colleagues have found that apolipoprotein E (Apo-E), the same protein that binds lipids into packets for transport in the blood, also goes into action when a nerve is damaged.

Figure 4 indicates that if the sciatic nerve is crushed during an accident, the body rushes microphages and immune system cells to the injury. In Figure 4 the microphages noted in Number 1 release Apo-E (Number 2) to mop up the lipids (Number 3) that pour out of the degenerating nerve stem and its outer sheath (Number 4). Part of the nerve dies, but the Apo-E ferries its lipids into Schwann cells (Number 5), where they are stored for use in their regenerating. In the new repair process, these Schwann cells, which surround neurons, release lipids and Apo-E which picks them up (Number 1) and ferries them to the regrowth site (Number 2); the lipids are used by the nerve growth bud. If an optic nerve is crushed, the Apo-E just disappears. Yet Dr. Schooter feels that the nerves of the spinal cord (central nerves) aren't that different from the peripheral nerves, and our task will be to figure out how this Apo-E can be kept around to do its work on the central nervous system. Obviously, this has implications for damaged brain cells that are directly implicated in mental retardation.

ENDOCRINOLOGY

Hormones affect not only our bodily functions, but our brain as well. Hormones, which are present in the immune system and interact with the brain, are giving researchers new hope regarding treatments and more information on diseases such as Alzheimer disease, diabetes, and acquired immune deficiency syndrome (AIDS). The 1986 Nobel Prize for medicine was awarded for research on hormonal-like growth factors and their connection with cancer.

The implications and potential of hormonal treatments is astounding for modern medicine and its curative approaches. Research in this area has just begun to touch on how hormones play a role in practically everything we do, think, feel, and, possibly, become.

Researchers have looked at the role hormones play in areas ranging from criminal behavior, depression, and psychiatric illnesses to Alzheimer disease, hypertension, and anorexia. In psychiatric illnesses, researchers have found that paranoid schizophrenics and manic-depressives have high levels of cortisol, noradrenaline, and thyroxine, but lower levels of testosterone. With this type of information, clinicians may someday be able to use an individual's hormonal profile for diagnosis and treatment.

Currently, one of the most extensive lines of research involves identifying the network of gene regulators within cells. An example of this is the

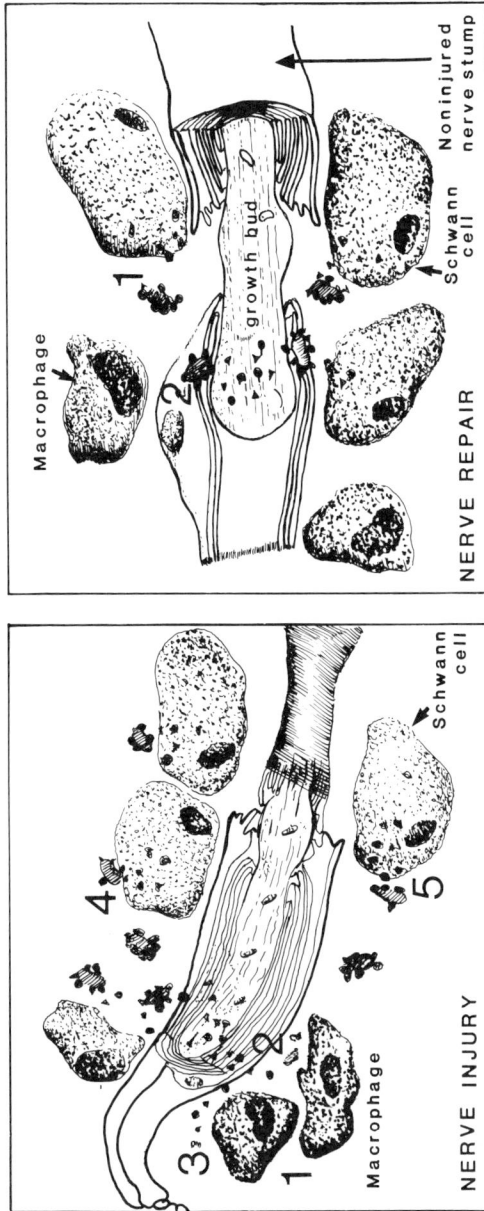

Figure 4. Illustration of nerve damage and repair, in which the body rushes macrophages and immune system cells to the injury site.

15

production of the hormone insulin for diabetics. Since every cell in the body contains exactly the same genes, it is thought that perhaps other insulin genes, in cells in other parts of the body besides the pancreas, could somehow be triggered to produce the insulin hormone. According to William Rutter of the University of California, this type of research will have great impact not only on efforts to cure diabetes but on regenerating other tissues and extending their functional life ("A user's guide to hormones," 1987).

Other exciting hormone research is continuing in the areas of immunology and endocrinology, as well as in the prevention and cure of disease, and may give us new insights into the "cure" of mental retardation.

INFECTIOUS DISEASES

Although this book does not closely examine infectious diseases and the role they play in the causation of mental retardation, it is not an area to be overlooked. For example, *Hemophilus influenzae* (H-flu) type b is the most common cause of meningitis and epiglottis in children. It is also one of the most common causes of infections in infants and children under the age of 2 years. Studies have indicated that H-flu type b meningitis in the United States results in 30–60 cases per 100,000 children under 5 years of age each year. The mortality rate for this influenza has been approximately 10% during the last 30 years and substantial neurological sequelae occur in at least one third of the victims. Those individuals under 2 years of age are the most severely affected. Only recently have we discovered that this influenza is contagious and that infants are particularly vulnerable. The American Academy of Pediatrics has recommended that nursery schools and day care centers administer a prophylaxis vaccination via rifampin. This vaccine has been developed, and is safe, for children over 2 years of age. Research is also close to being finalized for possible implementation of mass utilization of this vaccine for infants under 2 years of age.

Cytomegalovirus (CMV) is the leading infectious cause of mental retardation. CMV is a virus that lives in the body's circulating white blood cells and in the kidney tubule cells, which causes symptom-free infections in susceptible pregnant women, but results in severe brain damage and mental retardation in the fetus. In later life, acquired infections with this virus can cause paralytic disease, such as Guillain-Barré syndrome.

Probably no other medical problem has received as much public attention as the spread of the AIDS virus. Although the precise causes are not known, CMV is a leading contender for playing a role in AIDS. The Epstein-Barr virus, for example, is suspected to infect 100% of multiple sclerosis patients. Other viruses, such as herpes simplex virus I (HSV-I) and herpes simplex virus II (HSV-II) have emerged as major public health problems. Along with toxoplasma, rubella viruses, and CMV, these are the most frequently encountered organisms that affect the human fetus. There are now diagnostic neurological tests that have been assigned the acronym TORCH, which indicate past or recent infection or immunity. Diagnosis of recent infection can be demonstrated, via seroconversion, with such tests as enzyme immunoassay (EIA), indirect immunofluoresence (IFA), and indirect hemagglutination (IHA). Infections can also be assessed by identification by the IgG antibody. The focus on research viruses has taken on a new emphasis as a result of the AIDS scare, and also because of studies that point to the possibility that at least 25% of human cancers are caused by viruses. For example, it is felt by some researchers that viruses may even initiate this so-called autoimmune disease by tricking the immune system into attacking it's own body tissue. A major new solution to alleviating these viral diseases is demonstrated in the following three figures. In Figure 5, we see a variety of viruses from herpes simplex to mumps and the AIDS virus. In Figure 6, we see a conversion process that significantly helps the virus recognize and attach to a given cell. The life cycle involving this gene therapy is then listed in Figure 7, which illustrates the five various stages of viral infection that can be reversed.

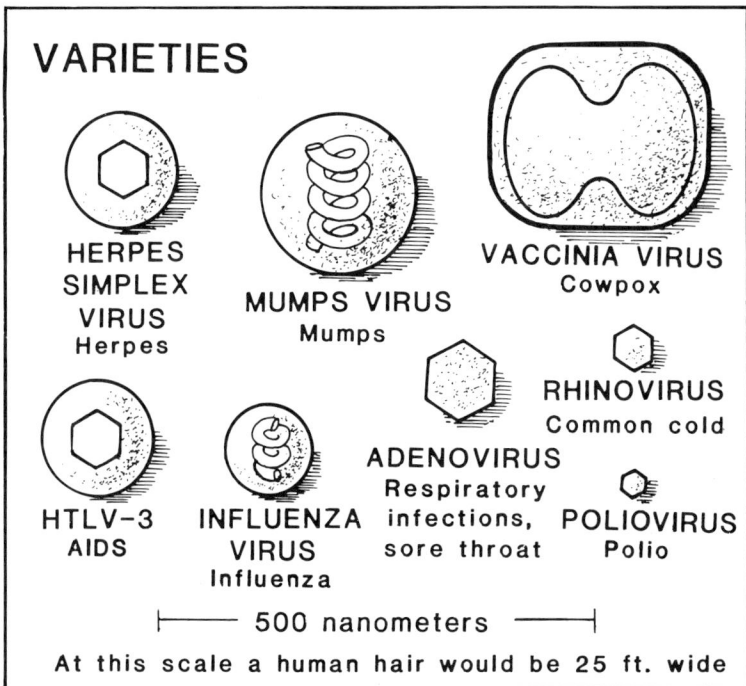

Figure 5.   Varieties of viruses, ranging from herpes simplex to poliovirus.

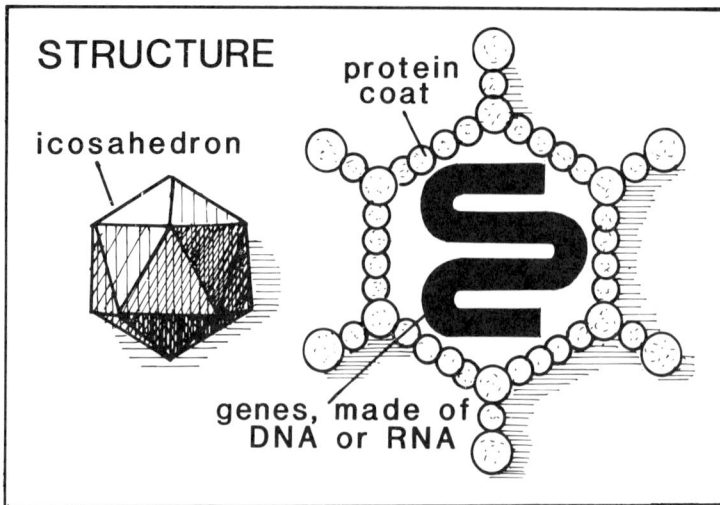

STRUCTURE   protein coat

icosahedron

genes, made of DNA or RNA

Figure 6.   The virus consists of a small number of genes (made of DNA or RNA) encased in a protective coat of protein. Many small viruses are built in the form of an icosahedron, which has 20 triangular facets. Spikes protruding from its outer surface help the virus recognize and attach to a cell.

There are other infectious diseases that have a definite effect upon the central nervous system. We have selected a few here that we hope will provide the reader with an example of promising new breakthroughs in this field, through development of new testing procedures, vaccinations, and gene therapy research.

NEUROTOXICITY

In addition to the information provided in the chapter by Angle and McIntire on developmental neurotoxicity (Chapter 9) and in the section on toxic syndromes in Davis's chapter (Chapter 7), the editors wish to emphasize three areas of concern that new research has indicated will play a more significant role in the causation of mental retardation than was previously thought: metal poisoning, fetal alcohol syndrome, and fetal tobacco syndrome.

Metal Poisoning

The effects of poisoning by heavy metals such as lead, mercury, and cadmium are becoming more apparent as our research methodology has significantly improved over the last 10 years, allowing us to better understand the impact of these toxins. It is also now known that additional studies have linked brain damage in children to lower levels of lead in the body. As a result, the National Center for Disease Control (CDC) has steadily lowered the threshold

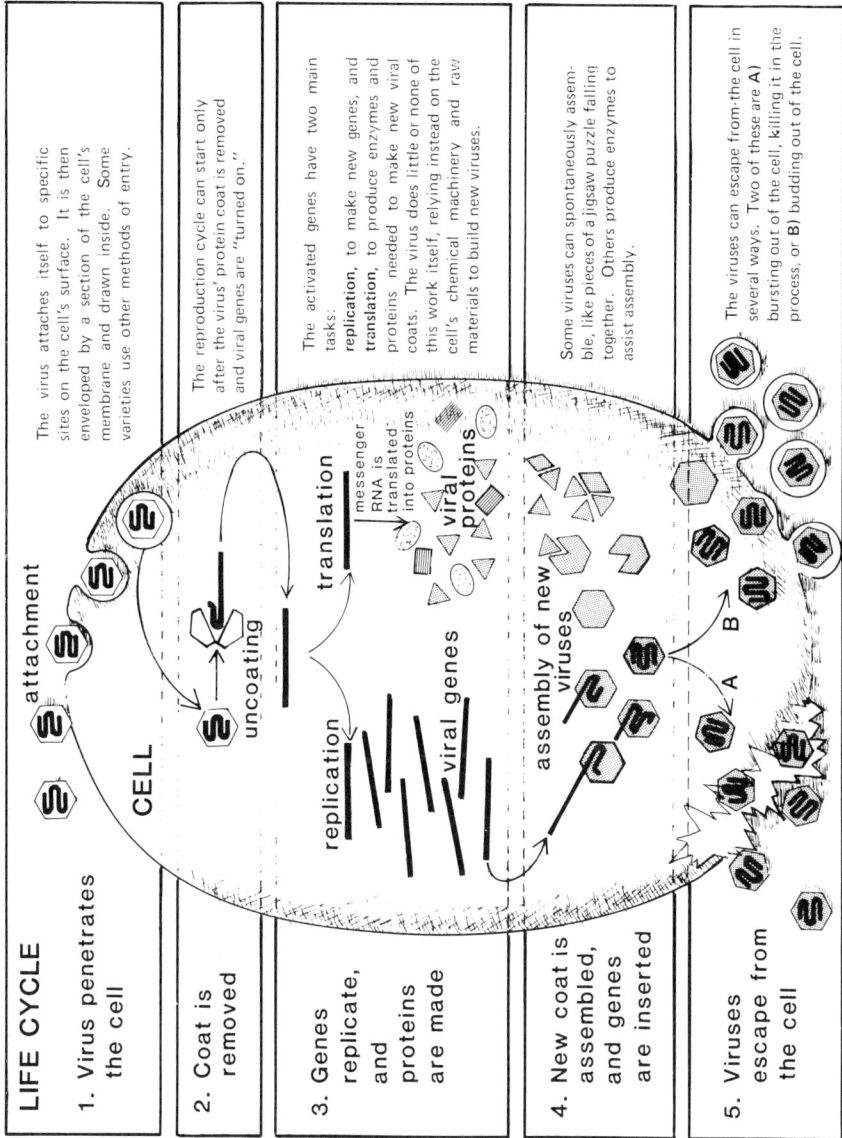

LIFE CYCLE

attachment

1. Virus penetrates the cell

The virus attaches itself to specific sites on the cell's surface. It is then enveloped by a section of the cell's membrane and drawn inside. Some varieties use other methods of entry.

CELL

uncoating

2. Coat is removed

The reproduction cycle can start only after the virus' protein coat is removed and viral genes are "turned on."

translation

messenger RNA is translated into proteins

viral proteins

replication

viral genes

3. Genes replicate, and proteins are made

The activated genes have two main tasks:

replication, to make new genes, and **translation,** to produce enzymes and proteins needed to make new viral coats. The virus does little or none of this work itself, relying instead on the cell's chemical machinery and raw materials to build new viruses.

assembly of new viruses

4. New coat is assembled, and genes are inserted

Some viruses can spontaneously assemble, like pieces of a jigsaw puzzle falling together. Others produce enzymes to assist assembly.

A

B

5. Viruses escape from the cell

The viruses can escape from the cell in several ways. Two of these are **A)** bursting out of the cell, killing it in the process, or **B)** budding out of the cell.

Figure 7. The five stages of viral infection that can be reversed.

19

of the amount of lead the body can safely tolerate. The latest "safe" lead level (as set in 1985) is 25 μg of lead per $\frac{1}{10}$ liter of blood. However, recent findings suggest that hearing impairment and other nerve damage can occur in children with blood levels as low as 12 μg. It would appear that the CDC will probably revise the standards downward again soon. Some individuals who are exposed to these higher levels of toxic metals (such as inner-city and lower socioeconomic status individuals) are included in the large group of individuals who have been identified as mildly retarded. We have come to realize that there may be no safe threshold for metals in the body. New research has indicated that tiny amounts of metal can adversely affect the brain and the nervous system. For example, the average American has 10–25 μg of lead per $\frac{1}{10}$ liter of blood. However, research by Schroeder (1987) and his colleagues has suggested that even 10 μg can destruct the production of hemoglobin (a component of blood that distributes oxygen throughout the body). This is particularly significant for young children, since their lungs are much larger in relation to the rest of their body, and 30% of the lead that they absorb ends up in the brain and softer tissues of the body where it interferes with the production of critical proteins necessary for nerve cell functioning.

Fetal Alcohol Syndrome

Concern over the deleterious effects of alcohol on the developing fetus can be traced back to the time of Aristotle, who observed that drunken women often bore children who were "feebleminded" (Warner & Rosett, 1975). This finding was once again observed during England's gin epidemic in the 18th century. But it was not until the early 1970s that researchers began to draw a direct correlation between prenatal exposure to alcohol and birth defects.

Current research shows that prenatal exposure to alcohol is associated with a distinct pattern of congenital malformations that have been collectively termed fetal alcohol syndrome (FAS). Characteristics associated with this syndrome are intrauterine and postnatal growth deficiency, a distinctive pattern of physical and mental malformations (including microcephaly, joint, limb, and cardiac anomalies), and behavioral/cognitive impairment (i.e., mental retardation and fine motor dysfunctioning). Mental retardation is now recognized as the most serious defect and probably the most sensitive indication and thereby manifestation of maternal alcohol abuse. The current trend seems to be approximately 5,000 FAS births per year in the United States, but many researchers feel that these figures are considerably underestimated. The increasing use of alcohol by pregnant women is disturbing. Little, Schultz, and Mandel (1976) report that about 2% of middle-class pregnant women consume about two drinks per day. Even higher rates of consumption during pregnancy are reported for women in the lower classes. One study indicated that 13% were estimated to be heavy drinkers (about 10 drinks per day) (Rosett, Ouellette, Winer, & Owens, 1978).

Fetal Tobacco Syndrome

Only in the last few years have we been able to collect valid amounts of data that clearly indicate concern over the consumption of tobacco during pregnancy. A consistent pattern of birth defects (comparable to that in FAS) is now known to be caused by cigarette smoking. It is called fetal tobacco syndrome (FTS). Research for quite some time has indicated that smoking produces small-birth-weight babies. But new research indicates that these low-birth-weight infants tend to remain that way throughout their life. Women who smoke two or more packs of cigarettes per day during pregnancy deliver infants who exhibit a higher than expected incidence rate of mental retardation, abnormal facial features, and heart defects. However, studies have not been significantly replicated due to sample sizes that tend to be small. It is certainly a fertile research field that will demand more attention in the coming years.

PSYCHOPHARMACOLOGICAL APPROACHES

Researchers have discovered a region deep in the brain where drugs can act to help control epileptic seizures. It has been known for quite some time that the administration of certain drugs can alter brain chemical levels and thus reduce the frequency of epileptic seizures. Yet, it is not known where in the brain all of this takes place. Researchers at Georgetown University have demonstrated that the site of this region may be the substantia nigra. Now there is hope that this will lead to a new drug that will selectively treat epilepsy without disturbing other brain functions.

Selective developmental drugs are a major focus of new pharmacological research. It has been discovered that nerve cells use several chemicals at a time to send messages to each other, rather than one chemical as was previously believed. For example, at the present time, drugs that are used to treat specifically anxiety, depression, schizophrenia, and other disease entities affect only four neurotransmitters. However, it is known that there are probably 50 neurotransmitters and that it should be possible to treat these disease entities with lower overall drug use and fewer side effects. In essence, pharmaceutical firms are developing selective drugs that will modify behavior in more specific ways. Scientists are also using enzyme inactivators to battle all types of illnesses. In effect, Figure 8 shows that each drug is a synthetic molecule that enters a disease bearing cell, such as a bacteria, and causes one of its enzymes to self-destruct. In essence, this molecule "tricks" the enzyme into binding to it because its structure resembles the substrate with which the enzyme normally interacts, resulting in the destruction of the enzyme in the cell.

Scientists are developing a plastic coating that will allow drugs to be ingested rather than injected and that will preclude enzymes of the stomach

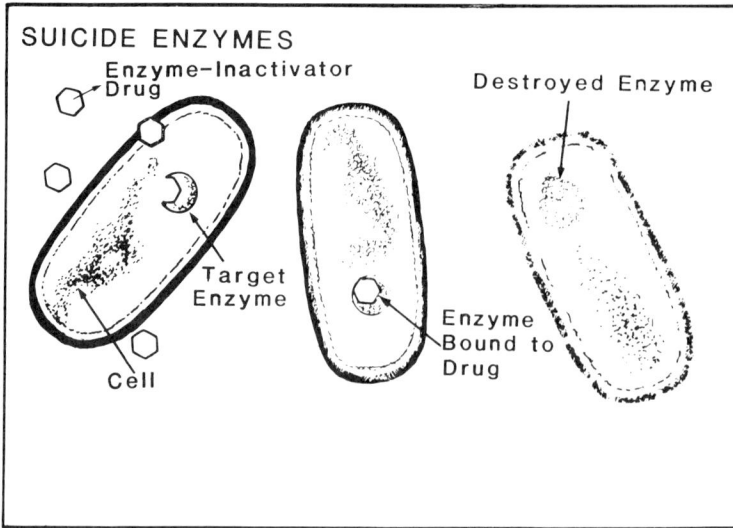

Figure 8. An enzyme-inactivation drug enters a disease-bearing cell, binding to a target enzyme, which is destroyed; so, often, is the cell.

from breaking them down. Electronic pumps will be used along with dermal patches, implantation, and the use of microcapsules. These microcapsules, which can contain a variety of drugs and be injected into diseased tissues, are tiny spheres made from molecules found naturally in the body. The microcapsules break down slowly and the drugs, therefore, can be more effective over a longer period of time.

NUTRITION

The National Institute of Child Health and Human Development is conducting extensive research on developmental nutrition, (including normal, excessive, and deficient amounts of nutrients during pregnancy, fetal development, and postnatal life) and the role of nutrition in physiological, intellectual, and behavioral development. The research has also focused on the nutrition of cell growth differentiation and function, as well as the development in utero of the immune processes, from the fetal period to early maturity. The role that nutrition plays in conjunction with economic and psychosocial interventions, and how these factors contribute to mental retardation and affect development from infancy to adolescence, is also currently being reviewed.

Studies on the nutritional efficacy of colostrum, human milk, formulas, and solid foods on physiological development, digestion, absorption, transport, metabolism, growth, development of the immune system, and allergic reactions to foods are also underway. Nutritional research is also focusing on the effects of protein-calorie malnutrition, specific nutrient deficiencies, nutrient idiosyncrasies, allergies and toxicity, and social and psychological development.

SOCIAL ECONOMIC FACTORS

Society has frequently failed to realize, or to acknowledge, the importance of poverty in its determinants of developmental outcomes in 75%–85% of persons with mild mental retardation for whom the organic origin of the retardation is not identifiable. Persons living in poverty are more vulnerable to the multiple variables that cause mental retardation. Such variables are:

Poor nutrition
Improper sanitation
Unsafe and substandard housing
Inadequate water supply
Late or absent prenatal care
Delayed medical treatment intervention
Use of walk-in emergency care rather than anticipatory health care
Lack of stimulation in education
Limited parenting
Limited developmental/educational opportunities
Underemployment
Limited resources of all types
Abuse or neglect
Lack of access to services
Depression or other mental disabilities
Lowered expectations
Poor synchrony with the surrounding cultural system
Misdiagnosis of low intelligence
Ignorance regarding good health practices and the need for prevention/intervention.

These data coincide with those presented by Dr. Hobel in (President's Committee on Mental Retardation, 1986) Chapter 8 that indicate that low-income pregnant women who do not receive regular prenatal care have approximately three times as many infant deaths as those who do receive such care. There are also studies that indicate that women who have limited financial resources have a significantly increased risk of having a child with low birth weight and other complications that take place in the 1st year of life. All of this suggests that many of the existing federally assisted support programs are incompletely utilized or undersubscribed. Greater outreach efforts are needed with funding levels that should make available the following: maternal and child health services, including prenatal and obstetrical care for low-income families, transients, and other populations at risk; immunization programs and nutritional programs; early intervention and parent training services; educational programs; day care; comprehensive medical care; social services; and housing assistance.

COGNITION AND MEMORY

Current research on Alzheimer disease and senescence has yielded important information that may be helpful in providing memory enhancers, that could be utilized, along with educational and psychological techniques, to strengthen the cognitive function of persons with mental retardation.

Senescence, for example, is a complicated process that is characterized by many morphological and chemical alterations in the brain. Cognitive functions decline with aging; the biochemical mechanism of this decrease is currently unknown. However, a number of studies have suggested that impaired cholinergic function may be an important factor in the production of memory deficits. Pharmacological manipulation of the cholinergic system in both animals and humans indicates an age-related decrement in cholinergic functioning. Neurophysiological studies also have demonstrated these reductions and have, in particular, found that such cholinergic receptors as choline acetyltransferase (CAT) and acetylcholinesterase (ACE) activities in the brain are reduced with aging and, even more significantly, in Alzheimer-type dementia. Similar results have also been documented in individuals with Down syndrome particularly with the loss of CAT and ACE in the cortical areas that contain plaques and tangles. Research by Dr. Kenneth Davis has demonstrated a significant 10%–25% increase in cognitive functioning with the use of physostigmine and arecoline. Additional research needs to be collected, and this will certainly open up new vistas of potential, particularly if one considers the transmutation of brain tissue from fetuses, which may provide more natural grafting and elicitation of natural neurotransmitters and, thus, preclude cognitive deficits such as the loss of memory, awareness, and concentration associated with depletion of acetylcholine (Christie, Shering, Ferguson, & Glen, 1981).

In addition, although research has progressed slowly, drug studies with rats and mice support the notion that drugs do indeed facilitate memory and retention. No specific drug has been identified, however, to improve learning. Three substances that facilitate retrieval and retention are strychnine, adrenocorticotropic hormone (ACTH), and vasopressin (Heise, 1981). Another drug, piracetam, seems to improve retrieval and maze-learning in rats.

BIOMECHANICS

Inventions for artificial body parts are becoming so ''real,'' that the distinction between body and machine is becoming less and less. For example, an artificial hand has been developed, complete with cosmetic veins and finger-nails, that can be attached to a stump and functions using the existing nerves and ligaments.

Following the same lines of form and function that are found in nature, biomechanics are used to design state-of-the-art inanimate objects, such as a robot holding a fuselage in place. Gideon Ariel, a biomechanician at California's Cots Research Center, has been working with ultra-high-speed film to help decipher the chain of complex acts in a human movement, such as swimmer's stroke. This information is then used to help athletes improve their form. Fascinating research will continue in biomechanics, integrating man and machine.

REFERENCES

A user's guide to hormones. (1987). *Newsweek, Jan. 12,* 50–59.

Christie, J. E., Shering, A., Ferguson, J., & Glen, A. (1981). Physostigmine and arecoline: The effects of intravenous infusions in Alzheimer pre-senile dementia. *British Journal of Psychiatry, 138,* 46–50.

Clewel, W. A., Johnson, M. L., & Meier, P. R. (1982). Surgical approach to the treatment of fetal hydrocephalus. *New England Journal of Medicine, 306,* 1320–1325.

Council on Scientific Affairs. (1983). Utero fetal surgery. *Journal of the American Medical Association, 250*(11), 1443–1444.

Editorial. (1987). *New England Journal of Medicine, 316*(10), 623–624.

Harrison, M. R., Globus, M. S., & Filly, R. A. (1981). Management of the fetus with a correctable congenital defect. *Journal of the American Medical Association, 246,* 774–777.

Heise, G. A. (1981). Learning and memory facilitators: Experimental definition and current status. *Trends in Pharmacological Sciences, June,* 158–160.

Little, R. E., Schultz, F. P., & Mandel, W. (1976). Drinking during pregnancy. *Journal of Studies on Alcohol, 37,* 375–379.

President's Committee on Mental Retardation. (1986). *The prevention of mental retardation related disabilities: A guide for state planning.* Washington, DC: Office of Human Development.

Rosett, H. L., Ouellette, E. M., Winer, L., & Owens, E. (1978). Therapy and heavy drinking during pregnancy. *American Journal of Obstetrics and Gynecology, 51,* 41–46.

Schroeder, S. (1987). *Mental retardation, neurobehavioral toxicity in teratology.* American Association of Mental Deficiency (monograph).

Warner, R., & Rosett, H. (1975). Effects of drinking on offspring: Historical survey of the American and British literature. *Journal of Studies on Alcohol, 36,* 1395–1420.

GENETIC AND DEVELOPMENTAL ASPECTS OF MENTAL RETARDATION

Introduction

Each year, more than 6% of all children are born with genetic diseases, representing some 250,000 children in the United States. These genetic diseases and related disorders account for approximately 25% of all inpatient hospital admissions and placement in long-term care facilities. The roster of these genetic anomalies includes such familiar ailments as sickle-cell anemia, diabetes, and cystic fibrosis. Many of the genetic conditions are also associated with mental retardation. Today, science (particularly as reported in this section) is on the brink of being able to cure some of these diseases, while holding great promise for cure of others over the next two decades.

Genetic diseases are caused by defective DNA. The instructions that describe how to assemble all of the components that go into making an animal or plant are encoded into the DNA, an extremely long molecular chain composed of shorter units called genes. All genetic diseases can be traced to these missing or defective genes. Genetic diseases can be divided into three major categories. First, genetic diseases such as congenital heart lesion, juvenile-onset diabetes, and neurotube defects are caused by complex interactions between one or more genes and the environment, oftentimes affected by a teratogen (an environmental agent that is harmful to the fetus). One third of all childhood deaths and admissions to pediatric inpatient programs are traceable to this type of genetic disease that is multifactorial. Second, genetic diseases such as Down syndrome are caused by chromosomal abnormalities, oftentimes affecting thousands of genes. These first two categories are considered by some to be too complex to be cured in the immediate future.

The third category includes genetic disorders that are caused by defects in a single gene, such as sickle-cell anemia, cystic fibrosis, and muscular dystrophy. Indeed, we know that there are 2,000 different single-gene defects—most notable of which is adenosine deaminase (ADA) deficiency, which results in the loss of immune function very similar to that caused by acquired immune deficiency syndrome. Many research scientists feel quite confident that in the next 10 years we will have widespread treatment for single-gene defects. Researchers have already succeeded in splicing a normal gene into a mouse DNA, and have successfully produced offsprings to prevent ADA. However, they have not yet been able to successfully splice (i.e., produce long-term effects) these genes into dogs and monkeys.

Indeed, gene splicing is a process that holds great promise. Although we lack adequate research paradigms to make significant scientific progress, some scientists, such as Dr. Ron Davis of Stanford, a molecular geneticist, are trying to accomplish this "scientific leap" by conducting research on yeast, microscopic single-cell fungi that live in colonies. Like humans, yeast has two genders and reproduces with cells similar to eggs and sperm. Each cell is a nucleus that separates its DNA from the viscous body of the cytoplasm. And, its 17 pairs of chromosomes behave remarkably like a human's 23 pairs. It can make the same mistakes during reproduction that in humans have led to some chromosomal disorders such as Down syndrome. Yeast manufactures enzymes similar to ours in that it carries them around inside itself and releases the enzymes in much the same way that our tissue cells do. Unlike normal human tissue, yeast thrives in a petri dish and divides once every 2 hours or so, whereas human and mouse cells take 12 hours or more. This means that experiments can be completed more quickly, and yeast has only about 10,000 genes, which is less than 3% of the 400,000 found in human cells, and can be more easily mapped and analyzed in fine detail.

Another major new approach to genetics is being developed by Dr. Charles Epstein and his associates at the Mental Retardation Research Center at the University of California, San Francisco. Although just established in September of 1982, this Mental Retardation Research Center has focused its investigative efforts on four major areas of research as it relates to Down syndrome and specifically trisomy 21: 1) an investigation of interferon in trisomy 21 cells and its effect on the trisomic immune system; 2) an analysis of the mechanism by which chromosome imbalance (technically referred to as aneuploidy) results in the deleterious effects on developmental function; 3) the establishment of an animal system for producing aneuploidy, resulting in the first animal model for trisomy 21 research; and 4) the investigation of gene deletions that produce severe mental retardation, which often leads to embryonic death early in gestation.

Trisomy 21 is the most frequent chromosomal abnormality, occurring in approximately 1 of every 800–1,000 newborns. Trisomy 21, the presence of an extra chromosome 21 in humans, causes a multitude of major and minor abnormalities that collectively create the phenotype referred to as Down syndrome. It is widely believed that no single gene on the human chromosome is thought to produce all of the alterations observed in Down syndrome individuals. Rather, the cumulative effects of an elevated dosage (or too many of a number of genes—probably in hundreds if not thousands) contribute to the major concern in by Down syndrome—mental retardation.

Epstein and his colleagues have established themselves as among the top major researchers in the world in the area of the neurobiology of Down syndrome (see Epstein, 1986). They distinctly point out that the prevalence of Down syndrome will not significantly fall in the foreseeable future, even with improved genetic counseling and prenatal diagnostic techniques and interventions. What is needed therefore (and is discussed in Chapter 2) is a new approach to investigating the mechanisms by which this chromosome imbalance, aneuploidy, results in abnormalities in development and function. One would expect that the word *aneuploidy* will become a more generic term among all disciplines in understanding this important new research focus. The elements of Down syndrome have been divided into three categories that are not mutually exclusive: 1) physical anomalies, 2) cellular alterations, and 3) functional abnormalities. Based upon the pioneering work of other researchers in the early 1970s, Epstein and his colleagues have been able to develop a successful animal model for better understanding the ways of preventing or reversing the physical, cellular, or functional deficits that could be directly related to human research. Their hypothesis is that many groups of genes closely linked to one another on individual human chromosomes are also closely linked to one another on single mouse chromosomes. Their basic approach has been to map genes known to be in human chromosome 21 onto the map genome, using conventional techniques. In essence, trisomy 16 in the mouse model is very similar to trisomy 21 in the human chromosome. However, the problem of the pathogenesis of Down syndrome is a complex one that results in the synthesis of 50% increased amounts of large numbers of gene products that lead to mental retardation and other symptoms. Nevertheless, Epstein and his colleagues remain optimistic about eventually arriving at an understanding of the structural and functional abnormalities associated with Down syndrome. Their ongoing work should make major contributions to advancing our knowledge in this area.

In 1908, Sir Archibald Garrod delivered a series of lectures in which he introduced the term "inborn errors of metabolism," which is still used today. With four metabolic disorders, he noticed that there were several features in common: 1) they appeared in the first few months of life, 2) they tended to be passed down along family lines, 3) those who were affected tended to live relatively long with minimal disability, and 4) there was a high occurrence of an inborn error in children of marriages of close relatives. In these biochemical-genetic disorders, the "errors" are disorders of the biochemical reactions that produce energy and vital substances. Figure 1 illustrates how: 1) genes in the body control the formation of enzymes; 2) the enzymes control the rate and the direction of the chemical reactions within the body; 3) the amount of substance B and substance C is controlled by enzymes 1 and 2, respectively; and 4) a mutant in gene 3 can cause a deficiency in enzyme 1 and a substance decrease in substance B leading to an increase in substances A and C.

The major theory is that gene mutations occur through deletions, substitutions, or transpositions. If any one of these processes occurs at a critical

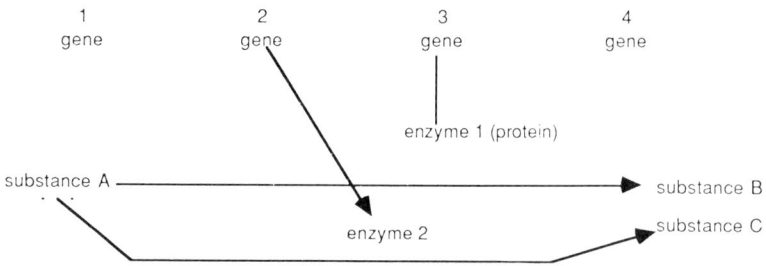

Figure 1. Genes, enzymes, and the formation of chemical substances within the body. (Adapted and reprinted from Menolascino, F., & Egger, M. [1978]. *Medical Dimensions of Mental Retardation.* Lincoln: University of Nebraska Press.)

stage, a defective enzyme will be made, resulting in an ''inborn error of metabolism.'' Such errors are nearly always inherited in an autosomal recessive fashion.

Of the several metabolism errors that are known, many are associated with mental retardation. These errors can be subclassified as: 1) disorders of protein metabolism, 2) disorders of carbohydrate metabolism, 3) disorders of lipid metabolism, and 4) connective tissue disorders. Figure 2 shows the biochemical imbalance caused by the defective enzyme.

The absence of one functioning enzyme (A) can result in deficiencies in the production of some compounds (B) and, by failing to use up the precursor substances (compound A), can overload the other chemical pathways for disposing of precursors, resulting in excesses of other compounds (compounds A, C, D, and E), which may be deleterious. The most important of the inborn errors of metabolism that cause mental retardation are phenylketonuria

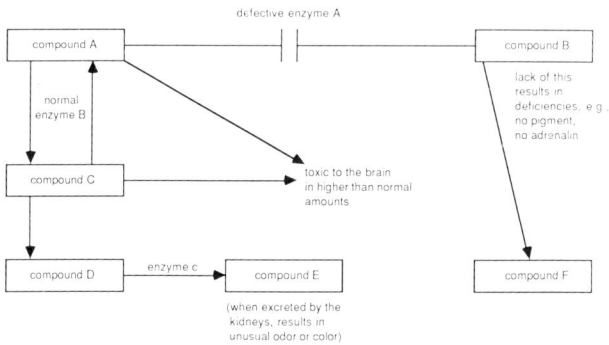

Figure 2. Biochemical imbalance caused by a defective enzyme. The absence of one functioning enzyme (A) can result in deficiencies in the production of some compounds (B) and, by failing to use up the precursor substances (compound A), can overload the other chemical pathways for disposing of the precursor, resulting in excesses of other compounds (compounds A, C, D, and E), which may be deleterious.

(protein metabolism), galactosemia (carbohydrate metabolism), maple syrup urine disease (MSUD), homocystinuria, and tyrosinemia.

During the last 30 years, Dr. Koch and his colleagues have been widely recognized as leading researchers in diagnosis and treatment of inborn errors of metabolism. In Chapter 3, they report on the national collaborative study of phenylketonuria, a disorder that if untreated can have devastating effects. Dr. Koch has conducted an extensive study involving treated and untreated phenylketonuria subjects in which comparisons were made on intellectual, academic, and neurological test instruments. The thesis of this research showed that while early initiation of treatment by dietary procedures was important, ongoing adherence to the diet, as measured by the rate of increase of blood phenylalanine over time, was also important. Recommendations for screening and follow-up procedures for such a population will be helpful to researchers and clinicians involved with this population.

Maple syrup urine disease, homocystinuria, tyrosinemia, and, particularly, galactosemia are commented on also as being rare but important metabolic disorders that need early diagnosis and prompt treatment. If strict dietary procedures are followed, the long-term prognosis is excellent. Dr. Koch and his colleagues demonstrate in Chapter 3 that multiple screening programs are contributing to our growing scientific knowledge base and that other inborn errors of metabolism should be added to screening programs for early treatment. Their recommendations and findings should serve as a valuable model for all those concerned with individuals who exhibit inborn errors of metabolism disorders.

REFERENCE

Epstein, C. J. (Ed.). (1986). *The neurobiology of Down syndrome*. New York: Raven Press.

Chapter 2

New Approaches to the Study of Down Syndrome

Charles J. Epstein

Chromosomal abnormalities constitute a frequent cause of moderate to severe mental retardation, and of these, trisomy 21 is the most common. Approximately 1 in 800–1,000 newborns is born with this condition and, with improved medical care and social management, a large fraction of these individuals survive well into the adult years. In contrast to the relatively short life expectancies quoted only a few decades ago, current estimates of life expectancy now go well into the sixth and seventh decades (Thase, 1982). Therefore, despite the modest reductions in the incidence of trisomy 21 that have resulted from the use of prenatal diagnosis and the changing demography of child bearing, it is likely that the prevalence of Down syndrome, the consequence of trisomy 21, will not fall significantly in the foreseeable future. Even if 50% of all pregnant women 35 years of age or older undergo prenatal diagnosis and all trisomic pregnancies are terminated, the reduction in the incidence of trisomy 21 at birth will only be 11% (Adams, Erickson, Layde, & Oakley, 1981).

It is apparent that present methods for the prevention of the birth of individuals with trisomy 21 will have only limited success. Therefore, better approaches to the treatment of affected persons will have to be developed if the burdens imposed by Down syndrome on individuals, families, and society are to be lightened. Aside from certain specific medical problems, such as congenital heart disease and, in a few cases, gastrointestinal obstruction, which are generally amenable to surgical correction, the major burden is that imposed by mental retardation. However, the central nervous system problems do not end here, since there is now mounting evidence that indicates that additional difficulties await the increasing number of individuals with Down syndrome who survive into and beyond the fourth decade of life. These difficulties are of two types. The first is a progressive loss of intellectual

This work was supported by grants from the National Institutes of Health (HD-17001), the American Cancer Society (CD-119), and the March of Dimes Birth Defects Foundation (1-760).

function so that certain cognitive and other skills (such as short-term memory, attention, and visuospatial ability) gradually diminish as the individual ages (Schapiro, Haxby, Grady, & Rapoport, 1986; Thase, Liss, Smeltzer, & Maloon, 1982). The second problem is the development, in all trisomy 21 individuals over the age of 35 years, of pathological changes resulting in Alzheimer disease (Ball, Schapiro, & Rapoport, 1986) and, in about 25% of these persons, of the clinical dementia associated with Alzheimer disease (Wisniewski, Wisniewski, & Wen, 1985). Whether the progressive loss of intellectual function is the result of the pathological changes in the brain or represents an independent phenomenon still remains to be determined.

The individual with trisomy 21 thus enters life with cognitive dysfunction resulting in mental retardation and ends life with gradual loss of intellectual function, pathological degenerative changes in the brain of the type found in Alzheimer disease, and, in some instances, with frank dementia. How then can one attempt to intervene therapeutically and to alter this situation? One approach, of course, is the use of empirical modes of therapy, therapies with little or no basis in theory or fact. Such therapies have abounded in Down syndrome, their most recent expressions being the injection of heterologous (foreign) cells and the administration of vitamins, minerals, and other nutrients in very large (''mega'') doses. Cell therapy has never been subjected to any form of controlled clinical trial; its efficacy is wholly unproven, and its safety has not been established (Karp, 1983). Although encouraging results with nutritional supplements have been reported (Harrell, Capp, Davis, Peerless, & Ravitz, 1981; Turkel, 1975), a controlled study (Smith, Spiker, Peterson, Cicchetti, & Justice, 1984) has not upheld the claims of rapid and dramatic improvements in IQ. Similarly, therapeutic attempts with more of a scientific basis, such as the administration of 5-hydroxytryptophan, a precursor of serotonin (5-hydroxytryptamine), have not met with any success (Weise, Koch, Shaw, & Rosenfeld, 1974).

It appears, therefore, that new strategies for the management and treatment of the neurological problems (which include the mental retardation) of Down syndrome will have to be developed. These strategies, which will hopefully be more rational than those employed thus far, will, in my view, have to be based on three types of approaches (Epstein, 1986c):

1. A definition of the anatomical and functional abnormalities of the nervous and other systems in Down syndrome
2. A consideration of the basic processes that could, if perturbed, lead to the abnormalities observed in Down syndrome
3. A delineation of the impact of imbalance of specific loci on human chromosome 21 on development and function

These three approaches, while stated separately, are not really independent of one another (see Figure 1). Knowledge in any one area will, of course,

TREAT, CURE, PREVENT
ABNORMALITIES OF
DOWN SYNDROME

DEFINE ABNORMALITIES   UNDERSTAND RELATIONSHIPS
OF DOWN SYNDROME   OF TRISOMY 21 TO ABNORMALITIES

UNDERSTAND BASIC PROCESSES
OF DEVELOPMENT AND
FUNCTION

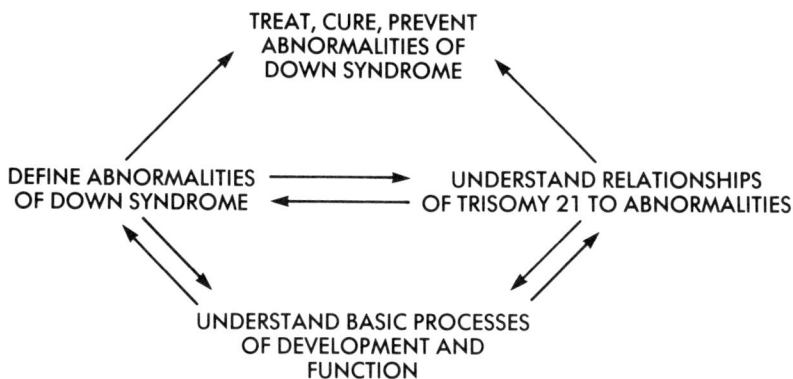

Figure 1. The interrelationships of several approaches to the development of methods for the treatment, prevention, and cure of the abnormalities resulting from trisomy 21.

influence studies and interpretations in the other. Nevertheless, from the point of view of investigation and analysis, it is convenient to consider each approach separately.

The basic premise underlying all of this work is that an understanding of the mechanisms by which aneuploidy (chromosome imbalance), in this case trisomy 21, produces its deleterious effects may permit us to develop strategies to counteract these effects. Such strategies will probably not be applicable to morphogenetic aberrations that are beyond the point of intervention by the time they are recognized. However, they may ultimately offer hope for counteracting some of the functional deficits brought about or associated with trisomy 21, the most significant in the long range being, of course, mental retardation.

ANATOMICAL AND FUNCTIONAL ABNORMALITIES IN DOWN SYNDROME

The aggregate of anatomical and functional abnormalities that result from trisomy 21 are the features that constitute the phenotype of Down syndrome. These phenotypic features, which are summarized in Table 1, can be divided into three categories: physical, cellular, and functional.

The *physical* features of Down syndrome are those that give affected individuals their distinctive appearance. For the most part, they are mild and fall into the category of minor congenital malformations or dysmorphic features. None of these features is necessarily unique to Down syndrome and any of them can appear in either normal individuals or in individuals with other types of multiple malformation syndromes of whatever etiology. Nevertheless, the total constellation or combination of features in Down syndrome

Table 1. Phenotype of Down syndrome

Frequency or amount	Features
	Physical
>80%[a]	Oblique palpebral fissures, loose skin on nape of neck
71%–80%	Narrow palate, brachycephaly, hyperflexibility
61%–70%	Flat nasal bridge, gap between first and second toes, short broad hands, short neck, abnormal teeth
51%–60%	Epicanthic folds, short incurved fifth finger, open mouth, Brushfield spots, furrowed protruding tongue, transverse palmar crease, folded/dysplastic ear
40%	Congenital heart disease
12%	Gastrointestinal malformations
	Cellular
3–15-fold[b]	Enhanced cellular sensitivity to interferon
5–9-fold	Exaggerated fibroblast cyclic AMP response to β-adrenergic agonists
3–5-fold	Increased adhesiveness of fetal lung and heart fibroblasts
1.4–6-fold	Increased cellular sensitivity to viral transformation
≤2-fold	Increased cellular sensitivity to radiation
0.4-fold	Decreased platelet serotonin
	Functional
	Mental retardation
	Hypotonia
	Presenile dementia (Alzheimer disease)
	Altered immune response
10–18-fold[c]	Increased frequency of leukemia (also leukemoid responses)
	Growth retardation

Data taken from Epstein (1986a).
[a]Proportion of individuals with Down syndrome who display feature.
[b]Increase of property in cells of individuals with Down syndrome.
[c]Increase in frequency over normal population.

is highly diagnostic of the presence of trisomy 21. And, although most of these features are without pathological significance, the abnormalities of the heart (most characteristic of which are endocardial cushion defects) and the gastrointestinal tract (in the form of duodenal atresia or megacolon) can be quite serious and may require surgical intervention.

The *cellular* phenotype of Down syndrome consists of those alterations in the metabolism and reactivity of cells that appear to be specific consequences of trisomy 21. Some of the changes from normal cellular behavior are quite large, as, for example, in the cellular sensitivity to interferon (Epstein & Epstein, 1983) and the enhanced responsiveness of fibroblasts to the cyclic AMP-inducing effect of β-adrenergic agonists such as isoproterenol (Sheppard et al., 1982). Other changes, such as those in the sensitivity of cells to viral transformation and to the chromosome-breaking effects of radiation, are much more subtle and their true existence and significance are still debatable. Nevertheless, cellular alterations of the type listed in the table—and there is undoubtedly a much larger number yet to be defined—are of still greater interest. They may represent more immediate and, ultimately, more accessible, in so far as detailed analysis is concerned, manifestations of the chromosomal imbalance and may in some instances be directly or indirectly involved in the pathogenesis of the functional or physical abnormalities that result from trisomy 21. A detailed review of the cellular phenotype of Down syndrome is given by Epstein (1986a).

The *functional* abnormalities in Down syndrome are quite diverse. They range from retardation of growth and an increased susceptibility to infection and to development of leukemia to the abnormalities of neurological function that have already been described. It is the latter group of abnormalities, and particularly those that affect cognition, that are, of course, of paramount concern with regard to potential therapeutic interventions. However, other functional abnormalities, which are considered in detail in Epstein (1986a), are once again of great importance for two reasons. One is that they do have clinical relevance. The other is that they, like the cellular abnormalities, may provide important clues to the nature of the molecular and developmental defects resulting from the presence of an extra chromosome 21.

Not included anywhere in the list of phenotypic features of Down syndrome presented in Table 1 are the specific anatomical changes in the nervous system. While there now seems to be agreement that degenerative changes of the same type—quantitatively, qualitatively, and geographically—as occur in Alzheimer disease occur late in life in individuals with Down syndrome (Ball et al., 1986), less clear-cut evidence of the nature of changes in the brain early in life has been forthcoming. Much of the neuroanatomy and neuropathology of the past, in so far as it applies to the central nervous system of fetuses, infants, and young children with Down syndrome, must be considered as being highly suspect. However, recent studies, particularly those of Wisniewski and her collaborators, do suggest that there may be significant and relatively specific abnormalities in the young Down syndrome nervous system. The most characteristic of these appears to be a reduction in the numbers of neurons and synaptic connections in certain parts of the brain (Wisniewski, Laure-Kamionowska, Connell, & Wen, 1986). The numbers of nerve cells in the occipital, temporal, and prefrontal cortices are decreased, as are neuronal densities. These decreases in neuronal density range from 20% to

50%. Of particular note are decreases in neurons in Layers II and IV of the prefrontal (entorhinal) cortex, neurons that project to the hippocampal cortex, and in the neurons of Layers II and IV of the temporal cortex itself. In addition to the decreases in neuron numbers and density, synaptic density was decreased from 1% to 29% in the visual cortex, but of possibly greater significance is a 20%–35% decrease in the mean surface area per synaptic contact.

The neuroanatomical alterations just described, when considered in terms of the functions subserved by particular regions of the brain, may, for the first time, give us some insight into the basis of the cognitive dysfunction in Down syndrome. For example, Nadel (1986) has pointed to the role of the hippocampus as an integrating region for higher thought processes. If this is in fact the case, the cellular defects of the type described by Wisniewski et al. (1986) could well be of importance in contributing to the development of mental retardation.

In addition to anatomical changes in the brains of young individuals with Down syndrome, electrophysiological alterations of the central nervous system have also been described both in vivo and in vitro and have been reviewed respectively by Scott (1986) and Scott, Becker, and Petit (1983), and by Galbraith (1986). At a minimum, these changes are reflections of underlying structural and functional alterations of the nervous system. However, it is not unlikely that they may, like the alterations in numbers of neurons and synapses, also play a role in the development of mental retardation.

BASIC PROCESSES OF DEVELOPMENT AND FUNCTION

A broad consideration of the basic processes that could, if perturbed, lead to the abnormalities found in Down syndrome (such as those described in the preceding section) is beyond the scope of this chapter. This subject has been reviewed in considerable detail in Epstein (1986a) for aneuploidy in general and in Epstein (1986b) for the central nervous system in Down syndrome. However, two points can be made.

The ability to identify which basic processes are involved in the pathogenesis of the manifestations of trisomy 21 depends, as is illustrated in Figure 1, on several factors. First, it is necessary to know exactly what is abnormal in Down syndrome. Therefore, studies of the type described earlier and summarized in Table 1 need to be expanded and extended. In particular, the lesions, both anatomical and functional, present in the central nervous system need to be more fully defined. And, in addition, the psychological deficits—the actual abnormalities of cognition that result in mental retardation—must be characterized in such a manner that they can ultimately be related to the neurobiological alterations. Second, knowledge of the identities and functions of the specific genes on chromosome 21 will make it possible to focus on particular developmental and functional processes that are likely to be perturbed by the presence of an extra copy of chromosome 21. How this approach can be used is discussed in the following section. And, third, there needs to be an expansion of information in the general fields of neurobiology and psychology and, hopefully, an increased understanding of the interrelationships between the two. It is this information and understanding that will ultimately make it possible to explain exactly what has gone wrong in Down syndrome.

The second point regarding basic processes is that, while specific ones that are perturbed cannot as yet be identified, it is possible to venture a guess about which might be particularly affected by a trisomic state. A list of such processes or systems is given in Table 2. Based on a consideration of mechanisms by which extra doses of genes (see below) might alter structure and function, it has been inferred that certain processes might be particularly vulnerable to perturbation (Epstein, 1986a). Chief among these are processes involving cellular interaction (recognition, adhesion, communication), growth factors and morphogens, and receptors (particularly those concerned with growth factors and morphogens). Precedent for the potential involvement of cellular interaction factors already exists for Down syndrome. Wright, Orkin, Destrempes, and Kurnit (1984) have demonstrated that the adhesivity of fibroblasts from the hearts and lungs of trisomy 21 fetuses is increased (Table 1), and Kurnit, Aldridge, Matsuoka, and Matthyse (1985) have provided theoretical arguments showing how such a change could lead to the occurrence of congenital heart disease. Likewise, both experimental studies (Hoffman & Edelman, 1983) and theoretical considerations (Epstein, 1986a; Rutishauser, 1986) have shown how small changes in the concentration of a cell surface recognition or adhesion molecule could have a profound impact on cellular interactions.

None of the considerations just discussed necessarily eliminates macromolecules, metabolic pathways (enzymes), transport systems, or regulatory systems from consideration as sites of abnormalities resulting from trisomy. In fact, particular attention has been devoted to such systems, particularly

Table 2. Mechanisms mediating the secondary effects of aneuploidy

System affected	Potential impact on phenotype in trisomy
Cellular interactions (recognition, adhesion, communication)	+ +
Receptors	+ +
Growth factors and morphogens	+ +
Regulatory systems (specific)	+
Assembly of macromolecules	±
Metabolic pathways (enzymes)	±
Transport of nutrients and metabolites	±

Modified from Epstein (1986a).

enzymes, in the study of trisomy 21 (see below). However, the experimental and theoretical information available suggests that these systems are, in general, less likely to be of great importance in a condition such as trisomy 21 (Epstein, 1986a).

IMPACT OF IMBALANCE
OF SPECIFIC LOCI ON HUMAN CHROMOSOME 21

The approach to the investigation of the abnormalities present in Down syndrome that I have personally been most interested in has been the analysis of the effects of unbalancing genes or loci known to be present on human chromosome 21. Of particular interest are those genes present on the distal half of the long arm of chromosome 21, in the region (21q22 → q22.2) that is specifically implicated in the genesis of the phenotype of Down syndrome (Rethoré, 1981; Summitt, 1981). The list of genes definitely or provisionally mapped to human chromosome 21 is relatively small (Table 3), but several of these genes appear to be in the Down syndrome region (Table 3; Figure 2): *SOD1* (superoxide dismutase-1), *PRGS* (phosphoribosylglycinamide synthetase, a purine biosynthetic enzyme), *PFKL* (phosphofructokinase, liver isoenzyme), and *IFRC,* now *IFNRA* (receptor for interferons α and β).

Table 3.   The genes on human chromosome 21

Gene symbol	Gene name	Regional assignment
	Confirmed[a]	
CBS	Cystathionine β-synthase	q21-q22.1
ADAP	Amyloid β protein	q21-q22.1
IFNRA	Interferon-α receptor	q21-qter
PRGS	Phosphoribosylglycinamide synthetase	q22.1
SOD1	Superoxide dismutase-1	q22.1
PFKL	Phosphofructokinase, liver type	q22.3
BCE1	Breast cancer, estrogen-inducible gene	q22.3
CRYA1	Crystallin, alpha-A2 polypeptide	q22.3
ETS2	Proto-oncogene, homologous to avian oncogene E26	q22.3
	Provisional	
PAIS	Phosphoribosylaminoimidazole synthetase	
MF13	Antigen (glycoprotein, MW 86K)	
MF14	Antigen (glycoprotein, MW 145K)	
MF17	Leukocyte-cell adhesion molecule (phorbol ester induced, MW 90K)	
S14	Surface antigen	

Data from Human Gene Mapping 8 (1985), Watson et al. (1986), and Lovett et al. (1987).
[a] Assignment to chromosome 21 made by two independent methods or investigators.

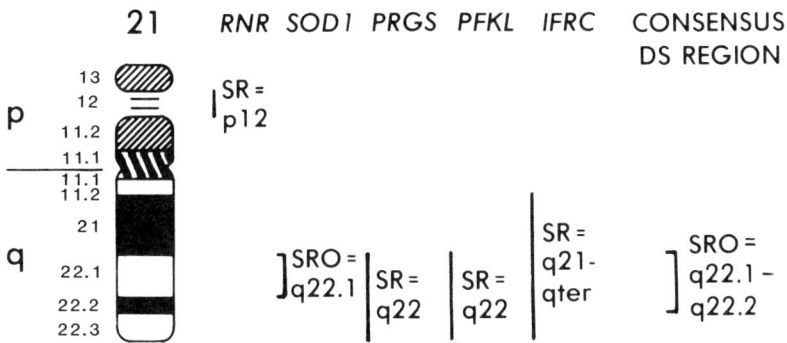

Figure 2. Regional mapping of genes on human chromosome 21. SR, smallest region; SRO, smallest region of overlap (of several partial duplications or deletions). The consensus region for the phenotypic features of Down syndrome is that defined by Rethoré (1981) and Summitt (1981). (Modified from Epstein 1986a.)

For the most part, studies of the genes on chromosome 21 have taken the form of determinations of the quantities of gene products and have demonstrated, for five known chromosome 21 genes, that the presence of an extra gene copy in trisomic cells is reflected in a proportional increase in the quantity of gene product, whether enzyme or receptor (Table 4). These *gene dosage effects* for chromosome 21 genes, with an overall mean increase of 1.55-fold, are consonant with the gene dosage effects observed for trisomies affecting a total of 37 human and 7 mouse loci, for which there were mean increases of 1.61 and 1.55, respectively (Epstein, 1986a). An increase of 50%, to 1.5 times the value present in nontrisomic (diploid) cells, is, of course, what would be expected in a trisomic state if, as appears to be the case, no system for dosage compensation exists.

Further explorations of the consequences of the increased dosage of chromosome 21 genes have been concerned with whether the extra amounts

Table 4. Gene dosage effects in trisomy 21

Locus	Function	Ts/2n[a]
CBS	Cystathionine β-synthase activity in stimulated lymphocytes	1.61
IFNRA	Interferon-α binding to fibroblasts	1.57
PFKL	Phosphofructokinase activity in red cells	1.47
PRGS	Phosphoriboglycinamide synthetase activity in fibroblasts	1.56
SOD1	Superoxide dismutase-1 activity in red cells, fibroblasts, platelets, lymphocytes, brain, granulocytes	1.52

Data from Epstein (1986a) and Arias, Paradisi, and Rolo (1985).

[a]Ratio of activities in trisomic (Ts) and diploid (2n) cells.

of gene products are reflected in detectable metabolic alterations. One locus, the interferon-α (IFN-α) receptor (*IFNRA*), has been studied directly and another, *SOD1*, both indirectly and directly. For the IFN-α receptor, trisomy 21 fibroblasts have the expected $\simeq$ 1.5 times the normal amount of receptor, as demonstrated by a 1.57-fold increase in the binding of IFN-α, and demonstrate proportional increases in the induction by IFN-α of the enzyme 2',5'-oligoisoadenylate synthetase and of eight intracellular peptides of unknown function (Figure 3). However, when the physiological effects of interferon treatment were examined, the responsiveness or sensitivity of trisomic cells to the antiviral effect of IFN-α was increased anywhere from 3- to 15-fold (mean = 6.3) and to all effects by 5-fold. We have attributed this functional amplification to the extra dose of the IFN-α receptor (Epstein, 1986a; Weil, Tucker, Epstein, & Epstein, 1983), although it still remains to be proven that this is in fact the case.

Much has been written about the increased concentration of superoxide dismutase-1 (SOD-1) in trisomic cells and tissues and its potential role in the pathogenesis of certain of the neurological abnormalities of Down syndrome (Sinet, 1982; Sinet, Lejeune, & Jerome, 1979). SOD-1 catalyzes the conversion (dismutation) of $O_2{}^-$ radicals to H_2O_2 and O_2. However, the evidence for functional alterations in the metabolism of oxygen compounds as a result of increased SOD-1 activity is quite sketchy. The most persuasive results are those of Groner and his collaborators (Groner et al., 1985). They found that cells overexpressing SOD-1 by 2- to 6-fold (after transfection with cloned *SOD1* genes) are more *resistant* to paraquat, an agent that leads to the generation of superoxide radicals. By contrast, it has been claimed by others that trisomic fibroblasts, with only 1.5 times more SOD-1 than normal, are more *sensitive* to the toxic effects of 95% oxygen, which are also attributed to superoxide generation, in terms of both decreased survival and increased lipid

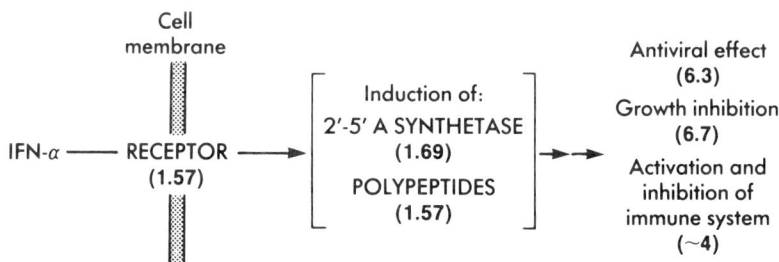

Figure 3. Effects of increased dosage of the interferon-α receptor in trisomy 21. The numbers in **boldface** represent the degree of increase in the binding of interferon (receptor) or in the induction of synthetase and polypeptides in trisomy 21 cells as compared with diploid controls, or the enhanced sensitivity of trisomic cells to various biological effects of interferon. 2'–5' A SYNTHETASE, 2',5'-oligoisoadenylate synthetase. (Data taken from Epstein & Epstein, 1983, and Weil et al., 1983.)

peroxidation (Mayes, Muneer, & Sifers, 1984). These contradictory results remain to be reconciled, but do lead to the possibility that an increase in SOD-1 activity could indeed have functional consequences, at least under conditions of oxidative stress that lead to the generation of superoxide.

The results obtained from studies of the interferon receptor and superoxide dismutase-1 systems in trisomy 21, as well as from the other genes studied both in trisomy 21 (Table 4) and in other trisomies and monosomies (Epstein, 1986a), indicate that the primary effects of all aneuploid states, which are themselves conditions in which there are abnormalities of gene dosage, are proportional alterations in the rates of synthesis of gene messenger RNAs (mRNAs) coded for by the unbalanced chromosome or chromosome region. Although one might expect that systems for regulating the rates of synthesis of mRNAs would exist, so that constant synthetic rates are maintained, no evidence for such regulatory systems has been obtained (Epstein, 1986a). Similarly, the 50% increases in synthetic rates found in trisomies appear, in all cases examined so far, to result in 50% increases in the concentrations of gene products. Posttranslational regulation of gene product concentration does not appear to occur. However, since virtually all of the products examined were enzymes, it is conceivable that the synthesis of other types of gene products might be more tightly regulated. However, no data in support of such a notion have as yet been obtained.

How are such proportional gene dosage effects translated into abnormalities of development and function? In the previous section, several systems that might be vulnerable to such effects are discussed, and Table 2 is based upon a consideration of what the molecular consequences of extra doses of gene products might be. At the present time, any discussion of how gene dosage effects result in developmental or functional abnormalities must be considered as being highly speculative in nature. However, the major inference that can be drawn is not. Any mechanism proposed to explain how trisomy 21 causes mental retardation, or hypotonia, or Alzheimer disease, must ultimately be able to begin with one or more specific chromosome 21 genes present in an extra dose, proceed through the demonstration of the existence of 50% more of the gene product or products coded for by these genes, and then relate the increased amount(s) of product to the genesis of a specific functional or morphogenetic abnormality (Figure 4). The last relationship, of increased gene product to specific abnormality, may either be a direct one or, more likely, an indirect one involving a series of intermediate events. Stated the other way around, any proposed pathogenetic mechanisms for neurological or other abnormalities in trisomy 21 must ultimately lead back to the quantitative imbalance of a specific gene or set of genes. Down syndrome, like the other aneuploid conditions, is a genetic disease resulting from abnormal gene dosage, not abnormal gene structure, and must ultimately be explicable as such.

TRISOMY 21

↓

1.5 x GENE DOSAGE

↓

1.5 x SYNTHESIS OF GENE PRODUCT(S)

↓
↓
↓

FUNCTIONAL OR MORPHOGENETIC ABNORMALITY

↓

MENTAL RETARDATION, HYPOTONIA, ALZHEIMER DISEASE

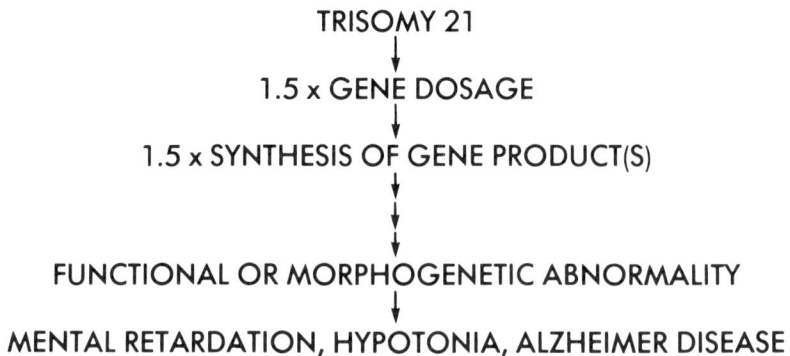

Figure 4. The chain of events relating the presence of an extra chromosome 21 to the neurological manifestations of Down syndrome.

Calculations based on the sizes of chromosome 21 and of individual genes suggest that the number of genes potentially involved in the neurological and other abnormalities of Down syndrome is anywhere from 100 to 1,000 (Epstein, 1986c). Such estimates might lead one to be pessimistic about being able to identify a set of genes responsible for the neurological abnormalities associated with trisomy 21, but this need not be the case. There is nothing implicit in the existence of such a large number of genes that excludes the possibility that a relatively small number of genes may play a disproportionately great role in determining the fate of the nervous system and other affected tissues and organs, at least under conditions of genetic imbalance. Once again, as the earlier discussion of the IFN-α receptor and SOD-1 indicates, it is not the imbalance itself that is injurious to the organism, but, rather, the way in which this imbalance alters development or function. Therefore, in a region the size of the distal half of human chromosome 21, there is still a reasonable possibility that imbalance of only a few genes is the major source of the difficulty—or at least of certain aspects of the problem. In this regard, however, it must not be assumed that the neurological abnormalities of Down syndrome are all of a piece, with a common cause. It is certainly not unreasonable to suspect that this may not be the case; the basis of the hypotonia may have nothing to do with that of the cognitive defect, and also may not be related to the Alzheimer disease type of degenerative changes that occur later in life.

ANIMAL MODEL OF HUMAN TRISOMY 21

The notion of developing mouse models for human autosomal aneuploidy became tenable when Gropp, Giers, and Kolbus (1974) and White, Tjio, Van de Water, and Crandall (1974) first described methods for generating trisomic mice. In these pioneering efforts, it was shown that a significant number of the progeny of mice heterozygous for Robertsonian fusion (translocation, metacentric) chromosomes would, as in the human situation, be trisomic. The power of the method was significantly increased when Gropp, Kolbus, and Giers (1975) showed that aneuploidy for specific individual autosomes could be induced at a high frequency (of the order of 15%–20%) when one parent, usually the male, is doubly heterozygous for two different Robertsonian chromosomes that share one chromosome arm in common (Figure 5). Using this

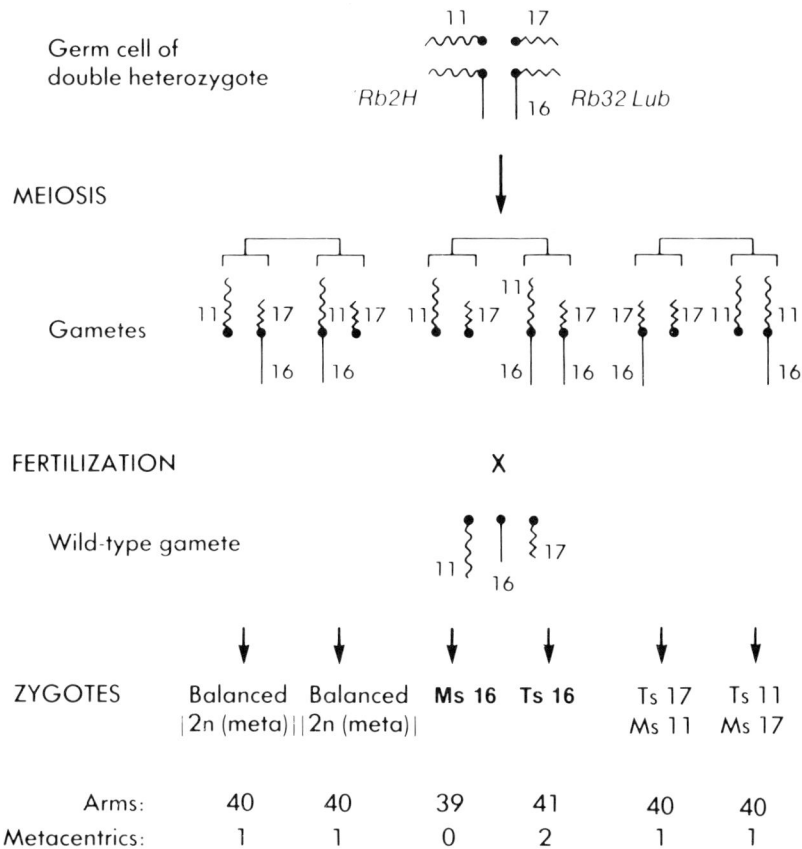

Figure 5. The generation of mouse embryos and fetuses with trisomy (Ts) or monosomy (Ms) for chromosome 16. A male carrying two Robertsonian fusion chromosomes, *Rb(11.16)2H* and *Rb(16.17)32Lub,* each of which contains chromosome 16, is mated with a wild-type female. Of the various segregation patterns possible in the male, one generates conceptuses with trisomy 16. The trisomic state is readily recognizable cytogenetically, even in unbanded preparations, by the presence of 2 metacentric fusion chromosomes and a total of 41 chromosome arms (the diploid number is 40). Only balanced and trisomy 16 embryos survive beyond implantation. (Modified from Epstein, 1985b.)

approach, Gropp and his collaborators systematically produced and studied mice trisomic for each of the 19 mouse autosomes (for review, see Epstein, 1985a, 1986a). As would be expected from what is known about human aneuploids, trisomic mice differ considerably from one another in their phenotypes and display a wide variety of congenital abnormalities of development. Furthermore, and again not unexpectedly if the human situation is kept in mind, nearly all of the mouse trisomics die sometime during gestation.

Given the ability to generate aneuploid mice with predictable types of chromosomal imbalance at a high frequency, it became possible to consider the production of trisomic mice that could constitute a model for human trisomy 21 (Epstein, 1981). The reasons for wanting to develop such a model were several. In general terms, one of the principal difficulties in studying human disorders of development, particularly if the nervous system is involved, is the inability, for both technical and ethical reasons, to study more than a very restricted number of tissues and developmental processes. The developing human fetus is inaccessible to any type of systematic study, and the brain can only be approached postmortem or, during life, by a limited number of noninvasive techniques. Therefore, to be able to study the mechanisms discussed above that underlie the development of abnormalities associated with trisomy 21, abnormalities both of prenatal somatic and neurological development and probably of postnatal neurological development and function as well, it is necessary to have experimental systems that lend themselves to convenient analysis. While initially directed toward issues of mechanism, such analysis could, if specific metabolic lesions are identified, ultimately also turn to considerations of therapy and, again, a model system would be most useful.

Our decision to attempt the development of a mouse model for human trisomy 21 was based on the premise that it should be possible to study the effects of increased doses of particular human chromosome 21 genes, or sets of such genes, by using mice that are trisomic for the particular mouse chromosome or chromosomes that carry the human chromosome 21 homologous loci. That it might be possible that these loci are actually present on just one or, at worst, a very few mouse chromosomes was suggested by the large number of data that demonstrate the existence of conserved syntenic regions in the mouse and human genome (for recent review, see Nadeau & Taylor, 1984). In other words, many groups of genes closely linked to one another on individual human chromosomes are also closely linked to one another on single mouse chromosomes. Given these precedents, the basic approach was to map genes known to be on human chromosome 21 onto the mouse genome, using conventional somatic cell genetic techniques.

Of the quite limited number of identified loci now known to be present on human chromosome 21, three (*SOD1*, *PRGS*, and *IFRC* [*IFNRA*]) had been mapped in the mouse by 1982, and all three were on mouse chromosome

16 (Cox, Epstein, & Epstein, 1980; Cox, Goldblatt, & Epstein, 1981; Francke & Taggart, 1979; Lin, Slate, Lawyer, & Ruddle, 1980) (Figure 6). That
all three of these human chromosome 21 genes are present on the same mouse
chromosome, and that two of them (*SOD1* and *PRGS*) are present on defined
small regions of each chromosome (Cox & Epstein, 1985) strongly suggested
that a human chromosome 21 region of significant size has, as hoped, been
evolutionarily conserved between man and mouse. This region is the same
one to which the phenotype of Down syndrome has been localized (Figure 6).
Recently, two additional genes have been mapped to human chromosome 21

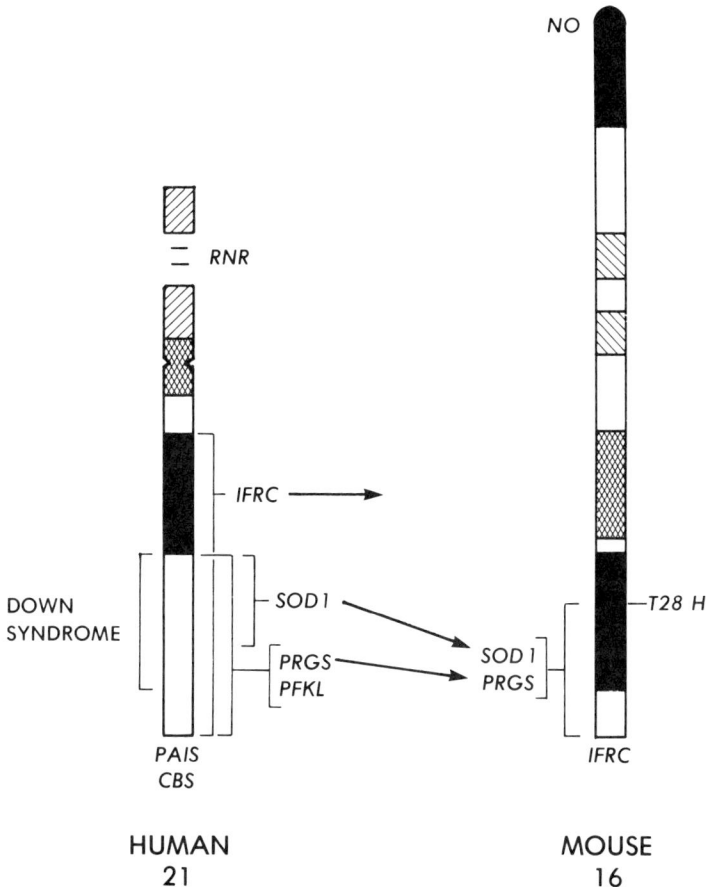

Figure 6.   The comparative mapping of mouse chromosome 16 and human chromosome 21. The regional localization of *SODI* and *PRGS* to the distal segment of mouse
chromosome 16, beyond the breakpoint of the *T28H* translocation, is shown. (From
Epstein, C. J. [1986a]. *The consequences of chromosome imbalance: Principles, mechanisms, and models.* New York: Cambridge University Press.)

and to the distal part of mouse chromosome 16: the protooncogene, *ETS2*, and the locus, *ADAP*, for the amyloid β protein precursor (Lovett et al., 1987; Watson et al., 1986). These bring the total number of homologous loci to five. It seems reasonable to infer that other homologous loci are also present on the two chromosomes in question and that we are dealing with many more than just the five genes mapped to date.

The salient aspects of the phenotype of mouse fetuses with trisomy 16 are summarized in Table 5. These animals are somewhat smaller than their sibs, by approximately 25% in weight, and have a distinctive phenotype. In midgestation they display a massive edema (Figure 7) that largely resolves by the end of gestation, leaving only a thick neck as an apparent residual. The neck is also short, the head smaller than normal, and the snout foreshortened (Figure 8). The eyelids, which should be closed, are open. Internally, the most prominent feature is congenital heart disease affecting the great vessels (usually overriding aorta, double outlet right ventricle, complete transposition, or persistent truncus arteriosus, either singly or in combination), but about half of the trisomic fetuses also have an endocardial cushion defect (Miyabara, Gropp, & Winking, 1982; Pexieder, Miyabara, & Gropp, 1981). The latter finding is of particular significance since the same lesion is found in about a third of all individuals with Down syndrome (Rehder, 1981). Neuroanatomical and neurochemical findings are indicative of retarded brain development that may lead to a reduced cortical surface and permanent deficiency of cortical neurons and to arrested development of the neurons within certain neurotransmitter systems (for review, see Coyle, Gearhart, Oster-Granite, Singer, & Moran, 1986; Oster-Granite, Gearhart, & Reeves, 1986).

The thymus of the trisomy 16 fetus is small, and the thymic lobes have not completed their descent into the thorax. There is a severe deficiency of thymocytes that appears to be the result of a marked reduction of prothymocytes entering the fetal thymus. In addition, there are moderate to severe deficiencies in the numbers of cells in the spleen and liver and in the total numbers of a variety of stem cells present in the liver, including the multipotential (CFU-S), granulocyte-macrophage (CFU-C), and erythroid (BFU-E and CFU-E) stem cells (Epstein, Hofmeister, Yee, Smith, Philip, Cox, & Epstein, 1985). Pre-B and B lymphocytes are also moderately reduced in the liver, and there is a very severe defect in the ability of fetal liver cells to be transformed in vitro with the Abelson virus.

While the trisomic embryos and fetuses are appropriate for studies on prenatal morphogenesis and development, they are not, of course, suitable for investigations of behavior and other aspects of postnatal central nervous system function. Therefore, to make the latter possible, trisomic cells have been combined with diploid ones in the form of postnatally viable trisomy 16 ↔ 2n chimeras or mosaics (Cox, Smith, Epstein, & Epstein, 1984). These

Table 5. Phenotype of mouse trisomy 16 compared with that of human trisomy 21

	Mouse trisomy 16 (fetal)	Human trisomy 21 (postnatal)
Survival beyond term	None	≤30% of conceptions
Growth in utero (weight)	Decreased 10%–25%	Reduced ~ 10% at birth
Edema in utero	Transient massive generalized edema	Transient edema of neck
Facies	Flat snout, short neck, open eyelids; retarded craniofacial development	Flat face, short neck, epicanthal folds
Congenital heart disease	Present in 96%, with aortic arch anomalies in >80% and endocardial cushion defect in ~50%	Present in ~45% with endocardial cushion defect in ~32% and aortic lesions in ~15%
Brain development	Weight reduced ~65%	Head circumference decreased ~2% at birth
	Decreased cell proliferation and migration in cortex	Deficiencies of cells in cortical layers
	Retarded development of cerebellar foliation and hippocampal fissure formation	Disproportionately small cerebellum; decreased neuron density in hippocampus
	Reductions in several neuronal neurotransmitter markers	Reduction in cholinergic markers in later life (associated with Alzheimer disease)
	Structural alterations of cochlear and vestibular portions of the inner ear	Anomalies of the inner ear
Immunological and hematological	Severe thymic hypoplasia	Thymic hypoplasia at birth
	Delayed maturation of thymic lymphocytes in vitro	Reduced T lymphocyte responses
	Reduction in pre-B and B lymphocytes	Decreased antibody responses

(*continued*)

Table 5. (*continued*)

	Mouse trisomy 16 (fetal)	Human trisomy 21 (postnatal)
	Reduced stem cell populations in liver (erythroid, granulocyte-macrophage, multipotential)	? Decreased circulating granulocyte-macrophage stem cells
	Poor lymphoid and erythroid cell survival in radiation and aggregation chimeras	Reduced proportion of trisomic lymphocytes in blood of trisomy 21/2n mosaics

Modified from Epstein, Cox, and Epstein (1985).

chimeras, which constitute the second form of the model, are the equivalent of human trisomy 21/2n mosaics which, when the proportion of trisomy 21 cells is high enough, display the functional and morphological phenotype of Down syndrome (Kohn, Taysi, Atkins, & Mellman, 1970). The trisomy 16 ↔ 2n chimeras that we prepared were normal in appearance and grossly

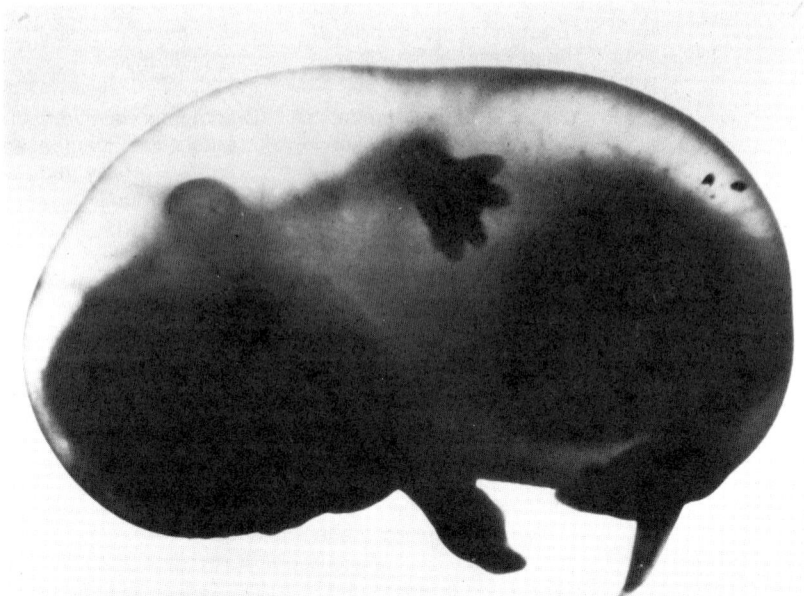

Figure 7. Mouse fetus with trisomy 16 at 14 days of gestation. The massive edema, which elevates the skin, is readily apparent. (From Epstein, C. J. [1984]. Early embryonic development: Normal and abnormal. In A. N. Schechter, J. Dean, & R. F. Goldberger [Eds.], *The impact of protein chemistry on the biomedical sciences* [pp. 331–348]. New York: Academic Press.)

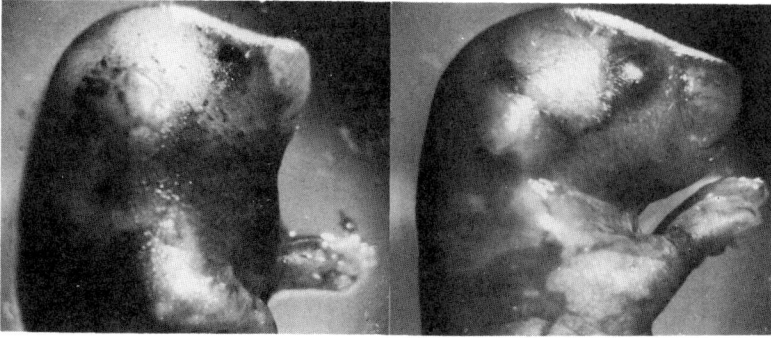

Figure 8. Facial appearance of trisomy 16 (left) and diploid sib (right) fetuses at day 18 of gestation. The trisomic fetus displays a short, thick neck, small ear, shortened snout, and open eyelid. (From Epstein, C. J. [1985a]. The mouse trisomies: Experimental systems for the study of aneuploidy. In H. Kalter [Ed.], *Issues and reviews in teratology* [Vol. 3, pp. 171–217]. New York: Plenum Press.)

normal in behavior, although systematic tests of behavior were not performed. In many organs, including the brain, kidney, liver, and heart, significant proportions (30%–60%) of trisomy 16 cells are present. However, not surprisingly in view of the immunological and hematopoietic cell deficits found in the trisomy 16 fetuses, the thymus, spleen, blood, bone marrow, and coat (pigment cells) of the chimeras are characterized by a marked deficiency of trisomy 16 cells. These findings suggest that the trisomic cells in the hematopoietic, lymphoid, and pigment cell lineages are unable to compete in a normal manner with diploid cells of the same type.

Coyle et al. (1986) recently reported preliminary data on the behavior of two trisomy 16 ↔ 2n chimeras that they prepared. In comparison to both chimeric and wild-type controls, these animals displayed increased spontaneous motor activity. This increased activity was particularly evident during the hours of darkness. These results indicate that behavioral differences may actually exist in the trisomy 16 ↔ 2n chimeras, thereby fulfilling one of the major objectives for developing the model system in the first place.

A comparison of the phenotypes of mouse trisomy 16 and human trisomy 21 is presented in Table 5. Many interesting parallels can be drawn, including the congenital heart disease, which has already been commented on, the retarded development of the brain and craniofacies with deficiencies in numbers of neurons, and the thymus and T lymphocyte abnormalities. Cultured dorsal root ganglion neurons from fetal trisomy 16 mice have been found to have specific changes in electrophysiological properties (Orozco, Smith, Epstein, & Rapoport, 1987). Nevertheless, we do not mean to imply that Down syndrome has actually been fully reproduced in the mouse. In fact, there are reasons for expecting that the mouse trisomy 16 and human trisomy 21 phenotypes could differ significantly from one another. The principal one, in addition to the species difference, is that mouse chromosome 16 and human chromosome 21 are clearly not completely homologous. Although the numbers of loci assigned to these two chromosomes are still relatively few, it is known that certain loci mapped to mouse chromosome 16 are present on human chromosomes other than 21. Furthermore, the genetic length of mouse chromosome 16 is of the order of ≈35% greater than that of human chromosome 21. It is possible, therefore, that some of the abnormalities found in the trisomy 16 mouse are the result of the imbalance of loci unrelated to human chromosome 21. Conversely, it remains to be proven that all of the loci in the "Down syndrome region" of human chromosome 21 are represented on mouse chromosome 16. While we believe that many certainly are, we still do not know how many.

The mouse trisomy 16 model for human trisomy 21 now permits the study of several problems related to the presence of extra copies of known human chromosome 21 genes, as well as analysis of phenotypic similarities, such as congenital heart disease (endocardial cushion defect) for which, as was noted earlier, mechanisms have been suggested even though the responsible locus or loci have not yet been identified (Wright et al., 1984). Nevertheless, since trisomy for all of mouse chromosome 16, as is produced in the current models, results in a degrees of genetic imbalance more extensive than occurs in human trisomy 21, an improved model would be an animal with a duplication of just the distal part of chromosome 16, the region in which *SOD1* and *PRGS* are located, or an animal with an extra dose of a single human chromosome 21 gene. Several lines of transgenic mice expressing the gene for human SOD-1 activity have recently been prepared (Epstein et al., in press). Being able to attribute a feature to imbalance of the putative homologous region would greatly strengthen its relevance to the study of human trisomy 21. However, even if not attributable to this region, the abnormalities produced by trisomy 16 are of interest in their own right as subjects for study with regard to the mechanisms by which aneuploidy produces its deleterious effects.

The ultimate extension of this "partial" trisomy approach would be the development of animals with an extra copy of just one or a few loci. This would permit an examination of the phenotypic consequences of the imbalance of individual loci and, in theory, a dissection of the aneuploid phenotype and assignment of features to specific loci or sets of loci (see Epstein, 1986a, for a discussion of the theoretical basis of this assertion). If the degrees of genetic imbalance were not too great, such animals would probably be viable beyond birth. The methodology for making animals with extra copies of specific loci has not as yet been developed. However, the approaches now being used for the creation of transgenic mice (Brinster, Ritchie, Hammer, O'Brien, Arp, & Storb, 1983) provide a basis for work in this direction, and the successes obtained so far give hope that it will eventually be possible to achieve the integration into the mouse genome and expression of sets of individual mouse genes homologous to genes on human chromosome 21. This would permit the realization of the prediction made by Lederberg (1966) that

> Human nuclei, or individual chromosomes and genes, will also be combined with those of other animal species. . . . Before long we are bound to hear of tests of the effect of dosage of the human twenty-first chromosome on the development of the brain of the mouse or the gorilla. . . . They need . . . just a small step in cell biology. (p. 10).

IS A CURE FOR THE NEUROLOGICAL PROBLEMS OF DOWN SYNDROME POSSIBLE?

Independent of the issues of the number and identities of the genes responsible for the neurological problems of Down syndrome is the question of whether, as is suggested in Figure 1, these problems are treatable, curable, or preventable, no matter how many genes are involved. One way to think about this question is to consider the neurological abnormalities of Down syndrome as falling into two categories: anatomical and functional. The former includes abnormalities of neuronal organization, both quantitative and qualitative, and of neuronal structure. Together these constitute what might be considered as the "wiring" of the brain, and their abnormality is the direct developmental consequence of the aneuploid state. However, it is also possible to visualize that, even though the development of the brain may be normal, its function may not be, because of a combination of major or minor derangements of metabolism, membrane properties, neurotransmitter synthesis and release, and electrical properties, which are not associated with visible defects. Many precedents from the inborn errors of metabolism testify to the severe effects of metabolic derangement on intellectual development and function.

Were the abnormalities to turn out to be primarily functional in nature, there would certainly be reason to hope that, with the development of increasingly more powerful and specific ways to affect the nervous system with pharmacological agents, therapeutic interventions would have a reasonable chance for success. Even small improvements in some aspects of deranged function could, over time, potentially lead to significant improvements in cognitive function. On the other hand, the existence of intrinsic defects in the "wiring" of the trisomic brain might lead us to be somewhat less optimistic about being able to ameliorate the neurological problems of Down syndrome, in that anatomical abnormalities would presumably be irreversible. However, the conclusion that anatomical abnormality is synonymous with lack of potential therapeutic benefit is not really warranted at this time, since we do not really know how much functional improvement the anatomically abnormal brain is capable of if appropriate measures are taken.

The problem of the pathogenesis of Down syndrome is a complex one, and it is not going to be easy to discover how the presence of an extra chromosome 21, which results in the synthesis of 50% increased amounts of a large number of gene products, leads to mental retardation and, ultimately, to Alzheimer disease. Nevertheless, as the summaries of recent conferences on the molecular structure of human chromosome 21 (Smith & Warren, 1985) and the neurobiology of Down syndrome (Epstein, 1986b) indicate—summaries that are illustrative of the tremendous amount of progress that is being made in the broad fields of human genetics and neuroscience relevant to Down syndrome—there is real reason to be optimistic about eventually arriving at an understanding of the pathogenesis of the structural and functional abnormalities associated with Down syndrome. And, from this understanding, it should ultimately be possible to devise rational approaches for treating and possibly even preventing or curing the mental retardation and other neurological abnormalities of Down syndrome.

REFERENCES

Adams, M. M., Erickson, J. D., Layde, P. M., & Oakley, G. P. (1981). Down's syndrome. Recent trends in the United States. *Journal of the American Medical Association, 246,* 758–760.

Arias, S., Paradisi, I., & Rolo, M. (1985). Cystathionine beta-synthase (*CBS*) location excluded from 21pter-q11, but confirmed to 21q, by gene dosage in trisomy 21. *Cytogenetics and Cell Genetics, 40,* 570.

Ball, M. J., Schapiro, M. B., & Rapoport, S. I. (1986). Neuropathological relationships between Down syndrome and senile dementia Alzheimer type. In C. J. Epstein (Ed.), *The neurobiology of Down syndrome* (pp. 45–58). New York: Raven Press.

Brinster, R. L., Ritchie, K. A., Hammer, R. E., O'Brien, R. L., Arp, B., & Storb, U. (1983). Expression of a microinjected immunoglobulin gene in the spleen of transgenic mice. *Nature, 306,* 332–336.

Cox, D. R., & Epstein, C. J. (1985). Comparative gene mapping of human chromosome 21 and mouse chromosome 16. *Annals of the New York Academy of Sciences, 450,* 169–177.

Cox, D. R., Epstein, L. B., & Epstein, C. J. (1980). Genes coding for sensitivity to interferon (*IfRec*) and soluble superoxide dismutase (*SOD-1*) are linked in mouse and man and map to mouse chromosome 16. *Proceedings of the National Academy of Sciences of the USA, 77,* 2168–2172.

Cox, D. R., Goldblatt, D., & Epstein, C. J. (1981). Chromosomal assignment of mouse *PRGS:* Further evidence for homology between mouse chromosome 16 and human chromosome 21. *American Journal of Human Genetics, 33,* 145A.

Cox, D. R., Smith, S. A., Epstein, L. B., & Epstein, C. J. (1984). Mouse trisomy 16 as an animal model of human trisomy 21 (Down syndrome): Formation of viable trisomy 16 ↔ diploid mouse chimeras. *Developmental Biology, 101,* 416–424.

Coyle, J. T., Gearhart, J. D., Oster-Granite, M. L., Singer, H. S., & Moran, T. H. (1986). Brain neurotransmitters: Implications for Down syndrome from studies of mouse trisomy 16. In C. J. Epstein (Ed.), *The neurobiology of Down syndrome* (pp. 153–169). New York: Raven Press.

Epstein, C. J. (1981). Animal models for human trisomy. In F. F. de la Cruz & P. S.

Gerald (Eds.), *Trisomy 21 (Down syndrome): Research perspectives* (pp. 263–273). Baltimore: University Park Press.

Epstein, C. J. (1984). Early embryonic development: Normal and abnormal. In A. N. Schechter, J. Dean, & R. F. Goldberger (Eds.), *The impact of protein chemistry on the biomedical sciences* (pp. 331–348). New York: Academic Press.

Epstein, C. J. (1985a). The mouse trisomies: Experimental systems for the study of aneuploidy. In H. Kalter (Ed.), *Issues and reviews in teratology* (Vol. 3, pp. 171–217). New York: Plenum Press.

Epstein, C. J. (1985b). Mouse monosomies and trisomies as experimental systems for studying mammalian aneuploids. *Trends in Genetics, 1,* 129–134.

Epstein, C. J. (1986a). *The consequences of chromosome imbalance: Principles, mechanisms, and models.* New York: Cambridge University Press.

Epstein, C. J. (Ed.). (1986b). *The neurobiology of Down syndrome.* New York: Raven Press.

Epstein, C. J. (1986c). Trisomy 21 and the nervous system: From cause to cure. In C. J. Epstein (Ed.), *The neurobiology of Down syndrome* (pp. 1–15). New York: Raven Press.

Epstein, C. J., Avraham, K. B., Lovett, M., Smith, S., Elroy-Stein, O., Rotman, G., Bry, C., & Groner, Y. (in press). Transgenic mice with increased CuZn-superoxide dismutase activity: An animal model of dosage effects in Down syndrome. *Proceedings of the National Academy of Sciences of the U.S.A.*

Epstein, C. J., Cox, D. R., & Epstein, L. B. (1985). Mouse trisomy 16: An animal model of human trisomy 21 (Down syndrome). *Annals of the New York Academy of Sciences, 450,* 157–168.

Epstein, C. J., & Epstein, L. B. (1983). Genetic control of the response to interferon in man and mouse. In E. Pick & M. Landy (Eds.), *Lymphokines* (Vol. 8, pp. 277–301). New York: Academic Press.

Francke, U., & Taggart, R. T. (1979). Assignment of the gene for cytoplasmic superoxide dismutase (SOD-1) to a region of the chromosome 16 and of Hprt to a region of the X chromosome in the mouse. *Proceedings of the National Academy of Sciences of the USA, 76,* 5230–5233.

Galbraith, G. C. (1986). Unique EEG and evoked response patterns in Down syndrome individuals. In C. J. Epstein (Ed.), *The neurobiology of Down syndrome* (pp. 109–119). New York: Raven Press.

Groner, Y., Lieman-Hurwitz, J., Dafni, N., Sherman, L., Levanon, D., Bernstein, Y., Danciger, E., & Elroy-Stein, O. (1985). Molecular structure and expression of the gene locus on chromosome 21 encoding the Cu/Zn superoxide dismutase and its relevance to Down syndrome. *Annals of the New York Academy of Sciences, 450,* 133–156.

Gropp, A., Giers, D., & Kolbus, U. (1974). Trisomy in the fetal backcross progeny of male and female metacentric heterozygotes of the mouse, I. *Cytogenetics and Cell Genetics, 13,* 511–535.

Gropp, A., Kolbus, U., & Giers, D. (1975). Systematic approach to the study of trisomy in the mouse, II. *Cytogenetics and Cell Genetics, 14,* 42–62.

Harrell, R. F., Capp, R. H., Davis, D. D., Peerless, J., & Ravitz, L. R. (1981). Can nutritional supplements help mentally retarded children? An exploratory study. *Proceedings of the National Academy of Sciences of the USA, 78,* 574–578.

Hoffman, S., & Edelman, G. M. (1983). Kinetics of homophilic binding by embryonic and adult forms of the neural cell adhesion molecule. *Proceedings of the National Academy of Sciences of the USA, 80,* 5762–5766.

Human Gene Mapping 8. (1985). Eighth International Workshop on Human Gene Mapping. *Cytogenetics and Cell Genetics, 40,* nos. 1–4.

Karp, L. E. (1983). New hope for the retarded? *American Journal of Medical Genetics, 16,* 1–5.

Kohn, G., Taysi, K., Atkins, T. E., & Mellman, W. J. (1970). Mosaic mongolism: I. Clinical correlations. *Journal of Pediatrics, 76,* 874–879.

Kurnit, D. M., Aldridge, J. F., Matsuoka, R., & Matthyse, S. (1985). Increased adhesiveness of trisomy 21 cells and atrioventricular malformations in Down syndrome: A stochastic model. *American Journal of Medical Genetics, 20,* 385–399.

Lederberg, J. (1966). Experimental genetics and human evolution. *Bulletin of the Atomic Scientists, 22*(8), 4–11.

Lin, P.-F., Slate, D. L., Lawyer, F. C., & Ruddle, F. H. (1980). Assignment of the murine interferon sensitivity and cytoplasmic superoxide dismutase genes to chromosome 16. *Science, 209,* 285–287.

Lovett, M., Goldgaber, D., Ashley, P., Cox, D. R., Gajdusek, D. C., & Epstein, C. J. (1987). The mouse homolog of the human amyloid β protein (AD-AP) gene is located on the distal end of mouse chromosome 16: Further extension of the homology between human chromosome 21 and mouse chromosome 16. *Biochemical and Biophysical Research Communication, 144,* 1069–1075.

Mayes, J., Muneer, R., & Sifers, M. (1984). Superoxide dismutase activity and oxygen toxicity in Down syndrome fibroblasts. *American Journal of Human Genetics, 36,* 15S.

Miyabara, S., Gropp, A., & Winking, H. (1982). Trisomy 16 in the mouse fetus associated with generalized edema, cardiovascular and urinary tract anomalies. *Teratology, 25,* 369–380.

Nadeau, J. H., & Taylor, B. A. (1984). Length of chromosomal segments conserved since divergence of man and mouse. *Proceedings of the National Academy of Sciences of the USA, 81,* 814–818.

Nadel, L. (1986). Down syndrome in neurobiological perspective. In C. J. Epstein (Ed.), *The neurobiology of Down syndrome* (pp. 239–251). New York: Raven Press.

Orozco, C. B., Smith, S. A., Epstein, C. J., & Rapoport, S. I. (1987). Electrophysiological properties of cultured dorsal root ganglion and spinal cord neurons of normal and trisomy 16 fetal mice. *Developmental Brain Research, 32,* 111–122.

Oster-Granite, M. L., Gearhart, J. D., & Reeves, R. H. (1986). Neurobiological consequences of trisomy 16 in mice. In C. J. Epstein (Ed.), *The neurobiology of Down syndrome* (pp. 137–151). New York: Raven Press.

Pexieder, T., Miyabara, S., & Gropp, A. (1981). Congenital heart disease in experimental (fetal) mouse trisomies: Incidence. In T. Pexieder (Ed.), *Perspectives in cardiovascular research: Vol. 5. Mechanisms of cardiac morphogenesis and teratogenesis* (pp. 389–399). New York: Raven Press.

Rehder, H. (1981). Pathology of trisomy 21—with particular reference to persistent common atrioventricular canal of the heart. In G. R. Burgio, M. Fraccaro, L. Tiepolo, & U. Wolf (Eds.), *Trisomy 21: An international symposium* (pp. 57–63). Berlin: Springer-Verlag.

Rethoré, M.-O. (1981). Structural variation of chromosome 21 and symptoms of Down's syndrome. In G. R. Burgio, M. Fraccaro, L. Tiepolo, & U. Wolf (Eds.), *Trisomy 21: An international symposium* (pp. 173–182). Berlin: Springer-Verlag.

Rutishauser, U. (1986). The potential effects of gene dosage on cell-cell interactions during development. In C. J. Epstein (Ed.), *The neurobiology of Down syndrome* (pp. 171–178). New York: Raven Press.

Schapiro, M. B., Haxby, J. V., Grady, C. L., & Rapoport, S. I. (1986). Cerebral glucose utilization, quantitative tomography (CT), and cognitive function in adult Down syndrome. In C. J. Epstein (Ed.), *The neurobiology of Down syndrome* (pp. 89–108). New York: Raven Press.

Scott, B. S. (1986). Electrophysiological studies of Down syndrome nervous tissue in vitro. In C. J. Epstein (Ed.), *The neurobiology of Down syndrome* (pp. 121–135). New York: Raven Press.

Scott, B. S., Becker, L. E., & Petit, T. L. (1983). Neurobiology of Down's syndrome. *Progress in Neurobiology, 21*, 199–237.

Sheppard, J. R., McSwigan, J. D., Wehner, J. M., White, J. G., Shows, T. B., Jakobs, K. H., & Schultz, G. (1982). The adrenergic responsiveness of Down syndrome cells. In J. R. Sheppard, V. E. Anderson, & J. W. Eaton (Eds.), *Membranes and genetic disease* (pp. 307–325). New York: Liss.

Sinet, P. M. (1982). Metabolism of oxygen derivatives in Down's syndrome. *Annals of the New York Academy of Sciences, 396*, 83–94.

Sinet, P. M., Lejeune, J., & Jerome, H. (1979). Trisomy 21 (Down syndrome). Glutathione peroxidase, hexose monophosphate short and IQ. *Life Sciences, 24*, 29–34.

Smith, G. F., Spiker, D., Peterson, C. P., Cicchetti, D., & Justice, P. (1984). Use of megadoses of vitamins with minerals in Down syndrome. *Journal of Pediatrics, 105*, 228–234.

Smith, G. F. & Warren, S. T. (1985). The biology of Down syndrome. *Annals of the New York Academy of Sciences, 450*, 1–9.

Summitt, R. L. (1981). Chromosome specific segments that cause the phenotype of Down syndrome. In F. F. de la Cruz & P. S. Gerald (Eds.), *Trisomy 21 (Down syndrome): Research perspectives* (pp. 225–235). Baltimore, MD: University Park Press.

Thase, M. E. (1982). Longevity and mortality in Down's syndrome. *Journal of Mental Deficiency Research, 26*, 177–192.

Thase, M. E., Liss, L., Smeltzer, D., & Maloon, D. (1982). Clinical evaluation of dementia in Down's syndrome: A preliminary report. *Journal of Mental Deficiency Research, 26*, 239–244.

Turkel, H. (1975). Medical amelioration of Down's syndrome incorporating the orthomolecular approach. *Orthomolecular Psychiatry, 4*, 291–303.

Watson, D. K., McWilliams-Smith, M. J., Kozak, C., Reeves, R., Gearhart, J., Nunn, M. F., Nash, W., Fowle, J. R., III, Duesberg, P., Pappas, T. S., & O'Brien, S. J. (1986). Conserved chromosomal positions of dual domains of the *ets* protooncogene in cats, mice, and humans. *Proceedings of the National Academy of Sciences of the U.S.A., 83*, 1792–1796.

Weil, J., Tucker, G., Epstein, L. B., & Epstein, C. J. (1983). Interferon induction of (2' - 5') oligoisoadenylate synthetase in diploid and trisomy 21 fibroblasts: Relation to dosage of the interferon receptor gene (*IFRC*). *Human Genetics, 65*, 108–111.

Weise, P., Koch, R., Shaw, K. N. F., & Rosenfeld, M. J. (1974). The use of 5-HTP in the treatment of Down's syndrome. *Pediatrics, 54*, 165–168.

White, B. J. Tjio, J.-H., Van de Water, L. C., & Crandall, C. (1974). Trisomy 19 in the laboratory mouse: I. Frequency in different crosses at specific developmental stages and relationship of trisomy to cleft palate. *Cytogenetics and Cell Genetics, 13*, 217–231.

Wisniewski, K. E., Laure-Kamionowska, M., Connell, F., & Wen, G. Y. (1986). Neuronal density and synaptogenesis in the postnatal stage of brain maturation in

Down syndrome. In C. J. Epstein (Ed.), *The neurobiology of Down syndrome* (pp. 29–44). New York: Raven Press.

Wisniewski, K. E., Wisniewski, H. M., & Wen, G. Y. (1985). Occurrence of neuropathological changes and dementia of Alzheimer's disease in Down's syndrome. *Annals of Neurology, 17,* 278–282.

Wright, T. C., Orkin, R. W., Destrempes, M., & Kurnit, D. M. (1984). Increased adhesiveness of Down syndrome fetal fibroblasts in vitro. *Proceedings of the National Academy of Sciences of the USA, 81,* 2426–2430.

Chapter 3

Inborn Errors of Metabolism and the Prevention of Mental Retardation

Richard Koch,
Eva Gross Friedman, Colleen Azen,
Elizabeth Wenz, Patricia Parton,
Xuanto Leduc, and Karol Fishler

Newborn screening for inborn errors of metabolism has become a part of newborn care in most countries of the world today. The thrust behind this effort has been a result of the pioneering work of Dr. Robert Guthrie (Guthrie & Susi, 1963), who developed the bacterial inhibition assay, which is used to test newborn blood for phenylketonuria (PKU), galactosemia, maple syrup urine disease, homocystinuria, and tyrosinemia. Screening received an additional impetus with the development of a newborn screening test for hypothyroidism. All 50 states screen for PKU and hypothyroidism and some 20 states do multiple test screening for the above diseases. While much has been accomplished from this prodigious effort over the past 20 years, there remains much more to be learned. The purpose of this chapter is to present the latest results of the National Collaborative Study of Phenylketonuria, clinical results on galactosemia from the Children's Hospital of Los Angeles, and some comments on maple syrup urine disease, homocystinuria, and tyrosinemia.

This work was supported by Grant NO. 5-RO1-HD09543 from the National Institute of Child Health and Human Development, National Institutes of Health, U.S. Department of Health, Education, and Welfare, Washington, DC.

PHENYLALANINEMIAS

Hyperphenylalaninemia is a disorder in which there is an impaired ability to convert phenylalanine to tyrosine because of a defect in the sequencing of the gene producing the enzyme phenylalanine hydroxylase. This impairment results in elevation of blood phenylalanine levels above 4 mg/dl, with normal blood tyrosine levels (0.4–1.6 mg/dl) and abnormal amounts of phenylalanine metabolites in the urine. Generally, three types of hyperphenylalaninemia have been distinguished: classical PKU, variant PKU, and benign hyperphenylalaninemia.

Individuals with classical PKU have blood phenylalanine concentrations persistently above 20 mg/dl; variants usually range between 10 and 20 mg/dl. PKU individuals excrete large amounts of phenylalanine and its metabolites in the urine, while variants may not, and they must be treated from near birth throughout early adolescence to prevent mental retardation. On the other hand, variants appear to attain near-normal to normal intelligence without treatment with the phenylalanine-restricted diet.

Benign hyperphenylalaninemia is the term applied to persons with blood phenylalanine concentrations between 4 and 10 mg/dl. Their urine is usually normal and blood tyrosine values are normal on a diet unrestricted in phenylalanine.

During the past several years, another group of inherited metabolic disorders presenting with hyperphenylalaninemia has been identified. These disorders are quite rare. They include dihydropteridine reductase deficiency, biopterin or cofactor defect, and dihydrofolate reductase defects (Kaufman, 1976; Kaufman, Holtzman, Milstien, Butler, & Krumholz, 1975; Kaufman et al., 1978). In persons with these disorders, dietary restriction of phenylalanine alone does not prevent the onset of neurological consequences. Treatment involves administration of the phenylalanine-restricted diet and the addition of neurotransmitters such as dopa and 5-hydroxytryptophan.

The focus of this chapter is on classical phenylketonuria, an autosomal recessive inherited metabolic disorder. The incidence of PKU in the United States is about 1 in 12,000 births. It is rare in blacks, Finns, and Ashkenazi Jews. The occurrence of the gene in the population is about 1 in 50.

Untreated PKU has characteristics that may be devastating. Children who have never received treatment for PKU usually are severely mentally retarded, often exhibit seizures and neurological sequelae, and may have other physical stigmata such as eczema. Normal growth and development, either physically or intellectually, is rare in untreated phenylketonuric children.

In 1947, Jervis reported that the genetic defect involved the enzyme phenylalanine hydroxylase and in 1953, Bickel, Gerrard, and Hickmans developed a diet that would allow PKU children to be treated with a synthetic formula low in phenylalanine content. With the development of the diet, and subsequent development of Guthrie's simple screening procedure, it was possible to undertake a large-scale effort to investigate scientifically the efficacy of dietary treatment.

During 1965 and 1966, clinicians from many centers throughout the United States met to establish the framework for a longitudinal evaluation of the efficacy of the treatment program. The Collaborative Study of Children Treated for Phenylketonuria was initiated in 1967. Initially, 19 centers in 12 states participated in the study.

The purpose of the first phase of the study, Phase A (Williamson, Dobson, & Koch, 1977), was to investigate prospectively the effects of the phenylalanine-restricted diet on physical, cognitive, and psychosocial development of PKU children through age 6 years. The second phase of the study, Phase B, was designed to compare the effects of dietary discontinuation with continuation between 6 and 10 years of age on the same group of children.

This initial phase of the study was funded by the Maternal and Child Health Section of the Bureau of Community Health Services, of the Department of Health, Education, and Welfare (Washington, DC). Phase B was funded by the National Institute of Child Health and Human Development, National Institutes of Health.

Dietary Treatment

In the PKU Collaborative Study, sample acquisition occurred between October 1, 1967 and October 1, 1972. For inclusion in the study, infants had to be identified through newborn screening, diagnosed as having PKU, and enrolled and treated prior to 121 days of age. They were randomly assigned to one of two treatment groups at entry into the study. Ideally, Treatment Group 1 children were to be treated so that their blood phenylalanine concentrations were maintained between 1.0 and 5.4 mg/dl and Treatment Group 2 children between 5.5 and 9.9 mg/dl.

There were two control groups. Control Group 1 consisted of previously untreated PKU siblings of the index case and contained only nine children. Due to the small numbers, this group was subsequently abandoned. Control Group 2 consisted of non-PKU siblings of the index case and contained approximately 200 children.

The investigation required a large range of disciplines involving the efforts of many health care professionals at each of the collaborating clinics, as well as the continued participation of the families. Table 1 represents the disposition of cases during Phase A of the PKU Collaborative Study. Between 1967 and 1972, 203 subjects qualified for the study, of which 116 were boys and 87 were girls. Nearly all of the infants were born at term; 97% were Caucasian; 50% were first-born. Subsequently, 36 of these children were identified as variants following a challenge procedure at 3 months or 1 year of

Table 1. Disposition of cases in Phase A

Diagnostic classification and study status	Number
Presumptive positive	216
Dx unconfirmed	13
Qualified for study	203
Variant Dx	36
Confirmed PKU	136
Inactive	33
Completed Phase A	134

age, and thus were excluded. One hundred and sixty-seven confirmed classical PKU children were available for study. By 1978, at the completion of Phase A, 134 children had participated fully for 6 years and entered Phase B. The mean maximum diagnostic serum phenylalanine level for PKU children was 48.3 mg/dl (ranging from a minimum of 22.6 to 98.4). For the children who were diagnosed as variants subsequent to study enrollment, the mean diagnostic serum phenylalanine level was 30.3 mg/dl (minimum 20.7 mg/dl, maximum 68.0 mg/dl).

The total sample began dietary treatment at a mean age of 21 days. The range in age of first treatment was from 3 days to 65 days. Thus, the study sample represents a very early treated group of PKU children. An Index of Dietary Control (IDC) was defined to monitor dietary compliance. The IDC for a given 6-month period is the median blood of all blood phenylalanine values for the individual during that period. Although Treatment Groups 1 and 2 differed significantly in IDC throughout Phase A, the average IDC of Treatment Group 1 children did not remain in the targeted range of 1.0–5.4 mg/dl. By 9 months of age their blood phenylalanine concentrations had moved into the range designated for Treatment Group 2. The average IDC for the total sample of 134 children who completed Phase A gradually increased to 12.5 mg/dl by 6 years of age, a 91% increase over 3-month values, as seen in Figure 1 (Williamson, Koch, Azen, & Chang, 1981).

Comparisons of selected demographic variables were made between families of children in adequate dietary control at age 6 (<15 mg/dl) and families of children in poor control. The children who were in poor dietary control at 6 years (approximately 28%) came from families exhibiting a greater degree of marital instability and unemployment. Mothers, on the average, were younger and exhibited lower intellectual quotients on the Wechsler Adult Intelligence Scale (WAIS). Factors that were not related to dietary control included father's age and IQ, mother's employment status, and parental education and socioeconomic status.

The medical findings (Johnson, Koch, Peterson, & Friedman, 1978) on 150 treated PKU children revealed essentially a normal population of children

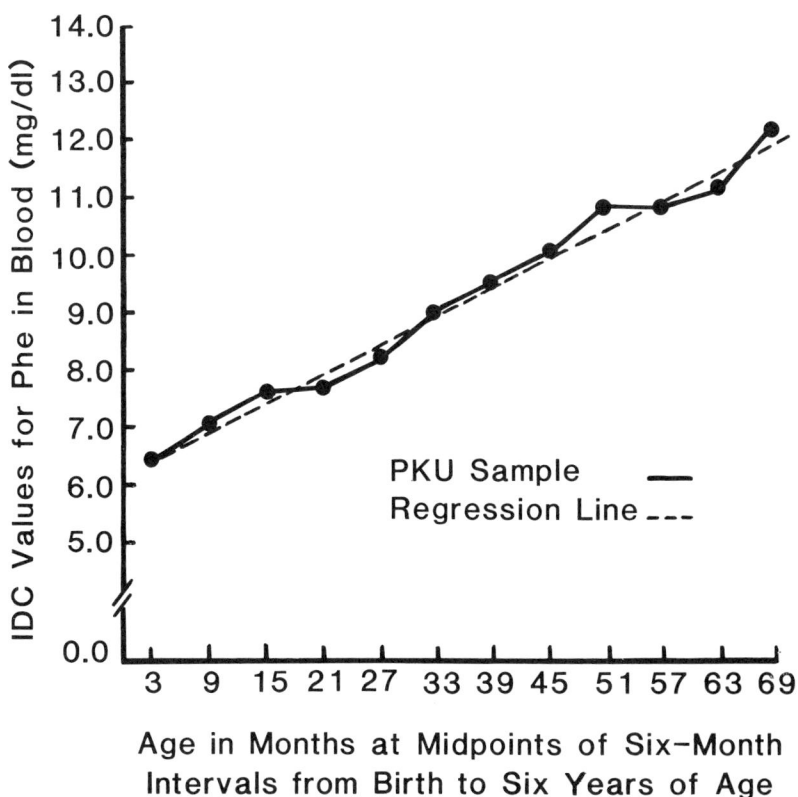

Figure 1. Values for indexes of dietary control (IDCs) regressed on age in months at midpoints of 6-month intervals from birth to 6 years of age for 132 early-treated children with phenylketonuria (PKU).

compared with normative data from the Fetal Life Study (McIntosh, Merritt, Richards, Samuels, & Bellows, 1954). When the PKU population was compared on selected abnormalities with a control population of 5,530 children, the only significant factor was that the incidence of pyloric stenosis was greater in the PKU group. Pyloric stenosis occurred in male children only. These findings suggest that perhaps a repeat phenylalanine test should be conducted on male infants who exhibit severe, excessive projectile vomiting.

Untreated PKU children usually exhibit severe EEG abnormalities. In the Collaborative Study, at the time of dietary inception, 19 children had abnormal EEGs. Children with initially abnormal EEGs also had higher diagnostic phenylalanine levels. By the time they were 1 year of age, their EEGs were normal. Hypsarrythmic patterns were not seen. This suggests that children treated with the phenylalanine-restricted diet improve and develop normally on this factor (Blaskovics, Engel, Podosin, Azen, & Friedman, 1981).

In untreated PKU, growth is stunted or substandard on height, weight, and head circumference (Holm & Knox, 1979). The PKU sample was compared with that of a group of normal children in the United States on whom corresponding longitudinal growth data had been collected at the Fels Research Institute (Holm, Kronmal, Williamson, & Roche, 1979). There were no significant differences in height, weight, or head circumference between the groups at any age, although there was a slight increase in weight of females as they became older. The importance of these findings is that children treated with a synthetic diet can grow normally.

Analyses on 5- and 6-year psychological assessments revealed no differences between the two treatment groups on any factors. Although the two groups differed significantly in mean phenylalanine level, they were not sufficiently distinct to warrant analysis as two separate groups. Subsequent analyses of Phase A data combined the two treatment groups into a single sample of early-treated PKU children who began treatment at various ages and experienced varying degrees of dietary restriction of phenylalanine throughout the first 6 years of life.

At 6 years of age, the PKU sample treated since an average of 21 days achieved a normal IQ of 98, as measured by the Stanford-Binet Intelligence Scale. As a group, the children performed within the normal range on the Wide Range Achievement Test (WRAT), the Frostig Test of Visual Perception, and the Illinois Test of Psycholinguistic Abilities. The Bender Gestalt Test, which measures perceptual ability and neurological development, was given at 6 years of age. The group was functioning at an age level of between 5 and $5\frac{1}{2}$ years; that is, from one half to a full year below normal expectation. Parents' IQs were slightly above the norm of 100. The mothers' mean IQ was 106 and the fathers' mean IQ was 109.

Comparisons of PKU subjects with their full nonaffected siblings should reveal true differences between PKU and non-PKU offspring from matings with heterozygous carriers for the PKU gene. Figure 2 depicts expected and observed frequency distributions of 6-year Stanford-Binet IQ scores for 63 PKU children and for composite scores of their matched non-PKU siblings. The outline associated with each histogram represents the expected distribution for the normal population.

The PKU children scored an average of 98 compared with their non-PKU siblings who had a mean IQ of 102. This difference is statistically significant, but not highly so. The higher scores achieved by the siblings are seen in the greater frequency of scores in the higher ranges of the distributions on Figure 2, in comparison with both the PKUs and the normal population.

There has been a great deal of debate as to which factors are the most critical contributors to, or predictors of, eventual IQ. Table 2 shows that early-treated PKU children had significantly higher IQs than late-treated PKU children. Children who began treatment in the 2nd month of life scored a

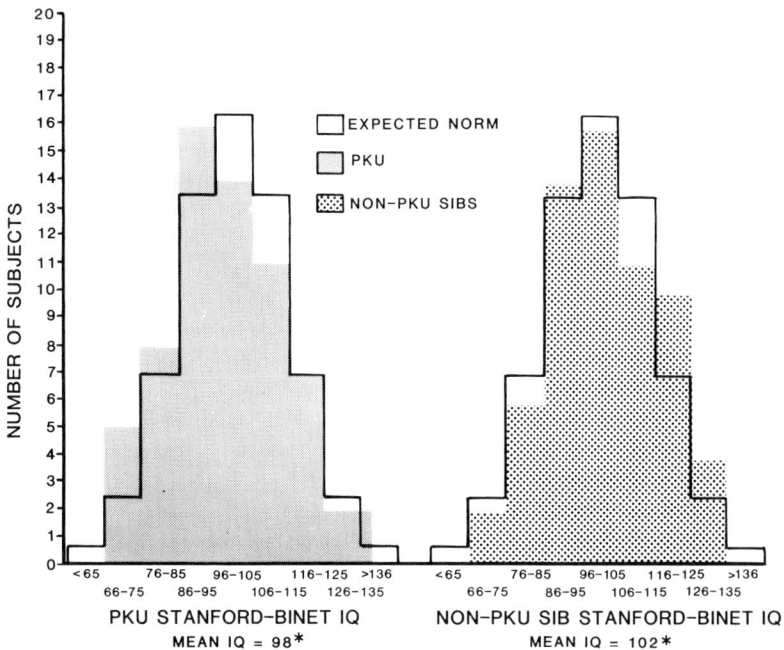

Figure 2. Histograms of expected and observed frequency distributions of 6-year Stanford-Binet IQ scores for 63 early-treated children with phenylketonuria (PKU) and composite scores of their non-PKU siblings. *, Paired ± test between PKU children and siblings was statistically significant ($p < .05$).

mean IQ of 89, whereas children who were treated in the 1st month of life scored a mean IQ of 100. Figure 3 depicts the results of analyses that demonstrated that the three most important predictors of 6-year IQs were mothers' WAIS IQ (which explained 25% of the variance), age at which the subjects were first treated (an additional 7%), and how well the subjects adhered to the low-phenylalanine diet (an additional 4%) (Williamson et al., 1981).

Thus, while early initiation of treatment was important, adherence to the diet, as measured by the rate of increase of blood phenylalanine over time, was also important. Those children who were out of control early did less well on subsequent IQ testing. This must be considered carefully when treating children with PKU.

Table 2. Intellectual performance of early- versus late-treated PKU children

	N	Mean age first treated	Stanford-Binet mean IQ[a]
Early-treated (<31 days)	105	15	100
Late-treated (31–65 days)	24	44	89

[a]$p < .01$.

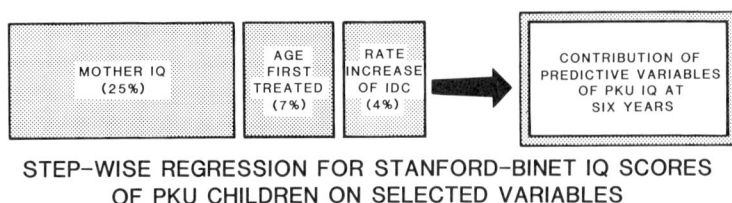

STEP-WISE REGRESSION FOR STANFORD-BINET IQ SCORES
OF PKU CHILDREN ON SELECTED VARIABLES

Figure 3. Stepwise regression for Stanford-Binet IQ scores of early-treated children with phenylketonuria on selected treatment and nontreatment variables.

Fifteen percent of the sample began treatment between 30 and 65 days of age and also had poorly controlled blood phenylalanine, consistently greater than 15 mg/dl. Despite the inclusion of these children with relatively poor treatment, the total sample achieved a normal IQ of 98. When the poorly controlled children were excluded from analysis, the sample had a normal mean IQ of 100 (Williamson et al., 1981).

Diet Discontinuation

There was much controversy concerning the issue of diet discontinuation. Some felt that diet should be discontinued at 4, 6, or 8 years of age (Hackney, Hanley, Davidson, & Lindsao, 1968; Holtzman, Welcher, & Mellits, 1975; Horner, Streamer, Alejandro, Read, & Ibbot, 1962; Hudson, 1967; Johnson, 1972; Kang, Sollee, & Gerald, 1970; Solomons, Keleske, & Opitz, 1966; Vandeman, 1963). Others thought that children should be treated throughout adolescence (Brown & Warner, 1976; Koch, 1964; Smith et al., 1978). In 1973, the participating clinic directors, after careful consideration of all the issues, agreed to age 6 years as the commencement of the Study of Diet Continuation/Discontinuation. At that time, there was no evidence that diet discontinuation at age 6 was harmful, and it was considered a good starting point for children entering school.

In 1973, Phase B was initiated, wherein each child, upon reaching his or her sixth birthday, was randomly assigned to either continue or discontinue the phenylalanine-restricted diet, subject to parental informed consent. Randomization was carried out utilizing a procedure stratified on sex, year of birth, and Phase A treatment group assignment. If the parents did not accept the random assignment, the child was placed in the group agreed upon by them and their data were analyzed accordingly. The target for treatment of children in the continuation group was to maintain the median blood phenylalanine level (IDC) between 2.0 and 12.0 mg/dl, as determined by the McCaman-Robins Fluorometric Procedure (McCaman & Robins, 1962). In children assigned to discontinue dietary therapy, an unrestricted diet was gradually achieved in 2 months. Children whose individual serum phenylalanine levels failed to reach 20.0 mg/dl on an unrestricted diet were reevaluated for possible diagnosis as hyperphenylalaninemic variants and excluded from the study when the data were consistent with this diagnosis. One child fell into this category.

One hundred and thirty-four children entered Phase B. All are currently 10 years of age or older. Seven children were dropped from Phase B prior to their 9th birthday, and an additional eight children withdrew at a later age. Of the 134 children entering Phase B, 65 had been randomized to continue and 69 to discontinue dietary therapy at age 6; 51 (78%) accepted continuation on the diet and 52 (75%) accepted discontinuation.

By age 10 years, 68 children (58%) had maintained their random assignment. For the analyses reported herein, children were grouped as continuers or discontinuers according to their blood phenylalanine concentrations at the time of follow-up evaluation, regardless of original random assignment. Statistical procedures, such as analysis of covariance, were employed whenever appropriate to minimize bias introduced by the breakdown of the randomized design.

Children who remained on the diet experienced a gradual increase in average IDC between 6 and 10 years. Discontinuers had higher mean IDCs than did continuers at age 6 years (an average of 11 versus 13 mg/dl) and markedly increased IDCs at age 8 through 10 years. Differences between the IDCs for the two groups were statistically significant at age 6. At ages 8, 9, and 10 the continuers averaged approximately 12 mg/dl and the discontinuers had a mean IDC of 26–27 mg/dl. The difference between the groups was statistically significant.

Evaluations of growth data indicate that both continuers and discontinuers maintained adequate linear growth as compared to data gathered by the National Center for Health Statistics. However, females, and to a lesser extent males, showed significantly higher weight to height ratios than expected.

The Wechsler Intelligence Scale for Children (WISC) was analyzed on 119 children and the WRAT was administered to 110 children at 10 years of age. Score comparisons based on phenylalanine levels of 10-year-old children showed that those with moderate phenylalanine levels (below approximately 19 mg/dl) achieved higher scores than those with higher phenylalanine levels on the WISC Verbal, Performance, and Full-Scale IQ. However, they functioned within the normal range of IQ.

Investigation of the relationship between IDC and WRAT standard scores revealed a marked difference in functioning at lower IDC levels as compared to higher IDC levels. On the Reading and Spelling subtests, functioning was within the normal range. However, all groups showed depressed performance of between 94 and 98 on the Arithmetic subtest.

Figure 4 depicts the percent distribution of school problems of 112 PKU children on whom school history information was collected. Nineteen children (17%) demonstrated mild problems, defined as repeating at least one

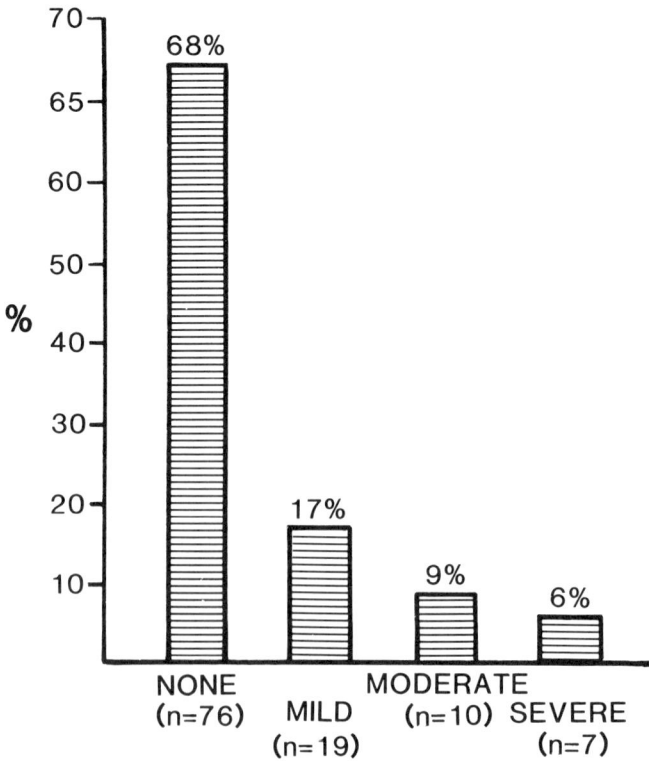

Figure 4. Percent distribution of school problems among 112 early-treated children with phenylketonuria (PKU).

grade in school or spending less than one half of their day in special classes. Ten children (9%) repeated at least one grade in school and spent more than one half of their day in a special class and were classified as having moderate problems. Seven children (6%) had severe problems requiring placement in special education classes. In addition to these 36 children, 14 children began first grade after the age of 6.9 years.

A comparison by sex of first and fourth grade PKU children with a national civilian, noninstitutionalized, white population that was based on 1981 Bureau of Census figures (U.S. Bureau of the Census, Current Population Reports, 1981) revealed that approximately 32% of the PKU first graders and approximately 34% of the PKU fourth graders were below grade expectation.

The Bender Gestalt Test for Young Children measures neurological impairment and may explain why PKU children are not functioning well in Arithmetic. For the 117 children evaluated, there were no significant differences between continuers and discontinuers at either 6 or 8 years of age on

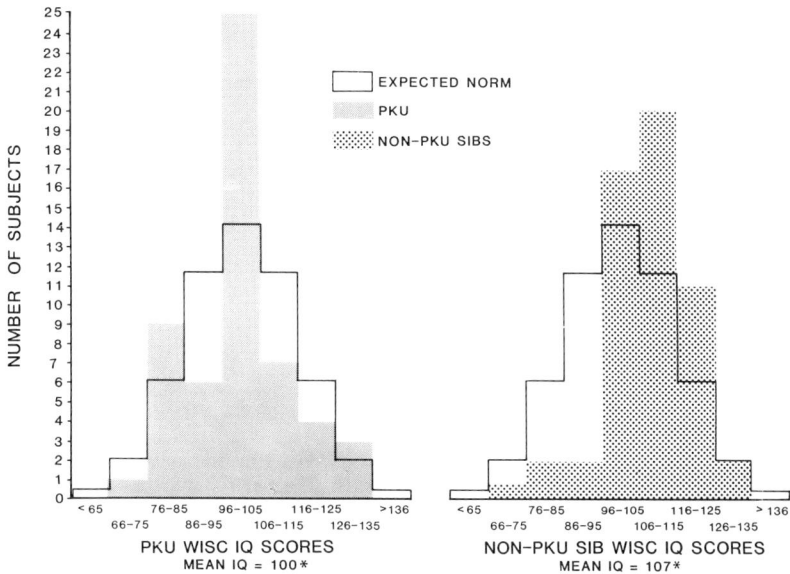

Figure 5.   Histograms of expected and observed frequency distributions of 8-year Full-Scale WISC IQ scores for 55 early-treated children with phenylketonuria (PKU) and their age-matched non-PKU siblings. *, Paired ± test between PKU children and siblings was statistically significant ($p < .001$).

the Koppitz score. However, approximately three out of four children in both groups scored below expectation for age at 6 and 8 years.

An evaluation of the effects of diet discontinuation was possible when an adequate sample of PKU children and their non-PKU full siblings were evaluated at age 8 years. Figure 5 compares the expected and observed frequency distribution of Full-Scale WISC IQ scores for 55 PKU children and their age-matched siblings. The black outline associated with the two histograms represents the expected distribution for the normal population. As a group, the PKU children had a mean IQ of 100 in comparison to a mean of 107 for their matched sibling controls. This difference is highly statistically significant. Notice that the distribution for the siblings is skewed to the left. Treatment parameters significantly correlated with sibling PKU IQ score differences included maximum diagnostic phenylalanine level and phenylalanine levels at age 6 and 8 years.

Figure 6 depicts paired comparisons of mean standard scores on the WRAT for 50 PKU subjects and their matched sibling controls. PKU subjects scored significantly lower on the WRAT Reading and Arithmetic subtests and lower, but not significantly so, in Spelling. The phenylalanine level at age 8 was significantly correlated with sibling PKU differences on all three WRAT subtests.

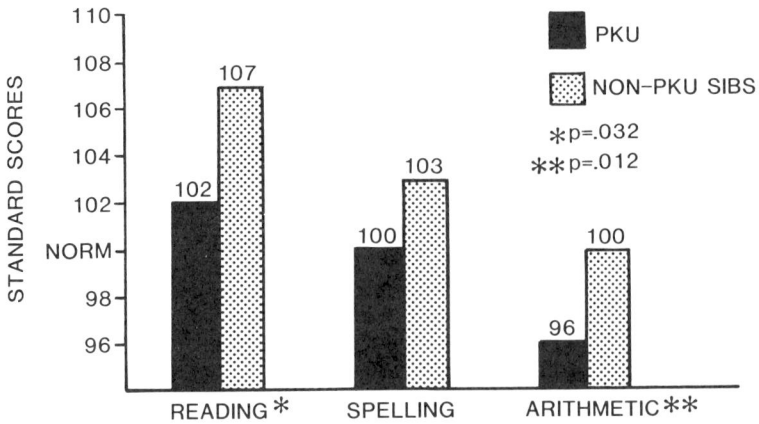

Figure 6. Bar graph showing differences between WRAT mean standard scores for 50 8-year-old treated children with phenylketonuria (PKU) compared with their age-matched non-PKU siblings.

Figure 7 depicts paired comparisons of the mean IQ scores on the WISC Verbal, Performance, and Full-Scale IQs. The left six bars represent on-diet comparisons and the right six bars represent off-diet cases. When the sample was grouped according to diet status at age 8, on-diet PKU children scored at or above the level achieved by their siblings on all three scales of the WISC, whereas the off-diet group scored from 10 to 13 points below their siblings on all measures. This difference was statistically significant.

Figure 8 depicts the same type of comparison for the Wide Range Achievement Test standard scores for Reading, Spelling, and Arithmetic

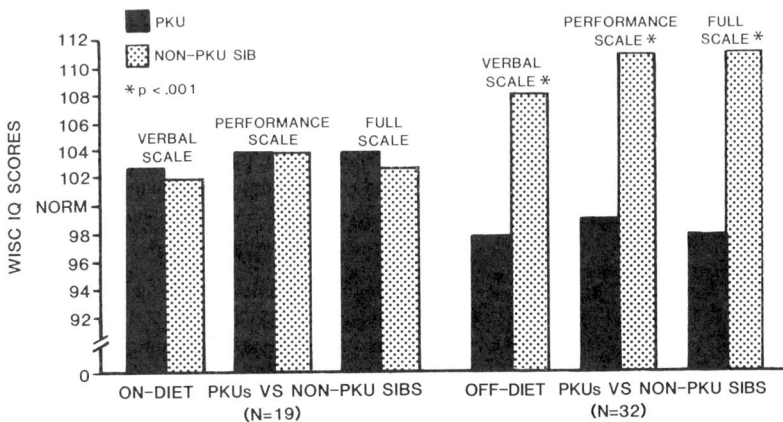

Figure 7. Bar graph showing differences in WISC Verbal, Performance, and Full-Scale mean IQ scores for early-treated children with phenylketonuria (PKU) grouped according to diet status at age 8 years compared with their age-matched non-PKU siblings.

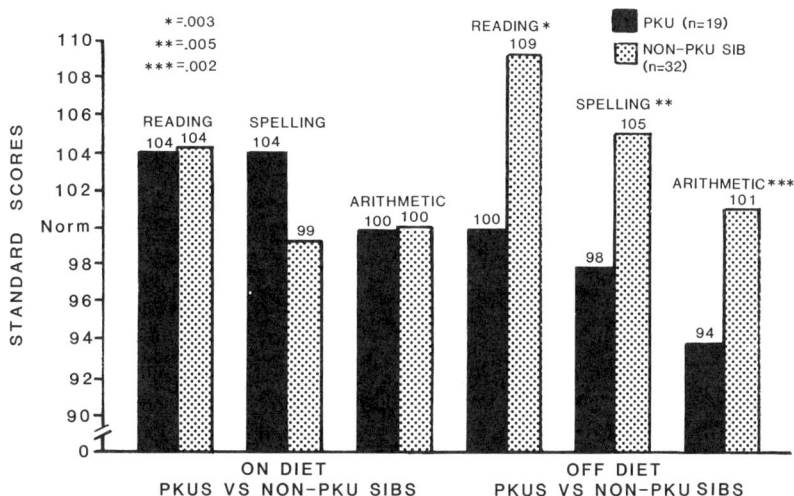

Figure 8.   Bar graph showing differences between mean standard scores on the WRAT Reading, Spelling, and Arithmetic subtests for early-treated children with phenylketonuria (PKU) grouped according to diet status at age 8 years compared with their age-matched non-PKU siblings.

subtests. Here again, the on-diet PKU children achieved the same or higher scores as their non-PKU siblings, while the off-diet PKU group scored significantly below their unaffected siblings. It is important to note that examination of the 6-year versus the 8-year WRAT scores for the PKU children showed that both the on-diet and off-diet groups maintained or improved their baseline Arithmetic standing, but the mean of the discontinuers dropped 4 points.

In conclusion, the data presented on dietary restriction of phenylalanine in PKU children suggest that:

1. It is recommended that PKU children continue the diet through the elementary school years. The lower the phenylalanine level, the better the outcome. We recommend the 2–12 mg/dl phenylalanine range. (Based on other studies [Hackney et al., 1968; Hanley, Linsao, Davidson, & Moes, 1970] overrestriction of phenylalanine level, that is, below 2 mg/dl, also seems to be detrimental to mental and physical development.)

2. The group averages suggest that discontinuation of the diet around age 6 does not allow optimum or expected growth in mental abilities. Some of the discontinuers had unacceptably high phenylalanine levels before age 6. Despite this, many of the discontinuers did well after age 6, especially if they had uniformly acceptable levels during the first 6 years of life. It is clear from the paired sibling data that diet continuers performed better than those children who discontinued the diet at age 6 years. Whether

these differences result from organic or functional changes in the brain remains to be answered.

3. The earlier the PKU infant is started on a phenylalanine-restricted diet, and the more uniformly the infant and preschooler maintains phenylalanine levels with the lower end of the desired therapeutic range, the better the child will do during the elementary school years.

4. Despite early and optimal treatment, high phenylalanine levels after age 6 do represent a risk factor for children off the diet. Therefore, the Collaborative Study recommends that the safer course for parents and physicians is to maintain children with PKU on a phenylalanine-restricted diet at least through adolescence.

The Future

Phase C of the study is designed to evaluate the same sample beginning at 10 years of age until 14 or 16 years. It will be important to follow this unique sample of children and their families through adolescence, especially in view of the impending problems posed by maternal PKU.

Data reported from a retrospective study by Drs. Lenke and Levy (1980) have demonstrated that untreated pregnancies (i.e., not restricted in phenylalanine intake) of PKU women resulted in serious effects on the offspring. The ratio of cord to maternal plasma phenylalanine concentrations is 1.2–2.25:1 (Brenton et al., 1981; Davidson, Isherwood, Ireland, & Rae, 1981; Ghadimi & Pecora, 1964; Levy, Kaplan, & Erickson, 1982; Lorijn, Sengers, & Trijbels, 1981; Michels & Justice, 1982), so that even with dietary restriction of phenylalanine, fetal phenylalanine levels are higher than levels in the mother. The data reported by Lenke and Levy (1980) showed that spontaneous abortion occurred in 24% of the pregnancies. Mental retardation occurred in 92% of the offspring; 73% of the offspring were microcephalic; 40% were of low birth weight; and 12% had congenital heart disease.

Early detection of PKU through statewide screening programs has nearly eradicated the devastating effects of the untreated disorder. Dr. Henry Kirkman (1979, 1982) has performed computer simulation of relative frequencies of new cases of mental retardation related to the frequency of PKU. He has demonstrated that the benefits of screening in reducing PKU-related mental retardation will be offset in one generation if PKU women reproduce at a normal rate without management of their diet to prevent mental retardation in their offspring (Kirkman, 1979, 1982).

This is clearly a problem borne out of the success of medical advances in the field and presents a new challenge to clinicians. Women should be evaluated for elevated phenylalanine levels if there is any suspicion that they have some form of hyperphenylalaninemia.

GALACTOSEMIA[1]

Galactosemia is a relatively rare metabolic disorder, but nonetheless is important to the pediatrician as an ideal model for the approach to treatment of children with inborn errors of metabolism. Early diagnosis and prompt treatment with a galactose-free diet can lead to excellent immediate results and a favorable long-term prognosis. In this regard, mass neonatal screening programs constitute an essential first step in reducing mortality and morbidity among galactosemic children.

Galactosemia has been an area of intensive research at Children's Hospital of Los Angeles for nearly 30 years, involving close collaboration of a multidisciplinary team of professionals. Our preliminary treatment results from treatment of galactosemic infants and children were reported in 1969 (Donnell, Koch, & Bergren, 1969). The present communication outlines new findings collected from 59 patients during the succeeding decade, including observations on some older patients during adolescence and early adult life.

Patients in the Study

Fifty-nine children with galactosemia from 47 families have been followed at Children's Hospital of Los Angeles from 1949 to 1978. Based upon the clinical findings and conventional biochemical studies, it has been assumed that the same defect in galactose metabolism exists in the whole sample. The age distribution of our patients is shown in Table 3. Approximately one half of the individuals are of school age, and one third are older and out of school. Twenty-seven are male and 32 are female. They range in age from 1 to 29 years. Forty-three (73%) are Caucasian, nine (15%) are Mexican-American, and seven (12%) are black. None are of Oriental or of American Indian origin. Seventeen of 59 were diagnosed at birth or within the first week of life; of these, 15 were born to families known to be at risk and two were identified by newborn screening programs. Of the remaining 42, 18 were diagnosed between 8 and 30 days of age and an additional 17 between 1 and 3 months. Seven were not diagnosed until after 4 months of age.

Three of the 59 have been lost to follow-up. Information concerning these individuals will be included as of the time they were last seen at the Children's Hospital of Los Angeles.

Factors in Management

The clinical manifestations of galactosemia are well known (Komrower, Schwarz, Holzel, & Goldberg, 1956; Nadler, Inouye, & Hsia, 1969). The find-

---

[1]Gratitude is expressed to George Donnell, M.D., and Won Ng, Ph.D., for permission to report these findings since they are associated with the Galactosemia Program at Children's Hospital of Los Angeles.

Table 3.   Present-age distribution

Status	Age	Number
Preschool	0–6	13
School	6–17	25
Postschool	17+	21

ings in this series were typical (see Table 4). With the exception of the 17 infants diagnosed at birth, all children were moderately to severely ill. Recurrent vomiting, weight loss, jaundice, and hepatomegaly occurred in the majority. Other features of the disorder varied.

As soon as the diagnosis was suspected, each patient was given a lactose-free diet (Koch et al., 1973). Milk, milk products, and all foods containing milk were eliminated; fortified soy protein isolate infant formulas or a casein hydrolysate[2] formula were substituted. Dietary restriction was rigid until early adolescence was reached, and then minor relaxation was allowed. Milk and foods obviously containing milk, such as ice cream, were still excluded, but small amounts were permitted. In some instances indiscretion became evident especially during adolescence, as demonstrated by monitoring erythrocyte galactose 1-phosphate values.

Discontinuation of the restricted diet was never recommended because adaptation to galactose never was documented. Galactose tolerance tests remained abnormal in all the subjects selected for study. An important factor in the decision against discontinuation was concern about the development of cataracts.

Progress of patients was assessed at regular visits by clinical evaluation, nutritional assessment, and psychological testing. Determination of erythrocyte galactose 1-phosphate was carried out routinely.

Dietary treatment is life-saving for individuals affected with galactosemia. Without removal of galactose many of the 59 patients could have become severely mentally retarded or even died in infancy.

At least half of the 59 individuals have developed very well; some have IQs ranging up to 125. Whether or not the development of children would have been better had they not been affected with galactosemia cannot be determined.

General Health

Most of the clinical evidence of the disorder was reversed in a few weeks after treatment was initiated. Usually jaundice disappeared in a few days, and weight gain was restored within 1–2 weeks.

Twenty-one children exhibited cataracts, two strabismus, and two severe hyperopia. Sixteen of 21 patients have minimal cataracts and do not require

---

[2]Nutramigen, manufactured by Mead Johnson & Co., Evansville, Indiana 47721, USA.

Table 4. Clinical data among 43 symptomatic galactosemic subjects

Major organ systems	Signs and symptoms	Number of subjects
General	Anorexia and weight loss (failure to thrive)	23
	Lethargy	7
	Pallor and/or cyanosis	6
Hepatic	Hepatomegaly	39
	Jaundice	34
	Ascites and/or edema	7
Gastrointestinal	Vomiting	17
	Abdominal distention	9
	Diarrhea	3
	Light stool	1
Ophthalmological	Cataracts	19
Spleen	Splenomegaly	6
Blood	Hemorrhagic phenomenon	3
Genitourinary	Dark urine	6
	Dysuria and frequency	1
Central nervous system[a]	Bulging anterior fontanel	4
	Neonatal anoxia suspected	1
	Mental retardation	2
	Cerebral palsy	1
	Speech delay	1
Infection	Sepsis	5
	Meningitis	1
	Septic joint	1
	Osteomyelitis	1
	Ethmoiditis	1
	Genitourinary	1

Note. The 17 individuals diagnosed and treated at birth remained symptom-free.

[a]Includes one individual diagnosed at 11 years of age who remained untreated (and not included in study except as noted in Table 6).

surgery. In one of the 16 children the cataracts have completely resolved. Strabismus was corrected by surgery in two children with this problem and the hyperopia was corrected by refraction.

Three children required surgery for cataracts, one an iridectomy (bilateral), one capsulotomy, and one lysis of cataracts by laser beam. The eye changes in the latter two progressed while on a well-controlled galactose-restricted diet. The individual with bilateral iridectomy has dense cataracts, but surgery has been refused because she is afraid of losing financial aid for the blind.

One patient had seizures, but whether or not the seizures were related to galactosemia remained uncertain. During the follow-up, there was no evidence of liver involvement in any of the children; however, gallstones were incidentally discovered and removed in one of the patients.

Ovarian insufficiency in galactosemia is a recognized sequelae of the disease in females (Gitzelmann & Steinmann, 1984; Kaufmann, Kogut, Donnell, Goebelsmann, March, & Koch, 1981).

Growth

The birth weights of the galactosemic patients were within normal limits. Data on eight males and eight females have been compared with normal standards developed by the National Center of Health Statistics (Figures 9 and 10).

The growth velocity for male and female patients was similar. In terms of height, all patients lagged behind normal standards until 18 years of age when they finally approached normal. The weight throughout the 18-year

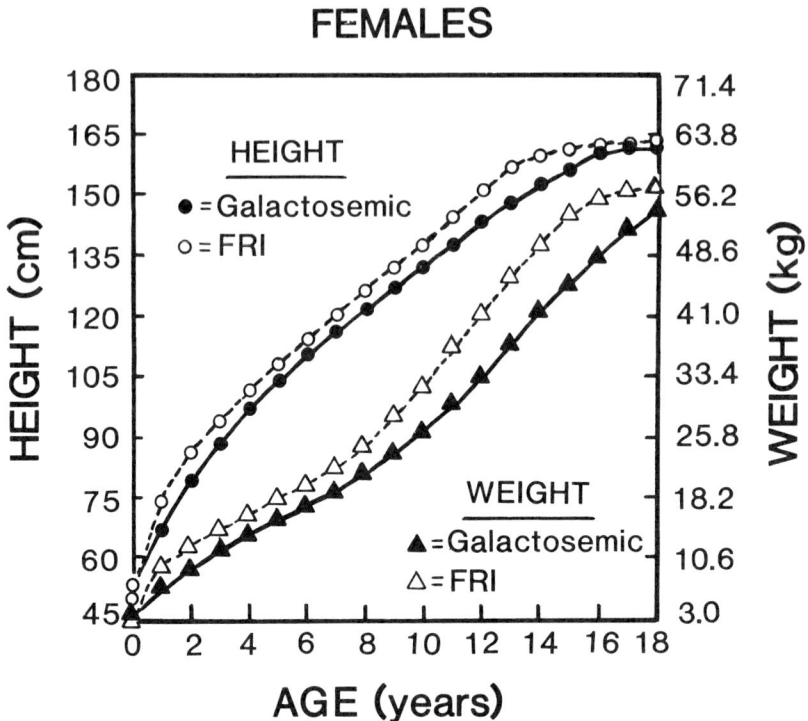

Figure 9. Growth patterns on galactosemic females from birth to 18 years. FRI,

MALES

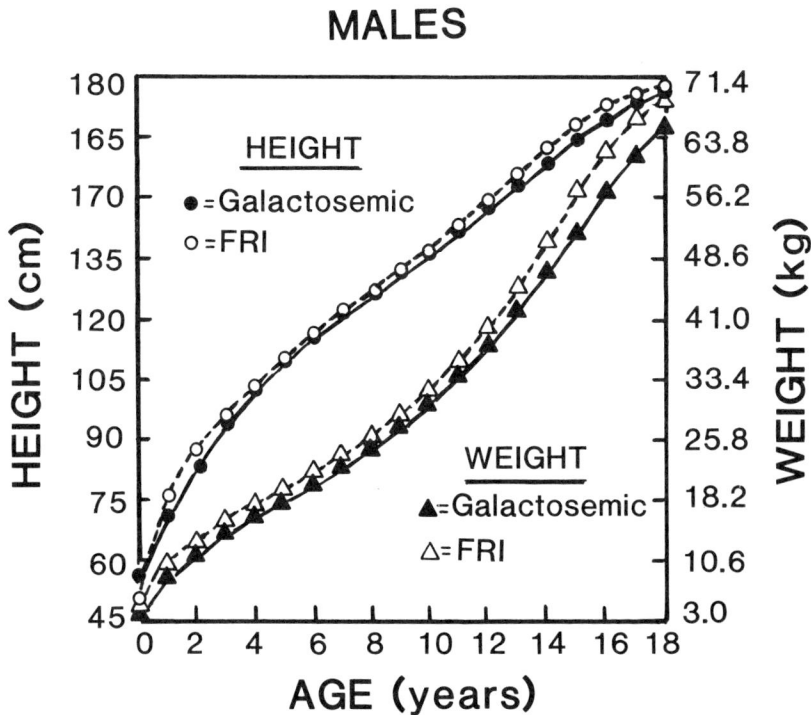

Figure 10. Growth patterns on galactosemic males from birth to 18 years. FRI,

span was slightly below that of the normals. Differences in height and weight, which might be construed as adverse effects of the disease or its treatment, did not emerge from a comparison of patient data with normal control data.

Intellectual Development

All patients were periodically assessed with the same developmental and psychological testing procedures. These studies were coordinated with medical, social, nutritional, and laboratory evaluations. The Gesell Developmental Scales were used for infants and children up to 3 years of age. Because estimates of early infant abilities are based on sensory and neuromuscular functions, they are reported as developmental quotient (DQ), rather than intellectual quotient (IQ). Intelligence, as determined by various mental functions, can be assessed only if verbal communication exists. DQ and IQ measures are not identical, but serial DQ measurements are useful in following developmental progress during infancy up to 3 years of age.

The Stanford-Binet Intelligence Scale was used for children from 3 through 7 years of age, and the Wechsler Intelligence Scale for Children (WISC) for children 8 years of age and older. After 16 years, the adult extension of the WISC and the Wechsler Adult Intelligence Scale (WAIS) were utilized. Interpretation of comparisons between age groups was subject to known differences among the testing instruments employed.

In addition, each child under the age of 5 was given the Seguin Form-board Test and a drawing test that included copying simple geometric forms (circle, cross, square, etc.). The Bender Gestalt Test, Raven's Matrices, and Draw-A-Person were administered routinely to older children. These tech-niques facilitated early identification of possible visual perceptual limitations. Earlier studies had suggested that such disabilities might be frequent among school-age galactosemia patients.

The overall findings are summarized in Table 5. For purposes of discus-sion, the sample has been divided into three groups, corresponding to the grouping in Table 3.

Group I is composed of 13 children from 5 months to $5\frac{1}{2}$ years. The range of DQ/IQ was from 70 to 125, with a mean of 102. In general, dietary control has been good to excellent. Visual-perceptual performance was normal for the four children who were old enough to be tested. Significant behavioral prob-lems were not identified. For the most part, they can be described as happy, sociable children.

Group II consists of 25 individuals from 6 to 17 years of age. Intelligence quotients varied from 50 to 117, with a mean of 91. All children attend school (Table 6). Of the 25 children, 12 are in the proper grade for their age. Of the remaining 13, four are in a regular class but in a grade lower than expected, four have been enrolled in the EMR program (Educable Mentally Retarded: IQ 50–70), two were in a TMR program (Trainable Mentally Retarded: IQ 30–50), two have attended the EH program (Emotionally Handicapped: IQ over 70), and one has been in a class for asphasic children. Eighteen of the 25 showed mild to moderate degrees of visual-perceptual difficulties, which may have had a bearing upon their academic progress. The specific school prob-lems most frequently encountered were difficulties in writing, reading, and arithmetic. Some require special tutoring and others require help with their school work.

Some of the older children are rather shy and restrained in interpersonal contacts even though basically they are friendly and cooperative. None of the

Table 5. Distribution of intelligence, visual-perceptual ability, and EEG findings in galactosemic patients

Group number	Number of cases	Age range (years)	DQ/IQ range	Mean DQ/IQ	SD
I	13	0–6	70–125	102	12.8
II	25	6–17	50–117	91	17.5
III	21	17–26	72–119	94	18.2
Total sample				95	16

Table 6. School status in galactosemic children

Elementary School (K–6):	7
Regular class:	5
1 Grade, held back:	1
2 Grade, held back:	0
Special class:	
EMR:	1
Secondary School (7–12):	**18**
Regular class:	7
1 grade held back:	2
2 grade held back:	1
Special class:	
EMR:	3
TMR:	2
EH:	2
Aphasic:	1

Note. EMR = educable mentally retarded; TMR = trainable mentally retarded; EH = emotionally handicapped; aphasic = language disordered.

children above the age of 12 years is described by school personnel as "hyperactive."

Group III includes the 21 individuals ranging from 17 to $29\frac{1}{2}$ years. Two in this group have been lost to follow-up. The mean IQ was 94 with a range of 72 to 119.

The six youngest attend high school, three in regular classes and three in special classes (two in EMR, one in TMR). Of the children in regular class placement, one is an "A" student who will enter college after graduation, another plans to enter college, and the other is considering this possibility.

Two of the 15 individuals who are beyond high school age are in college. Five are gainfully employed, including one in the Air Force, and one who is a program director for a radio station.

The oldest, a male, has joined a religious order. The two oldest females have married and have had four normal heterozygous children. One of these two has succeeded as housewife and mother of her one child in spite of borderline intelligence. The other is alcoholic and separated from her husband. She lives in a sociologically unfavorable environment and has emotional problems. Her three heterozygous children, all developmentally normal, have been placed in a foster home by court order. The reproductive status of galactosemic females was reported in 1981 by Kaufman et al.

One other patient, a male, has an unstable home background and a history of alcoholism. Two other adults, a brother and sister, have had difficulty establishing independence and are living at home. In addition to participating in household tasks they have established a home industry for selling canaries.

Discussion

Galactosemia, if untreated, usually results in early death for many affected children and creates the prospect of severe mental retardation for those who survive the early period (Clothier & Davidson, 1983). Among the families included in the present study, there was a history of 13 neonatal deaths prior to initial diagnosis of a galactosemia homozygote in the family. The deaths occurred at an average age of 6 weeks and were usually attributed to liver disease or infection. The history and autopsy findings were found to be consistent with galactosemia. Only one death from galactosemia occurred after the first diagnosis in a family. This was due to failure to inform the staff that the mother was pregnant so that early testing and treatment could be provided. A high rate of early death emphasizes the need to consider galactosemia in differential diagnosis of the sick neonate. *Escherichia coli* sepsis has been highlighted as a frequent complication.

One other individual, not included in the present study, was identified at age 11 years as a galactosemia homozygote at the time a much younger sibling was diagnosed. This older child was in an institution for persons with retardation. He had bilateral cataracts, cerebral palsy, and severe mental retardation. He remained in the institution until his death at age 24.

Galactosemia is a devastating disease. Treatment results in survival and reversal of the acute symptoms. However, the question of long-term outcome (intellectual development) has not been entirely certain. The experience gained in the present study has shown that many have developed very well, but others have had more or less severe problems. The causes of variability in response to treatment needs exploration.

Family differences related to genetic or sociological factors may account for some of these findings. Table 7 presents a comparison of the IQ results for homozygote galactosemics with those for fathers and mothers, normal brothers and sisters, and heterozygote siblings. These data are for a group and are not a comparison family by family. The spread of values within an individual group is broad and drawing conclusions from the means is difficult. However, the data provide a frame of reference. In considering individual patients in relation to their parents, there is a tendency, not apparent in the grouped data, for patients with higher IQ scores to come from parents with higher than average IQs.

Another determinant for outcome is the age at which diagnosis was made. The relationship between intellectual development and the time of

Table 7. Intellectual status of the parents and unaffected siblings of galactosemic patients

Subjects	Number	IQ range	Mean	SD
Fathers	33	87–138	110	12.7
Mothers	33	70–127	106	14.2
Normal siblings				
Brothers	5	92–114	103	8.9
Sisters	9	82–116	101	12.5
Heterozygote siblings				
Brothers	13	91–123	105	11.3
Sisters	13	86–125	105	11.1
Homozygote	59	50–125	95	16.0

initiation of dietary treatment is shown in Table 8. The data in this table tend to support the impression that a more favorable outcome results if the patients are treated at an earlier age. The mean IQs for the children in the first three groups are about the same. However, one of the patients included in the 0–7 day group of age at diagnosis was improperly treated elsewhere and was taken off diet at age 6 months. He has the lowest IQ of the group (56) and was not seen by us until 3–4 years of age. If this case were eliminated, the mean IQ for the remaining 16 would be 99.5. In patients treated after 4 months of age, there is a precipitous drop in mean IQ as compared to the first three groups. However, the number of patients comprising this group is small. Five individuals diagnosed at 4–11 months were all treated adequately after diagnosis, but the individuals in the last group did not receive adequate therapy. The

Table 8. Relationship between the age of diagnosis, intelligence, visual-perceptual status, and EEG results

	Age of diagnosis				
	Birth–7 days	8–30 Days	1–3 Months	4–11 Months	Over 11 years
Number of cases	17	18	17	5	3[a]
Mean IQ	97	94	91	62	57
Visual-perceptual status	7 N	6 N	8 N	0 N	1 N
	7 A	6 A	7 A	5 A	0 N
	3 NA	6 NA	2 NA	0 NA	2 NA
EEG results	11 N	7 N	9 N	2 N	2 N
	4 A	4 A	6 A	2 A	0 A
	2 NA	7 NA	2 NA	1 NA	1 NA

Note. N = normal; A = abnormal; NA = not available.

[a]Includes one individual diagnosed at 11 years of age who remained untreated (and not included in study except as noted in Table 2).

mean IQ value for the three individuals in this group (after 1 year of age) is biased by the inclusion of the patient (mentioned earlier) who was not diagnosed until age 11 years and who is not otherwise a part of this study. Another of the three, diagnosed at 17 months, received inadequate treatment due to poor compliance and subsequently was lost to the study.

Assessment of the relationship of late diagnosis to intellectual ability requires more data than there are available. However, it is reasonable to consider that onset of symptoms should be avoided and that diagnosis should be made and treatment instituted at the earliest possible age. Neonatal screening is an important step in this direction.

While diagnosis and treatment at birth are very desirable objectives, the possibility exists that galactosemic homozygotes may have experienced unfavorable intrauterine exposure to galactose or to its metabolites. This concept is supported by comparisons between the findings of homozygotes diagnosed at birth, who had no postnatal exposure to galactose, and of those on older siblings who were diagnosed and treated at varying intervals from $\frac{1}{2}$ month to as much as 11 months after birth (Table 9). Comparison of the mean IQ scores reveals that the mean values for the two groups are similar. Moreover, the mean IQ for the 17 galactosemic children treated at birth is 96; this is close to that for the sample as a whole. These results do not support the conclusions of our earlier studies, summarized in 1967, that patients treated from birth appeared to have a better outcome than those exposed to milk for varying short

Table 9. Comparison of 10 pairs of galactosemic siblings

Age diagnosed and treated (months)		Latest IQ		Visual-Perceptual		EEG	
Index case	Younger sib	Index case	Younger sib	Index case	Younger sib	Index case	Younger sib
3	Birth	119	118	N	N	N	N
3	$\frac{1}{2}$	106	79	N	A	N	N
$1\frac{1}{2}$	Birth	79	94	A	N	A	N
$1\frac{1}{2}$	Birth	92	80	N	A	N	N
$1\frac{1}{2}$	Birth	121	117	N	N	N	N
Birth	Birth	110	90	N	A	N	N
$\frac{1}{2}$	Birth	95	84	A	A	N	A
11	Birth	83	115	A	N	A	N
3	Birth	67	92	A	N	A	N
1	Birth	100	93	A	A	N	A
	Mean IQ: 97		96	$t = 0.16$		$p < .05$ N.S.	
	SD 11.6		15.1				

Note. N = normal; A = abnormal; N.S. = not significant.

periods of time. The data in Table 8, which related the visual-perceptual status of time of treatment, suggest that treatment at birth is beneficial.

Electroencephalographic findings were nonspecific and variable. Seventy-three percent of those diagnosed at less than 7 days of age exhibited normal tracing, whereas 50% of those diagnosed after the age of 4 months were abnormal. In view of the small sample size in the latter group, reliable interpretation of these data is not feasible. It is of interest that our oldest patient was diagnosed at 14 months of age and that his most recent electroencephalogram, at age 23, was normal.

Cord blood erythrocyte galactose 1-phosphate determination was obtained for 12 homozygotes (Table 10). All values demonstrated an accumulation of galactose 1-phosphate, which occurred during intrauterine life even though the mothers had been on a restricted lactose intake throughout pregnancy. The obvious inference is that the intrauterine environment is unfavorable for the homozygous fetus. That this is most likely the result of the metabolic processes of the fetus is suggested by the fact that the two treated galactosemia homozygote mothers have had clinically normal heterozygous children. This is in contrast to the problems experienced in untreated maternal phenylketonuria.

Conclusions

The outcome of dietary treatment of 59 individuals with galactosemia who were cared for at Children's Hospital of Los Angeles during the past 20 years, suggests that dietary management is effective. All patients survived and gen-

Table 10. Relationship of cord blood erythrocyte-galactose-1-PO_4 content and subsequent intellectual quotients

Case	Cord blood erythrocyte galactose 1-PO_4 content (mg%)	Latest IQ
1	24.6	103
2	17.7	97
3	16.4	103
4	12.7	110
5	12.7	115
6	11.6	100
7	9.1	97
8	9.0	107
9	8.7	93
10	4.7	81
11	4.7	100
12	3.9	128
	Average 11.3	Mean 102

eral health and growth approximate that of normal. Most have attained satisfactory intellectual development. For the remainder, the outcome has been less favorable for reasons that are ill understood.

Data from this study suggest that the intrauterine environment may be one factor in variability. Other variables may include age of diagnosis and treatment, family background, and genetic factors unrelated to the disease. The necessity for prolonged adherence to diet also poses problems in compliance and in the maintenance of nutritional adequacy. Finally, the affected individuals are offspring of families of varying economic status, which may influence the development independent of galactosemia and its treatment.

The principles of dietary management of galactosemia, in itself and as a model for other inborn errors of metabolism, remain simple. However, their application is more complex. There is no doubt that as we continue to gain experience, we will gain greater insight, and thereby improve the approach to management.

MAPLE SYRUP URINE DISEASE, HOMOCYSTINURIA, AND TYROSINEMIA

Some 20 states are now screening for these metabolic disorders. Due to their rarity, reliable data on the long-term results of treatment are still not available. It is clearly the general impression that dietary treatment is of value and clinicians generally are committed to treatment programs for these children. General reference textbooks, such as *The Metabolic Basis of Inherited Disease* by Stanbury, Wyngaarden, Fredrickson, Goldstein, and Brown (1983), have excellent chapters on each and it is not appropriate to take up the reader's time with a review of these disorders, but rather to indicate a few personal observations on these children to emphasize a few points in regard to management.

Maple Syrup Urine Disease

In maple syrup urine disease (MSUD) the time between birth and diagnosis with onset of treatment is critical. Without treatment, early death is the rule. In the absence of routine newborn screening, it is impossible to prevent brain damage because the newborn only comes to clinical attention due to lethargy, seizures, and coma. The maple syrup odor to the urine unfortunately is a late diagnostic clue in our experience, and was not the reason for referral in our patients. Due to the rarity of this disorder (1/250,000 births), State Health Departments have been reluctant to include MSUD in routine screening programs because of economic reasons. However, this is a philosophical problem as well. Why shouldn't we screen for rare diseases in order to help these affected individuals to live more meaningful lives? The authors are aware of two MSUD persons in our residential institutions in California who have never been treated and who have accounted for 40 years of institutional life at an exorbitant cost to society. Thus the authors are not convinced that the economic reasons for not screening are realistic and urge reconsideration of screening by states that have conscientiously made a decision not to screen. Furthermore, prenatal diagnosis is now available and, thus, once a family has been identified, prevention is feasible.

A word in regard to treatment is in order. Exchange transfusion and peritoneal dialysis are widely recommended as adjunctive therapy in the acutely ill newborn. Recently, we had the opportunity to treat a severely ill 10-day-old baby with MSUD with nasogastric feedings deficient in leucine, isoleucine, and valine and infusions of insulin with carbohydrates and appropriate electrolyte support. The dose of insulin used was 0.04 unit per gram of glucose administered intravenously. Blood sugars were monitored on an hourly basis initially, then less frequently as the blood sugar stabilized. Thiamine therapy was not effective in this infant. The leucine, isoleucine, and valine levels normalized within 4 days and the child at 2 years of age exhibits normal intelligence with mild spastic diplegia. Our preliminary impression is that this child has done as well as a previous infant treated with more aggressive measures.

Homocystinuria

The incidence of homocystinuria is also quite rare (1/250,000 births). When the infant has the defect sensitive to vitamin B_6, therapy is simplified considerably and the prognosis is excellent. The infant with the nonresponsive form requires lifetime dietary treatment with a methionine-deficient diet supplemented with cystine. The long-term prognosis for these patients is unclear. There is no question that they are aided by dietary therapy, but whether the outlook for complete normalcy is realistic is not known. Lack of treatment, however, clearly results in mental retardation, seizures, dislocation of the lenses of the eye, and osteoporosis. Thromboembolic phenomena are significant complications. Thus, dietary therapy should be instituted even though diagnosis is made late in childhood. Prenatal diagnosis is available.

Tyrosinemia

Tyrosinemia again is quite rare. The incidence is unknown. This is usually a devastating disease with a rapid progressive course and early death. Dietary therapy has been tried with poor results. The clinical presentation is with hepatomegaly, jaundice, and a bleeding diathesis. The blood methionine and tyrosine are elevated and the alpha-fetoprotein level is markedly elevated. The milder form of tyrosinemia with skin lesions, growth retardation, and eye complications is relatively easy to treat with a phenylalanine-tyrosine-deficient diet with good results. Prenatal diagnosis for both is available.

SUMMARY

In conclusion, there is no question that there remains much to be learned about phenylketonuria, galactosemia, maple syrup urine disorder, homocystinuria, and tyrosinemia. However, the multiple screening programs are contributing to the growth of scientific knowledge and that alone is a sufficient reason to promote their growth and effectiveness. As we become more knowledgeable, there will be newborn screening for more diseases. Cystic fibrosis, adrenogenital syndrome, and certain muscular dystrophies undoubtedly eventually will be added to the screening programs. As these programs develop, they will need wise leadership from the medical profession in order to achieve optimal effectiveness. It is hoped that the findings and recommendations contained in this chapter can lead to earlier intervention, prevention, and curative approaches to mental retardation.

REFERENCES

Bickel, H., Gerrard, J., & Hickmans, E. M. (1953). Influence of phenylalanine intake on phenylketonuria. *Lancet, 2,* 812–813.

Blaskovics, M., Engel, R., Podosin, R. L., Azen, C. G., & Friedman, E. G. (1981). EEG pattern in phenylketonuria under early initiated dietary treatment. *American Journal of Diseases of Children, 135,* 802–808.

Brenton, D. P., Cusworth, D. C., Garrod, P. Krywawych, S., Lachelin, L., Liburn, M., Smith, I., Thorburn, R., & Wolff, O. H. (1981). Maternal phenylketonuria treated by diet before conception. In H. Bickel (Ed.), *Maternal phenylketonuria: Problems, experiences, recommendations* (pp. 67–71). Heilbronn: Maizena Diat Gmb H.

Brown, E. S., & Warner, R. (1976). Mental development of phenylketonuric children on or off diet after the age of six. *Psychological Medicine, 6,* 287–296.

Clothier, C. M., & Davidson, D. C. (1983). Report: Galactosemia workshop. *Human Nutrition Applied Nutrition, 37A,* 483–490.

Davidson, D. C., Isherwood, D. M., Ireland, J. T., & Rae, P. G. (1981). Outcome of pregnancy in a phenylketonuric mother after low phenylalanine diet introduced from the ninth week of pregnancy. *European Journal of Pediatrics, 137,* 45–48.

Donnell, G. N., Koch, R., & Bergren, W. R. (1969). Observations on results of management of galactosemia patients. In D. Y. Y. Hsia (Ed.), *Galactosemia* (pp. 247–168). Springfield, IL: Charles C. Thomas.

Ghadimi, H., & Pecora, P. (1964). Free amino acids of cord plasma as compared with maternal plasma during pregnancy. *Pediatrics, 33,* 500–507.

Gitzelmann, R., & Steinmann, B. (1984). Galactosemia: Does long-term treatment change the outcome? *Enzyme, 32,* 37–46.

Guthrie, R., & Susi, A. (1963). A simple phenylalanine method for detecting phenylketonuria in large populations of newborn infants. *Pediatrics, 32,* 338–343.

Hackney, I. M., Hanley, W. B., Davidson, W., & Lindsao, L. (1968). Phenylketonuria: Mental development, behavior, and treatment of low phenylalanine diet. *Journal of Pediatrics, 72,* 646–655.

Hanley, W. B., Linsao, L., Davidson, W., & Moes, C. A. F. (1970). Malnutrition with early treatment of phenylketonuria. *Pediatric Research, 4,* 318–327.

Holm, V. A., & Knox, W. E. (1979). Physical growth in phenylketonuria: I. A retrospective study. *Pediatrics, 63,* 694–699.

Holm, V. A., Kronmal, R. A., Williamson, M., & Roche, A. F. (1979). Physical growth in phenylketonuria: II. Growth of treated children in the PKU collaborative study from birth to 4 years of age. *Pediatrics, 63,* 700–707.

Holtzman, N. A., Welcher, D. W., & Mellits, E. (1975). Termination of restricted diet in children with phenylketonuria: A randomized controlled study. *New England Journal of Medicine, 293,* 1121–1124.

Horner, F. A., Streamer, C. W., Alejandro, L. L., Read, L. H., & Ibbot, F. (1962). Termination of dietary treatment of phenylketonuria. *New England Journal of Medicine, 266,* 79–81.

Hudson, F. P. (1967). Termination of dietary treatment of phenylketonuria. *Archives of Diseases in Childhood, 42,* 198–200.

Jervis, G. A. (1947). Studies on phenylpyruvic oligophrenia. The position of the metabolic error. *Journal of Biological Chemistry, 169,* 651–656.

Johnson, C. (1972). What is the best age to discontinue the low phenylalanine diet in phenylketonuria? *Clinical Pediatrics, 11,* 148–156.

Johnson, C. F., Koch, R., Peterson, R. M., & Friedman, E. G. (1978). Congenital and neurological abnormalities in infants with phenylketonuria. *American Journal of Mental Deficiency, 82,* 375–379.

Kang, E. S., Sollee, N. D., & Gerald, P. S. (1970). Result of treatment and termination of the diet in phenylketonuria (PKU). *Pediatrics, 46,* 881–890.

Kaufman, S. (1976). Phenylkeonuria: Biochemical mechanisms. In B. W. Agranoff & M. H. Aprison (Eds.), *Advances in neurochemistry* (Vol. 2, pp. 1–132). New York: Plenum Press.

Kaufman, S., Berlow, S., Summer, G. K., Milstien, S., Schulman, J. D., Orloff, S., Spielberg, S., & Pueschel, S. (1978). Hyperphenylalaninemia due to a deficiency of biopterin. A variant form of phenylketonuria. *New England Journal of Medicine, 299,* 673–679.

Kaufman, S., Holtzman, N. A., Milstien, S., Butler, I. J., & Krumholz, A. (1975). Phenylketonuria due to a deficiency of dihydropteridine reductase. *New England Journal of Medicine, 293,* 785–790.

Kaufmann, F. R., Kogut, M. D., Donnell, G. N., Goebelsmann, U., March, C., & Koch, R. (1981). Hypergonadotropic hypogonadism in female patients with galactosemia. *New England Journal of Medicine, 304,* 994–998.

Kirkman, H. N. (1982). Projections of a rebound in frequency of mental retardation from phenylketonuria. *Applied Research in Mental Retardation, 3,* 319–328.

Kirkman, H. N., Jr. (1979). Projections of mental retardation from PKU. *Pediatric Research, 13,* 414 (abstract).

Koch, R. (1964). Letter to Vandeman. *American Journal of Diseases in Children, 107,* 537.

Koch, R., Donnell, G. N., Wenz, E., Fishler, K., Graliker, B., & Bergren, W. R. (1973). Galactosemia. In *Brennemann's Practice of Pediatrics* (Vol. I, pp. 1–12). Hagerstown, MD: Harper & Row.

Komrower, G. M., Schwarz, V., Holzel, A., & Goldberg, L. (1956). A clinical and biochemical study of galactosemia. A possible explanation of the nature of the biochemical lesion. *Archives of Diseases in Childhood, 31,* 254–264.

Lenke, R. R., & Levy, H. L. (1980). Maternal phenylketonuria and hyperphenylalaninemia. *New England Journal of Medicine, 303,* 1202–1208.

Levy, H. L., Kaplan, G. N., & Erickson, A. M. (1982). Comparison of treated and untreated pregnancies in a mother with phenylketonuria. *Journal of Pediatrics, 100,* 876–880.

Lorijn, R. H. W., Sengers, R. C. A., & Trijbels, J. M. F. (1981). Maternal phenylketonuria: The outcome of pregnancy. *European Journal of Obstetrics, Gynecology and Reproductive Biology, 12,* 281–285.

McCaman, M. W., & Robins, E. (1962). Fluorometric method for the determination of phenylalanine in the serum. *Journal of Laboratory and Clinical Medicine, 58,* 885–890.

McIntosh, R., Merritt, K. K., Richards, M. R., Samuels, M. H., & Bellows, M. T. (1954). The incidence of congenital malformations: A study of 5,964 pregnancies. *Pediatrics, 14,* 505–521.

Michels, V. V., & Justice, C. L. (1982). Treatment of phenylketonuria during pregnancy. *Clinical Genetics, 21,* 141–144.

Nadler, H. L., Inouye, T., & Hsia, D. Y. Y. (1969). Classical galactosemia: A study of fifty-five cases. In D. Y. Y. Hsia (Ed.), *Galactosemia* (pp. 127–139). Springfield, IL: Charles C Thomas.

Smith, I., Lobascher, M. E., Stevenson, J. E., Wolff, O. H., Schmidt, H., Grubel-Kaiser, S., & Bickel, H. (1978). Effect of stopping low-phenylalanine diet on intellectual progress of children with phenylketonuria. *British Medical Journal, 2,* 723–726.

Solomons, G., Keleske, L., & Opitz, E. (1966). Evaluation of the effects of terminating the diet in phenylketonuria. *Journal of Pediatrics, 69,* 596–602.

Stanbury, J. B., Wyngaarden, J. B., Frederickson, D. S., Goldstein, J. L., & Brown, M. S. (1983). *The metabolic basis of inherited disease* (5th ed.). New York: McGraw-Hill.

U. S. Bureau of the Census, Current Population Reports. (1981). Series P-20, No. 360, *School Enrollment—Social and Economic Characteristics of Students: October, 1979.* Washington, DC: U. S. Government Printing Office.

Vandeman, P. R. (1963). Termination of dietary treatment of phenylketonuria. *American Journal of Diseases of Children, 106,* 492–495.

Williamson, M., Dobson, J. C., & Koch, R. (1977). Collaborative study of children treated for phenylketonuria: Study design. *Pediatrics, 60,* 815–821.

Williamson, M. L., Koch, R., Azen, C., & Chang, C. (1981). Correlates of intelligence test results in treated phenylketonuric children. *Pediatrics, 68,* 161–167.

NEUROLOGICAL DEVELOPMENT
RELATIONSHIPS TO MENTAL RETARDATION

Introduction

Scientific disciplines of neurology, neuroanatomy, neurochemistry, neuroendocrinology, neuropathology, and neurophysiology are essential components of a major new field called developmental neurobiology, which has been used in the study of mental retardation during the last 10 years. This field essentially focuses on nerve cell growth and how it affects the overall functioning of the nervous system. It is shedding light on new knowledge about membrane structure and function and an understanding of nerve impulse transmission, cell to cell interactions, neurogenesis, synaptogenesis (growth and development of synapses), and receptor function. New diagnostic techniques are being developed that can help us to identify and understand the neurodegenerative diseases, particularly mental retardation, and how we can prevent or reverse this condition, particularly early in life.

The nervous system develops through a series of well-defined vents such as cell production, cell migration, cell differentiation, axon growth, establishment of cell pathway development, target recognition, synaptogenesis, and cell death. We know that prenatal and early postnatal life are exemplified by an explosive growth in the brain. As many as a quarter million neurons are generated per minute at the height of this maturation that mostly occurs prenatally. As we seek to find out what happens during development to cause an abnormal central nervous system that translates into mental retardation, we realize that one of the basic underlying problems of learning and memory function is a result of smaller structures such as neuron synapses and dendrites.

In his research at the Joseph P. Kennedy Mental Retardation Research Center at the University of Chicago, Dr. Huttenlocher has built upon findings in the early 1970s that critical synapses are already quite numerous at birth in the human fetal brain. Postnatally, during the first year of life there are further increases in synaptic density. This finding was especially significant because the cortex as a whole expands considerably during this period of time; the postnatal period is one of very rapid synaptogenesis in the human frontal cortex. By age 2 synaptic density is at its maximum. At about the same time, other components of the cerebral cortex are growing and approach the total brain weight of adulthood. After this period of time, synaptic density then declines, reaching by adolescence an adult value that is only 50% of the maximum. All of this is quite significant in that much of the research on early childhood intervention has proven most successful, particularly during the first few years of life. On the basis of these findings related to synaptogenesis in humans, one might predict that these would be the years in which brain plasticity is greatest and when external stimulation would most benefit brain organization and development. (Plasticity as used here and as defined by Jacobson [1978] implies, "certain types of adjustments of the developing nervous system to changes in the internal/external milieu, that are adaptive and tend to enable the system to function under changed conditions.") As Huttenlocher goes on to point out in his chapter, new quantitative techniques are now available to analyze growth and development of the human brain and what impact environmental stimulation can have, and also the deleterious effects of trauma upon the brain. For example, computer graphic analysis of dendritic trees has been used to study the development of cortical neurons and the microinjection of fluorescent dyes that help to establish specific pathways for connections such as that utilized in the study of animal models.

A better understanding of the cerebral plasticity in man is also addressed by Dr. David Coulter, a pediatric neurologist and past president of the American Academy on Mental Retardation. Dr. Coulter has also taught the popular symposium on the "Neurology of Mental Retardation" for a number of years at the American Association of Mental Deficiency. His chapter presents a way of looking at mental retardation that focuses on the structure and function of the brain. The neurological point of view is based primarily on a medical model that is intended to provide a scientific basis for both the diagnosis and treatment of brain dysfunctions. Dr. Coulter also recognizes the equally important psychological, educational, and rehabilitative models. He avoids the frequent criticism of such an approach as being too "physiological," which emphasizes a radical materialism approach. For example, he states, "the brain and mind are separate and the brain may be damaged while the mind is intact. Some aspects of mind, such as the ability to give and receive love and the ability to recognize transcendence or God, have very little to do with intelligence. In this respect, even the most severely retarded person may have as much of a human mind as an intellectually normal person."

Coulter's exhaustive and meticulous chapter focuses on four sections of the neurological analysis of mental retardation. First, he reviews normal brain development in order to examine the processes that may interfere with this development and lead to mental retardation. Coulter's analogy of building a house, along with his written and visual presentations, provide the reader with some insight into the ways of "curing" mental retardation through the prevention of adverse influences during critical periods of brain development. He postulates an interesting concept of the "hypoconnection syndrome" as possibly a major cause of mild mental retardation.

The second section of Dr. Coulter's chapter focuses on new diagnostic techniques that help confirm the cause of mental retardation and ways of preventing or reversing its symptoms. In 1895, the first X-ray photograph was taken by the German physicist, Wilhelm Konrad Roentgen. Since then, many techniques have been developed to intensify the X ray's image and improve its clarity resulting in detailed images. Some advanced X-ray machines (so named by Roentgen because of their unknown nature) digitize their data, allowing the image contrast to be mathematically enhanced in order to show subtle differences among tissues. The first such imaging technique referred to in this chapter is computed tomography (CT). The CT scanner produces a cross-sectional view of tissues within by penetrating the body with a thin fan-shaped X-ray beam. This is different from the conventional X-ray radiograph in which the body can be viewed from only one angle and can be difficult to interpret when shadows of bones, muscles, and organs are superimposed on one another. In Step 1, large molecules, such as calcium, absorb X rays as they pass through the body, partially masking whatever lies behind them. In Step 2, the CT machine views "a slice" of the body from many different angles by revolving an X-ray tube around the patient. In Step 3, a computer compares the many views to make a single video image via sensitive detectors on the opposite side that record what the scanner sees (see Figure 1).

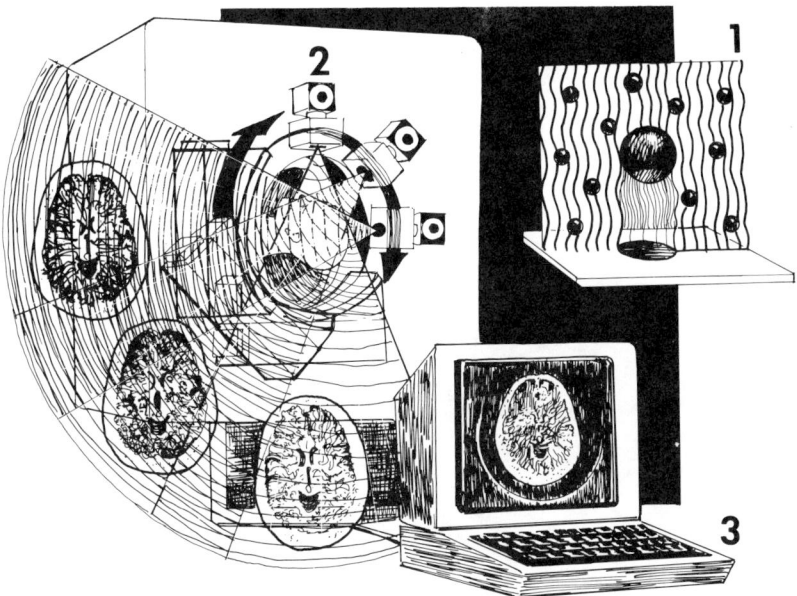

Figure 1.   Three-step process utilized by the computed tomography scanner.

The second imaging technique addressed in this chapter is magnetic resonance imaging (MRI), which reflects water by focusing on the behavior of hydrogen atoms in water molecules. This allows MRI to do things differently than CT scanners, such as distinguishing between the brain's white matter and water-rich grey matter. Teeth and bones, which contain little water, do not appear at all on the MRI process, thus enabling researchers to see tissue surrounded by bone, such as the spinal cord. The scanner, as depicted in Figure 2, surrounds the body with powerful electromagnets. Su-

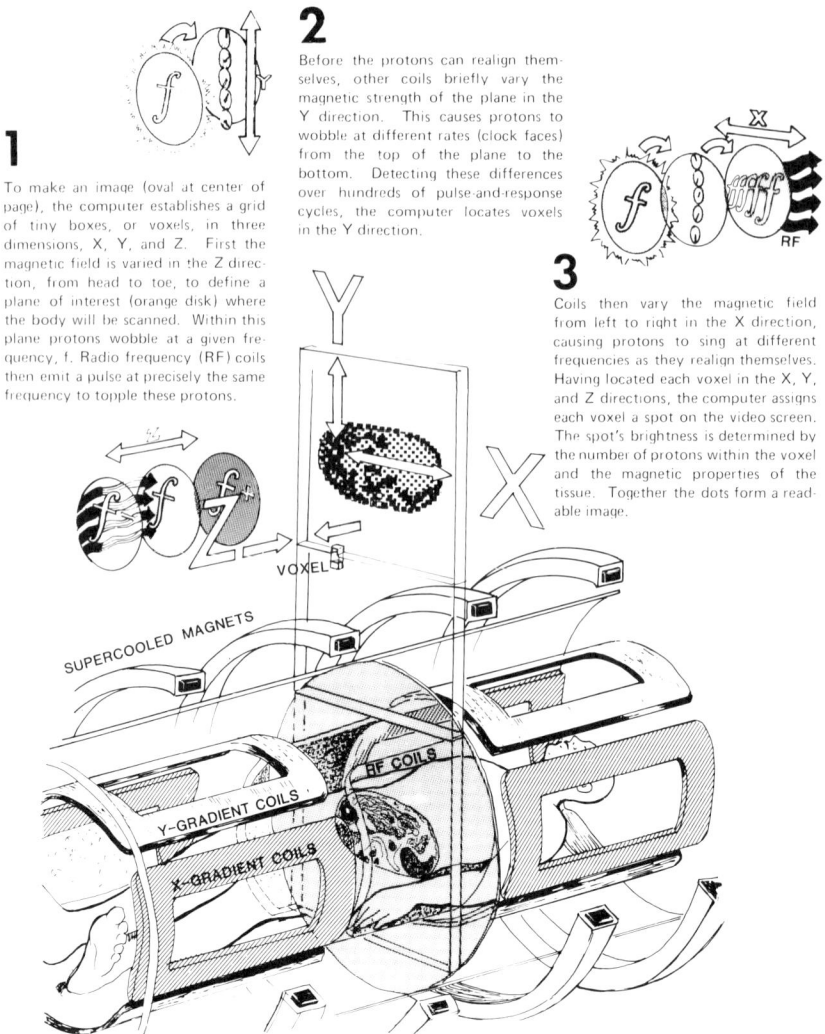

1

To make an image (oval at center of page), the computer establishes a grid of tiny boxes, or voxels, in three dimensions, X, Y, and Z. First the magnetic field is varied in the Z direction, from head to toe, to define a plane of interest (orange disk) where the body will be scanned. Within this plane protons wobble at a given frequency, f. Radio frequency (RF) coils then emit a pulse at precisely the same frequency to topple these protons.

2

Before the protons can realign themselves, other coils briefly vary the magnetic strength of the plane in the Y direction. This causes protons to wobble at different rates (clock faces) from the top of the plane to the bottom. Detecting these differences over hundreds of pulse-and-response cycles, the computer locates voxels in the Y direction.

3

Coils then vary the magnetic field from left to right in the X direction, causing protons to sing at different frequencies as they realign themselves. Having located each voxel in the X, Y, and Z directions, the computer assigns each voxel a spot on the video screen. The spot's brightness is determined by the number of protons within the voxel and the magnetic properties of the tissue. Together the dots form a readable image.

Figure 2.   Three-step process utilized by the magnetic resonance imaging scanner.

percooled by liquid helium, they create a magnetic field as much as 60,000 times as strong as that on the earth. This field has a profound effect on the nuclei of hydrogen atoms called protons (see Figure 3). Spinning like tops, these protons normally point in random directions such as in Figure 3A, but inside the scanner's magnetic field, as in Figure 3B, they align themselves in the direction of the field's poles. Even in alignment, however, they wobble with a certain frequency. The stronger the magnetic field, the greater the frequency $(f+)$. When the scanner excites these protons with the radio pulse timed to the same frequency as they are wobbling, it knocks them out of alignment, as in Figure 3C. Within a thousandth of a second, they spiral back into place, as in Figure 3D, putting out a faint radio signal of their own. The computer translates these signals into an image of the area scanned, made up of tiny dots converted to a readable image. This image then reveals varying intensities of hydrogen atoms and their interaction with surrounding tissues in a cross section of the body. Hydrogen has been selected as the basis for MRI scanning because of its abundance in the body and its prominent magnetic qualities. However, other elements are currently under investigation that could be used for specific diagnostic properties in other disease entities.

The third diagnostic imaging technique involves radioisotope imaging and is called SPECT (single-photon emission computed tomography), which

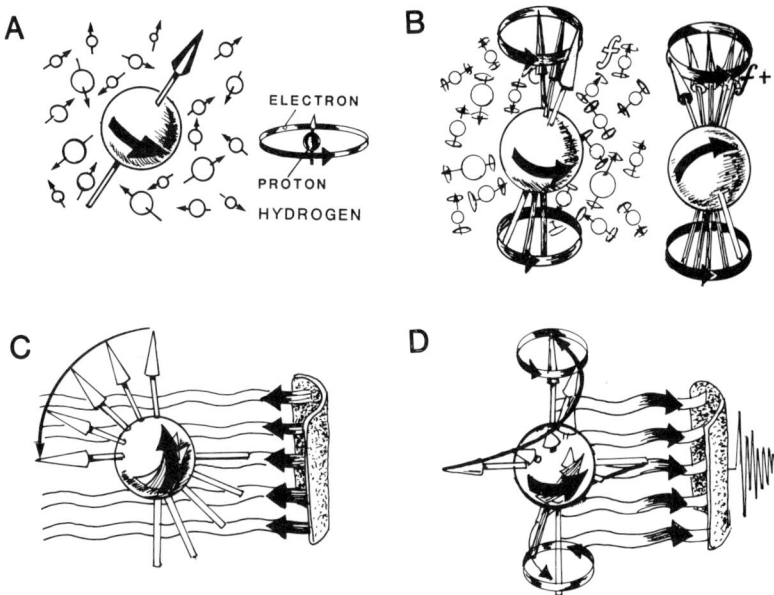

Figure 3.   The magnetic field of the MRI scanner and its effect upon protons. *A:* Proton in normal states. *B:* Proton inside scanner's magnetic field. *C:* Wobbling of proton due to increase in strength of magnetic field. *D:* Proton emitting a radio signal.

shows blood flow by image trace amounts of radioisotopes. However, a more versatile technique, PET (positron emission tomography) can also measure metabolism, revealing how well the body is working. The use of such radioactive tracers is well suited in such studies as epilepsy, schizophrenia, Parkinson disease, and other brain dysfunctions. As depicted in Figure 4, the PET scanner evaluates the way brain cells consume substances such as sugar. Substances are tagged with a radioisotope that is made in a small low-energy cyclotron. This isotope then has a short half-life, which means that it loses half its radioactivity within a short period of time (usually minutes or within hours of being developed). It is then injected into the body, usually intravenously, and its radioactive solution emits positrons wherever it flows. As these positrons collide with electrons, a burst of energy is released in the form of two gamma rays. As these rays shoot in opposite directions (Figure 4A), they strike the crystals in a ring of detectors (Figure 4B) around the patient's

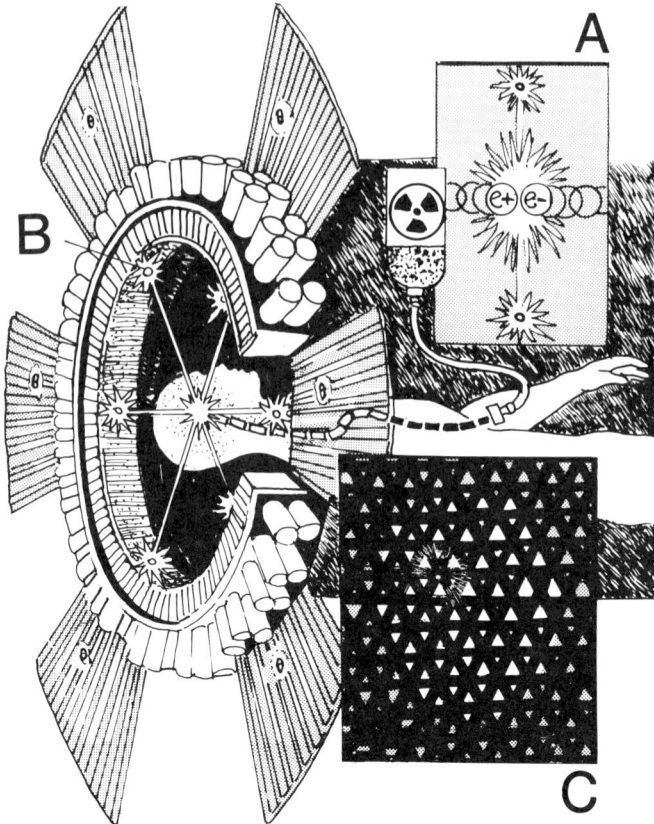

Figure 4.   Three-step process utilized by positron emission tomography.

head. This causes the crystals to light up. The computer then records the location of each flash and plots a source of radiation, translating that data into images (as in Figure 4C). The advantage of using SPECT is that it uses commercially available isotopes and thereby greatly reduces the cost by not having to use a cyclotron on site.

The last procedure, referred to as brain electrical activity mapping (BEAM), utilizes electroencephalographic (EEG) data, a color computerized picture of the brain's electrical activity. It can also be used with evoked potential techniques. In short, all of these techniques, CT, MRI, PET, SPECT, and BEAM, are powerful new techniques that will help greatly enhance progress toward the prevention and reversal or cure of mental retardation.

A third section of Dr. Coulter's chapter focuses on the treatment of seizure disorders, which are frequently one of the major health problems among individuals with retardation that often preclude their deinstitutionalization or lead to reinstitutionalization. New developments in the diagnosis and treatment of seizure disorders also provide great hope for significantly improving the functioning of individuals with mental retardation, since oftentimes learning and development cannot be significantly enhanced when frequent uncontrollable seizures occur.

Finally, Dr. Coulter's chapter focuses on a model of how the brain functions and also its dysfunction as it relates to movement disorders, thus providing an insightful and comprehensive view of treating these additional symptoms that magnify the cumulative effects of mental retardation.

REFERENCE

Jacobson, M. A. (1978). *Developmental neurobiology* (2nd ed., p. 19). New York: Plenum Publishing Corp.

Chapter 4

Developmental Neurobiology
Current and Future Challenges

Peter R. Huttenlocher

During the past decade, there has been tremendous progress in the field of developmental neurobiology. This has been aided and, to a large part, caused by development of new methods for studying the nervous system. Techniques that have proved to be particularly powerful for the study of developmental processes have included computer-assisted quantitation of various components of the brain. Development is to a large extent an increase in number and complexity of structures, such as neurons, synapses, and dendrites. Accurate, rapid methods for quantitation are essential for study of normal developmental processes as well as for investigation of the effects of various interventions and of disease processes on the developmental program. Some of these new quantitative techniques are applicable to the study of the human brain. Computer graphic analysis of dendritic trees has already been used to study the development of cortical neurons in the immature human brain (Purpura, 1983). A computer-assisted method for synapse quantitation has been applied to the study of normal synaptogenesis in man (Huttenlocher, DeCourten, Garey, & Van Der Loos, 1982). Similar approaches will be made to the investigation of developmental malformations once the ranges of normal have been established.

Another essential aspect of brain development is the establishment of specific pathways and connections. There are now extremely accurate and powerful methods for tracing connections, which utilize the microinjection and axonal transport of large molecules such as horseradish peroxidase and fluorescent dyes from terminal nerve endings to the cell body and dendritic tree. While these tracing techniques are not directly applicable to man, they can and have been utilized for the study of animal models of human disease. One such application is described later in this chapter.

The development of normal brain functions also depends on the formation of specific neurotransmitter systems such as the dopaminergic and central cholinergic system. Accurate neurochemical identification of neurons has become possible through immunohistochemistry with monoclonal antibodies to specific neurotransmitter enzyme proteins, such as choline acetyltransferase (Levey, Armstrong, Atweh, Terry, & Wainer, 1983). These techniques, while up to now employed mainly in animal studies, are presently being adapted for use in the human brain. The application of an immunochemical method for choline acetyltransferase to the study of Down syndrome represents a particularly exciting prospect. Cell changes resembling those of Alzheimer disease have been found in Down syndrome brains at much younger ages (Crapper, Dalton, Skopitz, Scott, & Hachinski, 1975). Such changes are known to be associated with degeneration of the cholinergic system that projects from basal forebrain to cerebral cortex (Whitehouse, Price, Clark, Coyle, & DeLong, 1981). Study of central cholinergic pathways in Down syndrome brains therefore may provide important new insights into the cause of the mental retardation in this disorder, and may eventually lead to therapeutic approaches.

Methods are now available for the investigation of cellular mechanisms underlying a wide variety of reactions of the immature nervous system. These include the responses of the immature brain to abnormal sensory input and to focal injury. It is well known that the developing brain reacts differently to focal damage than does the adult. These differences are of great importance for our understanding of mental retardation and other developmental disorders. Remarkable recovery or sparing of functions occurs after some types of perinatal and early postnatal injuries. This is usually ascribed to the "plasticity" of the developing nervous system. An example of plasticity in man is the recovery of language functions after destruction of the classical speech areas in the dominant hemisphere in the infant or young child. Permanent aphasia does not result if the language areas are damaged prior to about age 8 years (Woods & Teuber, 1978). The neurobiological basis for such remarkable recovery is presently unknown, but techniques now available are beginning to define specific cellular mechanisms.

Not all of the reactions of the immature brain lead to improvement in function. An example of a negative effect is the response of the immature visual cortex to lack of visual input or to abnormal input from one eye such as occurs in strabismus. The cortical connections from the abnormal eye either disappear or are never formed and the eye loses vision. No such visual loss occurs under similar circumstances in the adult (Hubel & Wiesel, 1970).

Knowledge concerning the cellular mechanisms of plasticity in man would be likely to lead to methods by which one could influence the response of the immature brain to injury in such a way as to maximize positive effects and minimize negative ones. Animal studies already have identified several possible mechanisms. One is the establishment of new connections by axonal sprouting. It occurs, for example, when the pyramidal tracts are damaged in the immature animal. There is regrowth of axons, which eventually find their correct targets in the spinal cord (Kalil, 1984). While axonal sprouting occurs under some circumstances in the adult central nervous system, it appears to be much more prominent in the developing brain.

A second cellular mechanism of plasticity is persistence of structures that would otherwise have been slated for elimination. It is now well established that during development of the nervous system there initially is overproduction of neurons. Nerve cells that do not find their target disappear in what has been called ''programmed cell death.'' This term may be somewhat of a misnomer, since the number of neurons that are eliminated is by no means fixed or preprogrammed, but can be changed by manipulation of the cells' natural target. A well-known example occurs in development of the spinal motor neurons in the chick embryo (Hollyday & Hamburger, 1976). Normally, about 50% of chick spinal motor neurons die during embryogenesis. Enlargement of the natural target of these neurons (i.e., skeletal muscle) through grafting of extra limbs results in decreased neuronal death and an increased number of surviving motor neurons in the mature animal. For a certain period in development, neurons that would otherwise disappear are able to establish connections and persist as functioning units, if free targets become available.

Rearrangement of synaptic connections is a more likely anatomic substrate for plasticity in cerebral cortex than is utilization of neurons that would otherwise have undergone programmed cell death. Most cortical neurons do not have specific peripheral targets, and elimination of one target still leaves many other opportunities for making synaptic connections. Programmed neuronal death, therefore, is less likely to occur in cerebral cortex than in spinal motor neurons, which have only a single natural target. The French neurobiologist Jean-Pierre Changeux has proposed an interesting theory of synaptic development in cerebral cortex that provides an explanation for plasticity during development related to the establishment of specific synaptic connections (Changeux & Danchin, 1976). Changeux argued that the great number of synaptic connections that are present in the brain rules out a genetic program for determination of each synaptic contact. Synapse formation, therefore, has to be to a large extent a random process initially. Many of these early connections are not specified for discrete functions. They are labile in Changeux's terminology. As the brain develops, some synapses become specified for defined functions, either because they become part of an afferent relay or of an internally generated electrical circuit. These connections become stabilized and persist. Connections that are not incorporated into functioning systems eventually disappear. Presence of labile connections in the immature brain would be a possible anatomic substrate for plasticity, in that these connections could become specified for functions normally subserved by other brain regions.

I have in my own work found confirmation for part of Changeux's theory, namely for initial overproduction and later elimination of synapses. The time course of these events in cerebral cortex of man is such as to make them a likely substrate for plasticity. In my studies, I utilized a method of quantitative histology aided by computer analysis. The work was performed at the Institute of Anatomy at the University of Lausanne in collaboration with Drs. DeCourten, Garey, and Van Der Loos (Huttenlocher et al., 1982). Human postmortem brain tissue was prepared by the alcoholic phosphotungstic acid method, which demonstrates synaptic profiles selectively. Synapses were counted in strips of cortex extending from pia to white matter, and synaptic density was calculated, utilizing a computer program. In a study of primary visual cortex (Area 17), it was possible to measure total volume of this area of cortex in addition to synaptic density. An estimate of total number of synapses in Area 17 at various ages could therefore be obtained.

At birth, synaptic density in visual cortex already is quite high, especially in Layers 4 and 5 where it approaches adult values. However, the volume of this cortical area is much smaller than in the adult, and the total number of synapses in Area 17 is only about 20% of the adult value. An interesting finding is the occurrence of a very rapid burst of synaptogenesis between ages 2 and 4 months, associated with rapid expansion of cerebral cortex. The total number of synapses rises above the adult number. Subsequently, there is a period of several years during infancy and early childhood during which synapses are lost from visual cortex. The adult number is approached by about age 4 years, after which the total number of synapses remains relatively stable until old age. This naturally does not rule out a dynamic system even in the adult. Synaptic contacts may continue to be eliminated and new ones may form; but these events, if they do occur, must be in balance.

The discussion of the possible functional significance of these findings follows. There can be little doubt that the sudden expansion of visual cortex and increase in synaptic contacts that occur between ages 2 and 4 months are closely related to the emergence of function in the visual system. This is the time during which visual alertness and acuity increase rapidly in the infant and during which such functions of visual cortex as stereopsis and stereoacuity first appear (Dobson & Teller, 1978). After age 6 months, the visual cortex appears to have most of the functional capacities of the adult. At least one difference, however, remains: the plasticity of the system with respect to visual input. Decreased or abnormal visual input to one eye in the young child, as from unilateral cataract or from strabismus, leads to amblyopia of that eye. This type of visual loss is preventable—by removal of the cataract or by patching of the "good" eye—until about age 5 years (i.e., approximately during the time when there is an excess number of synapses in visual cortex). The following schema provides a possible mechanism for amblyopia and for its prevention in the young child: Initially, there is overproduction of synapses. A large number of synaptic sites are available for afferent input from both eyes, although many of these are nonspecified or labile. Normally, an approximately equal number of synapses become specified for processing of inputs from each eye. Those synapses that are not specified for visual functions are eliminated. In the strabismic child, most synapses become specified for the processing of inputs from the dominant (nonsquinting) eye. As a result, not enough connections from the squinting eye to visual cortex remain for useful vision. This asymmetric specification of connections can be prevented by forcing the child to use the squinting eye, as by patching of the good eye, if patching is done prior to the critical age for synapse specification and elimination, which lies near age 5 years.

This schema suggests two important principles. The first is that development and maintenance of cortical connections in the young child are influenced by afferent input or by experience; to a certain extent experience determines the anatomy of the system. There can be little doubt that this is the case, both from clinical observation and from experimental work on the effects of visual input on functional connections of the developing visual cortex, largely the work of Hubel and Wiesel (Hubel & Wiesel, 1970; Hubel, Wiesel, & LeVay, 1977). The second principle is that of competition for synaptic sites during development. Under some circumstances, connections subserving one function seem to be able to crowd out connections related to another functional system. Both principles are important for our understanding of abnormal brain development as occurs in many conditions that are manifested by mental retardation, and for the eventual production of rational programs for training and rehabilitation.

A condition in which early competition for synaptic sites may have gone awry is the form of autism sometimes referred to as "idiot savant." Here one cortical function or ability—such as reading or calculation—develops very early in life and is associated with very poor performance in other areas of cognitive function (Huttenlocher & Huttenlocher, 1973). A possible explanation is that synaptic sites normally specified for other functions have been taken over by the one activity in which these children excel, perhaps partly influenced by early parental attempts to train this function.

Up to now, the discussion has concentrated on the situation in which abnormal afferent input leads to changes in connections in developing cerebral cortex. A second area of relevance to mental retardation is the reaction of the developing brain to damage. Here I would like to consider an animal model in which I have been studying this reaction, namely the animal in whom one cerebral hemisphere has been removed early in development. In this model one can look at the changes that occur in the remaining cerebral hemisphere in its attempt to "take over" functions otherwise subserved by the resected brain tissue. Such changes are likely to underlie the recovery of functions after hemispherectomy in the human infant, which is remarkable in many respects. For example, language functions develop to a near-normal level after removal of the dominant hemisphere in infancy (Woods & Teuber,

1978). As far as motor functions are concerned, the child in whom one cerebral hemisphere has been removed early in life has remarkable recovery of lower extremity functions. These children always learn to walk, and the gait pattern is often near normal with only a mild hemiparetic limp. This is in contrast to the situation in the adult where unilateral removal of motor cortex results in profound gait disturbance. The upper extremity fares less well. Finely coordinated movements of the fingers are severely affected after infantile hemispherectomy.

The animal hemispherectomy model has provided interesting insight into the mechanism for recovery of motor functions. In the rat, hemispherectomy done postnatally (usually in the first week) results in an animal that has only one pyramidal tract at the brain stem level. Distal to the decussation of the pyramids in the lower medulla there are bilateral pyramidal tracts, and the spinal cord looks essentially normal. This is achieved by formation of an uncrossed tract (i.e., only about half of the fibers in the remaining medullary pyramid cross over). The rest descend on the same side and innervate the ipsilateral anterior horn cells (Hicks & D'Amato, 1970; Leong & Lund, 1973; Sharp & Evans, 1983). The mechanism by which this compensation is achieved is not clear. Kalil (1984) at University of Wisconsin has demonstrated a remarkable capacity of damaged immature pyramidal tract fibers to sprout and to regrow and find their targets in the spinal cord. Sprouting of collaterals after hemispherectomy may lead to the uncrossed pyramidal tract. Alternatively, it may be formed by axons that had not yet reached the spinal cord level, even by some that otherwise would not have been destined to grow into the cord.

In collaboration with D. Rye and B. Wainer, I have recently initiated a study on the changes in motor cortex of the remaining hemisphere following neonatal hemispherectomy. Hemispherectomized rats and litter mate controls were allowed to grow to maturity. The cervical spinal cord then was injected with a mixture of wheat germ and horseradish peroxidase. Two days later, the animals were perfused and the cerebral cortex was examined for peroxidase-positive cells (i.e., neurons whose axons descended at least to cervical spinal cord). This study is in progress at the present time. Initial data show an expansion of the area of cortex specified for motor functions in the remaining hemisphere in hemispherectomized animals. It therefore appears that these animals compensate for loss of one motor cortex by enlarging the other one. How this is done is not yet clear. There is no evidence that the remaining hemisphere as a whole increases in size. Its weight is equal to that of a cerebral hemisphere in controls. Increase in size of the motor cortex, therefore, may be at the expense of other cortical areas, suggesting that some functions that may be less essential may be crowded out. Here again there is a suggestion that competition for neuronal circuits or synaptic sites may be an important aspect of plasticity, with some functions winning out while others may be further impaired.

At this point, one cannot be certain that the extrapyramidal tract neurons in the remaining hemisphere are cells that would have been specified for other functions had the opposite hemisphere been left intact. Another possibility is that these are neurons that would otherwise have disappeared by the process of programmed cell death. However, there is as yet no evidence that programmed cell death occurs in cerebral cortex. My colleagues and I found no evidence for it in our study of synaptogenesis in human visual cortex (De-Courten, Leuba, Huttenlocher, Garey, & Van Der Loos, 1982).

I have attempted to investigate the question whether the excess of synapses that are produced in immature cerebral cortex may become specified and may take over functions that have been lost due to lesions in other parts of cortex. In that case, the decrease in synaptic density that occurs during late cortical development should be less, and the synaptic density at maturity should be greater than in normal cortex. I again have utilized the rat hemispherectomy model for this study. As a first step, I had to determine whether synapse elimination occurs during development of cerebral cortex in the rat. I found that this was indeed the case, similar to the situation in man. There was an initial postnatal increase in synaptic density. The maximum was reached at about age 37 days and subsequently synaptic density declined (Layers 2 and 3, parietal cortex).

The results in the hemispherectomized animals differed in different cortical areas. In occipital cortex there was a significant increase in synaptic density in hemispherectomized animals as compared with controls. No significant differences were seen in frontal or parietal areas, although there was a trend toward higher synaptic density in the hemispherectomized animals. The difference between occipital cortex and the other areas may be related to the fact that there normally are no callosal connections in the occipital area. In other cortical regions, hemispherectomy results in removal of callosal inputs that account for 20%–30% of synaptic connections in some cortical layers. A passive reaction of cerebral cortex to hemispherectomy would lead to a decrease in synaptic density in areas that have callosal connections. Our data, therefore, suggest that specification and stabilization of synapses that would otherwise have been eliminated and specification of synapses for functions other than those normally subserved may both underly the reaction of the remaining hemisphere to hemispherectomy in the infant.

To sum up the results of the animal studies of plasticity, it is becoming clear that there are several cellular mechanisms underlying plasticity. These include: 1) axonal sprouting, 2) decrease in number of neurons undergoing programmed cell death, 3) specification of labile synapses that would otherwise have been eliminated, and 4) takeover of cortical areas for functions that normally would have been carried out by other regions. Turning to the situation of brain damage in man, the last mechanism—a shift of cortical representation to other areas—is the only one clearly documented. An example is the shift of language localization from the dominant to the nondominant hemisphere after early lesions in the speech areas. This compensation unfortunately is one that also carries a price. As some cortical functions find a new area of representation, others may be crowded out. Evidence for this is accumulating in studies of language and other cognitive functions in patients with early acquired unilateral brain lesions, including hemispherectomy. As I mentioned earlier, language recovers remarkably well in such patients even after complete destruction of the speech areas in the dominant hemisphere. Speech becomes represented in the nondominant hemisphere. However, this appears to occur to some extent at the expense of nonverbal, nondominant, hemisphere functions. St. James-Roberts (1981) recently summarized psychological test data from patients with hemispherectomy. They show that patients with early left hemispherectomy have a decrease in performance scores on the Wechsler test (i.e., in the functions normally subserved by the remaining hemisphere). There also is some indication that representation of nonverbal functions in the left hemisphere after early right hemispherectomy may depress verbal functions. The verbal IQ after right hemispherectomy in infancy appears to be lower than is verbal IQ after hemispherectomy in the adult, although the number of carefully studied adult patients is small. In collaboration with S. Levine, we have recently completed a study of 40 patients with unilateral brain damage dating from infancy that provides data that supplement the hemispherectomy data. Most of these patients had focal areas of destruction of cerebral cortex with formation of fluid-filled spaces, so-called porencephaly. Verbal IQ tended to be slightly higher than performance IQ, irrespective of whether the right or left hemisphere was damaged, suggesting that in the competition for cortical representation, language functions may have a slight edge. Even among language functions, recovery tended to be incomplete, especially when one considered those functions that normally emerge late. Here, left brain damage cases did worse than right brain damage cases, suggesting that plasticity may be limited for late-developing functions. In children that were old enough for testing, most were poor readers, and among the left-sided lesion cases, only a few had mastered the ability to analyze words phonetically.

The apparent absence of plasticity for late-developing functions, such as reading, provides an interesting parallel to the anatomical data on synapse elimination in human brain. If excess synapses were related to plasticity, then one would expect plasticity to decrease during the period of synapse elimination. In a study of middle frontal gyrus, which resembles the speech areas in its development, I found that synapse elimination begins during the early childhood years (Huttenlocher, 1979). The normal time for learning to read, therefore, may be past the time for maximum plasticity.

A central question for which there as yet is no clear answer is whether plasticity of the immature brain can be utilized to affect IQ. In patients with early-onset unilateral cerebral lesions, there is evidence of an IQ effect related to lesion size. In our study of infantile hemiplegia, we found lesion size to be the major predictor of IQ. The location of the lesion, occurrence of seizures, and EEG changes added little predictive value. IQ in patients with complete hemispherectomy is on the average about 20 points below the normal mean. Yet, there have been a few individual cases of hemispherectomy with normal and even superior IQ, suggesting that there is no absolute limit (Smith & Sugar, 1975).

The challenge clearly is to find methods for training children with brain damage that maximize positive effects of plasticity and that minimize the negative. At present, available data provide few clues as to what approaches are most likely to be successful. However, some hints exist. For example, we now know that children with left hemisphere damage are unlikely to learn to read well by standard methods. From what has been learned about plasticity, it can be suggested that, to be successful, reading instruction would have to be started early in such children, during the period when plasticity of cerebral cortex is still high and before areas required for reading are specified for other functions. One may have to make choices as to what functions to train early, since specification of brain areas for these early-acquired functions may impede others that should emerge later.

An exciting recent development is the prospect that one will be able to observe in vivo the effects of intervention programs on the localization of specific cognitive functions in cerebral cortex. There are now a number of methods, some quite noninvasive, that allow us to observe the effects of plasticity on cerebral localization. Positron emission tomography is one such method. However, its expense and the fact that it exposes the patient to some radiation hazard limit its applicability. Electrophysiological methods may provide similar data safely and less expensively. In this regard, I would like to mention a recent study by Neville and associates at Salk Institute (Neville, Schmidt, & Kutas, 1983). These investigators studied the distribution of visual evoked potentials over the scalp in patients with congenital deafness. Compared to controls, these patients had larger visual evoked responses in frontal and temporal regions that normally subserve auditory and spoken language functions. Apparently, visual processing takes over synaptic sites in such patients that would normally be specified for processing of auditory information.

Brain electrical activity mapping (BEAM), a technique developed by Frank Duffy at Harvard Medical School, also holds considerable promise for the in vivo study of altered cerebral localization related to brain plasticity. In this technique, brain areas with increased functional activity are identified by an increase in brain waves of fast (beta) frequencies using computer-assisted analysis of frequency spectra. In a study of normal children, Duffy and colleagues found activation of the left temporal areas while the children were listening to a story. Dyslexic children did not show left temporal activation during the same language task, suggesting that language functions may be aberrantly localized in other brain areas in such children (Duffy, Denckla, Bartels, & Sandini, 1980; Duffy & McAnulty, 1985).

This and similar techniques will undoubtedly be utilized to study cerebral localization of other specific cognitive tasks in normal and brain-damaged children. Such data will supplement and extend the histological data that can be gathered from animal models and from the occasional fortuitous human pathological specimen (Galaburda & Kemper, 1979). This combined approach should lead to a much better understanding of the extent and limits of cerebral plasticity in man. It may yield rational methods for early intervention designed to maximize the positive aspects of cerebral plasticity, and to thereby achieve the best possible functional outcome in brain-damaged children.

REFERENCES

Changeux, J. P., & Danchin, A. (1976). Selective stabilization of developing synapses as a mechanism for the specification of neural networks. *Nature, 264,* 705–712.

Crapper, D. R., Dalton, A. J., Skopitz, M., Scott, J. W., & Hachinski, V. C. (1975). Alzheimer degeneration in Down's syndrome: Electrophysiologic alterations and histopathologic findings. *Archives of Neurology, 33,* 618–623.

DeCourten, C., Leuba, G., Huttenlocher, P. R., Garey, L., & Van Der Loos, H. (1982). Volumetric, neuronal and synaptic development of human primary visual cortex. *Neuroscience Letters, Suppl. 10,* S135.

Dobson, V., & Teller, D. Y. (1978). Visual acuity in human infants: A review and comparison of behavioral and electrophysiological studies. *Vision Research, 18,* 1469–1483.

Duffy, F. H., Denckla, M. B., Bartels, P. H., & Sandini, G. (1980). Dyslexia: Regional differences in brain electrical activity by topographic mapping. *Annals of Neurology, 7,* 412–420.

Duffy, F. H., & McAnulty, G. B. (1985). The search for a physiological signature of dyslexia. In F. H. Duffy & N. Geschwind (Eds.), *A neuroscientific approach to clinical evaluation* (pp. 105–122). Boston: Little, Brown & Co.

Galaburda, A. M., & Kemper, T. L. (1979). Cytoarchitectonic abnormalities in developmental dyslexia: A case study. *Annals of Neurology, 6,* 95–100.

Hicks, S. P., & D'Amato, C. J. (1970). Motor-sensory and visual behavior after hemispherectomy in newborn and mature rats. *Experimental Neurology, 29,* 416–438.

Hollyday, M., & Hamburger, V. (1976). Reduction of the naturally occurring motor neuron loss by enlargement of the periphery. *Journal of Comparative Neurology, 170,* 311–320.

Hubel, D. H., & Wiesel, T. N. (1970). The period of susceptibility to the physiological effects of unilateral eye closure in kittens. *Journal of Physiology (London), 206,* 419–436.

Hubel, D. H., Wiesel, T. N., & LeVay, S. (1977). Plasticity of ocular dominance columns in monkey striate cortex. *Philosophical Transactions, 278,* 377–409.

Huttenlocher, P. R. (1979). Synaptic density in human frontal cortex: Developmental changes and effects of aging. *Brain Research, 163,* 195–205.

Huttenlocher, P. R., DeCourten, C., Garey, L. J., & Van Der Loos, H. (1982). Synaptogenesis in human visual cortex: Evidence for synapse elimination during normal development. *Neuroscience Letters, 33,* 247–252.

Huttenlocher, P. R., & Huttenlocher, J. (1973). A study of children with hyperlexia. *Neurology, 23,* 1107–1116.

Kalil, K. (1984). Development and regrowth of the rodent pyramidal tract. *Trends in Neuroscience, 7,* 394–398.

Leong, S. K., & Lund, R. D. (1973). Anomalous bilateral corticofugal pathways in albino rats after neonatal lesions. *Brain Research, 62,* 218–221.

Levey, A. I., Armstrong, D. M., Atweh, R. D., Terry, R. D., & Wainer, B. H. (1983). Monoclonal antibodies to choline acetyl transferase: Production, specificity and immunohistochemistry. *Journal of Neuroscience, 3,* 1–9.

Neville, H. J., Schmidt, A., & Kutas, M. (1983). Altered visual evoked potentials in congenitally deaf adults. *Brain Research, 266,* 127–132.

Purpura, D. P. (1983). Cellular neurobiology of mental retardation: Problems and perspectives. In F. J. Menolascino, R. Neman, & J. A. Stark (Eds.), *Curative aspects of mental retardation: Biomedical and behavioral advances* (pp. 57–67). Baltimore: Paul H. Brookes Publishing Co.

St. James-Roberts, I. (1981). A reinterpretation of hemispherectomy data without functional plasticity of the brain. *Brain and Language, 13,* 31–53.

Sharp, F. R., & Evans, K. L. (1983). Bilateral [14C] 2-[deoxyglucose uptake by motor pathways after unilateral neonatal cortex lesions in the rat. *Developmental Brain Research, 6,* 1–11.

Smith, A., & Sugar, O. (1975). Development of above normal language and intelligence 21 years after left hemispherectomy. *Neurology, 25,* 813–818.

Whitehouse, P. J., Price, D. L., Clark, A. W., Coyle, J. T., & DeLong, M. R. (1981). Alzheimer disease: Evidence for slective loss of cholinergic neurons in the nucleus basalis. *Annals of Neurology, 10,* 122–126.

Woods, B. T., & Teuber, H.-L. (1978). Changing patterns of childhood aphasia. *Annals of Neurology, 3,* 273–280.

Chapter 5

The Neurology
of Mental Retardation

David L. Coulter

Intelligence is a function of the brain, so there must be something different about a brain that functions in the mentally retarded range. The neurological point of view considers the symptom of mental retardation to result from a disturbance in the development of the brain prior to adulthood. Sometimes a brain that had developed normally up to a point is damaged by some identified adverse influence such as asphyxia, infection, or trauma. This is what is properly called "brain damage" and often results in sufficient cognitive dysfunction to cause mental retardation. In many cases, however, there is no obvious adverse influence, so one must suppose that the brain simply never developed properly. Brain development begins within the 1st month after conception and continues throughout childhood, so there are many opportunities for development to go awry. Aberrant brain development can also result in sufficient cognitive dysfunction to cause mental retardation. According to this point of view, mental retardation of any type or severity is a developmental brain dysfunction that begins during childhood and results in significantly subaverage intellectual and adaptive abilities.

This chapter first examines the causes of mental retardation according to the neurological point of view. This approach correlates knowledge of developmental neurobiology with known and hypothesized adverse influences that may result in mental retardation. Neuroimaging procedures are discussed to show how aberrant brain development and disordered brain function can be demonstrated during life. The management of seizure disorders is discussed in detail since this is a frequently associated neurological disorder. Persons with mental retardation often have other brain dysfunctions as well. A model of brain function and dysfunction is developed and applied to a consideration of movement disorders, which are a common dysfunction in persons with mental retardation. Finally, the limitations of this point of view are identified and placed in perspective with other approaches to persons with mental retardation.

CAUSES OF MENTAL RETARDATION

Mental retardation is the result of aberrant development and function of the brain. To understand the causes of mental retardation, one must first understand normal brain development. One can then examine influences and processes that may interfere with brain development and result in mental retardation. Detailed discussions of brain development are available (Jacobson, 1978; Purves & Lichtman, 1985).

Brain development is not a genetically programmed sequence of events or "unfolding" of a predetermined end result. One can think of it using the analogy of building a house. The blueprint is contained in the genetic code and serves to guide the subsequent construction of the brain. How the brain is actually put together—how this blueprint is executed—depends on the quality of the materials and the skill with which the work is done. A poor contractor and untrained workers build a house that doesn't work very well, even though the blueprint may have been a good one. In the same way, adverse influences during the process of cellular development of the brain may result in a brain that isn't put together the way it should be and that doesn't work very well. It follows that brain development cannot be thought of as exclusively "genetic" or "environmental." Genetic instructions may set the stage early in development, but their impact becomes more restricted as the cell specializes. From the very beginning, the brain develops as a result of the interaction between genetic programs and environmental influences that determines how the programs are executed. Attempts to separate the effects of "nature" versus "nurture" ignore this fundamental interaction in brain development.

Within the 1st month of gestation, the neural plate forms on the dorsal surface of the embryo and begins to fold over on itself to form the neural tube. The neural tube closes by the end of the 1st month. In the 2nd month, the rostral (head) end of the neural tube differentiates into the five primordial vesicles of the brain: telencephalon, diencephalon, mesencephalon, metencephalon, and myelencephalon. The telencephalon subsequently differentiates into the cerebral hemispheres. In the 3rd through the 6th month of gestation, the primary fissures of the cerebral hemispheres develop, but the surface of the brain is still smooth. Progressive development of the cerebral cortex in the 7th through the 9th month of gestation results in the folding of this smooth surface into cerebral convolutions or gyri. At birth, the brain looks much like an adult brain to the naked eye. Under the microscope, however, it is a very different story. The cellular development of the brain begins very early in gestation and continues long after birth and throughout childhood. Since aberrant brain function in mental retardation is related to disturbances in cellular development, these processes are considered in detail.

The primordial nerve cell (or neuron) begins by extending processes called growth cones outward from the cell body. These growth cones are directed by chemical gradients (nerve growth factors), positional influences, and interactions with other cells. When the growth cone encounters a favorable substrate, it attaches to it and retracts, pulling the cell body forward. In this way the growth cone can elongate as it seeks out and makes contacts with other cells that will later develop into specific connections or synapses. The cell body can also move or migrate as it is pulled along by the extending growth cone. The neurons that form the cerebral cortex first develop deep in the interior of the brain along the ventricular surface and then migrate to the surface through contact with specific radially oriented fibers that help guide the way. This process of cell migration results in neurons arriving at the cortex in the proper sequence and position. Having arrived at the cortex, the neurons can then seek out and make contact with other cortical neurons to develop the cortical architecture.

Since there is an excess of neurons early in development, some of these cells must die during the course of normal development. Cell death results from competition among a group of neurons that start as equals in which unsuccessful neurons die. The size of the target determines how many neurons competing to make contact with it will survive. Success and survival depend on the development of functional contacts that develop into synapses later. As many as 30%–75% of the original pool of competing neurons in some areas may die during the course of normal development.

As neuronal development proceeds, other cells in the brain also grow and differentiate to assume important roles that are necessary for normal neuronal function. These supporting cells (or glia) proliferate later than the neurons and so are even more susceptible to adverse environmental influences. Astroglia are cells that interface between the blood vessels and the neurons, presumably regulating the flow of ions and nutrients into and out of the nerve cell. Oligodendroglia are cells that form a myelin sheath around the axon, which promotes conduction of impulses along the axon and permits optimal communication between nerve cells. The formation of myelin occurs at different times in different areas of the brain but much of its occurs after birth, so adverse environmental influences can result in defective myelination.

Ultimately, synapse formation is the "name of the game" in brain development. These connections between nerve cells determine subsequent neuronal function. As the synapse forms, it induces specialization in the target neuron and also promotes the growth of the cell making contact with the target. The development of functional activity across these synapses promotes their survival, while nonfunctional synapses are progressively eliminated. There is evidence that synapses are made and broken throughout life. Sprouting of neuronal processes (axons) continues as long as appropriate stimulation occurs and is maintained by functional activity across the synapse. When contact is broken or functional activity does not occur, the synapse degenerates and the axon retracts. It should be apparent that deprivation of essential input results in lack of activity at the synapse and inadequate development of this vital connection between neurons. Since synapse formation occurs throughout childhood, adverse environmental influences (such as lack of stimulation) can result in aberrant brain development manifest as altered neuronal connectivity. Recovery is possible if the adverse influences are reversed or removed during a period in which that part of the brain is still developing (the critical period). In a theoretical sense, the cure of mental retardation depends on the prevention of these adverse influences or their reversal during the critical period of brain development.

Table 1 shows the relationship between the timing of normal brain development and the effect of adverse influences on this process. Table 2 lists some possible cellular mechanisms of altered brain development that may result in mental retardation. We will now consider specific causes of mental retardation according to the time of their influence on brain development. In accordance with the theme of this book, particular attention will be paid to prevent-

Table 1. Timetable of human brain development

Days of gestation	Normal event	Effect of adverse influence
0–18	Three germ layers elaborate	No effect or death
18	Neural plate and groove develop	Anterior midline defects
24–26	Anterior neuropore closed	Anencephaly, encephalocele
26–28	Posterior neuropore closed	Cranial bifidum, spina bifida
33–35	Five cerebral vesicles develop	Holoprosencephaly
30–150	Differentiation of cerebral cortex, neuronal migration	Microcephaly (30–130 days), abnormal cellular proliferation syndromes (30–175 days), migration defects (30 days to complete development of each brain subdivision)
70–100	Corpus callosum forms	Agenesis of corpus callosum
70–150	Primary fissures of cerebral cortex develop	Lissencephaly
140–175	Neuronal proliferation in cerebral cortex ends	Defects of cellular architectonics
9 months	Secondary and tertiary sulci form	Pachygyria, polymicrogyria, encephaloclasia
175 days through childhood	Neuronal outgrowth, glial cell production, myelin formation, axosomatic and axodendritic synaptic connections form	Hypoconnection syndromes

Table 2. Possible cellular defects in mental retardation

 1. Migration to the wrong position
 2. Failure to establish initial contacts (abnormal outgrowth)
 3. Absence or deficiency of growth (trophic) factors
 4. Abnormal cell surface markers to promote axon attraction and adhesion
 5. Excessive or inappropriate cell death
 6. Lack of specificity of connections (redundancy)
 7. Insufficient axon sprouting
 8. Inadequate synaptic activity
 9. Defective myelination of axon
10. Passing of critical period for adequate development

able or reversible influences. Detailed discussions of these diseases and disorders are available (Barlow, 1978; Grossman, 1983).

Table 3 lists adverse influences that affect brain development during gestation. Alterations in the genetic program, such as chromosomal abnormalities or single-gene disorders, often result in mental retardation. Prevention is available through genetic counseling, prenatal diagnosis of some conditions, and selective abortion of affected fetuses. The techniques of recombinant DNA genetics have been developed recently and may eventually offer the prospect of actual cure of some of these genetic disorders (Rosenberg, 1984). These techniques can result in the identification and purification of the actual defective gene in disorders such as phenylketonuria (PKU). Characterization of the abnormal gene product in PKU could provide the means to correct the defect in the gene itself. Healing the abnormal DNA in the PKU gene or providing a normal gene product would result in normal gene function. An individual born with PKU and treated in this way would be able to metabolize phenylalanine normally and thus would be "cured" of PKU. This is only a theoretical possibility at the present time, but future research may make it a reality for PKU and other genetic disorders.

Developmental defects reflect abnormalities in the processes described above, occurring prior to birth. In many such cases, the actual cause of the abnormal developmental process remains unknown, so that prevention is not yet possible. Many of these same developmental defects may result from the environmental influences listed separately in Table 3, however. Removing these adverse environmental influences would prevent both developmental defects and the mental retardation due to these influences. Thus, adequate maternal nutrition and abstention from alcohol, tobacco, and drugs during pregnancy would prevent many cases of mental retardation. It remains to be seen whether adequate treatment of maternal diseases, such as phenylketonuria, will also result in prevention of mental retardation in the children (Levy, Kaplan, & Erickson, 1982).

Table 3. Prenatal causes of mental retardation

I. Chromosomal abnormalities
   A. Autosomes
      1. Trisomy 21 (Down syndrome)
      2. Trisomy 13 (D)
      3. Trisomy 18 (E)
      4. Deletions
      5. Translocation
   B. Sex chromosomes
      1. X-linked MR (Fragile X)
      2. Turner syndrome (XO)
         Klinefelter syndrome (XXY)
      3. XYY syndrome
      4. Other multiple-X syndromes

II. Single-Gene disorders
   A. Neurocutaneous diseases
      1. Tuberous sclerosis
      2. Neurofibromatosis
      3. Sturge-Weber syndrome
   B. Neurotrichoses (Menkes disease)
   C. Other genetic syndromes

III. Developmental defects
   A. Neural tube closure defects
      1. Anencephaly/rachischisis
      2. Spina bifida
      3. Encephalocele
   B. Brain formation defects
      1. Holoprosencephaly
      2. Lissencephaly
      3. Pachygyria
      4. Polymicrogyria
      5. Schizencephaly
   C. Cellular migration defects
      1. Abnormal layering of cortex
      2. Heterotopias of gray matter
      3. Intraneuronal defects (microtubules, dendritic spines)
   D. Acquired brain defects (encephaloclasia)
      1. Hydranencephaly
      2. Porencephaly
   E. Primary microcephaly

(continued)

Table 3. (*continued*)

IV. Environmental influences
    A. Intrauterine malnutrition
        1. Maternal malnutrition
        2. Placental insufficiency
    B. Alcohol (fetal alcohol syndrome)
    C. Tobacco (cigarette smoking)
    D. Teratogenic drugs
    E. Maternal diseases
        1. Diabetes mellitus
        2. Phenylketonuria
        3. Myotonic dystrophy
    F. Irradiation during pregnancy
V. Other (nonspecific)

Table 4 outlines a variety of adverse influences that may affect the brain during the perinatal period immediately before, during, and after birth. Many of these are preventable through adequate prenatal care and prevention of teenage pregnancy and premature birth. To a large extent, these are socioeconomic and cultural influences, so that the most effective preventive efforts would be education and alleviation of poverty. A variety of postnatal events occurring during the first few months of life can also result in mental retardation. Transport of mothers with high-risk pregnancies to a regional medical center and transport of sick newborns to an intensive care nursery will result in optimal medical care and treatment of these conditions. Screening for selected metabolic diseases and attention to proper infant nutrition are also effective forms of prevention and treatment.

Table 5 lists conditions occurring during childhood that may result in mental retardation. Many head injuries are preventable. Education in child behavior, family support, and early protective intervention can prevent head injury due to child abuse. Mandatory seat belt use for children, effective penalties for driving drunk or speeding, and required use of motorcycle helmets would reduce head injury due to motor vehicle accidents. Prompt and appropriate medical treatment of infections, seizure disorders, and toxic or metabolic disorders can also prevent mental retardation in some cases. Better childhood immunization programs, including development of a safer pertussis vaccine, would prevent some cases of mental retardation. Adequate nutrition provides the "building materials" for brain development, so malnutrition can result in an abnormal brain and mental retardation. It is difficult to separate the effects of these various socioeconomic influences, including risk of infection, poor medical care, child abuse, exposure to toxins such as lead, lack of

Table 4.   Perinatal causes of mental retardation

I.   Asphyxia
   A.   Placental insufficiency
      1.   Acute
         a.   Abruptio placentae
         b.   Placenta previa/hemorrhage
         c.   Maternal hypotension
         d.   Toxemia
         e.   Twin-twin transfusion
      2.   Chronic (marginal reserve)
         a.   Maternal hypertension (infarcts)
         b.   Postmaturity (involution)
         c.   Erythroblastosis (edema)
         d.   Maternal anemia
         e.   Maternal diabetes
   B.   Abnormal labor and delivery
      1.   Premature rupture of membranes
      2.   Prolonged rupture of membranes and amnionitis
      3.   Maternal sepsis
      4.   Abnormal presentation (especially breech)
      5.   Delayed second stage (cephalopelvic disproportion)
      6.   Umbilical cord prolapse
      7.   Umbilical cord accidents (nuchal cord, true knot, avulsion)
   C.   Prematurity
   D.   Multiple gestation (especially smaller or second twin)
   E.   Obstetrical accidents
II.   Neonatal events
   A.   Hemorrhage
      1.   Subdural (tear bridging veins, sinuses, or falx-tentorial junction)
      2.   Subarachnoid (full-term)
      3.   Intracerebral (premature)
         a.   Parenchymal
         b.   Intraventricular
         c.   Brain stem
   B.   Respiratory disease (RDS)
      1.   Hypoxia
      2.   Mechanical ventilation
   C.   Infections
      1.   Sepsis
      2.   Meningitis (*E. coli,* Group B streptococcus)

(*continued*)

Table 4. (*continued*)

       3. Encephalitis (TORCH infections)
          a. Toxoplasma
          b. Rubella
          c. Cytomegalovirus
          d. Herpes simplex
    D. Head trauma
       1. Skull fractures
       2. Child abuse
    E. Metabolic disorders
       1. Hypoglycemia
       2. Hyperbilirubinemia
       3. Hypothyroidism
    F. Nutritional disorders
    G. Neonatal seizures
    H. Hydrocephalus
III. Inborn errors of metabolism

immunization, and malnutrition. All of them, separately or together, can interfere with normal brain development.

How can one understand the neurological basis of mental retardation resulting from adverse sociocultural influences? This category represents the majority of cases of mental retardation. When one considers that neuronal connections form and are maintained as a result of appropriate input or stimulation, and that this process continued throughout childhood, one can hypothesize that inadequate or inappropriate input during childhood could result in abnormal connections in the brain. This structural defect in connectivity could then result in the functional defect of mental retardation. The clearest example of this process is in the visual system, where lack of visual stimulation during the critical period of early infancy results in defective development of the visual cortex. A similar process may occur in the auditory cortex when children are born deaf or suffer from prolonged hearing impairment due to chronic otitis in infancy. It is interesting to note that children raised in the wild, deprived of exposure to human speech and communication during early childhood, are seldom able to learn to communicate effectively through speech. These experiences suggest that there are critical periods in childhood during which effective sensory input must occur in order for the appropriate connections in the brain to develop. Deprivation of these environmental inputs would then result in inadequate connectivity. Specifically, sociocultural influences that result in diffuse environmental deprivation might cause a deficiency of connections throughout the brain. Mental retardation attributa-

Table 5. Postnatal causes of mental retardation

I. Head injuries
   A. Cerebral concussion
   B. Skull fracture, cerebral contusion, and laceration
   C. Intracranial hemorrhage
      1. Epidural
      2. Subdural (acute or chronic)
      3. Subarachnoid
      4. Parenchymal
II. Infections
   A. Encephalitis (viral)
   B. Meningitis (hemophilus, pneumococcus, meningococcus)
   C. Fungal and parasitic infections
   D. Brain abscess
   E. Slow or persistent virus infections (measles, rubella)
III. Demyelinating disorders
   A. Postinfectious (measles, varicella)
   B. Postimmunization (pertussis)
   C. Schilder disease and variants
IV. Degenerative diseases
V. Seizure disorders
   A. Status epilepticus
   B. Acute infantile hemiplegia
   C. Infantile spasms
   D. Lennox-Gastaut syndrome
VI. Toxic/metabolic disorders
   A. Inborn errors of metabolism
   B. Lead intoxication
   C. Cerebral anoxia/cardiac arrest
   D. Dehydration
   E. Reye syndrome
   F. Toxic encephalopathy
VII. Malnutrition
VIII. Environmental deprivation
   A. Psychosocial disadvantage
   B. Child abuse and neglect
   C. Sensory deprivation
IX. Hypoconnection syndromes

ble to sociocultural influences could thus be considered as a "hypoconnection" syndrome.

Table 6 lists some possible mechanisms of hypoconnection. It should be apparent that the cellular defects listed in Table 2 could also result in hypoconnection. Some of these mechanisms have been shown to occur in certain cases of mental retardation using specialized histopathological techniques. For example, abnormal dendritic spines have been demonstrated in Down syndrome and unspecific cases of severe mental retardation (Huttenlocher, 1974; Purpura, 1979). One can only speculate whether milder degrees of dendritic abnormality would occur in cases of mild retardation (Huttenlocher, 1974). These issues were considered in detail in a previous volume (Caviness & Williams, 1983; Purpura, 1983; Williams, 1983). Many of the other mechanisms listed in Table 6 are possible (Caviness & Williams, 1979) but have

Table 6. Possible causes of hypoconnection

I. Neuronal
   A. Dendritic abnormalities
      1. Decreased number of spines
      2. Abnormally shaped spines
      3. Dendritic varices (neurotubule disarray)
      4. Meganeurites
   B. Cell body abnormalities
      1. Mismatch of excitatory and inhibitory inputs to the cell body
      2. Distorted spatial arrangement of inputs and their temporal convergence on the cell body
   C. Axonal abnormalities
      1. Altered cable properties due to size or myelination of axon
      2. Deficient axonal transport
      3. Abnormal axon collaterals
   D. Synaptic abnormalities
      1. Altered synthesis of transmitter
      2. Abnormal release or reuptake of transmitter
      3. Abnormal receptor function

II. Glial
   A. Defective myelination (oligodendroglia)
   B. Abnormal nutritive function (astroglia)

III. Circuitry
   A. Decreased numbers of axons
   B. Abnormal processing between neurons by:
      1. Axon collaterals
      2. Intercalated neurons
   C. Wrong target (axons end in wrong place)

not yet been shown to occur in mild mental retardation. Thus, hypoconnection as the mechanism of mild mental retardation is an unproven hypothesis, and its relationship to adverse sociocultural influences remains to be shown through further research. In general, hypoconnection can be thought of as the result of an abnormality in the interaction between genetic instructions and environmental influences in the process of neuronal development. The abnormality could occur at any time during brain development for a variety of reasons and would result in functionally deficient connectivity among nerve cells in the brain. This approach may be useful in explaining to families why their child is mentally retarded. Relating mental retardation to defective brain development and connectivity could provide a physical explanation that might relieve anxiety and guilt and alleviate confusion about the unknown. This approach could also explain why some people with mental retardation have other neurological deficits such as cerebral palsy, sensory impairments, or seizures (see below).

Consideration of mental retardation as a hypoconnection syndrome has implications for prevention, treatment, and cure. Many of the adverse environmental influences described above can be prevented. Early infant intervention, infant stimulation, and early childhood education programs are based on the concept that these processes are reversible, and dramatic improvements do occur. There are limits on what can be achieved, however. While stimulation can result in development of more effective connections in the brain during critical periods, its effect is limited by the severity of the disturbance and the timing of the intervention. We do not yet know the most effective form of intervention or its relationship to specific changes in the brain. More research is needed before we can "prescribe" specific treatments to reverse specific deficits in brain function. This is a challenge for the future that will require a much better understanding of normal and abnormal brain development and function.

IMAGING STRUCTURE AND FUNCTION

When the cause of mental retardation is in doubt or there is a need to confirm the clinical diagnosis, procedures are often used to provide an image of the pathological anatomy in the brain. The most commonly used imaging procedure is computed tomographic (CT) scanning of the brain. The technique of measuring nuclear magnetic resonance (NMR) has been developed recently to provide commercially available instrumentation for magnetic resonance imaging (MRI) scans of the brain. The use of MRI scanning to demonstrate structural brain abnormalities in mental retardation is only beginning, however.

Attempts to understand abnormal functioning of the brain in various neurological disorders have been enhanced recently by the development of positron emission tomographic (PET) scanning and brain electrical activity mapping (BEAM). These techniques offer the possibility of studying the functional anatomy of the brain in mental retardation. Such studies could provide a better understanding of how various areas of the brain function in mental retardation and how this differs from brain function in persons with normal intelligence.

CT Scanning

Gordon Hounsfield developed the first CT scanner, which was manufactured by the EMI Company of Great Britain and initially called the EMI Scanner (Hounsfield, 1973). The theory had been developed earlier by William Oldendorf (1980). In essence, the technique consists of taking numerous X rays of the head and using a computer to reconstruct the data into a picture of the interior of the brain. The total dose of X rays is 2–4 rads, which is approximately the same as in taking conventional skull X rays and carries approximately the same risk. In addition, a contrast material containing iodine is often injected intravenously during the scanning procedure. The contrast material outlines the blood vessels of the brain and can demonstrate vascular anomalies and malformations. The iodinated contrast material also leaks across a defective blood-brain barrier and can demonstrate where the capillary walls have been damaged. The contrast material is usually the same as that used in intravenous pyelography (IVP) studies of the kidney and carries the same risk of an allergic reaction to the iodine that it contains.

The actual technique begins with a conventional X-ray source. Instead of using the standard ''shower'' of X rays, however, a collimator is used to select a narrow beam of X rays that are allowed to leave the source. The X-ray beam, generally no more than a few millimeters wide, enters the head on one side and leaves on the other side, where the intensity of the emerging beam is measured. The beam is rotated 180 degrees around the head, while multiple measurements are taken in all positions. These measurements are entered into a computer, which analyzes the differences in intensity to create a two-dimensional image of the material through which the X rays have passed. In this way, a picture of a ''slice'' of the brain that is a few millimeters thick can be displayed on a video screen and ultimately reproduced on conventional X-ray film. By repositioning the moving beam of X rays on different planes of the head, multiple ''slices'' can be visualized, providing images of structures throughout the brain. Interpretation of these images requires knowledge of radiology, neuroanatomy, and clinical neurology. Unfortunately, all too often the CT scanner provides excellent images that may be misinterpreted by an inexperienced reader. Numerous technical problems and artifacts are possible that require skill to interpret. CT scanning is limited in certain areas of the brain where interference with bone is prominent, since bone is much denser than brain and absorbs more of the X-ray beam. Technical details are available in several sources (Kinkel, 1984; Weisberg, Nice, & Katz, 1984).

CT scans cost from $200 to $400 depending on the laboratory, the number of images, and whether contrast is used. This cost is justified when the procedure is necessary to make a diagnosis and when the choice of treatment depends on the results. For example, a CT scan can confirm the diagnosis of congenital viral infection or tuberous sclerosis (Figure 1). When a child with mental retardation has a large head, CT scanning can differentiate megalencephaly (which requires no treatment) from hydrocephalus (which requires a shunt) and it is useful in detecting shunt malfunction. When the etiology of mental retardation is unclear, CT scanning may demonstrate an unsuspected malformation of the brain such as holoprosencephaly (Figure 2). CT scanning has little to contribute in cases where the cause of mental retardation is obvious, as in severe birth asphyxia, but it is sometimes useful in defining the extent and distribution of brain damage. In every instance, the cost of CT scanning and the minimal risks associated with it must be balanced against the likelihood that the procedure will provide new information that will benefit the patient and the family.

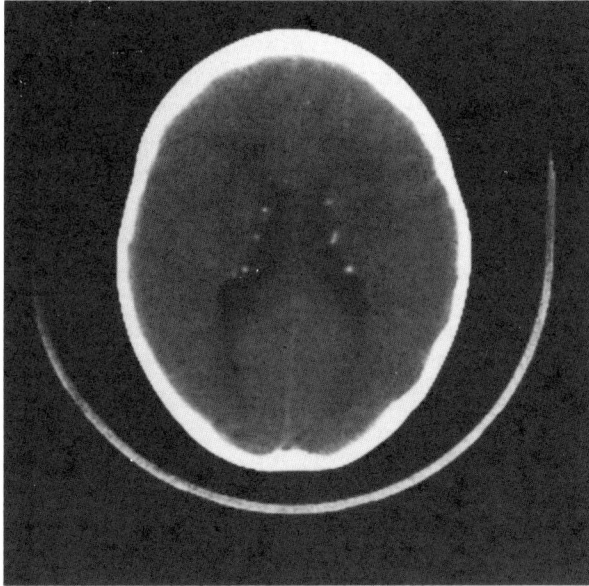

Figure 1. Computerized tomographic (CT) scan without contrast enhancement of a 6-year-old girl with tuberous sclerosis. Note numerous subependymal periventricular high-density (white) areas that are calcified tubers.

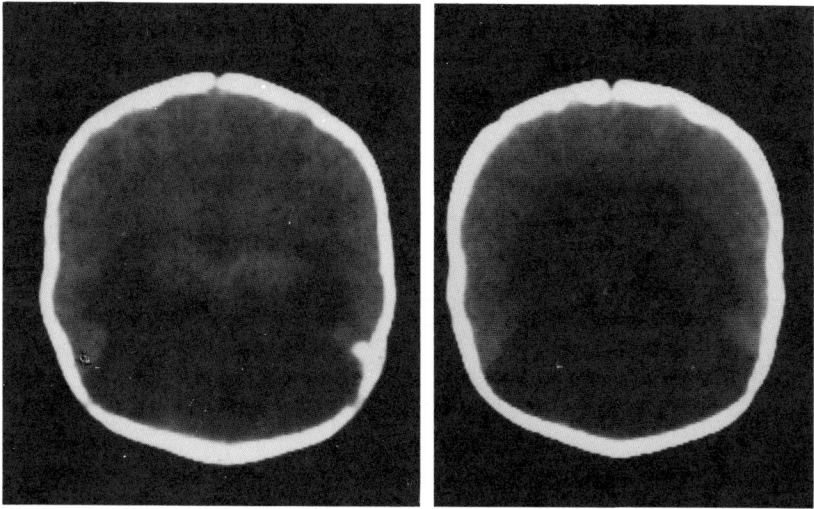

Figure 2. CT scan without contrast enhancement of a newborn baby boy born with a small head. Both sides of the brain are fused in front, and there is a single ventricle behind that extends to the back of the head. The findings are typical of alobar holoprosencephaly.

MRI Scanning

The phenomenon of NMR has been known to chemists for years, but its application to imaging of patients is very recent. MRI is based on the fact that when certain atoms are placed in a strong magnetic field and stimulated by a pulse of radio frequency radiation, they emit a characteristic signal that can be detected and measured. Very powerful magnetic coils are used in animal experiments, but human studies require weaker fields. MRI does not use any ionizing radiation (X rays), so it is safer than CT scanning. Because of the magnetic field used in MRI, the procedure cannot be performed on patients with ferromagnetic material in their body (certain types of surgical clips, sutures, or dental material, for example). Contrast material to enhance the MRI images has not yet been developed so the procedure is entirely painless. It often requires sedation for a child to keep still during MRI scanning, which is the only real risk of the procedure.

A patient who is to have an MRI scan is sedated (if necessary) and placed inside the magnetic coil. While the magnetic field is present, radio frequency pulses of varying sequence and time interval are used to stimulate protons in the tissue. The emitted signals are measured all over the brain at the same time and analyzed by a computer. Reconstruction of these data is performed to provide two-dimensional images in any plane, including the plane used for CT scanning as well as coronal or sagittal planes. Two types of images are usually produced. These are based on the time constants of the pulse used and are called relaxation times, reflecting the energy emitted as the proton "relaxes" from the radio frequency stimulation. Spin-lattice (T1) relaxation times produce saturation-recovery (SR) and inversion-recovery (IR) images, while spin-spin (T2) relaxation times produce spin-echo (SE) images. Since gray matter has a longer T1 than white matter, T1 images show the differences between these tissues very clearly. Typically, bone and cerebrospinal fluid appear dark, gray matter is gray, and white matter is bright. The fact that bone (with protons that are tightly bound) does not produce a signal in MRI permits visualization of tissues in areas where a lot of bone is present, such as the sella, posterior fossa, and spinal canal. This is a marked advantage over CT scanning, where bony artifacts in these areas often make interpretation difficult. T1 images provide a clearer view of brain anatomy than CT scanning and could demonstrate heterotopias and dysgenesis in cases of mental retardation. Diseased myelin has a higher water content than normal myelin, so that T2 images show high-intensity (bright) areas in leukodystrophies and demyelinating diseases. MRI is much more sensitive than CT in demonstrating these white matter diseases (Gabrielsen et al., 1985; Young et al., 1985).

Because of the high cost of installation of an MRI scanner and their relative scarcity at the moment, MRI scans cost the patient $750–$1,000. As with CT scanning, this cost must be balanced against the likelihood of discovering important diagnostic information that would influence case management. MRI has proven very useful in vascular disease (DeWitt, Buonanno, Kistler, Brady, Pykett, Goldman, & Davis, 1984) and it is the procedure of choice for visualizing plaques in multiple sclerosis (Gabrielsen et al., 1985). Because of its freedom from bony interference, it is also indicated for evaluating suspected Arnold-Chiari malformations and spinal lesions. In cases of mental retardation where the cause is unknown and CT scanning has not been helpful, MRI may provide useful information (see Figure 3).

PET Scanning

Although PET scanning also results in tomographic images or "slices" of the brain, it provides a fundamentally different kind of information from CT or MRI. PET scanning is based on the fact that tissues take up certain substrates during metabolism at different rates that reflect their level of metabolic activity. Thus, active tissue takes up more glucose than inactive tissue. In order to get an image of this regional variation in metabolic activity, the substrate (in this case, glucose) has to be prevented from undergoing any further metabolism. This is accomplished by using an analogue, 2-deoxyglucose, which is transported into the cell like glucose but which cannot be metabolized any further. Thus, 2-deoxyglucose accumulates in areas of greater metabolic activity. To measure this accumulation, a radioactive tracer (fluorine-18) is attached to the 2-deoxyglucose molecule. The tracer emits positrons whose

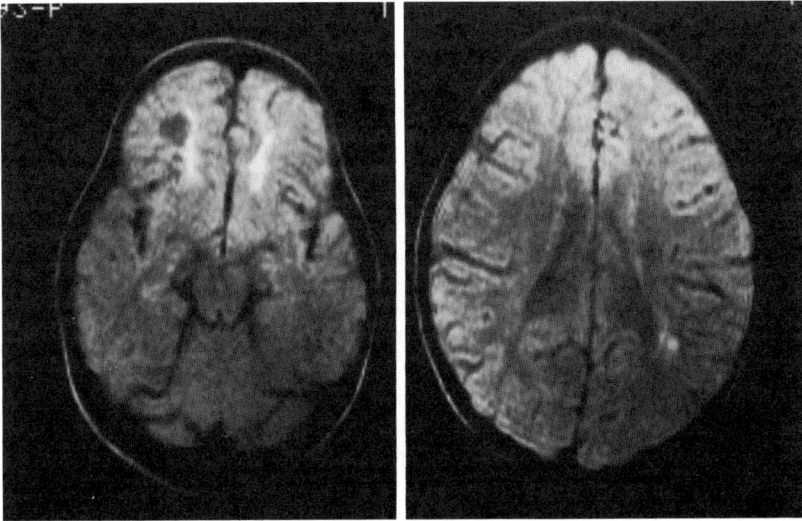

Figure 3. Magnetic resonance imaging (MRI) scan, T2 images, of a 3-year-old girl with postinfectious demyelination syndrome following chickenpox. Note a cystic (dark) lesion in the right frontal lobe, which was the only lesion visible on the CT scan. MRI showed in addition three separate (white) areas of demyelination, one adjacent to the cystic lesion, one in the left frontal lobe, and one in the left parietal lobe. MRI demonstration of these areas of demyelination established the correct diagnosis.

breakdown is detected externally. The intensity of positron emission is directly related to the degree of glucose-dependent metabolic activity (glycolysis) at the site during steady-state conditions. Extremely complicated equations are used to measure metabolic rates in the various tissues. As with CT and MRI, measurements from all over the brain are analyzed by a computer and the data are then reconstructed into tomographic images or "slices" that display the metabolic activity of the brain. These images are usually color-coded to show differences in metabolic activity, but the actual rates can also be obtained. Details of the theory, technique, and its application are available in the proceedings of a symposium held at the National Institutes of Health (Walker, 1984).

PET scanning is incredibly expensive and is currently available in only a few federally supported laboratories. It is not routinely available for clinical use and likely never will be. It is being used to study the function of different parts of the brain in normal persons undergoing various tasks and in certain disease states. For example, PET scanning shows increased metabolic activity in certain cortical areas during perceptual, sensory, and motor stimulation. When a positron-emitting radioactive tracer is attached to a drug that binds to specific receptors in the brain, PET scanning can show the distribution of these receptors in normal and diseased states. Preliminary results suggest that dopamine receptors and opiate receptors may be "mapped" in this way. Alterations in regional metabolism have been shown in stroke, Parkinson disease, Huntington disease, brain tumors, normal aging, Alzheimer disease, and epilepsy. Suggestive changes have also been found in Tourette syndrome, schizophrenia, and affective disorders. Details of these studies can be found in the symposium report noted above (see also Lenzi and Pantano, 1984).

PET scanning would undoubtedly provide very interesting results in cases of mental retardation, but this remains to be shown. The regional pattern of metabolic activity in autism is likely to be quite unique. PET scanning of retarded patients with a psychiatric disorder (so-called dual-diagnosis patients) might show different patterns from nonpsychiatric retarded patients, which could be useful in differentiating "organic" and "functional" conditions. The possibility that persons with retardation may use different parts of the brain when performing specific tasks could be confirmed with PET scanning, and these results could be used to test new methods of educational, training, and behavioral interventions. Collaboration between neuropsychology, special education, and neurology in PET studies of persons with mental retardation would be a particularly exciting framework for future research and could help to evaluate the effectiveness of early intervention and stimulation programs.

Single-photon emission computed tomography (SPECT) is much less expensive than PET scanning and is likely to become more available. SPECT can use radioactive tracers that are more available and more stable than PET scanning, similar to those used in conventional radionuclide brain scans. Its application at this point is limited to measurement of regional blood flow and disruption of the blood-brain barrier. If radioactive tracers are developed for SPECT that would measure regional metabolic activity, it could be very useful in studies of brain function (Cowan & Watson, 1980).

BEAM-SPM

Numerous attempts have been made over the years to correlate electroencephalographic (EEG) findings with brain function. Except for an excess of nonspecific abnormalities (Hughes, 1978), EEG studies have not been very useful in mental retardation, learning, or behavioral disorders. Duffy considered that the EEG actually contained too much information to be assimilated simply by visual "pattern recognition" of the paper record (Duffy & McAnulty, 1985). Processing of EEG data by a computer makes it possible to display relative voltages all over the head, using the procedure called brain electrical activity mapping (BEAM). This is topographical mapping of the surface of the head, unlike tomographic images of a "slice" through the head. From the patient's point of view, BEAM is similar to a routine EEG and carries the same negligible risk. BEAM maps can also be made of evoked potential voltages all over the head, using a comparable procedure.

BEAM begins by recording the individual voltages at each of 20 electrodes on the scalp (for evoked potential mapping, the mean voltage for each 4-msec interval after the stimulus is recorded at each scalp electrode). Using a fast Fourier transform, the EEG data are converted by spectral analysis into measures of the amount of EEG energy in each frequency band (delta, theta, alpha, beta). Values for areas on the head between electrodes are obtained by interpolation. The values are mapped over the entire scalp, using a color-coded scale to create a picture of the distribution of energy over the head. A map for each second of EEG data can then be computed and shown sequentially, reflecting instantaneous changes in brain electrical activity. When these raw BEAM data are compared to a well-defined normal population, the difference can be mapped using a variety of statistical measures. The result, called significance probability mapping (SPM), is a display of the instantaneous differences between the subject and the defined norms. Duffy has used BEAM-SPM studies of both EEG and evoked potential data to show that there are differences between dyslexic and nondyslexic boys (Duffy & McAnulty, 1985).

Modern computer technology has made BEAM capability fairly easy to add to a conventional EEG facility for approximately $100,000. Unfortunately, the scientific value of BEAM is limited by the fact that it is based on scalp EEG, which is a poor reflection of brain function. Nonetheless, BEAM is a relatively accessible technology for investigating differences in brain (surface) electrical activity in subjects with mental retardation.

All of the techniques described—CT, MRI, PET, SPECT, BEAM-SPM—are powerful tools for investigating brain structure and function in mental retardation. Their greatest power comes, not from studies of individual cases, but rather from well-designed tests of scientific hypotheses. In individual cases, they may yield nothing more than ''pretty pictures'' obtained at considerable expense. When used to test hypotheses about the nature of abnormal brain development or brain dysfunction, these procedures are capable of providing dramatic insights into the neurological basis of mental retardation.

SEIZURE DISORDERS

Seizures are fairly common events in persons with mental retardation, depending on the etiology and severity of the retardation. A minimum prevalance estimate would be 0.5%, which is the prevalence in the general (nonretarded) population (Epilepsy Foundation of America, 1975). Certain causes of mental retardation are very strongly associated with seizures. The prevalence in specific disorders varies from 28% in autism (Rutter, 1970) to greater than 90% in tuberous sclerosis (Gomez, 1979), for example. In the author's experience, approximately 40% of institutionalized retarded persons

(700 out of a total population of 1,700 in two state schools), most of whom are severely or profoundly retarded, require treatment for a seizure disorder. Recent advances in the diagnosis and treatment of seizures permit optimal management of these conditions, avoiding the risks of untreated seizures on the one hand and overmedication on the other hand.

To avoid confusion, it is necessary to define precisely what "seizure" and "epilepsy" mean. Both terms can be thought of as two-part definitions. A *seizure* is a sudden, excessive, and disorderly discharge of neurons associated with a simultaneous, observable, abrupt change in behavior, emotion, sensation, or motor activity. If a discharge is recorded by EEG but there is no simultaneous change in behavior, the EEG event cannot be considered a seizure. Thus, an abnormal EEG by itself without a history of clinical attacks of seizure-like activity is insufficient to make a diagnosis of seizures. On the other hand, if one observes a seizure-like behavior while an EEG is being performed and the EEG shows no change or no abnormality during this behavior, the behavior in question was not a true seizure. Such behaviors are often referred to as pseudoseizures (Gross, 1983). The EEG may be normal in between seizures, but it is always abnormal during a real seizure. The only exception to this rule is when seizures occur in premature or newborn infants (Coulter, 1986) or when the EEG is inadequate to record any possible abnormal discharge.

Epilepsy is a disorder caused by a chronic abnormal condition of the brain that increases the risk of seizure activity, and which has actually resulted in at least two or more clinical seizures. Acute brain disorders (such as meningitis or anoxia) and acute or chronic nonbrain disorders (such as hypoglycemia) may cause seizures, but this is not epilepsy. The brain disorder in epilepsy is usually a group of abnormal neurons that did not develop properly (Meencke & Janz, 1984) or that have been damaged in some way resulting in a "scar" or gliosis. Acute disorders such as those noted above may cause sufficient damage or scarring in the brain to result in epilepsy, but it is the brain damage that is the actual chronic disorder causing seizures. The increased risk of seizure activity is often referred to as a "low seizure threshold," but this is more of a theoretical than a measurable concept. In practice, an increased risk or "seizure tendency" is usually inferred from an EEG that demonstrates specific paroxysmal discharges (spikes and spike-waves). Nonspecific EEG discharges (focal or diffuse slowing or disorganized activity) do not necessarily indicate a seizure tendency. In any event, the diagnosis of epilepsy cannot be made unless the individual has actually had two or more true seizures. An abnormal EEG by itself (even if it shows spikes or spike-waves) is insufficient. This is a common error that results in prescription of anticonvulsant drugs to mentally retarded persons with psychiatric disorders who may have an abnormal EEG but who do not have true seizures. There is no scientific justification for this practice. Persons who have had only one seizure do not have epilepsy (by definition), but they may require treatment (see below).

Evaluation

Seizures may be difficult to recognize in persons with mental retardation. Table 7 indicates some guidelines that may be useful in deciding whom to refer for suspected seizure activity. These guidelines are based on the twin tests of true seizures: randomness and unresponsiveness. Seizures are usually random events that occur any time and any place (not only in school or only when bored or inattentive). Most patients are completely unresponsive during seizures, so that one cannot get the patient's attention until the seizure is over. This is distinguishable from simple daydreaming or stereotyped mannerisms that generally end when the patient is stimulated. In general, if one can put a "plus" in the "Seizure" column of Table 7 for at least four of the seven questions listed, the individual may be having real seizures and should be referred for diagnosis.

Table 7. Recognition of possible seizures

Description	Seizure	Nonseizure
Where do spells occur?		
Home and school	+	−
School	−	+
When do spells occur?		
School days as well as weekends/holidays	+	−
School days only	−	+
How do spells occur?		
Unresponsive (cannot get student's attention)	+	−
Responds when called	−	+
When are spells noticed?		
While talking (interrupts speech, then restarts)	+	−
While playing (stops)	+	−
While walking (may fall)	+	−
While bored only	−	+
While passive/inactive only	−	+
Associated motor events?		
(jerk, eye-blink, roll eyes, etc.)	+	−
Associated autonomic events?		
(pale, blue, sweaty, incontinent)	+	−
Subsequent altered behavior?		
(sleepy, headache, vomiting)	+	−

The evaluation of a patient suspected of having seizures begins with a complete description of the events or attacks in question. An experienced physician compares this description to that of other patients with true seizures to determine if the attacks "sound like" real seizures. Since the physician rarely sees the actual attacks, the diagnosis is based primarily on the description provided by others. This should include details of the time of occurrence, exacerbating factors, onset, frequency, duration, symptoms recalled by the patient (if possible), and observed behaviors noted by parents, teachers, friends, or attendants. The more details that are provided, the more accurate the diagnosis. When the description is insufficient, it is better to admit uncertainty and defer diagnosis, waiting to see if the attacks recur. Without treatment, epileptic seizures tend to recur, so that more accurate observations can be made the next time a seizure occurs. If the attacks do not recur, the patient probably does not have epilepsy.

A history of definite spontaneous seizures is sufficient to make the diagnosis of epilepsy. The next phase of the evaluation consists of an attempt to identify the nature of the causative brain disorder. The physician should elicit a history of the circumstances of pregnancy and birth, as well as any history of serious head injury, intracranial infection, or other acquired brain damage. In addition, a history of seizures or epilepsy in the family should be investigated. The physician should perform a complete physical examination looking for signs of acute infections, congenital anomalies, hepatosplenomegaly, neurocutaneous disorders, or other syndromes. A complete neurological examination should be performed to evaluate developmental status and to detect any focal deficits. If the cause of epilepsy is apparent (birth asphyxia, cerebral palsy, or tuberous sclerosis, for example), no further investigation is necessary. In doubtful cases or when no cause is apparent, some laboratory studies should be performed. In young infants, these should include serum glucose, electrolyte, calcium, magnesium, lactate, and ammonia concentrations, and screening for intoxications and inborn errors of metabolism. A lumbar puncture is usually unnecessary unless there is reason to suspect meningitis or encephalitis. CT scanning may be helpful in children if other studies are unrevealing or to confirm a diagnosis of tuberous sclerosis. CT scanning should always be performed when there is an unexplained focal neurological deficit or when seizures begin in adolescence or adulthood. The role of PET, MRI, or other imaging producers remains to be determined (see above).

A routine EEG is probably necessary in all cases since it may help classify the patient's seizures and determine the choice of therapy. This EEG should include recording during waking, drowsiness, and light sleep and should include performance of photic stimulation and hyperventilation if possible. Focal spikes suggest that the patient is having partial seizures, while diffuse spikes suggest that the patient is having generalized seizures. A complete EEG as described above will detect specific abnormalities in greater than 90% of patients with untreated absence (petit mal) seizures (Dreifuss, 1983), so that a normal EEG "rules out" this type of seizure in most cases. The EEG may be normal in between seizures in as many as 50% of patients with other types of seizures, however (Ajmone-Marsan & Zivin, 1970), so a normal EEG does not "rule out" a diagnosis of epilepsy if no actual seizures occurred during the EEG.

Classification

As a result of this evaluation, it should be possible to classify the type of seizure the patient is having (Dreifuss, 1981) and the type of epilepsy (Dreifuss, 1985). For practical purposes, the scheme in Figure 4 is sufficient to determine the choice of therapy. The first decision point is to identify how the seizure begins. If it begins in one part of the brain, it is called a *partial seizure*. Consciousness is not impaired during partial simple seizures, so that the patient can remember what happened and may be able to communicate during the seizure. Partial simple seizures may be characterized by focal twitching or jerking or focal numbness of one part of the body, special sensory symptoms (visual, auditory, olfactory, gustatory, or vertiginous), or autonomic or psychic symptoms (disturbed language, memory, thought, affect, or perception). Persons with mental retardation may not be able to recognize, recall, or describe these peculiar feelings, however, which makes recognition of partial simple seizures difficult. If consciousness is impaired during a partial seizure, it is called a partial complex seizure. Consciousness may be impaired at the onset (generally manifest by vacant staring), or it may follow within 1–2 minutes after the symptoms of a partial simple seizure described above. Automatic, semipurposeful behavior may occur during a partial complex seizure. This can include chewing, swallowing, lip-smacking, blinking, fumbling movements with the hands, or even a stumbling gait. These behaviors are termed automatisms, and by definition they are not intentional or goal directed (since the patient is not conscious during a partial complex seizure). Spontaneous violent behavior is extremely rare during such a seizure (Delgado-Escueta et al., 1981). Lawyers and psychiatrists may mistakenly characterize disturbed, hyperactive, violent, destructive, or antisocial behavior as partial complex seizure activity because such patients often have an abnormal EEG. Careful attention to the facts about epilepsy permits accurate diagnosis (Treiman & Delgado-Escueta, 1983). A seizure may begin as a partial simple or partial complex seizure and subsequently generalize into a tonic-clonic seizure. The category of partial seizures includes those previously known as focal, Jacksonian, psychomotor, or temporal lobe seizures.

If a seizure begins all over the brain at the same time, it is called a *generalized seizure*. When convulsive movements occur, it is called a generalized tonic-clonic (grand mal) seizure. The patient may cry out at the onset,

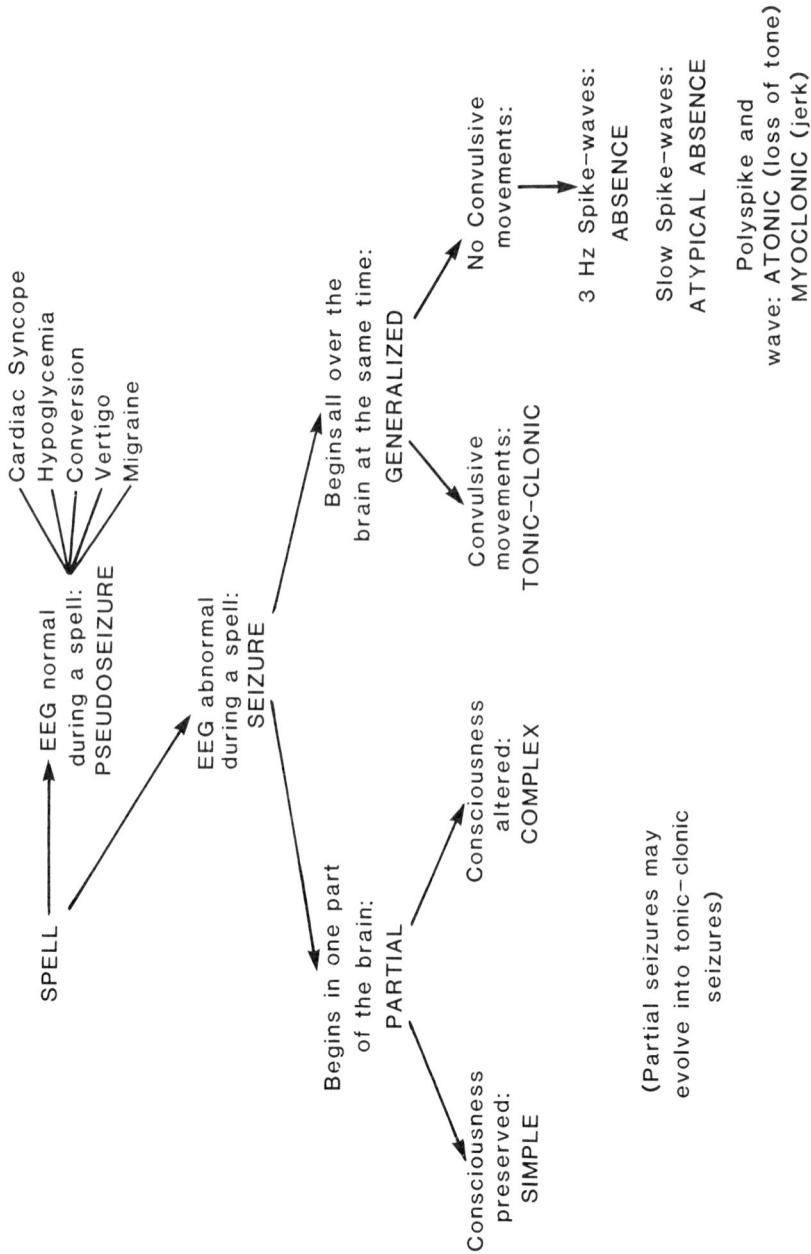

Figure 4. Determination of where a seizure begins in the brain will determine the choice of therapy.

then the eyes suddenly roll upward and consciousness is lost. There is usually an initial tonic stiffening of the limbs followed by clonic jerking. The initial tonic contraction may include the jaw muscle, resulting in biting the cheek or tongue. The seizure impairs ventilation so that breathing is labored and noisy and the patient often appears hypoxic and cyanotic. There is no truth to the myth that patients "swallow their tongue" however, so there is no reason to insert anything into the mouth during a tonic-clonic seizure. Patients often empty the bladder during such a seizure. When a tonic-clonic seizure ends after a few minutes, the patient is generally exhausted and goes to sleep for up to several hours. Tonic-clonic seizures are the most common type of seizure in patients with epilepsy.

Generalized nonconvulsive seizures are less common but are often more difficult to recognize. Differentiation between absence, atypical absence, atonic, and myoclonic seizures is best accomplished by recording the EEG during a seizure. Vacant staring and automatisms may occur in both partial complex and generalized absence seizures. The distinction is important since treatment depends on proper classification. Generally, absence seizures last for less than 1 minute; there is no warning or "aura" and the patient returns to normal immediately afterward. Partial complex seizures last for 1 minute or more; there may be an initial warning sensation and the patient is often mildly confused or sleepy afterward. In addition, brief stiffening, head turning, eye blinking, mild jerking of the limbs, or loss of muscle tone may occur during absence seizures (Penry, Porter, & Dreifuss, 1975).

Persons with mental retardation are particularly likely to have atonic or myoclonic seizures. While myoclonic seizures also occur in nonretarded persons (Delgado-Escueta & Enrile-Bacsal, 1984; Jeavons, 1977), they often occur in persons with retardation as part of the Lennox-Gestaut syndrome (Dreifuss, 1983). These seizures are also very brief, lasting less than 1 minute, but may recur many times a day. There is usually a sudden jerk of the body with flexion of the neck and hips, which may cause the patient to fall forward and injure the head. Sudden loss of postural tone may also occur and result in a fall to the ground. Atonic and myoclonic seizures are particularly likely to occur upon awakening, but may occur at other times as well. Infantile spasms are a special form of myoclonic seizure occurring in young infants and associated with mental retardation in the majority of cases (Lacy & Penry, 1976).

It should be noted that seizures in persons with severe and profound retardation sometimes are difficult to classify into the categories described above because of the marked extent of brain damage or abnormality that prevents typical expression of the epileptic phenomena. For these patients, it is usually sufficient to distinguish between partial seizures (of any type), convulsive seizures, and nonconvulsive seizures (of any type) in order to select proper treatment.

Difficulties in recognition and classification of suspected seizure activity can be resolved when the EEG is recorded during an actual attack. If the EEG is abnormal during the attack, it is a seizure; if not, it is a pseudoseizure. If the EEG shows a focal discharge at the onset, it is a partial seizure; if there is a diffuse discharge at the onset, it is a generalized seizure. Further sub-classification is possible when closed-circuit television (CCTV) cameras record the patient's behavior on videotape during the attack so that playback of the tape subsequently permits detailed observation of what actually happened. Simultaneous recording with EEG and CCTV is the best way to identify and classify suspected seizures. This technique is called EEG/CCTV monitoring and is usually carried out continuously for up to 24 hours or until an attack is recorded ("captured" on tape). The equipment is relatively inexpensive and available at many medical centers with specialists in epilepsy. EEG/CCTV monitoring is indicated if the diagnosis is unclear and attacks are occurring fairly often or occur predictably in response to specific exacerbating factors that can be reproduced in the laboratory. If the usual interval between attacks is less than the duration of EEG/CCTV monitoring (for example, daily), there is a good chance that an attack will be recorded. A different technique called ambulatory EEG monitoring is often used when video documentation of behavior is unnecessary. In this technique, the EEG is recorded continuously while the patient is ambulatory (at home, school, or work, for example), and EEG data are stored on a cassette that the patient wears on the belt. Playback of this cassette recovers the EEG documentation during any attack the patient may have experienced. Several recent reviews are available (Binnie, 1983; Mizrahi, 1984). EEG/CCTV monitoring of suspected seizures in persons with mental retardation showed that only 40% of the suspicious behaviors were actually seizures and that observation of the behavior alone was insufficient to distinguish between true seizures and pseudoseizures (Holmes, McKeever, & Russman, 1983). Thus, it is likely that many persons with retardation are receiving anticonvulsant drugs for attacks of abnormal behavior that are not in fact true seizures. EEG/CCTV monitoring would make it possible to eliminate unnecessary drug treatment in these cases. This technique should probably be used more extensively in centers that care for persons with mental retardation.

Treatment

Continuous anticonvulsant treatment may not be necessary when patients have only had one seizure or when it is unclear whether the attack actually was a seizure. As noted above, observation for possible recurrence may be sufficient. If the single seizure was particularly severe or prolonged (status epilepticus), drug treatment is probably indicated. If a person has a single seizure and the neurological examination is definitely abnormal (cerebral palsy or tuberous sclerosis, for example), or if the EEG shows a strong indication of a seizure tendency (frequent spikes or spike-waves), or if there is a strong history of epilepsy in a parent or sibling, drug treatment should be provided since the likelihood of seizure recurrence is high. The risk of recurrence is low in patients with a single seizure who do not meet these criteria (Hauser, Anderson, Loewenson, & McRoberts, 1982), so drug treatment can be deferred. Of course, treatment may be considered when the patient or family cannot accept even this low risk of recurrence.

Basic principles of drug therapy should be followed when continuous anticonvulsant drug treatment is prescribed for mentally retarded persons with epilepsy. These principles are described as follows:

1. Every drug has multiple effects on the body. This includes the desired effect as well as undesired (adverse) effects. No drug is completely free of adverse effects.
2. Risks and benefits of drug treatment should be balanced individually for each patient. The risk of adverse effects may be worth taking to experience the desired effect of seizure control. For some patients with very infrequent, mild, or resistant seizures, however, it may be more desirable to reduce or avoid drug treatment altogether than to use drugs that are likely to impair functional abilities or cause toxicity. The goal is the best possible seizure control with the fewest adverse drug effects.
3. Treatment should be started with the correct drug for the type of seizures that the patient is having. Current recommendations are provided in Table 8. Partial simple, partial complex, or generalized tonic-clonic seizures should be treated with phenytoin or carbamazepine (Porter, 1983). Generalized absence, myoclonic, or atonic seizures should be treated with ethosuximide or valproic acid (Dreifuss, 1983). In general, the most effective and least toxic drug should be used first.
4. Treatment should start with a single drug for each type of seizure that the patient has, or one drug effective against all types if possible. The dose should be increased until seizures are controlled or symptoms of toxicity emerge, whichever happens first. Each drug used should be given a fair trial (at least 1 month during which the serum level is in the therapeutic range) before switching to another drug because of failure to control seizures.
5. If the initial drug is ineffective, an alternative drug may be tried using the same principles as above. Ineffective drugs should be withdrawn gradually after the alternative drug has been added. Few (if any) patients need more than two drugs, and none should take more than three drugs for epilepsy (Shorron & Reynolds, 1979).
6. Serum drug levels should be used to monitor therapy. These levels should be obtained when the drug is at a steady state, usually at least 1 or 2 weeks after the most recent change in dosage. Drug levels are indicated

Table 8. Anticonvulsant drug selection

Type of seizures	First choice	Alternatives	Daily dose (mg/kd/day)	Therapeutic range (µg/ml)
Generalized tonic-clonic (grand mal)	Phenytoin or carbamazepine		4–7	10–20
Partial simple (focal)			20–30	6–12
Partial complex (psychomotor)		Phenobarbital	3–5	15–35
Partial onset with secondary generalization		Primidone	10–25	6–12
		Valproic acid	15–60	50–100
		Clorazepate	0.5–1.0	(Not known)
Generalized absence (petit mal)	Ethosuximide		20–40	50–100
Atypical absence		Valproic acid	15–60	50–100
		Clonazepam	0.01–0.2	0.01–0.07
Generalized myoclonic	Valproic acid		15–60	50–100
Generalized atonic		Clonazepam	0.01–0.2	0.01–0.07
		Ethosuximide	20–40	50–100
		Ketogenic diet		
Photomyoclonic		Acetazolamide	10–20	(Not known)

after a new drug is started or when the dose is changed, when toxicity is suspected clinically, when noncompliance is suspected, or when seizures are not yet controlled. In addition, all patients should probably have drug levels done routinely at least once or twice a year.

7. Virtually any adverse effect is possible with any drug, so one should always inquire about possible emerging adverse effects during drug therapy. These may be particularly difficult to recognize in very young children and in persons with mental retardation.

Proper classification of seizure activity and application of these principles when prescribing anticonvulsant drugs will result in improved or complete seizure control in the majority of patients with epilepsy. Additional details concerning management of specific types of seizures and use of specific anticonvulsant drugs are available in several recent texts (Dreifuss, 1983; Morselli, Pippenger, & Penry, 1983; Pedley & Meldrum, 1983, 1985).

Several authors have expressed concern that mentally retarded persons with epilepsy may be overmedicated (Bennett, Dunlop, & Ziring, 1983; Kaufman & Katz-Garris, 1979). Sedative anticonvulsant drugs have received particular attention because they often cause undesirable effects on learning and behavior and are not necessary to obtain seizure control in most cases (Theodore & Porter, 1983). Phenobarbital, primidone, and clonazepam may cause drowsiness, sedation, difficulty concentrating, impaired fine motor performance, poor memory, irritability, aggressiveness, sleep disturbances, and hyperactivity. Because persons with mental retardation may be particularly susceptible to these adverse effects that may interfere with adaptive functions, we investigated the effects of withdrawing these drugs from institutionalized mentally retarded persons with epilepsy (Coulter, 1985). A retrospective study demonstrated that sedative drugs could be withdrawn safely if seizure control was fairly good and if a nonsedating drug (phenytoin, carbamazepine, or valproic acid) was maintained with a serum level that was in the therapeutic range. A prospective study of the effect of withdrawing either phenobarbital or primidone from 26 patients who met the criteria described above confirmed these results, since 14 patients (54%) had the same or better seizure control after these drugs were withdrawn. Results were significantly better for phenobarbital than for primidone ($p < 0.05$), suggesting that caution be used when withdrawing primidone. Also, behavior often improved when sedative anticonvulsant drugs were withdrawn. On the basis of these results, we recommend that these drugs be avoided whenever possible. Seizure control can usually be obtained with phenytoin, carbamazepine, or valproic acid when the principles of drug therapy described above are followed. If patients are taking one of these nonsedating drugs as well as a sedating drug, and if the serum level of the nonsedating drug is within the therapeutic range, the sedating drug can be withdrawn gradually over a period of several months. If seizure control deteriorates, the dosage of the nonsedating drug can be increased or a second nonsedating drug can be added. In any event, we do not think that persons with mental retardation should ever take more than three drugs for epilepsy, although there may be individual exceptions to this rule.

ASSOCIATED BRAIN DYSFUNCTIONS

In a general sense, brain dysfunction refers to the consequences of damage, aberrant development, or altered connectivity in the brain. For each normal function of the brain, we can hypothesize a corresponding dysfunction. Thus mental retardation is a dysfunction of those processes that we measure as intelligence. Because brain development is diffusely altered in persons with mental retardation, we can expect that other processes may be affected as well. Indeed, deficient connectivity (hypoconnection) in other regions or pathways of the brain may account for these associated dysfunctions. Table 9 relates these associated dysfunctions to the corresponding normal function (see also Rapin, 1982). For a particular person, the observed complement of functions and dysfunctions would be unique and highly specific, reflecting the complex pattern of connection and hypoconnection throughout the brain. This pattern is probably different in each person, resulting from a unique set of genetic and environmental influences during the process of brain development. While some associated dysfunctions may occur more often in persons with mental retardation, it should be remembered that, theoretically, any combination is possible. Furthermore, we can only speculate about the significance of some possible combined dysfunctions. For example, the observed variability among persons with autism (Ritvo, 1976; Rutter & Schopler, 1978) could reflect various combinations of dysfunctional intelligence, language, affect, and sensory perception. Similarly, various combinations of dysfunctional intelligence, arousal, and affect could result in the psychiatric and behavioral disorders observed in persons with mental retarda-

Table 9. Brain dysfunctions

Function	Dysfunction
Intelligence	Mental retardation
Neuronal excitability	Seizure disorders
Movement	Cerebral palsy, movement disorders
Arousal	Attention deficit disorder
Sensory perception	Perceptual disorders
Vision	Cortical blindness
Hearing	Cortical deafness
Language	Communication disorders
Affect	Depression

tion (Menolascino & Stark, 1984). Disorders of movement are particularly interesting from a neurological point of view because of the prospect for relating knowledge of developmental neuropharmacology to specific treatments. Optimally effective treatment based on this knowledge may result in a cure of these dysfunctions.

When one thinks of specific dysfunctions, it is tempting to look for abnormalities in a specific part of the brain. The point-by-point correlation of function with location has been appropriately termed ''internal phrenology'' and reflects a misunderstanding of how the brain works. The approach in this chapter has emphasized connections between nerve cells, but one cannot deny that certain groups of neurons are more closely involved with certain brain functions. I suggest that a specific function reflects activity in many groups of neurons, including the primary area as well as other areas connected to it by incoming (dendritic) and outgoing (axonal) connections. According to this view, the brain consists of numerous ''modules'' composed of small groups of neurons specialized for processing of specific types of information, each of which is connected to many other modules through specific overlapping networks of connections throughout the brain. A specific type of brain activity (such as movement or speech) occurs when there is activation of the primary modules or areas and those to which it is connected. Thus, one can imagine millions of interconnected modules of neurons variably activated in a constantly changing pattern determined by the connections between them (Eccles & Robinson, 1985). Plasticity refers to the ability of certain modules to ''take over'' the function of damaged or dysfunctional areas by reorganization of the interconnecting network between them and other areas of the brain. When one recalls that connections form and disappear throughout life, based on the amount and type of activity in the entire network of interconnected modules (see above), one can visualize how recovery of function after injury could occur. Plasticity and recovery of function would depend on the integrity of the remaining network and its ability to reorganize itself and form new connections. It should be apparent that recovery would be more limited after a diffuse injury than a focal injury, because more of the modules and networks would be damaged. Since mental retardation generally reflects a diffuse brain abnormality, plasticity is not likely to permit much of a ''cure'' of mental retardation, although some improvement of intellectual function may be possible.

This model of brain function has several important implications for conceptualizing brain dysfunction. First, one can see that the model does not fit a computer analogy. The brain is constantly ''reprogramming'' and ''rewiring'' itself as well through the formation of new connections. Second, one can see how the effects of lesion and stimulation experiments can give misleading results. A specific lesion in one part of the brain may disturb a specific function, and stimulation of one part of the brain may accentuate a specific function, but this does not necessarily mean the observed function is ''located'' in the lesioned or stimulated area. In either case, the entire network of connections with the lesioned or stimulated area is affected by the experiment, so the observed result of the experiment reflects the overall effect on this entire network. In other words, the function is ''located'' in the network of connections or pathways and not necessarily just in the area of the lesion or stimulation. Third, one must realize that information is ''processed'' at many levels of the nervous system, which form a hierarchy of complexity from the lowest to the highest levels. Individual sensory receptors are connected to specific spinal neurons. Processing of these inputs begins within the spinal cord and continues in the thalamus, primary cortex, and association cortex, as the network of interconnections becomes progressively more extensive and elaborate. Similarly, voluntary motor activity begins as an intended movement in the supplementary motor area of the cortex, which then activates certain groups of neurons in the motor cortex and basal ganglia that organize the intended movement and activate, in turn, specific spinal neurons connected to the muscles needed to perform the desired movement. This view was first formulated by Jackson in 1880, who observed, ''The cortex knows nothing of muscles, it knows only of movements'' (Jackson, 1931). Thus, the consequence of damage in a specific area of the nervous system reflects the level of complexity of information processing at that area. Since the cortex represents the highest level of processing, cortical damage would result in very complex disturbances of higher level functions.

This model aids in the understanding of the dysfunctions that may be associated with mental retardation (Table 9). The diffuse abnormality of brain development in mental retardation could result in extensive and highly variable alterations in numerous networks of connections between cortical modules, which could be modified further through the effects of plasticity during subsequent brain development. The observed dysfunctions that result from these changes would likely be disturbances of complex functions requiring high-level information processing. Treatment of these dysfunctions would require augmentation or reorganization of the affected network of modules and connections without adversely affecting other potentially overlapping networks. Much more knowledge is needed before this kind of specific intervention or cure can become a reality.

Figure 5 represents a schematic interpretation of the network of connections between certain areas of the brain involved in movement. Further details are available in several recent reviews (Penney & Young, 1983; Swash & Kennard, 1985). The basal ganglia consist of the caudate, putamen, and globus pallidus. Input from the frontal (motor and premotor) cortex is bilaterally distributed primarily to the caudate and putamen, while input from the dorsomedial, central, ventral, and lateral nuclei of the thalamus is distributed to all of the basal ganglia. There is also input from the subthalamus, substan-

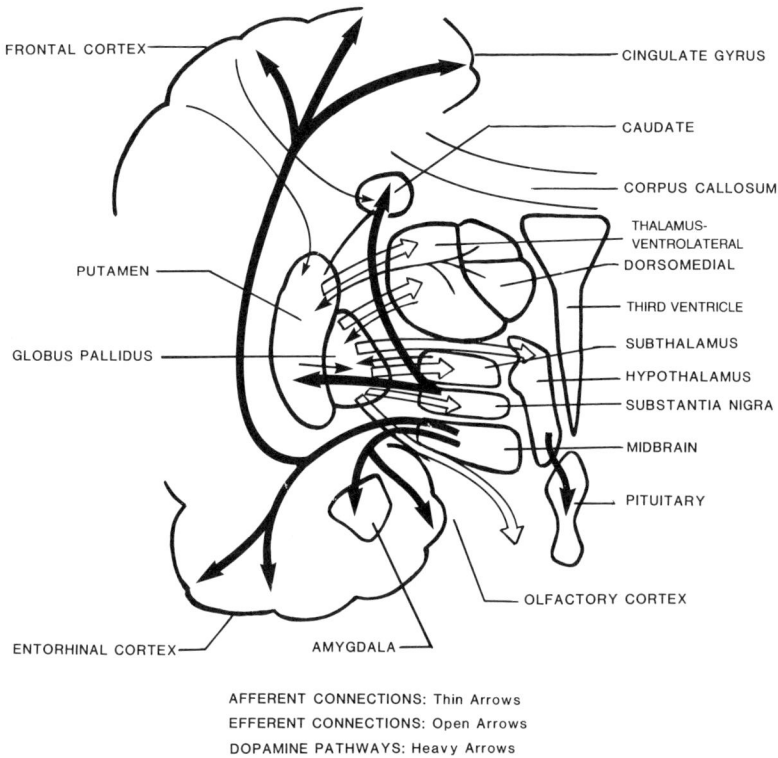

AFFERENT CONNECTIONS: Thin Arrows
EFFERENT CONNECTIONS: Open Arrows
DOPAMINE PATHWAYS: Heavy Arrows

Figure 5.   Schematic representation of the basal ganglia and their connections.

tia nigra, and raphe nuclei. The putamen receives input from the caudate, the globus pallidus receives input from the putamen, and the medial and lateral globus pallidus connect to each other. The output of the globus pallidus goes to the ventral nuclei of the thalamus, the hypothalamus, the subthalamus, the zona incerta, the fields of Forel, the substantia nigra, and the brain stem reticular activating system. The neurotransmitters in some of these pathways are known. Thus, input from the raphe is serotoninergic, input from the substantia nigra is dopaminergic, internuclear connections use acetylcholine and γ-aminobutyric acid (GABA), and output to the substantia nigra uses GABA. There are undoubtedly other neurotransmitters used in connections with the basal ganglia, including glutamate, norepinephrine, peptides, and endorphins, but the specific pathways are less certain.

Although the basal ganglia are interconnected with many other areas of the brain through several networks or pathways, the most important "circuit" of connections goes from the frontal (premotor) cortex to the basal ganglia to the thalamus to the motor cortex. This results in two primary functions: modulation of motor activity and automatic performance of learned movements (McDowell, Lee, & Sweet, 1984). The former serves to regulate posture, muscle tone, and voluntary movements. Dysfunction results in:

1. Increased tone (dystonia, rigidity)
2. Decreased tone (hypotonia)
3. Abnormal posture (simian posture, postural instability)
4. Unilateral postures (turning, circling)
5. Interrupted movement (tremor)
6. Irregular movement (tics, chorea, athetosis)
7. Reduced movement (akinesia)

The latter function serves to smooth out and simplify learned movements and reduce errors during their automatic performance. Dysfunction results in:

1. Loss of facial expression
2. Loss of variation in speech and control of speech
3. Reduced associated movements and postural defense movements
4. Slow initiation of movement (freeze)
5. Gait apraxia
6. Oculomotor apraxia and altered blinking

Thus, the consequence of altered development or injury to the basal ganglia and their connections would be a complex pattern of motor dysfunction, including any or all of the above symptoms individually or in combination.

Movement disorders are associated with mental retardation either as a consequence of altered brain development (cerebral palsy), injury (anoxia, encephalitis), or the use of neuroleptic drugs. Treatment of these dysfunctions has been attempted primarily with drugs that affect neurotransmitters used in the connections described above. Attempts to treat athetoid cerebral palsy in this way have been largely unsuccessful. Dystonia may improve with drugs that block acetylcholine (Fahn, 1983), but very large doses are required. Any administered drug is delivered to the entire brain, of course, including many areas and pathways not involved in the targeted dysfunction. Neurotransmitter-altering drugs may have the desired effect at the target site, but also undesired (adverse) effects arising from the influence of the drug at other sites. Treatment failure in cerebral palsy probably reflects the complexity of the dysfunction involving pathways using multiple neurotransmitters and the lack of specificity of the drug's effects.

Somewhat better results have been obtained with treatment of movement disorders caused by the use of neuroleptic drugs. Generally speaking, one can hypothesize a normal ''balance'' between the effects of acetylcholine, dopamine, and norepinephrine in the basal ganglia. Neuroleptic drugs act primarily by blocking dopamine receptors. Abrupt blockage of these receptors results in an imbalance with a relative excess of cholinergic influence. The clinical effect may be an acute dystonic reaction manifest as twisting of the head and neck, dystonic posturing of the limbs, and oculogyric movements of the eyes. This reaction can be treated by withdrawal of the dopamine-blocking drug and restoration of the normal balance by temporarily blocking acetylcholine receptors with an anticholinergic drug such as benztropine.

Chronic blockage of dopamine receptors with neuroleptic drugs may result in tardive dyskinesia or parkinsonism. The four dopaminergic pathways in the brain are shown in Figure 5. The majority of brain dopamine is found in the putamen and globus pallidus (corpus striatum), reflecting the dopaminergic pathway from the substantia nigra. This nigrostriatal pathway degenerates in idiopathic Parkinson disease and is presumably damaged in neuroleptic drug-induced parkinsonism. The neocortical pathway extends from the midbrain to frontal, entorhinal, and cingulate cortex. It is part of the median forebrain bundle and may be dysfunctional in schizophrenia and other psychiatric disorders. The mesolimbic pathway extends from the midbrain to the amygdala and olfactory cortex and may be altered in emotional disorders. The tuberoinfundibular pathway extends from the hypothalamus to the pituitary gland and regulates secretion of certain pituitary hormones, including prolactin and growth hormone.

Drugs such as haloperidol and the phenothiazines block dopamine receptors in all of these pathways. Over a period of time, the neuron attempts to overcome this blockage by increasing both the number and sensitivity to dopamine of these receptors. Tardive dyskinesia occurs when these compensatory responses result in a relative excess of catecholamine (dopamine and norepinephrine) effects relative to acetylcholine and GABA effects. The clinical consequences of this effect on the dopaminergic pathways in the brain include abnormal movements of the mouth, tongue, jaw, lips, cheeks, muscles of facial expression, neck, trunk, and limbs (Goetz & Klawans, 1984; Scheife & Growdon, 1982). Tardive dyskinesia is exacerbated by drugs that stimulate dopamine receptors, increase catecholaminergic transmission, or block cholinergic transmission. It is suppressed by drugs that block dopamine receptors, inhibit or deplete catecholamines, or increase GABA or cholinergic transmission. A variety of drugs with these putative neurotransmitter effects have been used to suppress tardive dyskinesia, including phenothiazines, tetrabenazine, reserpine, physostigmine, choline, lecithin, deanol, clonazepam, baclofen, and valproic acid. Results have been variable and inconsistent, however. The best approach is prevention (minimizing the use of neuroleptic drugs), early detection of emerging symptoms, and withdrawal of the offending drug if possible.

Chronic blockage of nigrostriatal dopamine receptors without compensatory receptor hyperplasia or supersensitivity may result in relative deficiency of dopamine effects compared to acetylcholine and GABA effects in the striatum. The clinical consequences are those of drug-induced parkinsonism. These include a resting "pill-rolling" tremor, bradykinesia, rigidity, cogwheeling, and disturbances in posture, gait, and oculomotor function. Treatment attempts to restore neurotransmitter balance in the basal ganglia by stimulating dopamine receptors with levodopa, Sinemet, or bromocriptine or blocking acetylcholine receptors with benztropine, trihexyphenidyl, and other anticholinergic drugs. Results have generally been successful and improvement can be expected in most cases (Burton & Calne, 1984).

Persons with mental retardation who have never received neuroleptic drugs may develop symptoms resembling tardive dyskinesia. One must then differentiate stereotyped movements and mannerisms, habit spasms, tics, Meige syndrome, blepharospasm, senile oropharyngeal movements, essential tremor, and Huntington disease. Parkinsonism may also occur in the absence of neuroleptic drugs as a result of intoxication with manganese or mercury, anoxia, encephalitis, or idiopathic nigrostriatal degeneration (Parkinson disease). The mechanism of these disorders presumably also reflects dysfunction in the pathways outlined in Figure 5.

This detailed discussion of one type of dysfunction that may be associated with mental retardation illustrates how the conceptual model of brain function and dysfunction described above can help explain specific clinical symptoms and their response to treatment. One could construct diagrams similar to Figure 5 to show the network of brain areas and interconnections involved in all of the functions listed in Table 9. These diagrams could then be used to understand the mechanisms, symptoms, and treatment of the corresponding dysfunctions. Research using the imaging techniques described above, especially PET, SPECT, and BEAM, should help to map the myriad functional connections in the brain in mentally retarded and intellectually normal persons. These studies should permit validation, correction, and elaboration of this model. The resulting improvement in our understanding of brain function and dysfunction should permit more specific and successful interventions, treatment, and eventual cure.

PITFALLS AND FALLACIES

One is reminded of the story of the six blind men and the elephant. The one who felt the tail thought an elephant was like a rope, the one who felt the side thought an elephant was like a wall, and so on. Similarly, the variety of professionals who work with persons with mental retardation all have their own way of looking at the person. The story teaches us that what we think we see may not be the whole thing.

This chapter presents a way of looking at persons with mental retardation that focuses on the structure and function of the brain. It is a neurological point of view based primarily on a medical model and is intended to provide a scientific basis for diagnosis and treatment of brain dysfunctions. There are other ways of looking at persons with mental retardation that are just as valid and useful within their own framework. The neurological viewpoint coexists equally with psychological, educational, social, rehabilitative, religious, and philosophical viewpoints. Standing in the middle of all this attention is the person with mental retardation whom we are all trying to understand and help. This person is as much of a person and as valuable as anyone else, despite arguments to the contrary (Lusthaus, 1985).

The philosophical pitfall of the neurological point of view is an exclusively materialistic outlook on the nature of personhood. This outlook interprets all human qualities as brain functions, so a person with a "defective" or dysfunctional brain would be "less human" than a person with a "normal" brain. It is not difficult to refute this radical materialism (Eccles & Robinson, 1985), and we emphatically reject the idea that all of the properties of the mind are functions of the brain. If the brain and mind are separate, then the brain may be damaged while the mind is intact. Some aspects of mind, such as the ability to give and receive love and the ability to recognize transcendence or God, have very little to do with intelligence. In this respect, even the most severely retarded person may have as much of a human mind as an intellectually normal person. The neurological point of view does not require a radical materialism because it only describes the brain and not the mind. I assert that all persons with mental retardation are fully valuable human beings, and nothing in this chapter should be misinterpreted to diminish or deny their personhood.

In conclusion, the neurological point of view is useful in helping to understand how the brain works and to show how aberrant brain development and brain dysfunction can explain many of the neurological aspects of mental retardation. We are only beginning to explore the frontier of neuroscience as it relates to mental retardation. This chapter attempts to describe what is known as well as what is not known and to suggest some testable hypotheses for further investigation. Much research needs to be conducted before we can anticipate the prospect of a cure for mental retardation, but the pace of present progress permits us to face the future with hope and optimism.

REFERENCES

Ajmone-Marsan, C., & Zivin, L. S. (1970). Factors related to the occurrence of typical paroxysmal abnormalities in the EEG records of epileptic patients. *Epilepsia, 11,* 361–81.

Barlow, C. F. (1978). *Mental retardation and related disorders.* Philadelphia: F.A. Davis.

Bennett, H. S., Dunlop, T., & Ziring, P. (1983). Reduction of polypharmacy for epilepsy in an institution for the retarded. *Developmental Medicine and Child Neurology, 25,* 735–737.

Binnie, C. D. (1983). Telemetric EEG monitoring in epilepsy. In T. A. Pedley & B. S. Meldrum (Eds.), *Recent advances in epilepsy* (Vol. 1, pp. 155–178). New York: Churchill Livingstone.

Burton, K., & Calne, D. B. (1984). Pharmacology of Parkinson's disease. *Neurologic Clinics, 2,* 461–472.

Caviness, V. S., & Williams, R. S. (1979). Cellular pathology of developing human cortex. In R. Katzman (Ed.), *Congenital and acquired cognitive disorders* (pp. 3–19). New York: Raven Press.

Caviness, V. S., & Williams, R. S. (1983). Normal and pathological development of the cerebral cortex: Cytogenesis and histogenesis. In F. J. Menolascino, R. Neman, & J. A. Stark (Eds.), *Curative aspects of mental retardation: Biomedical and behavioral advances* (pp. 43–55). Baltimore: Paul H. Brookes Publishing Co.

Coulter, D. L. (1985). *Withdrawal of sedative anti-convulsant drugs in mentally retarded persons.* Presented at the annual meeting of the American Association on Mental Deficiency, Philadelphia, PA.

Coulter, D. L. (1986). A proposal for the classification of neonatal seizures. *Journal of Child Neurology, 1,* 79.

Cowan, R. J., & Watson, N. E. (1980). Special characteristics and potential of single photon emission computed tomography of the brain. *Seminars in Nuclear Medicine, 10,* 335–350.

Delgado-Escueta, A. V., & Enrile-Bacsal, F. (1984). Juvenile myoclonic epilepsy of Janz. *Neurology, 34,* 285–294.

Delgado-Escueta, A. V., Mattson, R. H., King, L., Goldensohn, E. S., Spiegel, H., Madsen, J., Crandall, P., Dreifuss, F., & Porter, R. J. (1981). Special report: The nature of aggression during epileptic seizures. *New England Journal of Medicine, 305,* 711–716.

DeWitt, L. D., Buonanno, F. S., Kistler, J. P., Brady, T. J., Pykett, I. J., Goldman, M. R., & Davis, K. R. (1984). Nuclear magnetic resonance imaging in evaluation of clinical stroke syndromes. *Annals of Neurology, 16,* 535–545.

Dreifuss, F. E. (1981). Proposal for revised clinical and electroencephalographic classification of epileptic seizures. *Epilepsia, 22,* 489–501.

Dreifuss, F. E. (Ed.). (1983). *Pediatric epileptology.* Boston: John Wright-PSG.

Dreifuss, F. E. (1985). Proposal for classification of epilepsies and epileptic syndromes. *Epilepsia, 26,* 268–278.

Duffy, F. H., & McAnulty, G. B. (1985). Brain electrical activity mapping (BEAM): The search for a physiologic signature of dyslexia. In F. H. Duffy & N. Geschwind (Eds.), *Dyslexia: A neuroscientific approach to clinical evaluation* (pp. 105–122). Boston: Little, Brown & Co.

Eccles, J., & Robinson, D. N. (1985). *The wonder of being human: Our brain and our mind.* Boston: New Science Library.

Epilepsy Foundation of America. (1975). *Basic statistics on the epilepsies.* Philadelphia: F. A. Davis.

Fahn, S. (1983). High dosage anticholinergic therapy in dystonia. *Neurology, 33,* 1255–1261.

Gabrielsen, T. O., Gebarski, S. S., Gilman, S., Knake, J. E., Latack, J. T., & Aisen, A. M. (1985). The initial diagnosis of multiple sclerosis: Clinical impact of magnetic resonance imaging. *Annals of Neurology, 17,* 469–474.

Goetz, C. G., & Klawans, H. L. (1984). Tardive dyskinesia. *Neurologic Clinics, 2,* 605–614.

Gomez, M. R. (Ed.). (1979). *Tuberous sclerosis.* New York: Raven Press.

Gross, M. (Ed.). (1983). *Pseudoepilepsy: The clinical aspects of false seizures.* Lexington, MA: D. C. Heath.

Grossman, H. J. (1983). *Classification in mental retardation*. Washington, DC: American Association on Mental Deficiency.

Hauser, W. A., Anderson, V. E., Loewenson, R. B., & McRoberts, S. M. (1982). Seizure recurrence after a first unprovoked seizure. *New England Journal of Medicine, 307,* 522–528.

Holmes, G. L., McKeever, M., & Russman, B. S. (1983). Abnormal behavior or epilepsy? Use of long-term EEG and video monitoring with severely to profoundly mentally retarded patients with seizures. *American Journal of Mental Deficiency, 87,* 456–458.

Hounsfield, G. N. (1973). Computerized transverse axial scanning. 1. Description of system. *British Journal of Radiology, 46,* 1016–1022.

Hughes, J. R. (1978). Electroencephalographic and neurophysiological studies. In A. L. Benton & D. Pearl (Eds.), *Dyslexia: An appraisal of current knowledge* (pp. 205–240). New York: Oxford University Press.

Huttenlocher, P. R. (1974). Dendritic development in neocortex of children with mental defect and infantile spasms. *Neurology, 24,* 203–210.

Jackson, J. H. (1931). *Selected writings of John Hughlings Jackson*. London: Hodder and Stoughton, Ltd.

Jacobson, M. A. (1978). *Developmental neurobiology* (2nd ed.). New York: Plenum Press.

Jeavons, P. M. (1977). Nosological problems of myoclonic epilepsies in childhood and adolescence. *Developmental Medicine and Child Neurology, 19,* 3–8.

Kaufman, K. R., & Katz-Garris, L. (1979). Epilepsy, mental retardation and anticonvulsant therapy. *American Journal of Mental Deficiency, 84,* 256–259.

Kinkel, W. (1984). Computerized tomography in clinical neurology. In A. B. Baker & L. H. Baker (Eds.), *Clinical neurology* (Vol. 1, pp. 1–115). Philadelphia: Harper & Row.

Lacy, J. R., & Penry, J. K. (1976). *Infantile spasms*. New York: Raven Press.

Lenzi, G. L., & Pantano, P. (1984). Neurologic applications of positron emission tomography. *Neurologic Clinics, 2,* 853–872.

Levy, H. L., Kaplan, G. N., & Erickson, A. M. (1982). Comparison of treated and untreated pregnancies in a mother with phenylketonuria. *Journal of Pediatrics, 100,* 876–880.

Lusthaus, E. W. (1985). Involuntary euthanasia and current attempts to define persons with mental retardation as less than human. *Mental Retardation, 23,* 148–154.

McDowell, F. H., Lee, J. E., & Sweet, R. D. (1984). In A. B. Baker & L. H. Baker (Eds.), *Clinical neurology* (Vol. 3, pp. 1–67). Philadelphia: Harper & Row.

Meencke, H. J., & Janz, D. (1984). Neuropathological findings in primary generalized epilepsy: A study of eight cases. *Epilepsia, 25,* 8–21.

Menolascino, F. J., & Stark, J. A. (1984). *Handbook of mental illness in the mentally retarded*. New York: Plenum Press.

Mizrahi, E. M. (1984). Electroencephalographic/polygraphic/video monitoring in childhood epilepsy. *Journal of Pediatrics, 105,* 1–9.

Morselli, P. L., Pippenger, C. E., & Penry, J. K. (Eds.). (1983). *Antiepileptic drug therapy in pediatrics*. New York: Raven Press.

Oldendorf, W. H. (1980). *The quest for an image of the brain*. New York: Raven Press.

Pedley, T. A., & Meldrum, B. S. (Eds.). (1983). *Recent advances in epilepsy* (Vol. 1). New York: Churchill Livingstone.

Pedley, T. A., & Meldrum, B. S. (Eds.). (1985). *Recent advances in epilepsy* (Vol. 2). New York: Churchill Livingstone.

Penney, J. B., & Young, A. B. (1983). Speculation on the functional anatomy of basal ganglia disorders. *Annual Review of Neuroscience, 6,* 73–94.

Penry, J. K., Porter, R. J., & Dreifuss, F. E. (1975). Simultaneous recording of absence seizures with videotape and EEG: A study of 374 seizures in 48 patients. *Brain, 98,* 427–440.

Porter, R. J. (1983). Efficacy of anticonvulsant drugs. In A. A. Ward, J. K. Penry, & D. P. Purpura (Eds.), *Epilepsy* (A.R.N.M.D., Monograph No. 61, pp. 225–238). New York: Raven Press.

Purpura, D. P. (1979). Pathobiology of cortical neurons in metabolic and unclassified amentias. In R. Katzman (Ed.), *Congenital and acquired cognitive disorders* (pp. 20–44). New York: Raven Press.

Purpura, D. P. (1983). Cellular neurobiology of mental retardation: Problems and perspectives. In F. J. Menolascino, R. Neman, & J. A. Stark (Eds.), *Curative aspects of mental retardation: Biomedical and behavioral advances* (pp. 57–67). Baltimore: Paul H. Brookes Publishing Co.

Purves, D., & Lichtman, J. W. (1985). *Principles of neural development.* Sunderland, MA: Sinauer Associates.

Rapin, I. (1982). *Children with brain dysfunction.* New York: Raven Press.

Ritvo, E. R. (Ed.) (1976). *Autism: Diagnosis, current research and management.* New York: Spectrum Publications.

Rosenberg, R. N. (1984). Molecular genetics, recombinant DNA techniques and genetic neurological disease. *Annals of Neurology, 15,* 511–520.

Rutter, M. (1970). Autistic children: Infancy to adulthood. *Seminars in Psychiatry, 2,* 435–450.

Rutter, M., & Schopler, E. (Eds.). (1978). *Autism: A reapprasial of concepts and treatment.* New York: Plenum Press.

Scheife, R. T., & Growdon, J. H. (1982). Treating tardive dyskinesia. *Seminars in Neurology, 2,* 305–315.

Shorron, S. D., & Reynolds, E. H. (1979). Reduction in polypharmacy for epilepsy. *British Medical Journal, 2,* 1023–1025.

Swash, M., & Kennard, C. (1985). *Scientific basis of clinical neurology.* New York: Churchill Livingstone.

Theodore, W. H., & Porter, R. J. (1983). Removal of sedative-hypnotic antiepileptic drugs from the regimens of patients with intractable epilepsy. *Annals of Neurology, 13,* 320–324.

Treiman, D. M., & Delgado-Escueta, A. V. (1983). Violence and epilepsy: A critical review. In T. A. Pedley & B. S. Meldrum (Eds.), *Recent advances in epilepsy* (Vol. 1, pp. 179–210). New York: Churchill Livingstone.

Walker, M. D. (Ed.). (1984). Research issues in positron emission tomography: Proceedings of a conference sponsored by NINCDS. *Annals of Neurology, 15* (Suppl), S1–S204.

Weisberg, L. A., Nice, C., & Katz, M. (1984). Cerebral computed tomography: A text atlas. Philadelphia: W. B. Saunders.

Williams, R. S. (1983). Neuropathological abnormalities: Search for causative agents. In F. J. Menolascino, R. Neman, & J. A. Stark (Eds.), *Curative aspects of mental retardation: Biomedical and behavioral advances* (pp. 69–72). Baltimore: Paul H. Brookes Publishing Co.

Young, R. S. K., Osbakken, M. D., Alger, P. M., Ramer, J. C., Weidner, W. A., & Daigh, J. D. (1985). Magnetic resonance imaging in leukodystrophies of childhood. *Pediatric Neurology, 1,* 15–19.

NUTRITIONAL ASPECTS OF MENTAL RETARDATION

Introduction

What is the status of nutritional research in the United States and what are the implications for mental retardation? These are the questions addressed in Section IV. Nutritional research has gained a great deal of respectability in the last few years and has greatly influenced the field of mental retardation.

One can hardly pick up the newspaper today and not read about new breakthroughs in nutritional research. For example, we read how potassium has been linked to the prevention of strokes, how calcium is involved in the prevention of osteoporosis, how fish oil may decrease cardiovascular disease, and now how food, by initiating certain biochemical reactions in the brain, may also influence our moods. This last area of research indicates that carbohydrates, for example, eaten alone without protein, boost the production of tryptophan, a precursor to serotonin, which is a calming neurotransmitter (Wurtman, 1986). On the other hand, protein consumed alone would tend to increase the alertness transmitters, dopamine and norepinephrine.

The importance of nutrition can also be seen in its newfound emphasis in medical curricula. Up until a few years ago, nutrition was hardly reviewed in medical schools. Today, the emphasis has shifted to a solid month of learning nutrition, which is only offered as an interim course in the medical student's training. Indeed, we are seeing the establishment of a national nutritional research system in which centers are investigating the role nutrition plays in fetal and neonatal development, particularly in its interaction of the maternal and fetal genomes and their modulation by maternal nutrition. A whole new field, referred to as "developmental nutrition," has emerged, which looks at the normal, excessive, or deficient amounts of nutrients during pregnancy, fetal development, and postnatal life, as well as the role of nutrition in physiological, intellectual, and behavioral development. This line of research looks at the way in which nutrients potentiate growth and development via their role in cell growth, differentiation, and function, as well as the maintenance and decline of the immune process.

Dr. Resnick's chapter on nutrition, neurotransmitters, and developmental pharmacology discusses the neurobiological aspects of development and how nutrition affects neurotransmitter development, which in turn influences cognitive development. His findings are based on an investigation of the effects of varying protein diets of animal models.

A basic understanding of neurotransmitters is necessary to understand Dr. Resnick's research. First of all, synapses, neurotransmitters, and receptors have formed the basis of the psychobiological revolution. However, up until about 10 years ago neuroscientists believed that only two main classes of neurotransmitters were employed in the human brain—one class to excite neurons and one to inhibit them. As recently as 1970, only about 200 human hormones had been identified, and now researchers believe that the total number of neurotransmitters could range as high as 300. Hormones are no longer seen as just substances produced by specific glands for specific functions. Hormones (from the Greek word *"hormone"* [to set emotion]) are now defined as "anything produced by one cell that can get to another cell by any means and change what it does" (Wylie Vale, Head of the Neuropeptide Biology Lab at the Salk Institute in La Jolla, CA). It would appear that our definition of hormone is changing and the lines between hormones and other chemicals of the body are certainly blurring.

Definitely, endocrinology is now merging with neuroscience. For example, in the mid 1970s, researchers first determined that the brain itself is a gland, secreting its own hormones and reacting to others. The breakthrough came with the discovery of hormones called "opiates," which explain how people deal with pain and how they can accomplish certain feats. Since that time, we have been able to identify at least 45 separate hormones in the brain, many of which perform different tasks elsewhere in the body. Many of the hormones are identical to neurotransmitters (such as adrenaline and testosterone), which are produced by glands and which activate organs in the body. However, in the brain they are produced by neurons instead of glands, as seen in Figure 1.

It would appear that the brain needs so many of these transmitters to address specific control centers and organs and to obtain feedback about their readiness or effectiveness in order to vary the strength of synaptic signals. Discovering the identity of these neurotransmitters and their uses could help us in treating a host of neurological disorders. Complicating the whole picture is the fact that most neurotransmitters have a widespread distribution throughout the whole body. The amino acids aspartate and glutamate, for example, are currently thought to be chemicals responsible for excitatory impulses in the brain. But these small compounds are among the 20 standard molecules used in building proteins and are, therefore, present in virtually every tissue in the human body. In short, it is almost impossible to determine whether a given cell is using glutamate as a transmitter or as a protein component. Table 1 lists a few neurotransmitters and their probable functions.

The fundamental assumption of present-day drug research is based upon the fact that most mental disturbances, or incapacities, come from deficien-

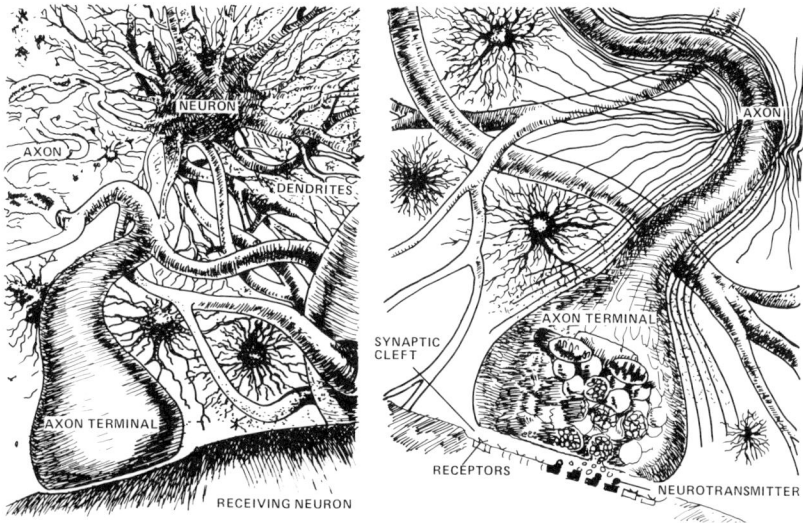

Figure 1. *Left:* In the intricate network of cells in the brain, neurons receive signals from each other through a dense array of dendrites and send out signals through their axons. *Right:* A schematic shows the synapse—the site where chemical messengers called neurotransmitters pass from one neuron to another to activate receptor molecules. (Adapted from artwork by Laszlo Kubinyi.)

cies or excesses of these neurotransmitters or receptors. In essence, every effective drug works in some way by affecting a neurotransmitter. Basically these neurotransmitter drugs seem to take on either an agonist or antagonist form. An agonist not only fits a receptor molecule but also activates it to initiate some operation in a cell. An antagonist, by contrast, plugs into the receptor but doesn't activate it. The antagonist just seems to sit there jamming the receptor so that natural neurotransmission cannot activate it either. Complicating it further is the fact that some drugs may combine the roles of both agonist and antagonist.

We recently came across an interesting NIMH research study that found that Chinese individuals appear to be more responsive to antidepressant drugs than Americans. It seems that for genetic reasons, Chinese individuals metabolize desipramine more slowly than their American counterparts, and thus this drug is more effective for them. Perhaps this is an example of Dr. Resnick's point that through nutritional development over generations, genetic encoding affects neurotransmitters, and this effect has tremendous implications for the development of psychopharmacological components.

Dr. Resnick's chapter discusses how protein malnutrition in developing individuals can tremendously affect reproduction, growth, and development. His research is focused primarily on an animal model in which he has investigated both prenatal and postnatal malnutrition and its implication for central

Table 1. Brain chemicals

Compound	Probable function
Aspartate	Excitatory neurotransmitter
Glutamate	Excitatory neurotransmitter
γ-Aminobutyric acid (GABA)	Inhibitory neurotransmitter—most important in brain
Glycine	Inhibitory neurotransmitter—most important in spinal cord
Acetylcholine	Slow excitation—important in memory
Norepinephrine and dopamine	Involved in arousal and motor activity
Serotonin	Involved in sleep, mood, appetite, and pain
Peptides (cholecystokinin, ACTH, substance P, enkephalins, etc.)	Various functions, many unknown. For example, substance P appears related to pain, and enkephalins to pain reduction.

nervous system delay. If one were to extrapolate these malnutrition data obtained in rats to man one would find that malnutrition during the first and second trimester may result in many irreversible central and peripheral changes. Exciting new findings are also postulated in this chapter; these perhaps will help us to understand the pervasiveness of mild mental retardation as a result of intergenerational effects of protein malnutrition. For example, based upon this animal model, Dr. Resnick found that mild protein restriction in the first generation becomes a more severe protein restriction in the second generation. Therefore, if we are to extrapolate from his findings ways in which we can prevent mental retardation, we realize that the times most important to these severe effects are during the first and second trimester and perhaps the most important periods for effective *rehabilitation* are at the third trimester and the first 2 years of life. Therefore, we need to focus on the value of nutritional supplementation at these times.

It is the coeditors' opinion that there is no chapter written to date that is more comprehensive than Dr. Davis's chapter on nutrition in the prevention and reversal of mental retardation. The purpose of Dr. Davis's chapter is to review the scientific status of and prospects for the prevention of mental retardation as well as the amelioration of mental retardation via nutritional factors. Dr. Davis's chapter takes us through a comprehensive and painstaking analysis of the current state of the art of nutritional therapy as it relates to primary and secondary prevention. It provides an in-depth analysis and critique to Dr. Harrell's study, which was initially hailed as a major breakthrough for the treatment of individuals with mental retardation. While providing us with insights into how nutrition can directly prevent mental retardation, he also shows that even though we can't prevent such disorders as

Down syndrome or fragile-X syndrome, or inborn errors such as phenylketonuria, nutritional approaches in combination with other approaches can prevent or ameliorate some *fraction* of mental retardation.

REFERENCE

Wurtman, J. (1986). *Managing your mind and mood through food.* Boston: Interneuron Corp.

Chapter 6

Nutrition, Neurotransmitter Regulation, and Developmental Pharmacology

Oscar Resnick

The vulnerability of the developing central nervous system to insults of prenatal protein malnutrition has been extensively investigated in recent years by
our research group (Resnick et al., 1979). We reported alterations in the
morphological, behavioral, electrophysiological, and biochemical profiles in
rats as sequelae of gestational protein malnutrition and lactational protein-
calorie malnutrition. Most of the sequelae of gestational protein malnutrition
proved to be irreversible. We believe that such information obtained with the
use of animals adds to the understanding of developmental disabilities and
mental retardation in humans. This information becomes even more important
when one considers that a large proportion of the world's population have
diets inadequate in "complete" protein. The study of prenatal protein malnutrition as a developmental stressor in animals may have implications for
other early developmental stressors. Many similar adaptations to various
kinds of developmental stressors have been reported in laboratory animals.
Extrapolations from animal data to human data are made wherever possible in
this chapter.

There is ample evidence that developing animals require "good quality"
or "complete" protein for normal reproductive performance, as well as
growth and development. Proteins found in cereal grains are incomplete and
will not support normal growth and development in rats (Chase & Jansen,
1976; Jansen & Chase, 1976). Good quality or complete protein is the least
available and most expensive foodstuff in the human diet, even in affluent
countries like the United States. This is exacerbated by the current popularity
of vegetarian diets that exclude animal and dairy products.

It has been reported that food intake in animals is depressed if individual
essential amino acids are deficient in the diet or if the essential amino acids

are not present in the diet in the proper proportions (Harper, 1967). When rats are fed a diet low in complete protein and high in fat, the animals compensate for the inadequate supply of protein by eating more food (Meyer, 1958). It has been demonstrated in humans that when diets are deficient in protein, more fats and carbohydrates are consumed. Taking into account the price and availability of good quality protein, as well as dietary fads and taboos, there is a good possibility that protein malnutrition may be a very serious problem, even in developed countries. In January 1972, the Worcester Foundation for Experimental Biology (WFEB) was awarded a program project entitled, "Maternal Protein Restriction and Mental Retardation," by the National Institute of Child Health and Human Development (NICHD). The aims of the program are:

1. To develop animal models whose diets are low in good quality or complete protein and high in carbohydrates and fats
2. To study the developmental consequences of such diets
3. To compare the developmental consequences of a mildly protein-restricted diet with those resulting from a severely protein-restricted diet
4. To determine which developmental consequences are reversible and which are permanent
5. To compare the consequences of prenatal protein malnutrition with lactational or postnatal protein malnutrition
6. To explore the possible implications of the animal data to the human condition

The animal models and the diets used in the program are fully described in the literature (Resnick, Morgane, Hasson, & Miller, 1982). It is generally understood that malnutrition and undernutrition in humans are associated with lack of sanitation, infectious diseases, low socioeconomic status, social and psychological stresses, and the like. As a result, retrospective and prospective studies in humans are confounded by many variables, thus making it difficult to ascertain the role of nutrition on the developing young. It is also very difficult to carry out rigidly controlled clinical studies on the effects of food supplementation on early development. Obviously, human studies are necessary and important to elucidate the role of nutrition on growth and development. These studies are, however, very difficult to carry out and are subject to many sources of error and confounding variables. For these reasons, the use of animal models is strongly indicated.

In order to make extrapolations from animal modes to humans, one must be able to compare results obtained at comparable developmental stages. For example, the brain growth spurt is essentially postnatal in the rat and coincides with the period of lactation. In humans, the brain growth spurt begins during the third trimester of pregnancy and ends at about 2 years of age. Thus, prenatal malnutrition in the rat is comparable to prenatal malnutrition during the first two trimesters of pregnancy in humans. Malnutrition during lactation in the rat is comparable to malnutrition during the last trimester of pregnancy and the first 2 years of life in humans. One must be able to compare, across species, the ontogenetic development of the central nervous system (CNS) and thus be able to define comparable periods of development in the various species. In addition, when extrapolating data from one species to another (e.g., rat to man), one must take into account timing, severity, and duration of the stressor or insult (e.g., malnutrition). These conditions may also apply when studying the developmental effects of many different forms of stressors, pharmacological agents, toxic agents, environmental pollutants, and the like. A brief description of the animal models and diets is as follows.

ANIMAL MODELS AND DIET

The experimental paradigm for the project's research is based upon a classic rat model for prenatal and postnatal malnutrition. The model, involving adaptation to the experimental diets of virgin female albino Sprague-Dawley rats for 5 weeks before mating, permits the use of an equilibrated pregnant rat during gestation. Thus, the confounding effects of maternal adaptation to the modified diets can be negated. Experimental diets are casein diets supplemented with methionine to assure that sufficient methionine is included to maintain a balanced mixture of amino acids. Casein is a mixture of related phosphoproteins occurring in milk. It is used as a source of protein in experimental diets for developmental studies in laboratory animals, such as the rat. Casein is deficient in the essential amino acid, methionine, needed for normal growth and development in the rat. Diets are isocaloric and supply about 4.3 calories per gram. The growth and reproduction results of these studies compare well with previous ones conducted along the same lines.

The experiments involved seven dietary models. The dams were fed either the control (25%), 8%, or 6% protein diets starting 5 weeks prior to mating and during gestation. The young were switched at birth or at weaning to one of the other diets or were maintained on the diet of their dams through lactation or through weaning and beyond. The experimental models were designed to produce prenatal protein deficiency, postnatal protein-calorie deficiency, or postweaning protein deficiency in various combinations of malnutrition and rehabilitation. In addition to experiments involving the F_1 generation, animal models have also been developed for looking at the intergenerational effects of malnutrition by the breeding of animals who have been malnourished from conception through reproduction and lactation. Again, a variety of combinations are used to provide animals who are either malnourished or rehabilitated at different times during this experimental period.

A great deal of experience has been gained by working with these models, and considerable data have been collected to support the contention that the effects obtained during prenatal malnutrition result from animals who are primarily protein deprived, while those suckled on protein-deficient mothers during lactation are both protein and calorie malnourished. Also, we have accumulated data on milk composition to suggest that there is a difference in the amount and the composition of the milks when comparing animals fed 8% casein diets, which we term "mildly malnourished," and those fed 6% casein diets, which we consider to be "severely malnourished." Considering the time period over which these diets and animal models have been used, it is fair to say that we are able to reproduce the models as required. On the basis of our data, the use of both 8% and 6% protein diets does permit us to describe the effects as "mild" and "severe."

Resnick et al. (1982) have shown that the mildly protein-malnourished dam that was fed the 8% isocaloric diet 5 weeks prior to mating and during gestation has a normal fertility rate and essentially a normal weight gain during pregnancy. These dams give birth to a normal number of pups per litter and the mean weight of the pups is essentially normal. When the 8% casein-derived pups are cross-fostered by normal dams, they show a normal growth curve (i.e., body and brain weights). Yet, these rats have lifelong central and peripheral effects—many of which cannot be reversed by dietary rehabilitation at birth. Thus, in rats, it is possible to have a normal pregnancy and to produce normal pups who can have a normal growth curve and yet have lifelong developmental disabilities (both central and peripheral). If this can be extrapolated to the human condition, then the implications are enormous. This is especially the case since complete protein is the one foodstuff liable to be deficient (even marginally) in our diets. They have also shown that the "severely" protein-malnourished dam that was fed the 6% isocaloric diet 5 weeks prior to mating and during gestation has a normal fertility rate but an abnormal weight gain during pregnancy. These dams show a marked reduction in weight gain during pregnancy, even though they consume more calories per gram of body weight than do dams fed the control (25% casein) diets. These dams give birth to a reduced number of pups per litter and the mean weight of the pups is considerably decreased. When the 6% casein-derived pups are cross-fostered by normal dams, they show a very depressed growth curve. The 6% casein-fed dams and their offspring are models for obvious or overt protein malnutrition. The 8% casein-fed dams and their offspring are models for hidden or covert protein malnutrition. These animal models are also important in that they demonstrate the need to develop predictors of risk in humans with essentially normal body and brain weights at birth, weaning, and at adulthood. This applies regardless of the developmental stressor. Such predictors are now being developed for both the rat and the human infant.

MODELS FOR MENTAL RETARDATION IN RAT

I would like to discuss some of the data obtained during the past 13 years, as well as some of the concepts that have been developed. It is very tempting to extrapolate some of the data and concepts to the human condition. However, I am fully aware of the pitfalls of such an exercise.

We have demonstrated many instances of retarded development in the central nervous system (CNS) of our developmentally malnourished animals (Resnick et al., 1979). Table 1 lists examples of such retarded development in the CNS. I am sure that there are many other instances of delayed maturation or retarded development in our animal models, which will be demonstrated in future studies. Can these observations in animals be extrapolated to human mental retardation? It is possible that we may have demonstrated, in animals, the underlying substrates of human mental retardation. In 95% or more of the cases of human mental retardation, there are no known pathognomic signs, as opposed to the aminoacidurias, hypothyroidism, and the like, which make up the remaining 5% of the cases. Perhaps an important factor may be a delay in maturation of parts of the CNS (e.g., delay in birth dates of neurons or a delay in migration of neurons), which could interfere with the normal development and synchrony of the many parts of the CNS.

MODELS FOR DEVELOPMENTAL DISABILITIES IN RAT

We have demonstrated a large number of chemical, physiological, anatomical, and behavioral changes in our animals from birth to 19 months of age (Resnick et al., 1979). Tables 2 through 5 list a few of these changes.

Table 1.   A partial list of instances of retarded development in the CNS of 8/8 and 6/6 rats

1.   Changes in latency and waveform in the visual evoked potential (returns to normal by 90 days of age)
2.   Increased latency in the transcallosal response (returns to normal by 21 days of age)
3.   Delayed maturation of several EEG bands, especially those of lower frequency spectrum, as measured by power spectral analysis of EEG ontogeny
4.   Delayed maturation of slow-wave sleep
5.   Rate of migration of neurons into the olfactory bulb was much slower in the the malnourished rats
6.   Delay in the birth date of neurons in the cortex
7.   Delay in the developmental change from activation to behavioral suppression in response to clonidine, an alpha-2-adrenergic agonist
8.   Delay in sensorimotor development (eye and ear opening)

Table 2. Partial list of chemical effects in 8/8 and 6/6 rats, from day 0 onward

1. Increased regional brain levels of serotonin
2. Increased regional brain levels of 5-HIAA
3. Increased regional brain levels of norepinephrine
4. Increased regional brain levels of tryptophan
5. Increased regional brain levels of phenylalanine
6. Increased depletion of regional brain levels of serotonin and norepinephrine following electroshock
7. Increased levels of plasma nonesterified free fatty acids
8. Increased levels of plasma-free tryptophan
9. Increased plasma levels of androgens in the males

Note. O. Resnick, Key Investigator.

All of these changes, and many others not mentioned, have their analogous counterparts in the clinical diagnosis of minimal brain dysfunction (MBD), which is a wastebasket classification of diverse symptoms. This may be the result of unitarian responses of the CNS to many different "subclinical" developmental stressors. Many of the adaptations seen in the ani-

Table 3. Partial list of neurophysiological effects in 8/8 and 6/6 rats

1. Increased susceptibility to electroshock-induced seizures
2. Slower spontaneous firing of single neurons in Layers III, IV, and V of the frontal cortex
3. Changes in latency and waveform in the visual evoked potential (returns to normal by 90 days of age)
4. Increased latency in the transcallosal response (returns to normal by 21 days of age)
5. Changes in waveform in contralateral cortex in thalamocortical evoked response studies
6. Delayed maturation of several EEG bands, especially those of lower frequency spectrum, as measured by power spectral analysis of EEG ontogeny
7. Delayed maturation of slow-wave sleep
8. Decreased light-dark ratios in REM sleep. A greater proportion of REM sleep occurred during the dark phase of the 24-hour recording period
9. A significant reduction of the low frequency power content in the cortical EEG obtained during slow-wave sleep
10. In single unit recordings made in thalamus and frontal cortical areas, there were fewer fast-firing cells, and overall lower discharge rates and altered firing patterns (fewer cells exhibit bursting) in the malnourished animals
11. Long-term hippocampal potentiation differs in normal versus malnourished rats
12. Increased peak power in theta band of hippocampal EEG

Note. P. J. Morgane, J. Bronzino, W. Stern, and W. Forbes, Key Investigators.

Table 4. Partial list of neuroanatomical effects in 8/8 and 6/6 rats

1. A decrease in synaptic spine density of cortical and subcortical neurons and a reduced dendritic length in some cortical and subcortical areas
2. Spine loss in Layer IIIb visual cortex cells, especially on basal and horizontal dendrites of pyramidal cells
3. A decrease in thickness of visual cortex, resulting in decreased length of apical dendrites
4. A decrease in apical dendrite thickness in visual cortex pyramidal cells
5. A marked lowering of spines on spine-poor cortical internuncial (stellate) cells
6. Reduction in vertical extent of dendritic tree in cerebellum
7. Decreased spines on cerebellar stellate cells
8. Decreased cell body size and decreased dendritic branching in cerebellar purkinje cells
9. Cerebellar basket cells show a decrease in dendritic length and a decrease in synaptic spine density
10. Decreased synaptic spine density on cells of neostriatum
11. Many changes seen in raphe dorsalis and locus coeruleus
12. Overall shrinkage of olfactory bulb
13. The rate of migration of neurons into the olfactory bulb was much slower in the malnourished rats

Note. T. Kemper and W. DeBassio, Key Investigators.

mals that were developmentally malnourished are also seen in animals that were developmentally exposed to low levels of lead, carbon monoxide, iron-deficiency anemia, and the like.

CONCEPTS DEVELOPED DURING COURSE OF PROGRAM

After obtaining data, using our rat models, it becomes necessary to develop a conceptual framework from which one may get an insight into the developmental consequences of an early stressor, such as protein malnutrition. It then becomes both challenging and useful to extrapolate such data and the concepts to humans. The following are several examples:

1. We have demonstrated many central and peripheral chemical changes, as well as neuroanatomical changes, in newborn 6% and 8% casein-derived pups—before they had a chance to nurse. These changes, which are the result of protein malnutrition of the mother, have nothing to do with lactation, nursing, or mother-infant interactions since the animals were sacrificed before nursing could take place. Examples of changes found in the newborn pups are: markedly elevated brain levels of phenylalanine (PhA), tryptophan (TR), norepinephrine (NE), serotonin (5-HT), 5-hydroxyindoleacetic acid (5-HIAA), and markedly elevated levels of plasma non-

Table 5. Partial list of behavioral effects in 8/8 and 6/6 rats

Behavioral effect	Nature of differences between dietary groups
Maternal-infant interactions	8% Litters spent more time actively nursing and less time out of nest
Copulatory behavior	8% Males showed increased frequencies of intromission
Circadian distribution of feeding	8% Group ate less during last half of light cycle and more during last half of dark cycle
Induction of oral behaviors by tail-pinch stress	Predominance of licking in 25% groups; predominance of gnawing in 8% groups
Response to the dopaminergic agonist apomorphine (stereotypy)	Subsensitivity of 8% rats to apomorphine as indicated by a shift to right in dose-response curve
Effects of the 5-HT agonist DMT on measures of motor coordination and acoustic startle	Subsensitivity of the 8% rats to DMT as indicated by a dose-response shift to the right
Effects of alpha-2 agonist clonidine in developing pups	Subsensitivity of pups of 6% diet at 5 and 10 days (motor activation); delay in the developmental change from activation to behavioral suppression normally seen between ages 15 and 20 days
Running-wheel activity	8% Groups were more active at older ages (> 120 days)
Climbing activity	8% Groups spend more time climbing in home cages
Escape from foot shock	8% Rats had shorter latencies to escape in a treadmill and in a tilt cage as a function of shock intensity
Size-intensity function of sciatic nerve compound action potentials with electrical stimulation of the foot pad	8% Rats showed enhanced evoked compound action potentials
Learning and retention of a bar-press delayed alternation response	Deficit of 8% group in relearning (retention); no deficits in acquisition
Learning of a rewarded spatial alternation	8% Rats showed an elevated number of perseverative errors
Spatial localization performance in a Morris maze	Mild acquisition deficit in 8% groups that are inexperienced with the task

Note. W. Stern, P. Hall, and C. Goodlett, Key Investigators.

esterified fatty acids (NEFA). In addition, we have demonstrated prenatal effects on birth date of neurons in the cortex.

These findings are important because they demonstrate, in the rat, that developmental consequences of early protein malnutrition on the CNS can result before the brain growth spurt, which is postnatal in the rat. According to Dobbing (1973), the prenatal period in the rat corresponds to the first two trimesters of pregnancy in humans. As is shown later, many of the central and peripheral effects due to prenatal protein malnutrition in the rat are irreversible. Thus, this period in the rat and presumably the first two trimesters of pregnancy in humans would seem to be the most vulnerable to developmental insults.

2. We have demonstrated changes in areas of the adult brain that show postnatal neurogenesis or cell migration in animals that were only prenatally protein malnourished. For example, we have reported dramatic effects on the firing of single neurons of Layers III, IV, and V of the frontal cortex in adult 8/25 rats cross-fostered at birth, who had normal body and brain weights at birth and who had normal growth curves. Those neurons studied were not in Layers III, IV, and V when the developing animals were protein malnourished in utero. Similar data were obtained in the olfactory system, hyppocampus, visual system, and myelination—all of which show postnatal development.

These data are extremely important because they demonstrate that prenatal protein malnutrition in the rat, imposed before the brain growth spurt, has long-term developmental consequences on the maturation of the CNS. This was demonstrated in animals that were cross-fostered at birth by normal dams. The implications for mental retardation and developmental disabilities are as follows: 1) one should look for stressors that occur early in development (first and second trimester); 2) rats and, presumably, humans can be at risk even if they have a normal birth weight and a normal growth curve; 3) the developmental consequences can occur quite late in development. This again emphasizes the need to develop predictors of risk in newborns, infants, and children.

These same changes were seen in adult 25/8 rats (normal pups nursed by 8% casein-fed dams) that hence suffered from lactational protein-calorie malnutrition. However, these effects could be reversed (completely or partially) in adulthood by dietary rehabilitation. These same effects caused by prenatal protein malnutrition could not be reversed from birth onward. Similar results were obtained when studying the elevated levels of brain PhA, TR, NE, 5-HT, and 5-HIAA. Thus, the reversibility or irreversibility of the effects studied is dependent on when the malnutrition took place. Timing is of the utmost importance. According to Dobbing (1968), the prenatal period in the rat is analogous to the first and second trimesters in humans, and lactation in the rat is analogous to the third trimester and the first 2 years of life in humans. Thus, prenatal malnutrition in the rat is analogous to prenatal malnutrition during the first two trimesters of pregnancy in humans. Malnutrition during lactation in the rat is analogous to malnutrition during the last trimester of pregnancy and the first 2 years of life in humans. If one were to extrapolate the data obtained in rats to humans, then malnutrition during the first and second trimesters may result in many "irreversible" central and peripheral changes. Malnutrition during the third trimester and the first 2 years of life may result in many "reversible" central and peripheral changes. In extrapolating data on the CNS from one species to another, one must be able to compare across species the ontogenetic development of the CNS and thus be able to define analogous periods of development. For example, the brain growth spurt is essentially postnatal in the rat and coincides with the period of lactation. In humans, the brain growth spurt begins during the third trimester of pregnancy and ends at about 2 years of age. In addition, when extrapolating data from one species to another, not only must one take into account time, but also severity and duration of the stressor or insult.

This may also have implications for other stressors. For example, in the fetal alcohol syndrome (FAS), irreversible changes are seen at birth. Yet, intravenous infusion of alcohol is used to stop premature labor, without causing FAS in the newborn. Thus, one might conclude that the FAS is a result of the action of alcohol on the developing organism during the first and second trimesters. The well-known treatment of infants with phenylketonuria (PKU) by removing phenylalanine in the diet and hypothyroidism by hormone replacement would seem to indicate that the deleterious effects on the developing CNS occur during the third trimester of pregnancy and the first 2 years of life. On the other hand, Tay-Sachs disease is irreversible at birth and would thus seem to indicate that the deleterious effects occurred during the first and second trimesters of pregnancy.

3.   Similar neurochemical and electrophysiological effects of developmental malnutrition were seen in adult rats that had normal body and brain weights at birth and normal growth curves (8/25 rehabilitated at birth), in adult rats that had normal body and brain weights at birth and abnormal growth curves (8/8 and 25/8 at birth), and in adult rats that were small for gestational age (SGA) at birth (markedly reduced body and brain weights) and had abnormal growth curves (6/6 and 6/25 at birth). Thus, in the rat, a normal body and brain weight at birth and a normal growth curve do not necessarily mean a normal development. Furthermore, in the rat, normal birth weights, brain weights, and growth curves are of no use in predicting normal development or a normal CNS (see Table 6) (Resnick & Morgane, 1983).

Human infants are considered normal if they weigh 2.5 kg and up, have a normal head circumference, and have a normal Apgar score. By analogous criteria, all of our 8% casein-derived newborn pups would be classified as normal. Yet, we have demonstrated dramatic changes in 8% casein-derived

Table 6. Conclusions derived from our studies

1. Similar central and peripheral chemical changes are seen in newborn pups with essentially normal body and brain weights (8% casein-derived) and in newborn pups with markedly decreased body and brain weights (6% casein-derived), albeit more pronounced. These changes occur before the brain growth spurt.

2. Similar central chemical and electrophysiological and peripheral chemical changes are seen in adult 8/25 rats who had normal birth weights and normal growth curves and in adult 6/25 rats who had markedly decreased birth weights and abnormal growth curves, albeit more pronounced.

3. The 8% casein-derived newborn pups had essentially normal body and brain weights. Yet we demonstrated many central and peripheral changes in the newborn 8% casein-derived pups, before they had a chance to nurse and before the brain growth spurt.

4. When the 8% casein-derived pups were cross-fostered by 25% dams at birth (8/25), they showed a normal growth curve. As adults, these 8/25 rats were shown to have irreversible central and peripheral effects.

5. In the rat, a normal body and brain weight at birth and a normal growth curve does not necessarily mean a normal development.

newborn pups before they had a chance to nurse. Furthermore, many of these central and peripheral changes were found to be irreversible. Since the outcome of most clinical prenatal supplementation studies is based on infant weight and head circumference at birth and since the outcome of most postnatal supplementation studies is based on growth curves, maybe these end points are not completely valid. There is a need for the development of predictors of risk in newborn infants with essentially normal body weights, head circumference, and Apgar scores. Such a predictor of risk is available for rats that have essentially normal body and brain weights at birth and that will have a normal growth curve: namely, rats born to mothers fed the 8% casein diet and nursed by control dams (8/25 rats). In the rat, plasma levels of nonesterified (free) fatty acids (NEFA) are elevated in newborn 8% casein-derived pups, and remain elevated throughout life—whether rehabilitated at birth or not (8/8 and 8/25 rats). In addition, plasma levels of NEFA can differentiate between pre- and postnatal malnutrition and between irreversible and reversible changes (Miller & Resnick, 1980).

4. The developmental effects of a severe protein malnutrition (6% casein diet) in the rat are similar to those resulting from a mild protein malnutrition (8% casein diet), only more marked. There are, however, a few notable differences. The 6% casein-derived pups are SGA at birth and have abnormal growth curves, even when rehabilitated at birth (6/25). Since the changes seen in the 6/25 animals are the same as those seen in the 8/25 animals, only more marked, then the use of the 8/25 rat as a model for an

infant at risk (IAR) is justified, even though this model has a normal body and brain weight throughout life (Resnick et al., 1982).

GENERATIONAL STUDIES

The most prevalent form of malnutrition in humans is characterized by its chronic and generational nature. Our studies to date (Resnick & Morgane, 1984) indicate that a mild protein restriction (8% casein diet) in the first generation becomes a more severe protein restriction in the second generation. This is based on weight gains of the dams during pregnancy; the mean number of pups (F_2) per litter; the mean pup (F_2) body weight and brain weight at birth; the growth curves; the levels of brain tryptophan, serotonin, and 5-hydroxyindoleacetic acid from birth to weaning; and the levels of certain plasma constituents, especially the nonesterified fatty acids.

It is of interest to mention at this time the report by Murthy (1984) that cytogenetic studies in fetal cells from pregnant rats given a 5% protein-restricted diet revealed a significant induction of structural chromosomal aberrations and sister chromatid exchanges (SCE). The chromosomal aberrations, which include chromatid breaks, gaps, fragments, and rings, and the SCE were associated with a rise in fetal mortality and decreased birth weights as expected with such a severe protein-restricted diet. Thus, we may conclude that a mildly protein-restricted diet (8% casein), as measured by its effects on the F_1 generation, produces the effects of a severely protein-restricted diet in the F_2 generation—even though the 8% casein diet was used in all of these studies. The biological significance of these findings is open to speculation.

EXTRAPOLATION OF ANIMAL
DATA TO HUMAN CONDITION

1. *Prevention:* The most important time may be the first and second trimesters.

2. *Rehabilitation:* The most important time may be the third trimester and the first 2 years of life.

3. *Most Important Factors:* 1) Nutritional history of mother before gestation; 2) maternal nutrition during gestation, especially the first and second trimesters. Several studies have indicated that maternal nutritional history before gestation may be even more important than maternal nutrition during gestation.

As mentioned earlier, animals require good quality or complete protein for normal reproductive performance and normal growth and development. Proteins found in cereal grains are incomplete. They are deficient in lysine and threonine and will not support normal reproductive performance or normal growth and development in rats. Not only must the diet contain normal amounts of the essential amino acids, but the essential amino acids must be present in proper proportions; such is the case in *eggs, dairy products, and meat*. For example, Stein, Susser, and Rush (1978) in their Harlem studies used casein diets that were not supplemented with methionine. Therefore, their results are based on the supplementation of an incomplete protein and their data should be so interpreted.

4. *A normal body and brain weight at birth and a normal growth curve does not necessarily mean a normal development*. As already mentioned, irreversible central and peripheral changes were noted in adult animals that had normal body and brain weights at birth and that had a normal growth curve (8/25 at birth). These animals were born to mothers that were mildly protein malnourished and were nursed by normal dams. Similar irreversible central and peripheral chemical and neuroanatomical changes were seen in newborn pups with normal body and brain weights (8%) and in newborn pups with markedly reduced body and brain weights (6%). The former were derived from mothers who were mildly protein malnourished, and the latter were derived from mothers who were severely protein malnourished. The changes were more pronounced in the latter (see Table 6).

Clearly, in animals at least, indicators other than body and brain weight are needed to signal potential developmental disabilities in the newborn. In our rat work, plasma NEFA levels seem to be such an indicator. If the rat data can be extrapolated to humans, then this becomes very important because birth weights and growth curves are the usual end points by which one assesses the value of supplementation either prenatally or postnatally. Finally, all chemicals (both endogenous or exogenous) may have different effects in animals that have been subjected to early developmental malnutrition and that show irreversible anatomical, physiological, chemical, and behavioral changes.

CONCLUSION AND SUMMARY

Any female who is subjected to a stressor(s) before or during pregnancy is potentially an "at-risk mother" and the offspring are potentially "at-risk infants." Data extrapolated from laboratory animals suggest that the first two trimesters of pregnancy in humans are the most critical in this respect, as measured by reversibility of deficits. This is discussed at great length in this presentation.

The use of prenatal protein malnutrition as a stressor in rats (which is analogous to the first two trimesters in humans) results in many instances of retarded development of the CNS. This may have implications for humans and may include a large variety of developmental stressors, including prenatal protein malnutrition.

There is a great need for the development of predictors of risk in newborn infants with essentially normal body weights, head circumference, and Apgar scores. This is especially true if such "normal" infants have a normal growth curve, yet show developmental disabilities at a later age—usually at the time they enter school. There is a tendency to assume that the developmental disabilities are the result of postnatal stressors. However, animal data suggest that it could very well be that the stressors occurred early in development, (i.e., during the first and second trimesters). This again points to the need for early predictors of risk. However, one recognizes that this is a most difficult task, albeit a very important one.

With respect to protein requirements during pregnancy for humans, as much complete protein as possible should be consumed in the absence of kidney disease. This is based upon the observations that ingested protein satiates the appetite quicker than carbohydrates and fats and that protein ingestion during pregnancy is likely to be decreased due to morning sickness. Of course, the diet should also contain sufficient vitamins, minerals, and calories to maintain fetal growth and development. It is now usually recommended that females gain 20–30 pounds during a normal pregnancy. Maternal nutrition during gestation, especially the first and second trimesters, is very important. Several clinical studies have also indicated that maternal nutritional history before gestation may be even more important than maternal nutrition during gestation. Thus, women of childbearing age should have the proper ratio of body fat to lean body mass. This assures a pool of calories for the developing fetus. If dietary protein intake is insufficient to meet the fetus' requirements, then the mother's own protein (usually, plasma albumin) will be used for the developing fetus. This results in edema.

There is a great need to study the generational effects of developmental stressors in humans. Animal data indicate that prenatal protein malnutrition can produce central and peripheral effects in the F_1 offspring. Some of these effects may also be seen in succeeding generations and may or may not be reversible by proper feeding over several generations. The implications of this work, if extrapolated to humans, are mind boggling.

REFERENCES

Chase, H. P., & Jansen, C. R. (1976). Effects of feeding lysine and threonine fortified bread during gestation and lactation on growth of the brain in rats. *Journal of Nutrition, 106,* 41–47.

Dobbing, J. (1968). Effects of experimental undernutrition on development of the nervous system. In N. S. Scrimshaw & J. E. Gordon (Eds.), *Malnutrition, learning, and behavior* (pp. 181–202). Cambridge, MA: MIT Press.

Dobbing, J. (1973). The developing brain: A plea for more critical interspecies extrapolation. *Nutrition Reports International, 7,* 401–406.

Harper, A. E. (1967). Effect of dietary protein content and amino acid on food intake and preference. In C. Code (Ed.), *Handbook of psychiatry: Sec. 6, Vol. 1. Alimentary Canal* (pp. 399–410). Washington, DC: American Physiological Society.

Jansen, C. R., & Chase, H. P. (1976). Effects of feeding lysine and threonine fortified bread during gestation and lactation on growth of the offspring in rats. *Journal of Nutrition, 106*, 33–40.

Meyer, J. H. (1958). Interactions of dietary fiber and protein on food intake and body composition of growing rats. *American Journal of Physiology, 193*, 488–494.

Miller, M., & Resnick, O. (1980). Tryptophan availability: The importance of prepartum and postpartum dietary protein on brain indoleamine metabolism in rats. *Experimental Neurology, 67*, 298–314.

Murthy, P. B. (1984). Elevated fetal chromosomal damage in malnourished pregnant rats. *Metabolism, 33*, 489–490.

Resnick, O., Miller, M., Forbes, W. B., Hall, R., Kemper, T., Bronzino, J., & Morgane, P. J. (1979). Developmental protein malnutrition: Influences on the central nervous system of the rat. *Neuroscience and Biobehavioral Review, 3*, 233–246.

Resnick, O., & Morgane, P. J. (1983). Animal models for small-for-gestational-age (SGA) neonates and infants-at-risk (IAR). *Developmental Brain Research, 10*, 221–225.

Resnick, O., & Morgane, P. J. (1984). Generational effects of protein malnutrition in the rat. *Developmental Brain Research, 15*, 219–227.

Resnick, O., Morgane, P. J., Hasson, R., & Miller, M. (1982). Overt and hidden forms of chronic malnutrition in the rat and their relevance to man. *Neuroscience and Biobehavioral Review, 6*, 55–57.

Stein, Z., Susser, M., & Rush, D. (1978). Prenatal nutrition and birth weights: Experiments and quasi-experiments in the past decade. *Journal of Reproductive Medicine, 21*, 287–297.

Chapter 7

Nutrition in the Prevention and Reversal of Mental Retardation

Donald R. Davis

> If all prospective human mothers could be fed as expertly as prospective animal mothers in the laboratory, most sterility, spontaneous abortions, stillbirths, and premature births would disappear; the birth of deformed and mentally retarded babies would be largely a thing of the past. (Williams, 1971, p. 51)

The greatest hope for nutrition and the problem of mental retardation almost certainly lies in preventing the birth of mentally defective babies. Although nutritional therapy in certain situations is scientifically more advanced than prevention, and even reversal of mental retardation has been demonstrated in rare cases, these successes are minor compared to the potential impact of improved nutrition on primary prevention.

Until recent decades, many believed that the environment of a human fetus is so well protected in its mother's body that no external influence could affect its genetically determined development. Even after the potentially disastrous effects of environmental toxins and maternal drugs were recognized, and even after the self-evident crucial importance of nutrient materials during gestation was granted, still the idea unfortunately lingered that a fetus is a "perfect parasite," able to take whatever nutrients it needs from its mother's body.

Now we have overwhelming proof in every species studied that myriad kinds of maternal malnutrition can readily induce virtually any imaginable neurological or physical defect in the offspring. Unfortunately, however, in humans we still can not answer the key question of what fraction of mental retardation and other birth defects occurring in our population is preventable by improved nutrition. Furthermore, the goal of prevention by nutritional means goes far beyond scientific issues and depends vitally on the individual human and social contexts in which knowledge must be transmitted and acted upon if it is to be useful.

The purpose of this chapter is to review the scientific status of, and prospects for, the prevention of mental retardation, as well as the amelioration of the tremendous burden of mental retardation that we have not been able to prevent. The picture presented is one of optimism, tempered with awareness of numerous factors that slow our progress. These factors include the complexity of the problem; the slow pace of needed research; the handicap of old, ingrained beliefs about the quality of fetal nutrition in developed nations; and, as mentioned, the gap that often exists between what we as a culture have learned and what we are able to apply.

NUTRITION AND PRIMARY PREVENTION

Prevention in Animals

The first clear demonstration that nutritional deficiencies can produce congenital malformations in a mammal is credited to a 1933 report of eyeless offspring from healthy but vitamin A-deficient sows. A tremendous body of evidence accumulated since then establishes that any animal will produce offspring with a wide variety of physical and neurological defects if its nutrition during reproduction is inadequate in quality or quantity. Deficiencies of single vitamins, minerals, or amino acids can all play havoc with reproduction, as can large excesses or imbalances of nutrients (Hurley, 1985; Williams, 1971; Winick, 1976).

An important lesson from animal experiments is that nutritional deficiencies can vary in many degrees from severe lacks in which no live offspring are produced, to marginal deficits in which only a few malformations occur. For example, an early experiment in France tested six different levels of pantothenic acid in the diets of 66 young female rats that produced 502 embryos (Lefebvres-Biosselot, 1954). Their fetuses were classified as shown in Table 1.

Significantly, the highest intakes—which still produced some defective offspring—are only about twofold less than the recommended intake for

Table 1. Congenital malformations and pantothenic acid intake in rats

Dietary intake (μg/day)	Resorbed (%)	Defective (%)	Normal (%)
0	100		
10	100		
20–25	58	19	24
30–35	46	16	38
40–45	17	10	72
50	3	1.5	95.5

Source: Lefebvres-Biosselot (1954).

reproduction in rats (National Research Council, 1978). As will be discussed further, comparable human deficiencies may occur in "well-nourished" countries; in a nationwide study of 36,000 typical Americans, 13%–23% of the population had estimated short-term intakes of half or less of the 1980 recommended dietary allowances for each of 6 out of 14 nutrients studied: vitamins A, B_6, and C, plus calcium, iron, and magnesium (U.S. Department of Agriculture, 1983).

Another well-established lesson from animal research is that birth defects and postnatal developmental defects can easily result from diets that are adequate to maintain health in adults. Gestation and the rapid development of infancy present the most severe tests of nutrition.

Animal studies also have shown the importance of interactions between nutrition and genetic factors (Hutt, 1953; Williams, 1956/1979). Differences in nutrient metabolism between different strains of the same species are clearly shown in nutritional studies of birth defects. Susceptibility to defects also varies among individuals of the same strain, and simple selective breeding techniques can produce substrains with increased or reduced susceptibility to defects caused by specific nutrient deficiencies (Hutt, 1953). Additional examples of nutrient-genetics interactions are cited later in relation to drugs and toxins and in the section on neural tube defects.

A striking nutrient-genetics interaction was discovered in the mutant "pallid" mouse (Erway, Hurley, & Fraser, 1966). The offspring of homozygous mothers showed, in addition to a pallid color, an irreversible congenital ataxia caused by defects of the inner ear. On customary diets, about two thirds of the offspring were affected. By increasing dietary manganese during gestation, the incidence of ataxia (but not the pallid color) was reduced. A 20-fold increase of dietary manganese prevented it entirely. This interesting kind of interaction between a gene and nutrition during gestation would be highly difficult to discover in humans. Some inborn errors of metabolism in humans are known to be helped by nutrients, but in these cases the gene-nutrient interaction is ameliorative rather than preventive as in the pallid mouse. Both kinds of nutrient-genetics interaction demonstrate a multifactorial causation that cannot be appropriately attributed to either genetics or nutrition alone.

Another kind of complexity is indicated by a recent disturbing finding that prenatal zinc deficiency in mice can have long-lasting effects on immune status, even in subsequent generations. When pregnant mice were given a moderately zinc-deficient diet during the last two thirds of gestation, their offspring had low immune functions for many months, even if they were nursed by normal mothers. Moreover, somewhat diminished immunocompetence persisted into the next two generations, despite provision of a normal diet (Beach, Gershwin, & Hurley, 1982). The mechanism of this astonishing effect and its possible relevance to human nutrition are presently unknown.

Animal studies gave us our first proof of the practical importance of nutrition in mammalian reproduction, and despite the uncertainties of relating animal results to humans, such studies continue to lead the way for human research and to provide vital information that is impossible or impractical to obtain with humans.

Prevention in Humans

Although mental retardation and other birth defects are most common in countries and in socioeconomic groups with the most malnutrition, and although other evidence also suggests that malnutrition contributes importantly to the incidence of mental defects, conclusive proof has been difficult to obtain in humans. Many authors grant little or no recognition to malnutrition in their estimates of the "known" causes of congenital defects. They typically attribute about 30%–40% of birth defects to inheritance, spontaneous mutations, maternal diseases or infections, drugs, and environmental toxins. The cause of the remaining 60%–70% is considered "unknown," at least in advanced nations (Brent, 1985). Nutritionists may note, however, that faulty nutrition may contribute to the incidence of several of these "known" causes, and some believe that the presently "unknown" majority of mental retardation in advanced nations will prove to be importantly linked to malnutrition (Hurley, 1985; Williams, 1971).

Starvation Conditions In developing countries or countries stricken with starvation and other obvious malnutrition, the incidence of mental retardation and other developmental defects is relatively high, and researchers are willing to include malnutrition among the known causes. For example, malnutrition together with infections (such as measles) is estimated to cause nearly half of mental disabilities in Nigeria (Adeyokunnu, 1985).

Numerous studies in developing countries worldwide have found that starvation (so-called protein-calorie malnutrition) during gestation or the first year or two of life is closely associated with mental retardation and other developmental defects (Brozek, 1977; Lloyd-Still, 1976; Manocha, 1972; Rush, Stein, & Susser, 1980; Somogyi & Haenel, 1982). Among infants who survive starvation during their first year of life and who then are re-fed, typically only a small fraction achieve normal intelligence in these countries, and their average IQ as adults may be only 60–70 (Winick, Meyer, & Harris, 1975). However, there is hopeful evidence that superior nutrition and environmental stimulation by age 5 can vastly improve on this record. Korean orphans who were severely starved for their first year of life but who were adopted by U.S. parents by age 3 had "normal" IQ (average 102) and school performance at age 10. This IQ was almost as high as for similar U.S.-adopted Koreans who had been "well nourished" all along (average 112). Later adoption (average age 5) was less beneficial (average 95), but nevertheless yielded far better intellectual development than was expected if the children had remained in Korea (Nguyen, Meyer, & Winick, 1977).

In these and other human studies, it is virtually impossible to assess the separate effects of nutrition and social environment because they are so closely associated in human populations. There is wide agreement, based partly on animal experiments, that either malnutrition or poor social environment alone *probably* can cause irreversible mental deficits, but that in practice, both factors interact strongly to produce the observed effects.

Unfortunately, protein-calorie malnutrition and its associated poor social environment are not restricted entirely to underdeveloped countries. Even in advanced nations, they may occur in children of those who are grossly ignorant of nutrition or who for various reasons lack the means or stability to provide minimally adequate nutrition during pregnancy and early growth.

Malnutrition in Advanced Nations Because of the ease with which obvious signs of food shortages may be seen in the poorest nations, or during war and natural disaster, some tend to regard serious malnutrition as easy to recognize and absent in advanced nations with abundant food. Full-figured citizens of such nations may be considered obviously "well nourished" or "overnourished." However, there are about 50 different nutrients that humans require, and virtually an unlimited number of ways that nutritional deficiencies, excesses, and imbalances can occur. The terms "undernourished," "well nourished," and "overnourished" are grossly inadequate to describe the vast complexities of nutrition.

Protein-calorie malnutrition (a misnomer because it also involves vitamin and mineral malnutrition) occurs usually in poor or stricken areas with inadequate *amounts* of otherwise relatively adequate foods. Other kinds of malnutrition that may occur readily in both poor and advanced nations involve inadequate *variety* and *quality* of foods selected.

Although technological advancement and abundant food supplies may nearly banish certain kinds of malnutrition, they unfortunately permit other kinds that are unlikely or impossible in less developed nations. The most important cases in point are malnutrition made possible by declining energy ("calorie") needs and by the "partitioning" or "dismembering" of large and increasing portions of the diets consumed in advanced western nations (Davis, 1983; Mertz, 1983). The major "dismembered" foods are purified sugars, separated fats (extracted vegetable oils and animal fats), highly milled grains, and distilled alcohol. Sugars, shortening, and milled grains are inexpensive, store well, and can be made into appealing products. They are the dominant ingredients in most cereal products, soft drinks, sweets, snacks, dips, and other fabricated foods. Although dismembered foods are among the most concentrated sources of energy, they supply little or none of the dozens of other nutrients present in all whole foods. Excessive consumption of such foods fosters types of deficiency and imbalance that are unlikely in more active and less developed nations.

It is a little-appreciated fact that dismembered foods constitute well over half of the dry weight and energy content of most diets in advanced western nations. In the United States, purified sugars, separated fats, and milled grains each supply 15%–20% of the food energy consumed nationally, and alcohol supplies another 5%–10% (U.S. Department of Agriculture, 1978). Our wide availability of fresh, whole plant and animal foods helps mitigate this situation, but there remain unfortunate opportunities for malnutrition fostered by low energy requirements, nutritional ignorance and complacency, and the taste appeal and convenience of foods fabricated from dismembered ingredients. These facts help make understandable what has been to some the surprising evidence of widespread marginal malnutrition in developed nations, including during pregnancy.

Nutrition Surveys in North America   National nutrition surveys in the United States and Canada have consistently found a substantial incidence of poor dietary habits and marginal biochemical measures of nutritional status. A few studies have focused on pregnant women, with similar results.

Early surveys in the United States assessed dietary intakes of households. A 1965 survey used recollections of 7-day food purchases in 7,500 representative households (U.S. Department of Agriculture, 1969). Nutrient intakes were calculated and compared with the recommended dietary allowances (RDAs). Only half of the households had "good" diets estimated to meet the RDAs for all nine nutrients studied. Twenty-one percent had "poor" diets that supplied less than two thirds of the RDA for one or more nutrients. High income facilitated good diets, but "high income alone was no assurance of good diets." Ten years earlier in 1955, consumption of milk, vegetables, and fruit was higher, and consumption of soft drinks, chips, pastries, and sweets was lower than in 1965. As a result, "Fewer households had good diets in 1965 than in 1955—50% in 1965 compared with 60% in 1955. The proportion with poor diets increased from 15% to 21% over the 10-year period" (p. 1).

Two larger surveys in the United States and Canada attracted wide attention, partly because they included biochemical assessments of nutritional status in addition to estimated nutrient intakes. The Ten-State Nutrition Survey of primarily poor individuals "indicated that a significant proportion of the population surveyed was malnourished or was at high risk of developing nutritional problems" (U.S. Department of Health, Education, and Welfare, 1972, p. 8). "Low or deficient" biochemical status for one or more of six nutrients studied was found in 27%–67% of individuals in various subgroups (p. IV-292).

The Canadian survey sampled the broad population and found that "communities classified above the poverty line have the same prevalence of nutrition problems as those in the poverty zone" (Sabry, Campbell, Campbell, & Forbes, 1974, p. 12). Among pregnant women, 5%–43% were judged to show moderate or high risk of nutritional deficiencies by *each* of eight biochemical measures: serum protein, hemoglobin, hemoglobin/hematocrit, transferring saturation, serum folate, serum calcium, serum vitamin A, and serum vitamin C (Nutrition Canada, 1973). Three other biochemical measures were relatively satisfactory: urinary thiamin, riboflavin, and iodine.

Further studies have found similar results, including the recent U.S. Department of Agriculture (1983) survey cited earlier. Surveys of magnesium status are mentioned in the following section.

Smaller studies focusing exclusively on middle-class pregnant women in Quebec have been reported by Vobecky and co-workers. In a preliminary study of dietary habits, they concluded that the women's diets predisposed significant numbers of them to the possibility of nutritional deficiencies. Later, they assessed biochemical measures of nutritional status at the end of pregnancy (Vobecky et al., 1982). Blood was taken at the time of delivery from 556 dominantly middle-class mothers who had uneventful pregnancies. *Average* serum levels of all nutrients were well above those generally considered adequate. However, 20% of the women were judged "deficient" in one or more nutrients. Including subjects with "marginal" serum levels, 5%–21% were found at risk regarding each of five nutrients (protein, vitamin C, folic acid, calcium, and iron as measured by hematocrit or hemoglobin). Only vitamin E and serum-free iron were marginal in less than 5% of subjects. The authors concluded that their data, "demonstrate the risk of nutritional deficiency in the newborn even with uneventful pregnancies in an economically favored population" (p. 640). These findings have implications about nutritional status during both pregnancy and early postnatal development.

Citizens of western nations surely have the *potential* to obtain good nutrition. However, widespread ignorance and complacency (both public and professional) are largely responsible for a continuing major consumption of low-nutrient "dismembered" foods. Consequently substantial portions of North Americans have marginal nutrient intakes and unsatisfactory biochemical measures of nutritional status. These facts need increased recognition by those who seek to understand and prevent mental retardation and other failures of reproduction.

Prevention of Preeclampsia and Eclampsia Preeclampsia (previously called "toxemia of pregnancy") is a serious complication of late pregnancy characterized by hypertension and urinary albumin, usually with edema. In the United States it occurs in about 5% of pregnancies, kills over 35,000 babies annually, and leaves many thousands more mentally retarded or crippled. Contraction or spasm of the blood vessels restricts circulation to many organs, including to the placenta and fetus. Fetal growth retardation and premature delivery are common unfavorable outcomes. In its advanced forms, preeclampsia involves clotting disorders, widespread maternal organ damage, and grave danger to the fetus. Mental retardation due to preeclampsia probably relates to various factors. These include restricted circulation and fetal malnutrition, oxygen deprivation, premature birth, and premature separation of the placenta—an emergency in which the baby must be delivered immediately if it is to survive undamaged. Preeclampsia also threatens the mother who may experience severe seizures (eclampsia), stroke, blindness, and even death.

This ancient scourge of pregnancy has been called the "disease of theories," reflecting the remarkable variety of causes that have been proposed (Chesley, 1978). Maternal malnutrition is currently considered suspect by authors of medical texts (de Alvarez, 1982; Pritchard, MacDonald, & Gant, 1985). However, some practicing physicians consider it beyond dispute that malnutrition is intimately involved in preeclampsia (Brewer, 1966; Hamlin, 1952), although in ways that cannot be determined from their work. Current research promises that understanding and proof of nutritional factors will be forthcoming. However, before considering this evidence we should note that, as with all metabolic disorders, complex interactions of nutrition with genetic and other environmental factors must be expected. In fact, hereditary influences are suggested for preeclampsia, and its peculiar tendency to occur primarily in first pregnancies also points to multiple causative factors.

Hamlin (1952) cited the incidence of seizures (eclampsia) in various British commonwealth hospitals as one case in 200–600 pregnancies. These rates had changed little over the years, with or without conscientious prenatal care. Between 1936 and 1947, the rate of eclampsia was one case in 350 pregnancies (106 in 36,700) at an Australian women's hospital where Hamlin became the medical superintendent. After 3 years of a diet-centered prevention program, the rate dropped dramatically, reaching zero seizures in 5,000 consecutive patients the third year. Serious preeclampsia also declined sharply, and there were no cesarean deliveries in preeclampsia patients the last year.

In 1963, Brewer began a similar diet-oriented prevention program at his county prenatal clinics for low socioeconomic class women in California (Brewer, 1966). The diet emphasized high protein and whole foods: dairy products, meat, seafood, fruits and vegetables, nuts and seeds, and whole grains, with salt to taste. Weight gain was not restricted, and drugs were avoided. Over half of the patients belonged to ethnic minorities (black, Mexican, American Indian, Oriental), and two thirds of those having their first babies were teenagers. Usually these groups of poor women have high rates of preeclampsia (up to 30% in some areas). But in over 7,000 pregnancies during the 12 years of this project, Brewer reported preeclampsia in only 0.5%, far below the national average, with not a single case of eclampsia (Brewer & Brewer, 1977).

What seems even more remarkable than these results is the disinterested reception they received from medical scientists. Many hundreds of sophisticated studies have focused on the most minute details of the *pathology* of preeclampsia, including clinical, histological, immunological, biochemical, and hormonal aspects. Many more studies have dealt with various aspects of *early diagnosis* and *treatment,* including drugs. But surprisingly, very little research has focused on *prevention,* especially on following up Hamlin's and Brewer's dramatic evidence that prevention is possible.

Follow-up studies are surely needed, because Hamlin's and Brewer's methods might well be improved, and their success might not have been entirely or even primarily for the reasons they thought (high protein intake). Unfortunately, during the time when such studies might have begun, a generation of pregnant women was given unproven low-salt and weight-restricting diets to prevent preeclampsia, often with diuretic drugs—all of which are now abandoned as worthless and harmful (Hemminki, 1984; Lindheimer, 1980; Pritchard et al., 1985).

Magnesium Over 60 years ago, it became accepted that injected magnesium sulfate can prevent or stop the seizures of eclampsia. Large doses of injected magnesium are still considered by obstetricians to be the preferred "anticonvulsant drug" in severe preeclampsia or eclampsia. Recent research indicates that this treatment works by partially correcting magnesium deficiency, which causes abnormal contractions of "smooth" muscles in maternal and fetal blood vessels and elsewhere (Altura, Altura, & Carella, 1983). The effect of magnesium ion on muscle tone may reflect the ion's essential role in regulating the permeability of cell membranes to calcium ion. Too little magnesium permits entry of excess calcium into cells, causing abnormal contractions.

Magnesium deficiency also may lead to deficient production of prostacyclin (prostaglandin I_2), a potent smooth muscle relaxant and inhibitor of platelet aggregation that is known to be deficient in preeclamptic women (Watson, Moldow, Ogburn, & Jacob, 1986). By causing abnormal platelet "stickiness," magnesium and prostacyclin deficiency may also contribute to the dangerous clotting disorders of preeclampsia.

Besides consuming adequate magnesium, another way to increase deficient prostaglandin levels might be to consume more of their fatty acid precursors. In a recent exploratory study, 4 g/day of evening primrose oil plus selected other nutrients (not including magnesium) were given to pregnant women. The supplements did not affect normal blood pressure, but they reduced the pregnancy-induced hypertensive reaction to angiotensin II (O'Brien, Morrison, & Broughton Pipkin, 1985). This suggests that dietary fatty acids and/or the other nutrients also may affect susceptibility to preeclampsia.

Until recently, dietary deficiencies of magnesium were widely assumed to be rare. However, recent knowledge about the magnesium content of foods and diets shows that marginal intakes predominate in the United States and that clearly deficient intakes readily occur with diets low in whole foods. It is not widely appreciated that all whole foods contain significant magnesium in relation to their calorie content, whereas all dismembered foods do not (Davis, 1983). In a national survey by the U.S. Department of Agriculture, 80%–85% of women had magnesium intakes below the recommended dietary allowance (RDA) (Morgan, Stampley, Zabik, & Fischer, 1985). Several studies of pregnant or lactating women have found that average magnesium intakes are only about half of the RDA (Moser, Issa, & Reynolds, 1983).

Altura et al. (1983) cite evidence that serum magnesium levels often fall in late pregnancy, especially in preeclampsia, and that placentas from women with preeclampsia and eclampsia exhibit depressed magnesium levels. They suggest also that magnesium deficiency might help explain the high incidence of infant mortality and congenital malformations in regions with soft water and magnesium-poor soils.

Direct human evidence was presented recently that small or moderate (RDA) amounts of magnesium supplementation during pregnancy help prevent preeclampsia (July 1985, International Symposium on Magnesium). The supplements reduced the incidence of pregnancy-induced hypertension, fetal growth retardation, and premature deliveries (Conradt, Weidinger, & Algayer, 1985). Other reports supported these findings and gave evidence that modest magnesium supplements also help prevent other obstetrical disorders, including muscle cramps, premature labor, and premature rupture of amniotic membranes (abstracts in *Journal of the American College of Nutrition,* 1985, *4,* 319–321, 375–376.)

Other Nutrients   The recent surge of interest in magnesium is surely valuable. However, it should be balanced with the knowledge that individual nutrients always function in conjunction with others, and that diets that are low in magnesium are likely to be low in other nutrients. Excessive concern with a single nutrient is potentially detrimental, because balance is needed among various nutrients, especially minerals. Heavy magnesium supplementation of a broadly poor diet, for example, might aggravate shortages of calcium, zinc, iron, and possibly vitamin B_6. This is one of the key advantages of emphasizing a variety of whole foods as the foundation for good nutrition. When supplements are used, consideration should be given to avoiding unnecessarily large dose levels and to ensuring the kind of balance among nutrients that exists in well-chosen food.

Probably other nutrients will eventually receive some of the attention magnesium is beginning to attract. Dietary precursors of prostaglandins are mentioned above. Calcium is another nutrient that may play a role in preventing preeclampsia, and it is well known to function in conjunction with magnesium. Pregnant women who had hypertension (but not preeclampsia) showed slightly depressed serum levels of ionized calcium and parathyroid hormone (Varner, Cruikshank, & Pitkin, 1983). Belizan and colleagues have reviewed evidence suggesting the importance of calcium in preventing preeclampsia and have shown that calcium supplements tend to lower blood pressure in normal pregnant women and in animals (Belizan et al., 1983).

Vitamin B_6 metabolism seems to be disturbed in preeclampsia (Klieger, Evrard, & Pierce, 1966). Ellis, a practicing physician, has reported that large doses of vitamin B_6 often control edema of pregnancy and preeclampsia (Ellis & Presley, 1973). (Ellis is also a pioneer in reporting benefits from magnesium supplements in preeclampsia.) Interestingly, vitamin B_6 supplements strongly increase the magnesium content of plasma and red blood cells in women (Abraham, Schwartz, & Lubran, 1981).

Others have suggested roles for thiamin and iron (Chadhuri, 1970), and folic acid (Hibbard, 1964; Shojania, 1984).

Clearly, much remains to be learned about the role of nutrition in the prevention of preeclampsia-eclampsia and the mental retardation that it can cause. However, it also seems clear that we already know enough empirically to hope that basic nutritional improvements to commonly marginal U.S. diets can greatly reduce the incidence of this major crippler of children. The time seems near when medical texts will no longer say that the etiology of preeclampsia is "unknown."

Prevention of Neural Tube Defects   Evidence for dramatic prevention of neural tube defects by nutritional means has been accumulating since 1980, following suspicions that began about 15 years earlier. The recent evidence comes from studies in the British Isles where these malformations of the brain and spinal cord are the most common serious congenital abnormality (3–10 per 1,000 births, a few times higher than in the United States). Dietary improvements or modest nutritional supplements were prescribed in several hundred women who had previously given birth to an affected child. Compared to untreated controls who had the expected recurrence rate of about 5%, treated women had less than 1% recurrences.

The significance of this apparent breakthrough is twofold. First, it indicates a simple means to prevent a notable cause of mental retardation and crippling physical defects. In the United States there are about 5,000 live births per year with significant neural tube defects (spina bifida and anencephaly). Roughly three times as many more cases miscarry or spontaneously abort. About half of the 5,000 live babies die shortly after birth, and the survivors have varying degrees of physical and mental handicaps, usually including hydrocephalus.

Second, and more importantly, this discovery promises to be the first unquestionable proof *in humans* that a significant congenital defect is related to inadequate nutrition. This demonstration should convince many who have been reluctant to accept the implications of animal research and nutrition knowledge. It should also encourage a broad search for nutritional factors in most other birth defects, especially among the two thirds of defects for which the cause is still unknown. If this search is as successful as many nutrition scientists hope, it will give us the means (but not necessarily the practical ability) to prevent at least half of all congenital mental retardation now occurring in developed nations.

Folic acid (folacin) is the nutrient currently receiving the most attention regarding neural tube defects in the British Isles, but the probable limiting role of other vitamins or minerals is under study. Several kinds of evidence suggest that deficiency of the trace mineral zinc causes neural tube defects (Bergmann, Makosch, & Tews, 1980; Buamah, Russell, Bates, Ward, & Skillen, 1984; Cavdar, Arcasoy, Baycu, & Himmetoglu, 1980; Sever, 1975). Sandstead (1984) has reviewed evidence that zinc deficiencies also impair learning and cause brain malformations of other kinds.

The most critical time for preventing neural tube defects presumably occurs during the first few weeks of pregnancy when the neural tube forms and closes to make an enclosure for the brain and spinal cord. Therefore, needed dietary improvements or supplements should begin before a woman knows she is pregnant, and preferably well before she conceives. Prevention of these defects (and potentially many others) is an educational and social issue, not one amenable to ordinary prenatal care.

Several authors have reviewed the emergence of this discovery (Dobbing, 1983; Laurence, 1985; Main & Mennuti, 1986; Nevin, 1985). Key observations included: evidence of complex genetic and environmental influences, strong association with low socioeconomic status, association with conception in the winter and early spring when supplies of some foods are limited, similarity with birth defects in folic acid-deficient animals, a few cases associated with use of folic acid antagonists during pregnancy, low blood levels of folic acid and other nutrients in the first trimester of pregnancies with a neural tube defect, association with poor diet, prevention of recurrences in women advised to improve their diet before conception, and prevention of recurrences in two large-scale (but imperfectly controlled) studies of supplementation before conception, either with folic acid alone or with folic acid combined with other nutrients.

The evidence is sufficiently strong that many observers now recommend vitamin supplementation prior to conception, at least in women who are at high risk (Main & Mennuti, 1986; Smithells, 1984). Also, placebo-controlled experiments are now generally considered both unethical and impractical— the latter because few informed women will consent to such experiments.

Skeptics remain, however, and British researchers under the auspices of the Medical Research Council are conducting a 5-year, randomized clinical trial (Wald & Polani, 1984). It measures recurrences in women who are given various kinds of supplements, including minerals without folic acid. Other confirming studies are in progress in the United States. If these studies support the prior findings, they will hasten a major shift coming in scientific and medical opinion about the potential of improved nutrition to prevent human birth defects in western nations. An example of the kinds of new research to be expected are a few studies that suggest that preconceptional vitamin supplements can reduce the recurrence rate of cleft lip and cleft palate (Tolarova, 1982).

Nutrition-genetics interactions must always be expected. In the case of neural tube defects, a genetic influence has long been indicated, and a recent abstract suggests a possible mechanism for such influence (Yates et al., 1985). Twenty women who had borne two or more infants with neural tube defects showed considerably less folic acid in their red blood cells than did a matched control group. Yet there was no significant difference between these groups in serum folic acid or other vitamins, and little difference in dietary intake of folic acid or other vitamins. Depressed red cell folic acid may reflect an elevated metabolic need that is associated with susceptibility to offspring with neural tube defects. If so, these and some other susceptible women may have above-average folic acid requirements, and the cited nutritional interventions may have succeeded in part by meeting such elevated needs.

Drugs and Toxins   Drugs and toxins exert their effects (desired and undesired) by interfering with various aspects of metabolism, including the enzymes that govern nearly all chemical changes in the body. Drugs and toxins never act alone, but always in the context of an individual's metabolism. Because the whole range of nutrients enters into all metabolism—including the building and function of all enzymes—nutritional status always interacts with the metabolic effects of drugs and toxins. When these substances act to produce mental retardation (either congenitally or postnatally), superior nutrition is potentially able to prevent or limit the retardation, and able to help reverse it if it is reversible. Examples discussed here include various nutrients that reduce susceptibility to drug-induced birth defects and nutrients that protect against and help reverse the neurotoxicity of lead and other heavy metals.

It should be emphasized that genetically based individual differences in metabolism also affect the actions of drugs and toxins as well as the response to nutritional factors. It is seldom, if ever, appropriate to consider mental retardation to be caused solely by any single factor. Generally, there is a complex interaction between multiple genetic factors, environmental stresses, and nutritional status (Hackman & Hurley, 1984; Williams, 1971). This multifactorial causation presents both challenges and opportunities for those seeking to prevent or treat mental retardation by nutritional means—challenges to deal with the complexities and opportunities such as the ability to alter environmentally the effects of unalterable genes.

Even when a single agent, such as the drug thalidomide, seems to be the obvious ''cause'' of birth defects, important nutritional and genetic interactions must be expected. This greatest recognized episode of drug-induced birth defects (about 8,000 births from 1959 to 1962) most likely involved disturbed fetal nutrition during early pregnancy. There is excellent evidence from animals and microorganisms that thalidomide interferes with biochemical processes involving riboflavin, niacin, and pantothenic acid (Frank et al., 1962; Fratta, Sigg, & Maiorana, 1965; Friedman, Shue, & Hove, 1965; Leck & Millar, 1962; Rauen, 1963; Riva & Uboldi, 1964). Low levels of these vitamins and the mineral zinc (Jackson & Schumacher, 1979) enhance the interfering effects of thalidomide. The human fetuses most damaged by thalidomide presumably came from those mothers with the lowest status of these nutrients and possibly others.

Genetic influences apparently have not been studied or noted for thalidomide except for the tragic fact that this drug did not produce birth defects in premarketing tests with some species of (well-nourished) animals.

Drugs Many drugs capable of inducing birth defects in animals are known to interact strongly with nutritional and genetic factors. This knowledge has been accumulating for over three decades, but its human implications are not well appreciated by many researchers and policymakers. Runner (1967) reviewed early studies of drug-nutrient-genetic interactions. More recent reviews emphasize interactions with several B vitamins, ascorbic acid, calcium, potassium, zinc, copper, manganese, and iron (Hackman & Hurley, 1984; Roe, 1976). An important example is the finding in rats that aspirin-related birth defects are fostered by marginal zinc intake and depend also on rat strain. Aspirin is a most commonly taken drug during pregnancy, and its use is suspected to induce birth defects in humans (Roe, 1976). Hackman and Hurley (1984) emphasize the relevance of existing research to the potential prevention of human birth defects and conclude, "women who have marginal deficiencies of essential nutrients may be more susceptible to the teratogenic effects of drugs than are those in good nutritional status. . . . Carefully controlled human studies are needed" (p. 322).

Human research on drug-nutrient interactions during pregnancy is poorly developed, but a pioneering series of advances illustrates its promise. Infants of epileptic mothers have long been known to have elevated rates of major congenital malformations—about 2%–11%, or roughly double or triple "normal" rates in the United States. The malformations include primarily heart defects, neural tube defects, cleft palate, and mental retardation. Some believe these malformations are often caused by the disease of epilepsy, rather than by the drugs used to treat it. However, at least one anticonvulsant, diphenylhydantoin (Dilantin), is known to produce birth defects in rodents and probably in humans (Monson et al., 1973; Speidel & Meadow, 1974). Diphenylhydantoin, phenobarbital, and primidone (all anticonvulsants) are also well known to reduce blood levels of folic acid (Roe, 1976). However, as late as 1984 it was argued that there was no basis for increasing folic acid intake in pregnant women receiving anticonvulsant drugs (Hackman & Hurley, 1984).

Suggestive evidence for the value of folic acid supplementation came from Israel that same year. Biale and Lewenthal (1984) reported results of a small prospective study of folic acid supplementation (2.5–5 mg/day) before and during pregnancy in women taking anticonvulsive drugs. No malformations occurred in 33 children born to 22 supplemented mothers, whereas up to about five were expected according to their retrospective controls who took no folic acid. If this finding is confirmed in larger and more rigorous studies, it will apparently be the first direct proof in humans that nutritional improvements can reduce the incidence of drug-related birth defects. Confirmation also would emphasize the value of animal research and encourage further studies in humans regarding other drugs.

Another aspect of drug-nutrient interactions probably needs increased public and professional (Brent, 1982) recognition more than it needs further research: Strictly avoiding *all* drugs whenever possible during pregnancy and somewhat before pregnancy is the surest way to prevent drug-related fetal malnutrition and birth defects.

Alcohol Drinking during pregnancy is a double risk to the unborn. Alcohol is a drug capable of disrupting fetal metabolism and development, *and* it is potentially a major source of food energy (''calories'')—energy very deficient in the nutrients that every mother needs to consume for her developing child. Both the drug and ''empty calorie'' aspects of alcohol conspire against optimal fetal development.

Alcohol consumption during pregnancy has been suspected since ancient times to cause mental and physical birth defects (Abel, 1984). Remarkably, however, the dangers of drinking during pregnancy were not significantly recognized in the modern era until 1973, when alcohol-induced defects were independently discovered, given the name ''fetal alcohol syndrome,'' and prominently published in the scientific literature. Since then many hundreds of reports have confirmed and extended these findings, as reviewed by several authors (Abel, 1984, 1986; Colangelo & Jones, 1982; Hill & Kleinberg, 1984; Streissguth, Landesman-Dwyer, Martin, & Smith, 1980). This difficulty of recognition by scientists is noteworthy and disquieting because alcohol is now generally considered to be a leading cause of congenital defects in the western world, seriously affecting at least 4,000 births annually in the United States.

Fetal alcohol syndrome consists primarily of small size at birth; low growth rate; malformations of the brain, heart, and other structures; mental deficits; and a distinctive pattern of facial anomalies. Small brain size, mild to moderate mental retardation, and behavioral disturbances are common, with the severity generally correlated with the mother's alcohol intake. The characteristic facial features include narrow forehead, short palpebral fissures (eye openings), epicanthal (corner of eye) folds, short nose, low nasal bridge, indistinct philtrum (the ridges between nose and mouth), thin upper lip, and rotated ears. The retardation and behavioral effects such as irritability and short attention span persist even in children given remedial help and foster care at birth; hence these effects cannot be attributed to being raised by an alcoholic mother, as they were in past decades.

Although the distinctive facial features of fetal alcohol syndrome (FAS) have attracted attention, maternal alcoholism seems to cause mental impairments even in the absence of visible FAS. Some of this retardation might be caused by postnatal influences associated with maternal alcoholism, but available evidence suggests that congenital brain malformations and mental retardation can occur independently of the facial features and slow growth of FAS.

Prevalence of the full FAS is now estimated at about 2.5%–3% of live births from alcoholic mothers, and much higher, about 10%, for partial effects (Colangelo & Jones, 1982). These figures exclude the high incidence of damaged fetuses that die during pregnancy or near birth. Earlier estimates of 20%–40% incidence of FAS were based on samples of the most extreme alcoholic mothers. Expressed in terms of all births, the prevalence of FAS is commonly estimated at 1 in 750 births in the United States.

Besides alcohol consumption, many other factors yet to be assessed presumably affect the incidence of FAS, including genetic susceptibility, nutritional status (Colangelo & Jones, 1982; Hackman & Hurley, 1984), and maternal use of other drugs and tobacco. Although dietary improvements or nutritional supplements in alcoholics might reduce the incidence of FAS, a favorable outlook for alcohol-drugged pregnancy seems beyond reach. If so, the potential value of research on the nutrient lacks associated with FAS may be of more academic than practical value.

The mechanisms of alcohol damage remain unknown. Worrisome animal experiments reviewed by Graham (1985) suggest that there may be a critical time during gestation when the fetus is especially vulnerable, and that a single, ill-timed "binge" of alcohol consumption might produce FAS or mental retardation. The most critical time in animals corresponds to about the third week of human pregnancy, a time when many women are not yet aware they are pregnant.

Heavy drinking during pregnancy is now universally agreed to be dangerous and important to avoid. There is somewhat less agreement about the risks of social or moderate alcohol consumption during pregnancy, and about what to recommend to prospective mothers. The full FAS apparently requires heavy maternal drinking, but lesser "fetal alcohol effects" seem to occur even with moderate levels of alcohol consumption (two or three drinks per day). These effects include miscarriage and stillbirth, low birth weight, congenital anomalies, and a variety of behavioral disturbances (Colangelo & Jones, 1982; Graham, 1985). Based on this suggestive evidence, most observers recommend against all alcohol consumption by women attempting conception and during pregnancy, at least until "safe" levels may be determined.

This advice is in line with the general principles of restricting "empty calorie" foods and avoiding all possible drugs during pregnancy. Unfortunately, those women who could most benefit from such advice are probably the least likely to hear it or heed it. The problem of alcohol-induced mental retardation well illustrates the gap mentioned at the outset between what we know and what we can apply (Nathan, 1983). Nevertheless, the current extensive interest and research in FAS reflects our belief that millions of women are vitally interested in learning *and* applying all they can to produce healthy babies. At least for them, the recently recognized dangers of alcohol consumption during pregnancy are a great step forward.

Lead We turn now to environmental toxins that cannot be avoided in the way that drugs usually can. Lead is regarded by many as the most important industrial pollutant because of its current high levels in humans and its propensity to cause mental retardation, mental impairment, and many other adverse effects. Lead's conceivable significance to mental retardation can be compared with the thalidomide disaster. If lead contributes significantly to only 1% of all mental retardation in developed nations, it would be claiming about as many victims *every year* as did thalidomide for a brief time (several thousand births).

This order of magnitude seems plausible or conservative because of growing evidence that lead is associated with measurable mental impairment in most children from industrial nations, and with serious risk in a few percent of them (Bryce-Smith, 1986; Charney, 1982; Lin-Fu, 1982; Needleman, 1980; Needleman, Geiger, & Frank, 1985; Needleman et al., 1979; Thatcher & Lester, 1985; Yule, Lansdown, Millar, & Urbanowicz, 1981). The emerging consensus holds that lead has serious effects on the central nervous system at levels that only two decades ago were believed safe. Fetuses and infants are especially vulnerable to the neurotoxicity of lead because of their rapidly developing nervous systems and because children usually absorb lead much more efficiently than adults (Chisolm & O'Hara, 1982).

In a recent study, the "normal" range of umbilical cord blood levels at birth correlated inversely with infant mental development during the first year of life in middle- and upper middle-class populations (Bellinger, Leviton, Needleman, Waternaux, & Rabinowitz, 1986). Similarly, a preliminary report indicates that placental lead and cadmium correlate inversely with birth weight and head circumference in obstetrically normal births (Bryce-Smith, 1986).

Excessive lead exposure during pregnancy has long been linked to congenital mental retardation and a variety of other common birth defects (Beattie et al., 1975; Needleman, Rabinowitz, Leviton, Linn, & Schoenbaum, 1984). Recent research indicates that lead toxicity also contributes significantly to many minor physical anomalies at birth (Needleman et al., 1984). However, compared with the available assessments of lead-related minor physical and mental impairments in the broad population, little is known about lead's contribution (pre- or postnatally) to the incidence of overt mental retardation.

Studies of children with mental retardation in the United States, Scotland, and Greece have found significantly elevated blood or hair lead levels compared with controls, including equally retarded controls living in the same institution but whose retardation was attributable to causes other than lead (Beattie et al., 1975; David, Hoffman, McGann, Sverd, & Clark, 1976; Marlowe, Folio, Hall, & Errera, 1982; Moore, 1980; Youroukos, Lyberatos, Tsomi, Philippidou, & Gardikas, 1978). Although these studies together strongly suggest a causative role for lead, they do not permit unambiguous interpretation. Elevated body lead levels might be caused *by* the retardation rather than be a cause *of* it (from pica or exaggerated hand-to-mouth contamination). High body levels in the children might reflect lead in the mother's environment during gestation, which caused the retardation prenatally and incidentally also later led to high levels in the child. Or the high lead levels might reflect postnatal or ongoing damage from excessive lead acquired since birth. That ongoing damage plays some part is suggested by reports that lead removal by chelating drugs often improves behavior and sometimes raises IQ in retarded children who have no known brain damage (Moncreiff et al., 1964). Further research seems urgent to clarify the role of lead in congenital and postnatal mental retardation, because of the possibly large numbers of children involved, and because lead toxicity is largely preventable.

As suggested above, two aspects of lead toxicity may be distinguishable. One aspect involves an ongoing metabolic toxicity that would be reversible if it were possible to remove or inactivate the lead. The second aspect involves irreversible developmental defects caused during gestation or postnatal growth, defects that would remain even if the offending lead were removed. Currently active toxicity may predominate in the minor mental impairments documented so far, but congenital and other past damage may be equally or more important in frank mental retardation, and probably will be more difficult to prove. Innovative research methods may be required to evaluate these potential contributions of lead to mental retardation and to find the most effective methods of prevention and therapy, including nutritional methods.

Because of the growing evidence of widespread harm from current lead levels, the U.S. Environmental Protection Agency reduced lead amounts permitted in gasoline in 1982 and 1985, and it proposes an accelerated total elimination by 1988 (Sun, 1985). (Some regard these actions as long overdue for political reasons [Bryce-Smith & Stephens, 1980; Schoenbrod, 1980].) The value of these steps is indicated by the report that average blood lead levels in the United States fell by about one third between 1976 and 1980, paralleling the declining use of leaded gasoline (Mahaffey, Annest, Roberts, & Murphy, 1982). However, lead from gasoline still contributes perhaps half of the lead intake in most Americans, primarily through contamination of food and air. Other lead sources include old paints, soldered food cans, ingestion of contaminated dust, some pottery glazes, and water pipes in some countries. Lead was eliminated from most paints produced in the United States after the early 1940s, but large amounts remain in many old houses, and paint is still considered the most common source of serious lead toxicity in children (Lin-Fu, 1982). A recent finding of ubiquitous high levels in soils of an inner city suggest that ingestion of city dust and soil also may contribute importantly to the lead problem (Mielke et al., 1983).

Steps to reduce lead exposure are fundamental, but worldwide lead pollution is great (100–1,000 times preindustrial levels [Patterson, 1980]), and superior nutrition is potentially the most important protection against lead pollution. Improved nutrition is especially desirable in the low socioeconomic groups that have the highest levels of body lead and the poorest diets (Mahaffey et al., 1982; O'Hara, 1982). Nutrition's foreseeable role is primarily preventive, because removal of body lead is difficult, and the most serious toxic effects appear irreversible.

A large body of animal and human research shows that nutritional factors afford substantial protection against lead toxicity (see reviews by Fox, 1975; Mahaffey, 1982; Mahaffey & Michaelson, 1980; Sandstead, 1977). Nutrients act primarily to reduce lead absorption and deposition and to increase its excretion. Calcium may be the most important protective nutrient, but good evidence indicates that phosphate, iron, zinc, magnesium, and fiber (Rose & Quarterman, 1984; Wapnir, Moak, & Lifshitz, 1980) are also protective. Except for phosphate, these nutrients are commonly ingested in the United States at less than recommended levels. Hence there is much room for increased resistance to lead toxicity by nutritional improvements, which are desirable for other reasons as well.

Still other nutrients also probably play protective roles, including selenium, chromium, and vitamins E and C (Mahaffey, 1982; Sandstead, 1977). In calves, large doses of injected thiamin (about 20 times usual intakes) prevented toxic symptoms from orally administered lead and greatly reduced deposition of lead in all tissues examined, especially kidney, liver, and brain (Bratton, Zmudzki, Bell, & Warnock, 1981). The authors note that lead is one of the most common sources of accidental poisoning in cattle, and that thaimin seems to have therapeutic as well as protective value.

Lead absorption is affected importantly not only by what is eaten but also by how frequently it is eaten. Lead ingested with a balanced meal or within 2 or 3 hours after eating is absorbed far less efficiently than lead ingested on an empty stomach (James, Hilburn, & Blair, 1985). Skipped meals may be among the dietary factors that contribute to observed variations in body lead levels.

Nutritional factors that increase lead absorption include low protein consumption, and—at least in rats—high fat intakes such as humans commonly consume in developed nations (Mahaffey, 1982). Unfortunately the protective value of the calcium in milk is partially offset by lactose and other milk components that aid lead absorption.

Although nutrients have been commonly regarded as protective rather than therapeutic for lead toxicity (Mahaffey, 1982), dietary and nutritional therapies are receiving renewed attention. Chemical chelating agents such as ethylenediaminetetraacetic acid (EDTA) and d-penicillamine are helpful and even life saving, but their use is limited to brief periods by side effects, including removal of unintended minerals. Nutritional treatments are potentially useful in combination with chelation therapy (Burgan, 1982; Flora, Singh, & Tandon, 1986; Goyer & Cherian, 1979) and could be safer alternatives in cases of mild toxicity.

Little is known yet about the effectiveness of these and other potential nutritional therapies. Abnormally high blood lead levels in battery workers dropped 25% after 4 months of treatment with high doses of zinc and vitamin C (60 and 2,000 mg/day, respectively), even though the workers remained on the job and exposed to lead (Papaioannou, Sohler, & Pfeiffer, 1978). The same regimen similarly reduced blood levels, other measures of toxicity, and behavior problems in psychiatric outpatients with moderately elevated but "normal" initial blood levels (Sohler, Kruesi, & Pfeiffer, 1977). Goyer and Cherian (1979) reported that vitamin C in combination with EDTA is more than twice as effective in rats as either agent alone, and that removal of lead from the central nervous system is especially benefited by this combination. The latter finding is potentially most significant. Remarkably similar synergistic effects are recently reported for thiamin combined with EDTA (Flora et al., 1986). Thiamin alone may have therapeutic potential also, as cited above. Nutritional therapies for lead toxicity have certainly not been thoroughly explored, and a broad approach using all potentially helpful nutrients seems most promising. Compared with drugs, nutrients have the great advantage that they are native to our bodies, and in judicious amounts can be used safely for indefinite periods.

Cadmium and Mercury Cadmium is another toxic metal implicated in mental dysfunctions including congenital defects (Capel, Pinnock, Dorrell, Williams, & Grant, 1981; Thatcher & Lester, 1985; Thatcher, Lester, McAlaster, & Horst, 1982). Body cadmium levels, like lead levels, are positively correlated with dyslexia, low cognitive functioning, poor school achievement, and abnormal electroencephalograms and evoked potentials. Also like lead, the detrimental effects of cadmium are dose dependent and appear to have no threshold. Elevated cadmium levels usually correlate strongly with elevated lead levels in children, and possibly cadmium is responsible for some of the effects associated with lead. However, lead and cadmium seem to be related to somewhat different aspects of mental functioning (Thatcher & Lester, 1985; Thatcher et al., 1982).

What causes elevated cadmium levels is uncertain. The known large effect of nutrition on lead absorption and the correlation between cadmium and lead levels in children suggest that cadmium is as widespread in the environment as lead, and that common nutritional factors are important in limiting the absorption of both metals. A study of 150 children found that cadmium in hair strongly correlated with consumption of refined carbohydrates (sugar and white flour products) (Lester, Thatcher, & Monroe-Lord, 1982). If refined carbohydrates "cause" increased body cadmium levels, they presumably do so indirectly by their lack of protective nutrients and their displacement from the diet of more wholesome foods. Further research is needed to determine the contribution of cadmium to mental deficiencies and congenital retardation in humans and to determine the role of nutrition in preventing and ameliorating cadmium's adverse effects. Extensive studies (mostly in animals) suggest that zinc, calcium, selenium, iron, vitamin C, and copper are most important (Fox, 1975; Sandstead, 1977; Thatcher & Lester, 1985).

Mercury is another heavy metal capable of causing severe brain damage and congenital mental retardation—most memorably in a village near Minamata Bay, Japan between 1953 and 1961. Organic mercury from industrial wastes flushed into the Bay severely affected adults and older children as well as infants born to mothers who ate contaminated fish during pregnancy. Serious incidents of neurological damage and death also have resulted from human and livestock consumption of seed grain treated with methyl mercury-containing fungicides (Kitamura, Sumino, Hayakawa, & Shibata, 1976).

A recent study found that modest elevations of hair mercury correlate with mild mental retardation, learning disabilities, and behavior disorders in children (Marlowe et al., 1986). Unfortunately, the authors failed to report lead or cadmium levels that might also account for or contribute to their findings. Much further research is needed to assess the role of mercury in mental retardation. Selenium is the nutrient best known to counter mercury toxicity, but others, including zinc, are probably important as well (Sandstead, 1977).

Uncontrolled Studies of Nutrition and IQ

"U" Series Nutrients and Drugs   Since 1940 Henry Turkel has treated several hundred Down syndrome subjects and some other retarded children with the "U" series of nutrients and drugs. The "U" series presently contains about 30 nutrients plus digestive enzymes, thyroid hormones, decongestants, antihistamines, a diuretic, and other drugs—all intended to promote physical and mental development and to counteract the metabolic abnormalities of Down syndrome and some other inborn disorders.

Turkel reports long-term physical and mental improvements in most Down subjects, including IQ gains and changes apparent in radiological and photographic records for a few subjects (Turkel, 1975; Turkel & Nusbaum, 1985). He also has reported striking mental and physical improvements in two children with other types of retardation (Turkel, 1981; Turkel & Nusbaum,

1985). One girl had initial IQ scores of 44 and 49 at ages 4 and 5. Treatment began at age 5½. She scored 72 at age 6, 65 at age 7, 64 at nearly 8, 85 later at age 8, and 82 at age 14. Initially retarded growth, short attention span, and severe strabismus (crossed eyes) improved greatly, and she graduated with average grades from a regular high school.

Apparently, the only independent report published in North America on the "U" series comes from Bumbalo, Morelewicz, and Berens (1964). They carried out a brief (1-year) double-blind trial of a modified "U" series in Down syndrome subjects and reported "no improvement" in the 12 treated subjects. Unfortunately, this one-page report curiously lacks data and statistical analysis needed to support its conclusion, and Turkel and Nusbaum (1985) point to other reasons for questioning it. Adequate evaluation of Turkel's approach has been hampered by premature judgments and by rancorous controversy between Turkel and the medical community and the U.S. Food and Drug Administration (Turkel, 1975; Turkel & Nusbaum, 1985).

Meanwhile, there are positive reports (some of uncertain publication) from studies in Japan by Makoto Iida of the Japanese National Institute of Mental Health and others. A practicing physician, T. Kurita (1977) reported better-than-expected survival, physical and mental gains, and parental satisfaction, but he acknowledges the difficulty of scientific interpretation due to lack of an untreated control group. Translations of reports by Iida and Ichiko Kurita (1969) and by T. Tomada (1974) are available from Turkel or a parents' group that supports his work (US for DS, 3323 Club Dr., Los Angeles, CA 90064). According to these translations, several thousand Down syndrome patients have been treated with a restricted "U" series in Japan since 1964, with benefit to most. Iida and Kurita report that 26 of 50 subjects showed IQ gains of 10 points or more after treatment for 2 years or more.

This extensive and long-term Japanese experience with the "U" series in Down syndrome should be an invaluable source of data, but regrettably it has not been adequately reported. Proponents of the "U" series might advance their case by scientific publication of long-term results from Japan, preferably in English and preferably with comparison to untreated Down children in Japan. Also, Turkel and other physicians who use the "U" series might promote further evaluation of this treatment if they supplemented Turkel's reports of a few dramatic cases with concise summaries of their entire experience with many hundreds of Down syndrome subjects.

A physician from Kyoto University noted the complexity of Turkel's regimen and decided to try large doses of 11 vitamins alone in about 60 Down syndrome children (Tanino, 1966). He reported both physical and mental improvements (including "almost normal level of mentation") in many subjects, especially in young boys treated for 5 years or more.

If the large gains reported by Turkel and the Japanese workers are replicable in significant numbers of other children with retardation, they are certainly important, but basic scientific questions would remain: What are the contributions (if any) of the nutrients and the various drugs, and what doses are needed? How much is lost by omitting the drugs as done by Tanino (1966)? Controlled studies are needed to answer such questions.

However, another question may be asked: Is it possible that the physician and parental expectations and stimulation alone cause most of the gains reported? If so, new kinds of scientific studies are needed, because traditional controlled studies merely *eliminate* such factors, without assessing their possible importance.

Controlled Studies of Nutrition and IQ

Controlled studies of nutrition and IQ have focused on glutamic acid or glutamine, vitamins, and multivitamin and mineral combinations, sometimes with thyroid supplements.

Glutamic Acid Reports in the 1940s of improved personality and mental acuity in children receiving glutamic acid for petit mal seizures led to almost 50 studies of mental functioning in children with retardation who were given either glutamic acid or a salt such as sodium glutamate. These studies have been reviewed by Astin and Ross (1960) and by Vogel, Broverman, Draguns, and Klaiber (1966). The two reviews present contrasting conclusions.

Astin and Ross (1960) selected (without noting the fact) only about half of the available literature for review. They observed that most of the selected positive studies used no control group and that when a control group was used, most of the studies were negative. They concluded that no benefit had been convincingly demonstrated. This certainly understandable view prevails today. Less understandably, however, no research to clarify the contradictory results seems to have been published.

Vogel et al. (1966) found many more positive studies with controls (14) than did Astin and Ross (6). They also corrected Astin and Ross's data in other ways and disputed Astin and Ross's assessment of even the selected studies originally reviewed. They noted that the positive studies tended to: 1) use noninstitutionalized subjects who were in school, 2) consider individual differences between different types of subjects with mental retardation, 3) vary the dosage levels for individuals, and 4) use glutamic acid, not a glutamate salt. They recommended more sophisticated and rigorous studies using subjects and experimental conditions that proved most favorable in the prior, positive experiments. Unfortunately, no such clarifying research appears to have been done.

Glutamine Rogers and Pelton (1957) contributed a promising sidelight to the glutamic acid issue, a sidelight that also has not been adequately pursued. They noted evidence that L-glutamine, the amine of glutamic acid, has essential metabolic functions that are poorly performed by glutamic acid. Glutamine is the dominant form in serum and cerebrospinal fluid, and plays a major role in brain metabolism. Rogers and Pelton (1957) suggested that some mental retardation may involve inadequate synthesis of glutamine from glutamic acid, and that relatively small doses of glutamine might work better or more reliably than glutamic acid. They carried out a brief (6-week) preliminary double-blind trial in 30 institutionalized children with retardation using a modest 1 g/day. They found an average IQ gain of about 4 points relative to the controls. Correction of the authors' understated statistical significance gives $p < 0.05$ by one-tailed t test or Mann-Whitney test. This finding was supported by Beley, Caustier, and Olievenstein (1964), and it would seem to call for longer term studies, preferably with noninstitutionalized children in school.

Vitamins Using nonretarded subjects, Kubala and Katz (1960) found that average IQ was 4.5 points higher in 72 students with plasma ascorbic acid levels exceeding 1.1 mg/dl than in 72 other students matched by socioeconomic criteria but with plasma ascorbic acid levels less than 1.1 mg/dl. When both groups were given supplemental orange juice for 6 months, most of this difference in IQ was abolished. From these statistically significant results, they concluded that some of the variance in IQ test performance is determined by the temporary nutritional state of intellectually normal individuals.

Maseck (1980) reported significant benefits in a partially controlled study of a modest multivitamin supplement given to students in a class for slow readers. The benefits included increased reading test scores and IQ (7 points by a "blind" tester), plus large reductions in absenteeism and disruptive behaviors compared to controls (nonblind). This type of study lends itself well to testing by rigorously controlled methods.

In a 6-month study of improved diet and vitamin supplements in 20 children with learning disabilities, the improved diet—with or without supplements—apparently produced large benefits in a variety of school behaviors (Kershner & Hawke, 1979). However, interpretation of this finding is uncertain due to lack of a control group with unchanged diet. The limited supplements (large doses of four vitamins) yielded no statistically significant additional benefits. However, a suggestive IQ increase of 4.6 points occurred only in the vitamin-supplemented group. These results warrant further studies of dietary improvements and supplements in children with learning disabilities.

Harrell Study This report of substantial IQ gains and other benefits in children with mental retardation grew out of unpublished work of Mary B. Allen (Harrell, Capp, Davis, Peerless, & Ravitz, 1981). Its findings attracted wide interest, controversy, and several follow-up studies. Sixteen school-age children living at home (IQ 17–70) received dietary advice and nutritional supplements or placebos during a planned 8-month study. Desiccated thyroid was also given throughout to 13 of the subjects, as required to maintain morning axillary temperature at 36.6°C or above (Barnes method). The supplement contained 11 vitamins, most in large amounts, and 8 minerals in moderate amounts.

During the first 4-month period (double blind), the 5 children receiving supplements (and thyroid) recorded average IQ gains of 5–10 points, depending on the investigator. However, the 11 placebo (and thyroid) subjects showed negligible average change (1 point), indicating that thyroid alone did not increase IQ in this experiment. During the second 4-month period, both groups received supplements (and thyroid). The IQs of the prior placebo subjects increased a reported 10 points on average, especially in the younger subjects, while some of the previously supplemented group showed additional gains. Three of four Down syndrome subjects recorded IQ gains of 11–24 points and showed physical changes toward normal. Other behavioral and health benefits also were reported.

Disappointingly, seven later studies using nearly the same nutritional supplement with about 125 retarded children and adults have all reported no significant average IQ gains (see Table 2). Furthermore, with the exception of one 18-point gain in a placebo subject, the later studies all reported no individual gains exceeding 10 points, whereas Harrell jointly with her co-testers reported gains over 10 points in many subjects (5 of 16 after 4 months and about 9 of 16 after 8 months). Also, apparently none of the later studies have found the academic, behavioral, or physical improvements Harrell noted. However, it is difficult to evaluate conclusions without data, such as, "no consistently striking reports of observed improvements" (Smith, Spiker, Peterson, Cicchetti, & Justine, 1984).

The discrepancies between the results of Harrell and seven later studies seem clear-cut, and they beg for exploration. Four of the follow-up studies involved institutionalized adults much older than Harrell's subjects (Table 2; groups led by Ellis, Coburn, Ellman, and Chanowitz). As noted by some of these researchers, the age and low IQ of the subjects and their relative lack of stimulation from school and home all made them unpromising candidates for quick improvements. Although worthwhile, these four experiments do not test the reproducibility of Harrell's findings in home-living children.

The remaining three studies more nearly approached the age and IQ of Harrell's subjects (Table 2; groups led by Bennett, McClelland, Kriegsmann, Andrus, & Sells, 1983; Smith et al., 1984; and Weathers, 1983). All three used entirely Down syndrome subjects who were more predominantly male than Harrell's subjects, but these two differences seem unable to explain the

Table 2. Comparison of the Harrell Study and seven follow-up studies

Author & date[a]	Subjects (No.)	Male (%)	Mean age & range	Mean IQ & range	Home living	Thyroid used	Design[b]	Group	IQ Change: mean (range)		IQ Tests
									4 Months	8 Months	
Harrell (1981)	16 4 Down	38	9.5 5–15	48 17–70	Yes	Desiccated, Barnes method, 0.5–2 grains/day	ST1 ST1 PT ST2 (ST2)	ST1 ST2 PT	5 (−2/10) 10 (2/22) 1 (−7/5)	14 (6/22) 16 (2/24)	S. Binet 84% WISC-R 10% Cattell 6%
Ellis (1983)	40 10 Down	60	29 21–40	26 12–40	No	No	S (7 mo.) P (7 mo.)	S P	— —	−1 (?/>4) −1	S. Binet
Weathers (1983)	47 All Down	66	11.4[c] 6–17	46 30–67	Yes	No	S P	S P	1 (−9/7)[c] 3 (−5/18)	—	S. Binet
Bennett (1983)	20 All Down	50	10.5 5–13	49 26–76	Yes	No	S P	S P	— —	−1 (−6/9) 1 (−7/6)	S. Binet
Coburn (1983)	38 9 Down	74	24 16–30	29 10–49	No	No	S (20 weeks) P (20 weeks)	S P	0 0	— —	S. Binet
Ellman (1984)	20 4 Down	50	22 16–24	39 22–56	No	No	S (6 mo.) P (6 mo.)	S P	1 (−4/7) 1 (−9/8)	— —	Leiter 95% S. Binet 5%
Smith (1984)	56 All Down	71	11.2 7–15	46 28–76	Yes	No	S S P P	S P	0 0	−1 (−9/9) −1 (−8/?)	WISC-R 50% WPPSI 50%
Chanowitz (1985)	37 ?	?	26 ?	15? ?	No	l-thyroxin[d], 0.15 mg/day	ST SP PT PP	ST SP PT PP	1 mo. MA[e] 0 mo. MA 0 mo. MA 0 mo. MA	—	Cattell 57% S. Binet 43%

[a]Harrell, Capp, Davis, Peerless, and Ravitz (1981); Ellis & Tomporowski (1983); Weathers (1983); Bennett, McClelland, Kriegsmann, Andrus, and Sells (1983); Coburn, Schaltenbrand, Mahuren, Clausman, and Townsend (1983); Ellman, Silverstein, Zingarelli, Schafer, and Silverstein (1984); Smith, Spiker, Peterson, Cicchetti, and Justine (1984); Chanowitz, Ellman, Silverstein, Zingarelli, and Ganger (1985).

[b]S = supplement; P = placebo; T = thyroid gland or hormone. S modifications: no biotin (Harrell); 1/3 vitamin A after 4 months (Smith).

[c]Weathers, J.C., Ph.D. dissertation, Georgia State University, 1982.

[d]Said to approximate 1.5 grains/day of desiccated thyroid.

[e]MA = mental age.

discrepant results, because Harrell's Down syndrome and male subjects did as well as the others. The major experimental difference in these three studies (which also applies to the adult studies, except perhaps one that used *l*-thyroxin) is their omission of the desiccated thyroid given to 13–15 subjects who needed it according to the Harrell protocol. This omission and possible synergistic interactions between thyroid and nutrients may be the only hope that Harrell's findings can yet be reproduced in unselected groups.

The "thyroid explanation" receives perhaps slight support from a 7-point IQ gain in one subject coincidentally taking thyroid in the study by Ellman et al. (1984) and from a recent anecdotal report (Rimland & Davis, 1986). However, it is weakened by average 13-point IQ gains in the two Harrell subjects who didn't take recommended thyroid. An important experiment in progress led by Menolascino includes thyroid (although in uniform dose) and will provide the first near replication of Harrell's study (see Chapter 1). (Some of the later researchers described their work too loosely as attempted "replications"; some failed to mention their omission of thyroid; and one downplayed the omission by misrepresenting Harrell's use of thyroid as "intermittent.")

Thyroid was omitted in the later studies mainly because of objections to the unorthodox method of prescribing it in the Harrell study. The Barnes functional method calls for giving thyroid to many individuals who do not need it according to current biochemical methods based on serum levels of thyroid hormones. Also, Harrell's thyroid-plus-placebo group showed no significant IQ change, and this fact regrettably led at least one research group to the unwarranted conclusion that "therefore, thyroid medication did not influence [Harrell's] final results" in the thyroid-plus-supplement group (Davis & Capp, 1985).

Other explanations for the discordant findings have been suggested or implied. The Harrell study was not fully double blind after the first 4 months, and strong investigator expectations may have affected half of the IQ tests at 8 months as well as other outcomes reported. Significantly, however, blind and skeptical independent testers reported IQ gains of 11–16 points in 4 or 5 of 15 subjects (S.R., T.C., D.D., S.O., R.S., who all took thyroid). This proportion of large individual gains contrasts sharply with the tiny incidence of gains over 10 points in the studies led by Weathers, Bennett et al., and Smith (1 out of 123; $p < 0.0005$ by Fisher's exact test).

The several large individual gains in Harrell's report are also inconsistent with the implication of Smith et al. (1984) that their superior matching of supplement and placebo groups and control of other variables could explain the discrepant findings (Davis & Capp, 1985). No amount of matching or variable control with Harrell's subjects could change their large IQ gains, which are the crucial and unexplained differences between the results of the Harrell group and the others.

Attention should now focus first on whether the several 11–24-point IQ gains recorded for the Harrell subjects were accurate. If Harrell and the licensed and certified independent testers were all incorrect, there may be no conflict with the three subsequent studies in children, and no need for further explanation. On the other hand, if the independently verified gains were accurate, the problem becomes one of discovering why they occurred and whether they can be reproduced. If the gains were accurate and were facilitated by factors such as thyroid or investigator belief and enthusiasm, then the Harrell study is an important discovery (or rediscovery) with broad implications requiring further elucidation.

If Harrell's reported gains were accurate but cannot be reproduced *by true replications* in other groups of children with retardation, then the Harrell study probably has little significance beyond her subjects. For example, Harrell's subjects from Norfolk, Virginia might represent a selected population of unusual retarded children with nutrient-responsive metabolic defects or heavy metal toxicity as discussed elsewhere in this chapter. (Many of Harrell's subjects had hearing, vision, or motor handicaps or diseases such as epilepsy, which apparently would have excluded them from at least some of the follow-up studies.) Further deliberation and research should focus on distinguishing these and any other warranted interpretations of the Harrell and follow-up studies.

Inborn Errors of Metabolism

When Garrod first called attention to four inborn errors of metabolism in 1908, genetically transmitted metabolic disorders were considered rare curiosities. Now we recognize nearly 4,000 disorders transmitted by defects in single genes, and new ones are reported at the rate of about 130 per year (McKusick, 1986). Although inborn errors of metabolism are individually rare, collectively they occur in at least 10 out of 1,000 births and account for more than 5% of pediatric hospital admissions in the United States. Roughly half of these disorders (over 1,500) can cause mental retardation, usually beginning by age 3, but sometimes not until adolescence or even adulthood. Somewhat outdated studies attribute 3%–7% of severe mental retardation to inborn errors of metabolism (Moser, 1982).

Often the serious consequences of inborn errors can be reduced or even eliminated by nutritional adjustments such as restricting dietary protein or particular amino acids or by increasing intake of a specific vitamin. If treatment begins early enough, mental retardation may be prevented. In rare cases, retardation has been reversed by nutritional supplements.

These nutritional approaches to inborn errors of metabolism represent extreme examples of the "genetotrophic" principle first enunciated by Williams and co-workers in 1950: "Every individual organism that has a distinctive genetic background has distinctive nutritional needs which must be met for optimal well-being" (Williams, 1956/1979, p. 167). Less extreme inborn *variations* of metabolism occur in all individuals and, as discussed earlier, they interact with diet to affect individual resistance to preeclampsia, birth defects, and myriad other conditions. The emerging science of nutrition that focuses on these important individual differences has been termed "differential nutrition" (Williams & Davis, 1986).

The two most common and treatable inborn errors of metabolism are routinely detected by mass screening tests of newborn infants in the United States: hypothyroidism (1 in 3,500 births) and phenylketonuria (PKU) (1 in 11,000). Galactosemia is another for which mass screening is practical and useful (1 in 75,000 births). The latter two are eminently treatable by diet.

Detection of the remaining 1,000-plus inborn errors that cause mental retardation is presently difficult and haphazard. When they are found, usually it is by specialized, sometimes costly, diagnostic studies undertaken in response to suggestive clinical observations. Although most of these other inborn errors occur once in only 50,000 to 500,000 or more births, and although many are now untreatable, correct and timely diagnosis of treatable errors can be very important to the child and family involved. Recent excellent reviews are designed to help alert practicing physicians and clinics to this rapidly progressing field and to guide them in obtaining needed diagnostic services (Ampola, 1982; Moser, 1982). Other reviews are more biochemically oriented for specialists and scientists (Cockburn & Gitzelmann, 1982; Milunsky, 1979; Stanbury, Wyngaarden, Fredrickson, Goldstein, & Brown, 1983).

Prenatal diagnosis is now possible for about 100 inborn errors of metabolism, permitting abortion of affected fetuses (Milunsky, 1979; Patrick, 1983). Unfortunately, prenatal testing is costly and slightly risky to the fetus. It is therefore practical only when one knows in advance that a particular defect is likely, usually because a couple has already produced one affected child.

Nutritional therapies fall into two main categories (Ampola, 1982; Collins & Leonard, 1985). The most common therapy limits dietary intake of substances for which there is defective metabolism and which therefore produce toxic accumulations. For example, most kinds of phenylketonuria respond well to special diets low in phenylalanine, and mental retardation is prevented if blood levels are well controlled during the years of brain maturation, especially before age 6. Several defects involve toxic accumulation of ammonia in the blood due to impaired metabolism of all amino acids (urea cycle defects). When the impairment is not too severe, restriction of dietary protein can prevent retardation if treatment is begun early, usually within a few days or weeks of age. Other examples are galactosemia (restrict galactose, found in lactose from milk) and maple syrup urine disease (restrict leucine, isoleucine, and valine; supplement thiamin in some cases).

The other common nutritional therapy for inborn errors is to supply a vitamin cofactor in doses ranging from 5 to over 1,000 times usual requirements (Ampola, 1982; Bartlett, 1983; Duran & Wadman, 1985). About 25 vitamin-responsive inborn errors are well studied, involving vitamin B_6, vitamin B_{12}, biotin, folic acid, thiamin, and riboflavin. Often the metabolic error causes the protein part of an enzyme to bind weakly to its vitamin cofactor, and large vitamin concentrations are able to compensate and produce adequate amounts of functioning enzyme. In other cases, the high intakes are needed to overcome defective absorption or metabolism of the vitamin, or they may augment a normal, secondary metabolic pathway that bypasses a defective primary pathway.

Inborn errors of metabolism are highly variable and unpredictable in their clinical features and response to treatment. Several different enzyme defects requiring different treatments can lead to the same biochemical finding, for example, of abnormal urinary excretion of homocystine. Some variants of homocystinuria are helped by low methionine diets, about half respond to vitamin B_6 in doses ranging from 25 to 1,000 mg/day, some require folic acid supplements, and some are helped by a methyl donor such as betaine. Recently two variants were reported that responded to the hydroxy form of vitamin B_{12} (Schuh et al., 1984; Shinnar & Singer, 1984). Usually the only way to determine vitamin responsiveness is empirical—large doses are tried for a few weeks or months, and if there is a response the dose is reduced gradually until the amount needed is found.

The latter report is one of the rare cases in which mental retardation was dramatically reversed by nutrient therapy (Shinnar & Singer, 1984). The 14-year-old girl had been a straight-A student in excellent health until the last year, during which her speech and work deteriorated to the first grade level and her IQ fell to 40. After 3 weeks of vitamin B_{12} therapy her IQ rose to 84, and in 6 weeks she was judged to be functioning at a level appropriate for her age. Her impaired gait was improved but not as fully as her mental functioning.

The diagnosis and treatment of inborn errors of metabolism has seen tremendous progress in the last two decades, and we may hope for much further progress to come. The primary goals ahead are to improve diagnosis and treatment so that more of these individually rare and highly variable disorders can be found and appropriately treated at the earliest possible stage.

Fragile-X Syndrome

Fragile-X syndrome is a major inherited disease of males, second only to Down syndrome as an identified cause of mental retardation (about 1 in 1,200–2,000 males) (de la Cruz, 1985; Madison, Mosher, & George, 1986). Remarkably, the syndrome was not recognized as a distinct entity until 1969, when it was found to involve instability of the X chromosome in cells grown in tissue culture. If the culture medium is made low in folic acid and thymidine, the long arms of X chromosomes often appear constricted or broken—hence the name of the syndrome.

Fragile-X syndrome is quite variable in its symptoms. Mental retardation is the rule; usually it is moderate to severe. Most victims also have highly enlarged testes after puberty, large rotated ears, a long, narrow face, and other physical features. Common behavior problems include poor expressive ability, hyperactivity, and autistic-like symptoms. (About 8% of "autistic" males have been found to have fragile-X chromosomes [Brown, Jenkins et al., 1986].)

The syndrome is inherited as a sex-linked recessive disease: Sons of an affected male are unaffected, but all daughters are carriers, and half of their sons have the disorder and half of their daughters are carriers. Some carriers seem to have mild mental deficits. Prenatal diagnosis is under investigation.

In 1981, French workers reported that oral folic acid supplements reduce the frequency of altered X chromosomes in cells from fragile-X patients and also remarkably seem to ameliorate many of the behavior abnormalities. Since then, many reports have confirmed that folic acid supplements reduce or eliminate the "fragility" of X chromosomes in tissue culture.

Numerous uncontrolled and controlled studies have investigated the behavioral effects of folic acid supplements in fragile-X syndrome. The largest double-blind trial to date well illustrates the findings and limitations of these studies (Hagerman et al., 1986). Twenty-five males ages 1 to 31 were given 10 mg/day of folic acid or placebo for 6 months, after which the placebo and supplement groups were switched. Psychological, language, and behavioral evaluations were recorded, along with reports from parents or caregivers. While on folic acid, four subjects "improved remarkably" in attention span, activity level, and frequency of tantrums, including two subjects who were removed from the study by their caregivers when their behavior deteriorated badly on placebo. Nine subjects improved mildly in behavior and 10 showed no change. The improvements occurred mostly in the prepubertal boys.

IQ tests showed no statistically significant overall difference between the folic acid and placebo groups. Likewise, no group differences were seen in the language and behavior evaluations. Nevertheless, a few individuals seemed to clearly improve on folic acid, mainly among the young subjects, and statistical significance was achieved for the eight prepubertal boys in the study. The most striking improvement was in a 2-year-old whose development quotient (DQ) went from 63 to 86 in 6 months on folic acid and then to 100 on placebo, although some other measures deteriorated on placebo. A 4-year-old went from a measured IQ of 54 to 75 while on folic acid, with dramatic improvements in behavior. His IQ also may have improved during the placebo period (to 80), but behavior worsened. Both subjects have maintained their DQ or IQ in the normal range for 1–2 years while continuing folic acid treatment.

In this study, behavior improvements began after 2–4 weeks on folic acid, and deterioration began after 2–3 weeks on placebo. However, as mentioned, some subjects' developmental and IQ measures seemed to continue improving for months after folic acid was discontinued. This phenomenon may relate to a slow removal of large doses of folic acid from some cells (6–8 weeks for red blood cells) (Zettner, Boss, & Seegmiller, 1981). Recently, Wells and Madison (1986) reported clear behavior benefits of folic acid in a 7-year-old, but they (probably unnecessarily) judged their evidence "equivocal" because the gains failed to regress after 18 days on placebo.

Another recent report is consistent with the large study described above. A double-blind trial of 250 mg/day of folic acid for three 3-month periods was presented as showing "little support" for treatment by folic acid (Brown, Cohen et al., 1986). However, as the authors noted, three subjects exceeded the age that seems likely to respond (14, 21, and 26). The two youngest subjects (8 and 13) did show noteworthy IQ increases, and the failure of the IQ values to deteriorate during 3 months on placebo seems to be a common phenomenon. Other studies also found folic acid to be beneficial in some children, but not usually in adolescents or adults (Froster-Iksenius et al., 1986; Gustavson et al., 1985). No benefit was seen in 14-year-old twins (Rosenblatt et al., 1985).

Fragile-X syndrome thus seems in most ways like many nutrient-responsive inborn errors of metabolism—heterogeneous in expression, with nutrient responsiveness unpredictable and most likely in young children. However, no metabolic error has been found yet, and the biochemical nature of the syndrome and its apparent response to folic acid remain a puzzle.

FUTURE DIRECTIONS

Prevention

The greatest hope for nutrition and mental retardation, as mentioned at the outset, is that improved nutrition before and during pregnancy can prevent the birth of *most* of the mentally defective babies currently being born in the United States and throughout the world. Although this hope may still seem extravagant to many, it is rooted in several decades of research by experts in mammalian nutrition. It is also grounded on substantial knowledge about the complexities of human nutrition and about the marginal nature of most human diets in western nations that derive less than half of their food energy from whole foods. Finally, this hope is beginning to be substantiated by progress in the prevention of neural tube defects and by recognition of nutritional factors in the prevention of preeclampsia.

At a scientific level, the most important future direction is to seek nutritional factors in the prevention of the majority of human birth defects whose cause is still "unknown." Another important future direction is research on the prevention of some known causes of mental retardation, such as preeclampsia, which in turn are of "unknown origin." A related need is to study the role of nutrition in the prevention and treatment of developmental deficits that arise during infancy and childhood, including those associated with lead and other environmental toxins.

At the practical level—which is as important as the scientific level—a crucial future direction is to gain greater public and professional awareness of nutrition and the scientific knowledge we already have. Here we must overcome decades of nutritional illiteracy and staunch complacency, unfortunately even among some of our respected leaders in nutrition. While many were defending the "balanced diets" that they were *sure* that North Americans generally were eating, large and increasing portions of the population were and are consuming poor to marginal diets. These diets consist primarily of just three refined ingredients that are never fed in quantity to prized animals: purified sugars, separated fats, and highly milled grains (not to mention alcohol). The resulting incidence of low blood and urine levels of nutrients has been documented, but it has not yet produced the new directions in nutrition education that seem needed at all levels.

It is certainly possible (but of course not yet provable) that widely teaching *and* applying the nutrition knowledge that we already have would make great inroads into the problems of congenital and developmental retardation—without any further scientific research of the kinds suggested above, and without reference to the research already done, for example on neural tube defects. In other words, basic nutritional improvements, which can be defended solely on narrow nutritional grounds, seem likely to markedly reduce the incidence of mental retardation as well as many other health problems (Weir, 1971). Thus a promising future direction would be simply to apply the basics of good nutrition, and study what happens. The experiences cited earlier by Hamlin and Brewer with thousands of pregnant women are but one encouragement for this approach. It could be initially tested and developed on a scale no larger than their experiments.

Secondary Prevention and Treatment

There seems little or no grounds for optimism that improved nutrition can prevent disorders such as Down syndrome, fragile-X syndrome, or inborn errors of metabolism such as phenylketonuria. Fortunately, there are other approaches to the primary prevention of these conditions. However, it is clear that nutritional approaches, perhaps combined with others, can prevent or ameliorate *some fraction* of the mental retardation associated with such disorders.

The most important future directions in this field seem twofold: first, to learn how large this ameliorated fraction can be made by means of sophisticated nutritional-biochemical approaches; and second, to work toward practical early diagnosis and individualized treatment for these highly variable disorders. In this regard, traditional clinical trials may lead us astray when they tacitly depend on the assumption that all subjects have about the same metabolic need, whether it be for glutamine, folic acid, or large doses of other vitamins. Each of these nutrients and others may be extremely valuable in *some* retarded individuals or identifiable subgroups, and we need to develop better ways to identify responsive individuals. "*N* of 1" studies may be valuable in this search (Guyatt et al., 1986).

REFERENCES

Abel, E. L. (1984). *Fetal alcohol syndrome and fetal alcohol effects.* New York: Plenum Press.

Abel, E. L. (1986). *Fetal alcohol syndrome: An annotated bibliography.* New York: Praeger Publishers.

Abraham, G. E., Schwartz, U. D., & Lubran, M. M. (1981). Effect of vitamin B-6 on plasma and red blood cell magnesium levels in premenopausal women. *Annals of Clinical and Laboratory Science, 11,* 333–336.

Adeyokunnu, A. A. (1985). The role of malnutrition in common forms of physical and mental congenital defects among Nigerian Africans. In M. Marois (Ed.), *Prevention of physical and mental congenital defects* (Part B). New York: Alan R. Liss.

Altura, B. M., Altura, B. T., & Carella, A. (1983). Magnesium deficiency-induced spasms of umbilical vessels: Relation to preeclampsia, hypertension, growth retardation. *Science, 221,* 376–378.

Ampola, M. G. (1982). *Metabolic diseases in pediatric practice.* Boston: Little, Brown & Co.

Astin, A. W., & Ross, S. (1960). Glutamic acid and intelligence. *Psychological Bulletin, 57,* 429–434.

Bartlett, K. (1983). Vitamin-responsive inborn errors of metabolism. *Advances in Clinical Chemistry, 23,* 141–198.

Beach, R. S., Gershwin, M. E., & Hurley, L. S. (1982). Gestational zinc deprivation in mice: Persistence of immunodeficiency for three generations. *Science, 218,* 469–471.

Beattie, A. D., Moore, M. R., Goldberg, A., Finlayson, M. J. W., Graham, J. F., Mackie, E. M., Main, J. C., McLaren, D. A., Murdoch, R. M., & Stewart, G. T. (1975). Role of chronic low-level lead exposure in the aetiology of mental retardation. *Lancet, 1,* 589–592.

Beley, A., Caustier, M., & Olievenstein, A. (1964). Action favorable du monoamide de l'acide 1-glutamique (levoglutamine) sur les capacites d'efficience de l'ecolier debile mental (Recherches portant sur deux groupes egaux avec apairages et placebos). *Annales Medico-psychologiques, 122,* 585–591.

Belizan, J. M., Villar, J., Zalazar, A., Rojas, L., Chan, D., & Bryce, G. F. (1983). Preliminary evidence of the effect of calcium supplementation on blood pressure in normal pregnant women. *American Journal of Obstetrics and Gynecology, 146,* 175–180.

Bellinger, D., Leviton, A., Needleman, H. L., Waternaux, C., & Rabinowitz, M.

(1986). Low-level lead exposure and infant development in the first year. *Neurobehavioral Toxicology and Teratology, 8,* 151–161.

Bennett, F. C., McClelland, S., Kriegsmann, E. A., Andrus, L. B., & Sells, C. J. (1983). Vitamin and mineral supplementation in Down's syndrome. *Pediatrics, 72,* 707–713.

Bergmann, K. E., Makosch, G., & Tews, K.-M. (1980). Abnormalities of hair zinc concentration in mothers of newborn infants with spina bifida. *American Journal of Clinical Nutrition, 33,* 2145–2150.

Biale, Y., & Lewenthal, H. (1984). Effect of folic acid supplementation on congenital malformations due to anticonvulsive drugs. *European Journal of Obstetrics, Gynecology, and Reproductive Biology, 18,* 211–216.

Bratton, G. R., Zmudzki, J., Bell, M. C., & Warnock, L. G. (1981). Thiamin (vitamin B_1) effects on lead intoxication and deposition of lead in tissues: Therapeutic potential. *Toxicology and Applied Pharmacology, 59,* 164–172.

Brent, R. L. (1982). Drugs and pregnancy: Are the insert warnings too dire? *Contemporary OB/GYN, 20,* 42–49.

Brent, R. L. (1985). The magnitude of the problem of congenital malformations. In M. Marois (Ed.), *Prevention of physical and mental congenital defects* (Part A). New York: Alan R. Liss.

Brewer, G. S., & Brewer, T. (1977). *What every pregnant woman should know: The truth about diets and drugs in pregnancy.* New York: Random House.

Brewer, T. H. (1966). *Metabolic toxemia of late pregnancy: A disease of malnutrition.* Springfield, Il: Charles C Thomas.

Brown, W. T., Cohen, I. L., Fisch, G. S., Wolf-Schein, E. G., Jenkins, V. A., Malik, M. N., & Jenkins, E. C. (1986). High dose folic acid treatment of fragile (X) males. *American Journal of Medical Genetics, 23,* 263–271.

Brown, W. T., Jenkins, E. C., Cohen, I. L., Fisch, G. S., Wolf-Schein, E. G., Gross, A., Waterhouse, L., Fein, D., Mason-Brothers, A., Ritvo, E., Ruttenberg, B. A., Bentley, W., & Castells, S. (1986). Fragile X and autism: A multicenter study. *American Journal of Medical Genetics, 23,* 341–352.

Brozek, J. (Ed.). (1977). *Behavioral effects of energy and protein deficits.* Washington, DC: U.S. Government Printing Office.

Bryce-Smith, D. (1986). Environmental chemical influences on behaviour and mentation. *Chemical Society Reviews, 15,* 93–123.

Bryce-Smith, D., & Stephens, R. (1980). *Lead or health.* Surrey, England: Conservation Society.

Buamah, P. K., Russell, M., Bates, G., Ward, A. M., & Skillen, A. W. (1984). Maternal zinc status: A determination of central nervous system malformation. *British Journal of Obstetrics and Gynaecology, 91,* 788–790.

Bumbalo, T. S., Morelewicz, H. V., & Berens, D. L. (1964). Treatment of Down's syndrome with the "U" series of drugs. *Journal of the American Medical Association, 187,* 361.

Burgan, P. (1982). Role of the pediatric intermediate care facility in the treatment of children with lead poisoning. In J. J. Chisolm, Jr., & D. M. O'Hara (Eds.), *Lead absorption in children.* Baltimore: Urban & Schwarzenberg.

Capel, I. D., Pinnock, M. H., Dorrell, H. M., Williams, D. C., & Grant, E. C. G. (1981). Comparison of concentrations of some trace, bulk, and toxic metals in the hair of normal and dyslexic children. *Clinical Chemistry, 27,* 879–881.

Cavdar, A. O., Arcasoy, A., Baycu, T., & Himmetoglu, O. (1980). Zinc deficiency and anencephaly in Turkey. *Teratology, 22,* 141.

Chadhuri, S. K. (1970). Correlation of toxemia with anemia of pregnancy. *American Journal of Obstetrics and Gynecology, 106,* 255–259.

Chanowitz, J., Ellman, G., Silverstein, C. I., Zingarelli, G., & Ganger, E. (1985). Thyroid and vitamin-mineral supplement fail to improve IQ of mentally retarded adults. *American Journal of Mental Deficiency, 90,* 217–219.

Charney, E. (1982). Sub-encephalopathic lead poisoning: Central nervous system effects in children. In J. J. Chisolm, Jr., & D. M. O'Hara (Eds.), *Lead absorption in children.* Baltimore: Urban & Schwarzenberg.

Chesley, L. C. (1978). *Hypertensive disorders in pregnancy.* New York: Appleton.

Chisolm, J. J., Jr., & O'Hara, D. M. (Eds.). (1982). *Lead absorption in children.* Baltimore: Urban & Schwarzenberg.

Coburn, S. P., Schaltenbrand, W. E., Mahuren, J. D., Clausman, R. J., & Townsend, D. (1983). Effect of megavitamin treatment on mental performance and plasma vitamin B_6 concentrations on mentally retarded young adults. *American Journal of Clinical Nutrition, 38,* 352–355.

Cockburn, F., & Gitzelmann, R. (Ed.). (1982). *Inborn errors of metabolism in humans.* Lancaster, England: MTP Press.

Colangelo, W., & Jones, D. G. (1982). The fetal alcohol syndrome: A review and assessment of the syndrome and its neurological sequelae. *Progress in Neurobiology, 19,* 271–314.

Collins, J. E., & Leonard, J. V. (1985). The dietary management of inborn errors of metabolism. *Human Nutrition: Applied Nutrition, 39A,* 255–272.

Conradt, A., Weidinger, H., & Algayer, G. (1985). Magnesium deficiency, a possible cause of pre-eclampsia: Reduction of frequency of premature rupture of membranes and premature or small-for-date deliveries after magnesium supplementation (abstract). *Journal of the American College of Nutrition, 4,* 321.

David, O., Hoffman, S., McGann, B., Sverd, J., & Clark, J. (1976). Low lead levels and mental retardation. *Lancet, 2,* 1376–1379.

Davis, D. R. (1983). Nutrition in the United States: Much room for improvement. *Journal of Applied Nutrition, 35,* 17–29.

Davis, D. R., & Capp, R. H. (1985). Vitamins and minerals in Down syndrome. *Journal of Pediatrics, 106,* 531.

de Alvarez, R. R. (1982). Preeclampsia-eclampsia & other gestational edema-proteinuria-hypertension disorders (GEPH). In R. C. Benson (Ed.), *Current obstetrics & gynecologic diagnosis & treatment* (4th ed.). Los Altos: Lange Medical Publications.

de la Cruz, F. F. (1985). Fragile X syndrome. *American Journal of Mental Deficiency, 90,* 119–123.

Dobbing, J. (Ed.). (1983). *Prevention of spina bifida and other neural tube defects.* New York: Academic Press.

Duran, M., & Wadman, S. K. (1985). Thiamine-responsive inborn errors of metabolism. *Journal of Inherited Metabolic Disease, 8,* 70–75.

Ellis, J. M., & Presley, J. (1973). *Vitamin B_6: The doctor's report* (chap. 7). New York: Harper & Row.

Ellis, N. R., & Tomporowski, P. D. (1983). Vitamin/mineral supplements and intelligence of institutionalized mentally retarded adults. *American Journal of Mental Deficiency, 88,* 211–214.

Ellman, G., Silverstein, C. I., Zingarelli, G., Schafer, W. P., & Silverstein, L. (1984). Vitamin-mineral supplement fails to improve IQ of mentally retarded young adults. *American Journal of Mental Deficiency, 88,* 688–691.

Erway, L., Hurley, L. S., & Fraser, A. (1966). Neurological defect: Manganese in phenocopy and prevention of a genetic abnormality of inner ear. *Science, 152,* 1766–1768.

Flora, S. J. S., Singh, S., & Tandon, S. K. (1986). Chelation in metal intoxication XVIII: Combined effects of thiamine and calcium disodium versenate on lead toxicity. *Life Sciences, 38,* 67–71.

Fox, M. R. S. (1975). Protective effects of ascorbic acid against toxicity of heavy metals. *Annals of the New York Academy of Science, 258,* 144–150.

Frank, O., Baker, H., Ziffer, H., Aaronson, S., Hutner, S. H., & Leevy, C. M. (1962). Metabolic deficiencies in protozoa induced by thalidomide. *Science, 139,* 110–111.

Fratta, I. D., Sigg, E. B., & Maiorana, K. (1965). Teratogenic effects of thalidomide in rabbits, rats, hamsters, and mice. *Toxicology and Applied Pharmacology, 7,* 268–286.

Friedman, L., Shue, G. M., & Hove, E. L. (1965). Response of rats to thalidomide as affected by riboflavin or folic acid deficiency. *Journal of Nutrition, 85,* 309–317.

Froster-Iskenius, U., Bodeker, K., Oepen, T., Matthes, R., Piper, U., & Schwinger, E. (1986). Folic acid treatment in males and females with fragile-(X)-syndrome. *American Journal of Medical Genetics, 23,* 273–289.

Goyer, R. A., & Cherian, M. G. (1979). Ascorbic acid and EDTA treatment of lead toxicity in rats. *Life Sciences, 24,* 433–438.

Graham, J. M. (1985). The effects of alcohol consumption during pregnancy. In M. Marois (Ed.), *Prevention of physical and mental congenital defects* (Part C). New York: Alan R. Liss.

Gustavson, K.-H., Dahlbom, K., Flood, A., Holmgren, G., Blomquist, H. K., & Sanner, G. (1985). Effect of folic acid treatment in the fragile X syndrome. *Clinical Genetics, 27,* 463–467.

Guyatt, G., Sackett, D., Taylor, D. W., Chong, J., Roberts, R., & Pugsley, S. (1986). Determining optimal therapy—randomized trials in individual patients. *New England Journal of Medicine, 314,* 889–892.

Hackman, R. M., & Hurley, L. S. (1984). Drug-nutrient interactions in teratogenesis. In D. A. Roe & T. C. Campbell (Eds.), *Drugs and nutrients: The interactive effects.* New York: Marcel Dekker.

Hagerman, R. J., Jackson, A. W., Levitas, A., Branden, M., McBogg, P., Kemper, M., McGavran, L., Berry, R., Matus, I., & Hagerman, P. J. (1986). Oral folic acid versus placebo in the treatment of males with the fragile X syndrome. *American Journal of Medical Genetics, 23,* 241–262.

Hamlin, R. H. J. (1952). The prevention of eclampsia and pre-eclampsia. *Lancet, 1,* 64–68.

Harrell, R. F., Capp, R. H., Davis, D. R., Peerless, J., & Ravitz, L. R. (1981). Can nutritional supplements help mentally retarded children? An exploratory study. *Proceedings of the National Academy of Sciences, 78,* 574–578.

Hemminki, E. (1984). Diuretics in pregnancy: A case study of a worthless therapy. *Social Science & Medicine, 18,* 1011–1018.

Hibbard, B. M. (1964). The role of folic acid in pregnancy with particular reference to anemia, abruption and abortion. *Journal of Obstetrics and Gynecology of the British Commonwealth, 71,* 529–542.

Hill, L. M., & Kleinberg, F. (1984). Effects of drugs and chemicals on the fetus and newborn. *Mayo Clinic Proceedings, 59,* 755–765.

Hurley, L. S. (1985). Trace elements and their interactions as causes of congenital defects. In M. Marois (Ed.), *Prevention of physical and mental congenital defects* (Part B). New York: Alan R. Liss.

Hutt, F. B. (1953). *Genetic resistance to disease in domestic animals.* Ithaca: Cornell University Press.

Jackson, A. J., & Schumacher, H. J. (1979). The teratogenic activity of a thalidomide analogue EM_{12} in rats on a low-zinc diet. *Teratology, 19,* 341–344.

James, H. M., Hilburn, M. E., & Blair, J. A. (1985). Effects of meals and meal times on uptake of lead from the gastrointestinal tract in humans. *Human Toxicology, 14*(4), 401–407.

Kershner, J., & Hawke, W. (1979). Megavitamins and learning disorders: A controlled double-blind study. *Journal of Nutrition, 109,* 819–826.

Kitamura, S., Sumino, K., Hayakawa, K., & Shibata, T. (1976). Dose-response relationship of methylmercury. In G. F. Nordberg (Ed.), *Effects and dose-response relationships of toxic metals.* Amsterdam: Elsevier.

Klieger, J. A., Evrard, J. R., & Pierce, R. (1966). Abnormal pyridoxine metabolism in toxemia of pregnancy. *American Journal of Obstetrics and Gynecology, 94,* 316–321.

Kubala, A. L., & Katz, M. M. (1960). Nutritional factors in psychological test behavior. *Journal of Genetic Psychology, 96,* 343–352.

Kurita, T. (1977). [Treatment of Down's syndrome]. *Pediatrics* [Japanese], *18,* 791–798. Translated in Turkel & Nusbaum (1985).

Laurence, K. M. (1985). Prevention of neural tube defects by improvement in maternal diet and periconceptional folic acid supplementation. In M. Marois (Ed.), *Prevention of physical and mental congenital defects* (Part B). New York: Alan R. Liss.

Leck, I. M., & Millar, E. L. M. (1962). Incidence of malformations since the introduction of thalidomide. *British Medical Journal, 2,* 16–20.

Lefebvres-Biosselot, J. (1954). [The influence of slight pantothenic acid deficiency on the results of gestation in the rat.] *Comptes-Rendus, 238,* 2123–2125.

Lester, M. L., Thatcher, R. W., & Monroe-Lord, L. (1982). Refined carbohydrate intake, hair cadmium levels, and cognitive functioning in children. *Nutrition and Behavior, 1,* 3–13.

Lin-Fu, J. S. (1982). The evolution of childhood lead poisoning as a public health problem. In J. J. Chisolm, Jr., & D. M. O'Hara (Eds.), *Lead absorption in children.* Baltimore: Urban & Schwarzenberg.

Lindheimer, M. D. (1980). Current concepts of sodium metabolism and use of diuretics in pregnancy. *Contemporary OB/GYN, 15,* 207–216.

Lloyd-Still, J. D. (Ed.). (1976). *Malnutrition and intellectual development.* Littleton, MA: Publishing Sciences Group.

Madison, L. S., Mosher, G. A., & George, C. H. (1986). Fragile-X syndrome: Diagnosis and research. *Journal of Pediatric Psychology, 11,* 91–102.

Mahaffey, K. R. (1982). Role of nutrition in prevention of pediatric lead toxicity. In J. J. Chisolm Jr., & D. M. O'Hara (Eds.), *Lead absorption in children.* Baltimore: Urban & Schwarzenberg.

Mahaffey, K. R., Annest, J. L., Roberts, J., & Murphy, R. S. (1982). National estimates of blood lead levels: United States, 1976–1980. *New England Journal of Medicine, 307,* 573–579.

Mahaffey, K. R., & Michaelson, I. A. (1980). Interaction between lead and nutrition. In H. L. Needleman (Ed.), *Low level lead exposure: The clinical implications of current research.* New York: Raven Press.

Main, D. M., & Mennuti, M. T. (1986). Neural tube defects: Issues in prenatal diagnosis and counseling. *Journal of the American College of Obstetricians and Gynecologists, 67,* 1–16.

Manocha, S. L. (1972). *Malnutrition and retarded human development.* Springfield, IL: Charles C Thomas.

Marlowe, M., Folio, R., Hall, D., & Errera, J. (1982). Increased lead burdens and trace-mineral status in mentally retarded children. *Journal of Special Education, 16,* 87–99.

Marlowe, M., Moon, C., Errera, J., Jacobs, J., Brunson, M., Stellern, J., & Schroeder, C. (1986). Low mercury levels and childhood intelligence. *Journal of Orthomolecular Medicine, 1,* 43–49.

Maseck, D. (1980). Vitamins: The get-smart pills? *Journal of Orthomolecular Psychiatry, 9,* 58–65. (See also statistical analysis and other information in D. R. Davis, *ibid,* 196.)

McKusick, V. A. (1986). *Mendelian inheritance in man: Catalogs of autosomal dominant, autosomal recessive, and X-linked phenotypes* (7th ed.). Baltimore: Johns Hopkins University Press.

Mertz, W. (1983, March/April). Our most unique nutrients. *Nutrition Today, 18,* 6–10, 27–29.

Mielke, H. W., Anderson, J. C., Berry, K. J., Mielke, P. W., Chaney, R. L., & Leech, M. (1983). Lead concentrations in inner-city soils as a factor in the child lead problem. *American Journal of Public Health, 73,* 1366–1369.

Milunsky, A. (Ed.). (1979). *Genetic disorders and the fetus.* New York: Plenum Press.

Moncrieff, A. A., Koumides, O. P., Clayton, B. E., Patrick, A. D., Renwick, A. G. C., & Roberts, G. E. (1964). Lead poisoning in children. *Archives of Diseases in Children, 39,* 1–13.

Monson, R. R., Rosenberg, L., Hartz, S. C., Shapiro, S., Heinonen, O. P., & Slone, D. (1973). Diphenylhydantoin and selected congenital malformations. *New England Journal of Medicine, 289,* 1049–1052.

Moore, M. R. (1980). Prenatal exposure to lead and mental retardation. In H. L. Needleman (Ed.), *Low level lead exposure: The clinical implications of current research.* New York: Raven Press.

Morgan, K. J., Stampley, G. L., Zabik, M. E., & Fischer, D. R. (1985). Magnesium and calcium intakes of the U.S. population. *Journal of the American College of Nutrition, 4,* 195–206.

Moser, H. W. (1982). Mental retardation due to genetically determined metabolic and endocrine disorders. In I. Jakab (Ed.), *Mental retardation.* New York: Karger.

Moser, P. B., Issa, C. F., & Reynolds, R. D. (1983). Dietary magnesium intake and the concentration of magnesium in plasma and erythrocytes of postpartum women. *Journal of the American College of Nutrition, 2,* 387–396.

Nathan, P. E. (1983). Failures in prevention. Why we can't prevent the devastating effect of alcoholism and drug abuse. *American Psychologist, 38,* 459–467.

National Research Council. (1978). *Nutrient requirements of laboratory animals* (3rd ed.). Washington, DC: National Academy of Sciences.

Needleman, H. L. (Ed.). (1980). *Low level lead exposure: The clinical implications of current research.* New York: Raven Press.

Needleman, H. L., Geiger, S. K., & Frank, R. (1985). Lead and IQ scores: A reanalysis. *Science, 227,* 701–704.

Needleman, H. L., Gunnoe, C., Leviton, A., Reed, R., Peresie, H., Maher, C., & Barrett, P. (1979). Deficits in psychologic and classroom performance of children with elevated dentine lead levels. *New England Journal of Medicine, 300,* 689–695.

Needleman, H. L., Rabinowitz, M., Leviton, A., Linn, S., & Schoenbaum, S. (1984). The relationship between prenatal exposure to lead and congenital anomalies. *Journal of the American Medical Association, 251,* 2956–2959.

Nevin, N. C. (1985). The role of periconceptional vitamin supplementation in the prevention of neural tube defects. In M. Marois (Ed.), *Prevention of physical and mental congenital defects* (Part B). New York: Alan R. Liss.

Nguyen, M., Meyer, K. K., & Winick, M. (1977). Early malnutrition and "late" adoption: A study of their effects on the development of Korean orphans adopted into American families. *American Journal of Clinical Nutrition, 30,* 1734–1739.

Nutrition Canada. (1973). *Nutrition: A national priority.* Ottawa: Information Canada.

O'Brien, P. M. S., Morrison, R., & Broughton Pipkin, F. (1985). The effect of dietary supplementation with linoleic and gammalinolenic acids on the pressor response to angiotensin II—a possible role in pregnancy-induced hypertension? *British Journal of Clinical Pharmacology, 19,* 335–342.

O'Hara, D. M. (1982). Social factors in the recurrence of increased lead absorption in children. In J. J. Chisolm, Jr., & D. M. O'Hara (Eds.), *Lead absorption in children.* Baltimore: Urban & Schwarzenberg.

Papioannou, R., Sohler, A., & Pfeiffer, C. C. (1978). Reduction of blood lead levels in battery workers by zinc and vitamin C. *Journal of Orthomolecular Psychiatry, 7,* 94–106.

Patrick, A. D. (1983). Inherited metabolic disorders. *British Medical Bulletin, 39,* 378–385.

Patterson, C. C. (1980). Lead pollution in the human environment: Origin, extent, and significance. In *Lead in the human environment.* Washington, DC: National Academy of Sciences.

Pritchard, J. A., MacDonald, P. C., & Gant, N. F. (1985). *Williams Obstetrics* (17th ed., p. 540). New York: Appleton.

Rauen, H. M. (1963). Are thalidomide and its biological metabolites vitamin antagonists? *Arzneimittel-Forschung, 13,* 1081–1084.

Rimland, B., & Davis, D. R. (1986). Letter to the Editor (Dr. Hoffer). *Journal of Orthomolecular Medicine, 1,* 28–29.

Riva, G., & Uboldi, L. (1964). Pantothenic acid and coenzyme A concentrations in fetuses and offspring from thalidomide-treated female rats. *Atti della Accademia Medica Lombarda, 19,* 301–303.

Roe, D. (1976). *Drug-induced nutritional deficiencies.* Westport, CT: AVI Publishing Co.

Rogers, L. L., & Pelton, R. B. (1957). Effect of glutamine on IQ scores of mentally deficient children. *Texas Reports on Biology and Medicine, 15,* 84–90.

Rose, H. E., & Quarterman, J. (1984). Effects of dietary phytic acid on lead and cadmium uptake and depletion in rats. *Environmental Research, 35,* 482–489.

Rosenblatt, D. S., Duschenes, E. A., Hellstrom, F. V., Golick, M. S., Vekemans, M. J. J., Zeesman, S. F., & Andermann, E. (1985). Folic acid blinded trial in identical twins with fragile X syndrome. *American Journal of Human Genetics, 37,* 543–552.

Runner, M. N. (1967). Comparative pharmacology in relation to teratogenesis. *Federation Proceedings, 26,* 1131–1136.

Rush, D., Stein, Z., & Susser, M. (Eds.). (1980). *Diet in pregnancy: A randomized controlled trial of nutritional supplements.* New York: Alan R. Liss.

Sabry, Z. I., Campbell, J. A., Campbell, M. E., & Forbes, A. L. (1974, January/February). Nutrition Canada. *Nutrition Today, 9,* 5–13.

Sandstead, H. H. (1977). Nutrient interactions with toxic elements. In R. A. Goyer & M. A. Mehlman (Eds.), *Toxicology of trace elements.* Washington, DC: Hemisphere Publishing Corp.

Sandstead, H. H. (1984). Zinc: Essentiality for brain development and function. *Nutrition Today, 19* (Nov/Dec.), 26–30.

Schoenbrod, D. (1980). Why regulation of lead has failed. In H. L. Needleman (Ed.), *Low level lead exposure: The clinical implications of current research.* New York: Raven Press.

Schuh, S., Rosenblatt, D. S., Cooper, B. A., Schroeder, M.-L., Bishop, A. J., Seargeant, L. E., & Haworth, J. C. (1984). Homocystinuria and megaloblastic anemia responsive to vitamin B_{12} therapy. *New England Journal of Medicine, 310,* 686–690.

Sever, L. E. (1975). Zinc and human development: A review. *Human Ecology, 3,* 43–57.

Shinnar, S., & Singer, H. S. (1984). Cobalamin C mutation (methylmalonic aciduria and homocystinuria) in adolescence. *New England Journal of Medicine, 311,* 451–454.

Shojania, A. M. (1984). Folic acid and vitamin B_{12} deficienty in pregnancy and in the neonatal period. *Clinics in Perinatology, 11,* 433–459.

Smith, G. F., Spiker, D., Peterson, C. P., Cicchetti, D., & Justine, P. (1984). Use of megadoses of vitamins with minerals in Down syndrome. *Journal of Pediatrics, 105,* 228–234.

Smithells, R. W. (1984). Rational use of vitamins. *Lancet, 1,* 1295.

Sohler, A., Kruesi, M., & Pfeiffer, C. C. (1977). Blood lead levels in psychiatric outpatients reduced by zinc and vitamin C. *Journal of Orthomolecular Psychiatry, 6,* 272–276.

Somogyi, J. C., & Haenel, H. (Eds.). (1982). *Nutrition in early childhood and its effects in later life.* New York: Karger.

Speidel, B. D., & Meadow, S. R. (1974). Epilepsy, anticonvulsants and congenital malformations. *Drugs, 8,* 354–365.

Stanbury, J. B., Wyngaarden, J. B., Fredrickson, D. S., Goldstein. J. L., & Brown, M. S. (Eds.). (1983). *The metabolic basis of inherited disease* (5th ed.). New York: McGraw-Hill.

Streissguth, A. P., Landesman-Dwyer, S., Martin, J. C., & Smith, D. W. (1980). Teratogenic effects of alcohol in humans and laboratory animals. *Science, 209,* 353–361.

Sun, M. (1985). EPA accelerates ban on leaded gas. *Science, 227,* 1448.

Tanino, Y. (1966). Improvement of children with mongolism through the effect of large doses of various vitamins (2nd report). *Annales Paediatrici Japonici, 12,* 31–45.

Thatcher, R. W., & Lester, M. L. (1985). Nutrition, environmental toxins and computerized EEG: A mini-max approach to learning disabilities. *Journal of Learning Disabilities, 18,* 287–297.

Thatcher, R. W., Lester, M. L., McAlaster, R., & Horst, R. (1982). Effects of low levels of cadmium and lead on cognitive functioning in children. *Archives of Environmental Health, 37,* 159–166.

Tolarova, M. (1982). Periconceptional supplementation with vitamins and folic acid to prevent recurrence of cleft lip. *Lancet, 2,* 217.

Turkel, H. (1975). Medical amelioration of Down's syndrome incorporating the orthomolecular approach. *Journal of Orthomolecular Psychiatry, 4,* 1–14.

Turkel, H. (1981). Treatment of a mucopolysaccharide type of storage disease with the "U" series. *Journal of Orthomolecular Psychiatry, 10,* 239–248.

Turkel, H., & Nusbaum, I. (1985). *Medical treatment of Down syndrome and genetic diseases* (4th ed.). Southfield, MI: Ubiotica.

U.S. Department of Agriculture. (1969). *Dietary levels of households in the United States, Spring 1965.* Washington, DC: U.S. Government Printing Office.

U.S. Department of Agriculture. (1978). *Food consumption, prices, expenditures* (Table 39). Washington, DC: U.S. Government Printing Office.

U.S. Department of Agriculture. (1983). *Nutrient intakes: Individuals in 48 states, Year 1977–78.* Washington, DC: U.S. Government Printing Office.

U.S. Department of Health, Education, and Welfare. (1972). *Ten state nutrition survey, 1968–1970.* Washington, DC: U.S. Government Printing Office.

Varner, M. W., Cruikshank, D. P., & Pitkin, R. M. (1983). Calcium metabolism in the hypertensive mother, fetus, and newborn infant. *American Journal of Obstetrics and Gynecology, 147,* 762–765.

Vobecky, J. S., Vobecky, J., Shapcott, D., Demers, P.-P., Cloutier, D., Blanchard, R., & Fisch, C. (1982). Biochemical indices of nutritional status in maternal, cord, and early neonatal blood. *American Journal of Clinical Nutrition, 36,* 630–642.

Vogel, W., Broverman, D. M., Draguns, J. G., & Klaiber, E. L. (1966). The role of glutamic acid in cognitive behaviors. *Psychological Bulletin, 65,* 367–382.

Wald, N. J., & Polani, P. E. (1984). Neural-tube defects and vitamins: The need for a randomized clinical trial. *British Journal of Obstetrics and Gynaecology, 91,* 516–523. (See also correspondence in *ibid.,* 1984, *92,* 185–186.)

Wapnir, R. A., Moak, S. A., & Lifshitz, F. (1980). Reduction of lead toxicity on the kidney and the small intestinal mucosa by kaolin and pectin in the diet. *American Journal of Clinical Nutrition, 33,* 2303–2310.

Watson, K. V., Moldow, C. F., Ogburn, P. L., & Jacob, H. S. (1986). Magnesium sulfate: Rationale for its use in preeclampsia. *Proceedings of the National Academy of Sciences, 83,* 1075–1078.

Weathers, C. (1983). Effects of nutritional supplementation on IQ and certain other variables associated with Down syndrome. *American Journal of Mental Deficiency, 88,* 214–217.

Weir, C. E. (1971). *An evaluation of research in the United States on human nutrition: Report No. 2. Benefits from human nutrition research.* Washington, DC: U.S. Department of Agriculture.

Wells, T. E., & Madison, L. S. (1986). Assessment of behavior change in a fragile-X syndrome male treated with folic acid. *American Journal of Medical Genetics, 23,* 291–296.

Williams, R. J. (1971). *Nutrition against disease* (chap. 4). New York: Pitman.

Williams, R. J. (1979). *Biochemical individuality* (chap. 10). Austin: University of Texas Press. (Original work published 1956. New York: Wiley).

Williams, R. J., & Davis, D. R. (1986). Differential nutrition—a new orientation from which to approach the problems of human nutrition. *Perspectives in Biology and Medicine, 29,* 199–202.

Winick, M. (1976). Maternal nutrition. In R. L. Brent & M. I. Harris (Eds.), *Prevention of embryonic, fetal, and perinatal disease.* Washington, DC: U.S. Government Printing Office.

Winick, M., Meyer, K. K., & Harris, R. C. (1975). Malnutrition and environmental enrichment by early adoption. *Science, 190,* 1173–1175.

Yates, J. R. W., Ferguson-Smith, M. A., Shenkin, A., Guzman-Rodriguez, R., White, M., & Clark, B. J. (1985). Vitamin status and neural tube defects (abstract). *Journal of Medical Genetics, 22,* 394.

Youroukos, S., Lyberatos, C., Tsomi, A., Philippidou, A., & Gardikas, C. (1978). Increased blood lead levels in mentally retarded children in Greece. *Archives of Environmental Health, 33,* 297–300.

Yule, W., Lansdown, R., Millar, I. B., & Urbanowicz, M. A. (1981). The relationship between blood lead concentrations, intelligence and attainment in a school population: A pilot study. *Developmental Medicine and Child Neurology, 23,* 567–576.

Zettner, A., Boss, G. R., & Seegmiller, J. E. (1981). A long-term study of the absorption of large oral doses of folic acid. *Annals of Clinical and Laboratory Science, 11,* 516–524.

EARLY BIOMEDICAL INTERVENTION

Introduction

In this section we turn our attention to early intervention strategies, with a major focus on the biomedical sciences. Chapter 8 is written by Dr. Cal Hobel, Director of the Maternal-Fetal Medicine Unit and Co-Director of the Department of Obstetrics and Gynecology at the respected Cedars-Sinai Medical Center, who has an international reputation for his research in obstetrics and perinatology. Dr. Hobel has recently received considerable media attention because of his development of the West Los Angeles Premature Prevention Program. Just how important is this area to the prevention of mental retardation? Consider this alarming figure: Each year approximately 250,000 premature babies are born in the United States with approximately 8% (or 20,000) of them weighing less than 1,000 g. Many of these children don't survive and those who do are often faced with severe disabilities; this fact presents an enormous challenge in our primary and secondary prevention efforts.

Dr. Hobel presents us with some historical figures that indicate that during the 1950s and 1960s there was a tremendous focus on reducing infant mortality. However, during the last 15 years there has been much more of an effort on preventing morbidity. Researchers have made significant gains in this process, primarily due to the development of a new medical speciality, perinatology, which bridges the disciplines of obstetrics and pediatrics. In these highly specialized fields of obstetrics and perinatalogy, we have seen some significant technological breakthroughs, such as intrauterine fetal transfusions that were first attempted in 1963. This was followed by the development of the Rh immunoglobulin in 1969. The development of fetal surgery in the late 1970s also seemed promising, but now the results seem to be a bit equivocal and intrauteral surgery seems to be stalled. In addition to the tremendous assistance of fetal monitoring and the establishment of neonatology units, regionalization of perinatal programs in the United States is the first national effort that has brought about a significant reduction in perinatal mortality and morbidity.

Dr. Hobel points out that the three conditions that make the biggest contribution toward poor developmental outcomes (primarily mental retardation and associated cerebral palsy) are: 1) low birth weight or prematurity, 2) genetic disorders, and 3) structural abnormalities. In order to prevent these conditions, Dr. Hobel describes a systems delivery service approach that he has helped to establish. The program effectively demonstrates that the establishment of these model perinatal programs can continue to significantly reduce the incidence of prematurity and also provide a tremendous cost savings to individual states. However, Dr. Hobel is a realist and understands that during these difficult fiscal times, the establishment of preventative programs is costly, yet he develops an excellent rationale and model for accomplishing this goal by focusing on a state with 1½ million people who spend $90 million a year for their residents who have developmental disabilities. The reader of this chapter should find his analysis and model program of tremendous use, particularly if one is considering the establishment of such programs on a local or statewide basis.

The editors of this book have been privileged to know and work with Drs. Angle and McIntire, the authors of Chapter 9, "Developmental Neurotoxicity." We have long respected their research contribution and their combined 60 years of experience in the clinical training of medical students and residents, as well as direct clinical services as pediatric specialists. Recently, they were asked by the prestigious *New England Journal of Medicine* to write an editorial on the topic of developmental neurotoxicity. How important is this area of emphasis on the overall picture of preventing mental retardation? Consider these statistics: The National Research Council estimates that human beings are exposed to some 53,000 distinct chemicals in the form of pesticides, drugs, food additives, cosmetics, and commercial substances each year. Almost none are tested for their neurobehavioral effects. The federal government, through its National Institute for Occupational Health and Safety, has set occupational standards for only 588 chemicals. Of these, only 167 (or 28%) are regulated because of the effects that they have on the central nervous system, often discovered after they have produced significantly disabling side effects. Most disturbing about this entire process is that we seem to react rather vigorously to chemicals that cause physical deformities, yet we seem to be remiss in our efforts to develop an effective program to alleviate toxins that lead to subtle neurological damage over decades of exposure. For example, studies have shown that children exposed to moderate levels of lead score 5 IQ points lower than children exposed to little or no lead. Although this may not seem like much, statistically, this would represent a decrease by almost 50% of those individuals with an IQ of 130 or above who are considered to be in the gifted classification range (i.e., 2 standard deviations above the mean). The fact that chemicals can poison our nervous system has been known for a long time. For example, the neurotoxic effects of lead have been documented before the time of Christ and the side effect of mercury ingestion was noted over 4 centuries ago. Despite this knowledge, it wasn't until the early 1970s that the federal government began to reduce the level of lead allowed in gasoline. Because of these adverse findings on the research of children's intellectual functioning, the level of lead in gasoline has dropped by 90% in 1987.

In 1972 the Federal Drug Administration set up a National Center for Toxicological Research (NCTR) and later, in 1976, passed the Toxic Substances Control Act. Today at NCTR there are 600 full-time and contract employees who are conducting over 100 experiments on the side effects of chemicals, ranging from the effects on fetal development to the subtle effects on elderly adults.

Biomedical scientists and behavioral specialists (in two new fields, behavioral teratology and behavioral toxicology) are joining forces in an interdisciplinary effort to address these critical issues. Drs. Angle and McIntire point out the complex challenges facing this new field of developmental neurotoxicity in conducting research. For example, of the 3,000 chemicals that have been tested for teratogenicity, at least 1,000 have been found positive in animals. Despite this, only 14 groups of chemicals were documented as having teratogenetic effects in the human fetus. This of course does not include the subtle latent neurological sequelae that can often times manifest themselves several years later. The major problem, however, facing this area is the ability to conduct scientific research on animal models. For example, even though a potential hazard is indicated by one third (1,000 out of 3,000) of the teratogenetic studies in animals, we have only been able to document human risk in 6 of these 1,000, for a 0.6% incidence rate. As these two researchers point out, what have been identified as human teratogens range from positive responses of 85% in the mouse down to 30% in the primate. Of the 165 compounds specifically recorded as having absolutely no evidence of human teratogenicity, 41% were found positive in more than one animal species.

The following statistic also points out the tremendous need for research in neurotoxins: At the present time, environmental chemicals account for only 2%–3% of teratogenetic effects observed in humans, and 65%–70% of all developmental anomalies continue to have unknown causes. These authors go on to write an in-depth analysis of lead, mercury, hydrocarbons, and insecticides and their unique neurotoxic effects and what needs to be done to prevent or reverse reactions. Finally, they posit two critical conclusions as they relate to this emerging field of study. First, even though drugs and chemicals have been in use for many years, it does not exonerate them from producing subtle neurotoxic effects that show up many years later. As we continue to try to understand the structural toxicity relationship of the chemical structure and reaction within the brain, it would appear that the adverse effects of neurotoxins will become the dominant disease entity and focus of research in the 21st century. Second, developing nervous systems seem particularly sensitive to the neurotoxins. This has important implications, particularly for the person with mild mental retardation. In addition to the sociocultural factors, lack of educational opportunities, and nutritional deficits, we need to have a better understanding of the effects of teratogenetic and neurotoxic substances, since we may be able to develop primary and secondary prevention strategies that may bring about the reversibility of the symptom of mental retardation or at least contribute partially to this.

Chapter 8

Obstetrics and Perinatology

Implications for Prevention
in Mental Retardation

Calvin J. Hobel

During the past 20 years, few areas in clinical medicine have changed as rapidly as those in obstetrics and perinatology. Without question, advances in genetics, immunology, pharmacology, and biophysics have provided us with new concepts about the manipulation of various perinatal events to improve outcome. Before the role of obstetrics and perinatology in the prevention of mental retardation is discussed, it is important to understand the conditions that contribute to various types of mental handicaps. Beginning in 1950, the primary thrust was the reduction in perinatal and infant mortality. Only during the past 15 years has there been a clear focus on preventing morbidity. When one isolates the events occurring during pregnancy and the newborn period, one can identify some conditions that are associated with various disorders in children. The terminology, however, is not often clear. Therefore, it is necessary to clarify this apparent confusion.

Next, there is considerable interest in the components of our health care delivery system that account for improvements in outcome. Setting aside the contributions of technology, the systems approach appears to be playing a very important role. Perinatology bridges the disciplines of obstetrics and pediatrics, yet, other disciplines become involved as the seriousness and complexity worsen. Health care planning is beginning to play an important role in the identification of those conditions most suited for prevention. Today in perinatology, three conditions make the biggest contribution toward poor outcome. They are: low birth weight (both prematurity and intrauterine growth retardation), genetic problems, and structural abnormalities.

During the past 5 years, considerable attention has been directed toward the escalation of health care costs. Special attention has been directed toward the initial high cost of care for low birth weight infants. Follow-up care and the cost of long-term disability, as well as loss of productivity, contribute heavily to the total cost of conditions that contribute to perinatal "waste." If the disciplines of obstetrics and perinatology could significantly reduce the incidence of both cerebral palsy and mental retardation, a significant cost savings would be realized, and the mental and social stigma of the family who must care for a person with disabilities would be avoided.

HISTORICAL PERSPECTIVE

Prior to 1960, the inaccessible fetus was referred to as a "Mount Everest in utero." Intrauterine fetal transfusions (Liley, 1963) for treating fetal anemia were the first therapeutic measure that made the fetus accessible for therapy. Prior to fetal transfusion, the fetus would either die in utero from severe anemia or, if delivered early, succumb secondarily to respiratory distress syndrome. The development of Rh immunoglobulin in 1969, passively immunizing women to prevent Rh sensitization (Freda, Gorman, Pollack, & Bowe, 1975), is yet another step in the history of preventative medicine.

Most obstetrical and newborn care during the late sixties was crisis oriented. Technicological advances, however, began to provide new methods for the management of the critically ill newborn. Consequently, special care units developed to provide care for the critically ill newborn began to provide an environment for clinical research to study new methods for reducing morbidity and mortality. Obstetrical fetal monitoring (Hobel, 1971; Hon, 1959), coupled with other risk assessments (Hobel, Hyvarinen, Okada, & Oh, 1973), provided a new and easy method of categorizing the risk status of patients during labor. During the early 1970s, a dramatic reduction in infant mortality was realized (see Figure 1). In 1973 the March of Dimes published a monograph, "To Improve Pregnancy Outcome," that began to focus on the need to provide a means of integrating obstetrical and newborn health services (March of Dimes, 1973). This resulted in the development of the concept of regionalization of perinatal care. To test this new concept, the Robert Wood Johnson Foundation funded eight regional perinatal programs in the United States to study the value of developing extensive linkages between various levels of care. An important component of these regional programs was the utilization of risk assessment techniques facilitating the deployment of services. In 1985, a report summarizing data from these projects (McCormick, Shapiro, & Starfield, 1985) suggested that these regional programs were effective in reducing perinatal morbidity and mortality. However, reports from these regional programs (Hack, Merkatz, Jones, & Fanaroff, 1980; Shapiro, McCormick, Starfield, Krischer, & Bross, 1980) began to focus on low birth weight as a significant component responsible for perinatal morbidity and mortality.

After a period of relatively little change in infant mortality rate during the 1960s, it began to rapidly decline (see Figure 1). The infant mortality rate was

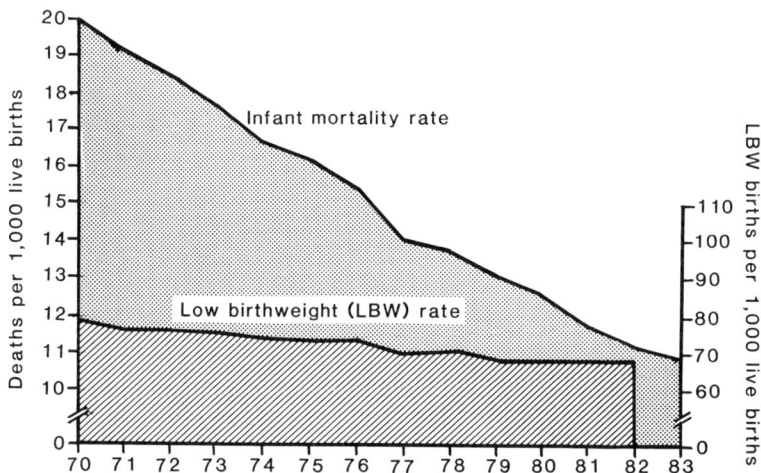

Figure 1. Infant mortality and low birth weight rates, 1970–1983. (Reproduced with permission from the Robert Wood Johnson Foundation Annual Report, 1984.)

13.1 per 1,000 live births, a 47% decrease from the rate in 1965. This change was primarily the result of a decrease in neonatal mortality. A major factor in this rapid decline was the increased survival of low birth weight infants due in part to improvements in neonatal intensive care and obstetrical care. The regionalization of services was thought to play an important role in facilitating these changes. This decline in the neonatal mortality is now beginning to plateau. If we want to maintain the previous decline, we must focus on the prevention of low birth weight (prematurity and intrauterine growth retardation—both of which contribute significantly to cerebral palsy and mental retardation). During the past 15 years, the incidence of low birth weight has decreased slowly, only 11% (approximately 1% per year) (Institute of Medicine, 1985). Since low birth weight is the leading cause of poor outcome, we must focus on the prevention of prematurity in order to sustain this decline in perinatal morbidity and mortality.

ETIOLOGY OF POOR OUTCOME

Frequently, terminology to describe poor outcome is ambiguous and, if the terms of the discussions are not clearly stated, one may become confused as one applies the current knowledge and understanding about poor outcome. Table 1 provides percentages for three conditions: infant mortality, cerebral palsy, and mental retardation. Prenatal conditions (early pregnancy, prior to 20 weeks) contribute significantly more to mental retardation than to infant mortality or cerebral palsy. Meanwhile, perinatal conditions (from 20 weeks to 28 days newborn life) contribute equally to infant mortality, while there are

Table 1.   Percentage of poor outcome for infant mortality, cerebral palsy, and mental retardation

	Infant mortality	Cerebral palsy	Mental retardation
Prenatal	20	20	72
Perinatal	52	56	10
Postnatal	19	—	3
Other	9	3	3
Unknown	0	21	12

J.M. Freeman (Ed.). Compiled by author from data published in *Prenatal and perinatal factors associated with brain disorders.* U.S. Department of Health and Human Services, Public Health Service (NIH Publication No. 85-1149), 1985.

still significant unknowns in the etiology of cerebral palsy and mental retardation. Therefore, if one is to launch a clinical program, one must focus on early prenatal care services for the prevention of mental retardation, and perinatal programs must focus on the reduction of infant mortality and cerebral palsy. The author cautions the reader not to assume that there is a clear distinction between each of these conditions.

Infant Mortality

It is difficult to identify the causes of stillbirths and infant death. Often there is no single cause, but interrelated causes leading to death. Recent technologies such as ultrasound, fetal monitoring, and biochemical tests, however, have helped to identify the cause of at least 80% of perinatal deaths. Table 2 identifies the most common causes (*Monthly Vital Statistics Report,* 1983). Perinatal conditions account for 48%, while congenital anomalies account for 20%. Thus, perinatal and congenital factors account for two thirds of infant death.

Table 2.   Causes of infant mortality

Cause	Percentage
Low birth weight[a]	27
Congenital anomalies	20
SIDS	12
Neonatal (other than low birth weight)[a]	9
Delivery process[a]	8
Infections	9
Pregnancy[a]	4
Accidents	3
Other	8

Derived from *Monthly Vital Statistics Report* (1983).
[a]Perinatal condition accounts for 48%.

Cerebral Palsy

Cerebral palsy is a descriptive term referring to nonprogressive motor deficit of early onset. Table 3 lists the attributed risks for cerebral palsy. Almost every epidemiological study has found a strong association between low birth weight and cerebral palsy. However, low birth weight infants are not a homogeneous group. It is comprised of prematurity and fetal growth retardation and accounts for one third of cerebral palsy cases. The next most common attributed causes are prenatal (genetic and fetal deprivation) and perinatal asphyxia. Again, these two conditions occur at two distinctly different time periods in the pregnancy-infancy continuum and require distinctly different intervention schemes for prevention. "Fetal deprivation of supply" is a term Hagberg (1978) used, referring to a condition resulting from maternal-fetal vascular insufficiency during pregnancy that probably causes placenta insufficiency and chronic fetal distress.

Mental Retardation

For our purposes, mental retardation is defined as lower cognitive functioning (i.e., an IQ score of 2 standard deviations below the mean and lower social/adaptive functioning). The best data available to assess the etiology of mental retardation are the data from Sweden (see Table 4) (Gustavson, Hagberg, Hagberg, & Lewerth, 1977; Moser, 1985). Prenatal conditions account for approximately 73% of the cases of mental retardation. The majority of these cases (43%) are chromosomal and genetic. "Fetal deprivation of supply" also plays an important role. Relatively few of the cases of mental retardation are attributed to perinatal factors, that is, those related to the time period between 20 weeks of fetal life and 28 days of neonatal life.

As with most conditions in medicine, a mixture of disabilities exists. Among those infants with mental retardation (Susser, Hauser, Kiely, Paneth, & Stein, 1985), about one fifth also have cerebral palsy, and among those with cerebral palsy, more than four fifths also have mental retardation.

Table 3. Proportion of cerebral palsy cases attributed to various factors

Factor	Relative risk	Attributed risk (%)
Prenatal etiology (fetal deprivation and genetic)	3.5	20
Prematurity	9.0	25
Fetal growth retardation	2.3	6
Perinatal asphyxia	10.0	25
Other		3
Unknown		21

Adapted from table by M. Susser et al., Chapter 10 in John Freeman, *Prenatal and Perinatal Factors Associated with Brain Disorders*, NIH Publication 85-1149, 1985, p. 400.

Table 4. Etiology of severe mental retardation

Cause	Percentage
Prenatal	
Chromosomal and genetic	43
Congenital anomalies	20
Acquired infection, diabetes, SGA	10
Perinatal	10
Postnatal	11
Childhood	3
Unknowns	12

Revised from table by H. Moser, Chapter 4, in John M. Freeman, *Prenatal and Perinatal Factors Associated with Brain Disorders*, NIH Publication T5-1149, 1985, p. 122.

SYSTEMS APPROACH TO HEALTH CARE

Several years ago the "risk approach" was adopted by the World Health Organization as a managerial device (World Health Organization, 1977) to facilitate the planning and implementation of integrated maternal and child health services. The purpose of this approach was the accomplishment of a rational distribution of resources that would ensure "something for all and more for those in greater need." The strategy involved in the risk approach is the development of an intervention program based on valid data about costs, resources, risk of disease, and the effectiveness of different types of health care activities provided by different types of personnel. This systematic method includes the activities listed in Table 5.

Each step of the risk approach has been accomplished by the West Los Angeles Perinatal Program. In 1970, we began to collect data using a newly developed perinatal record-keeping system. By 1973, we identified perinatal

Table 5. Activities for systematic planning and implementation of health development projects

1. Study baseline data
   Morbidity—mortality
   Factors influencing outcome
2. Select problems to be dealt with
   Priorities
3. Select indicators of risk
4. Develop a risk assessment system
5. Review health strategies and resources
6. Develop a strategy of care according to level of risk
   Emphasis on early and appropriate intervention
7. Implement, monitor, and evaluate

From World Health Organization (1977).

morbidity and mortality (Hobel et al., 1973) as our major problem and identified those risk factors primarily associated with poor outcome. Using those risk factors, we developed a risk assessment system to identify patients at risk. Beginning in 1975, we implemented one of the eight Robert Wood Johnson Foundation projects to study the role of regionalization of services based on the risk approach. By 1979, five major perinatal problems were identified as significantly contributing to perinatal morbidity and mortality (Hobel, 1979). These five problems were: prematurity, intrauterine growth retardation, genetic abnormalities, hypertension, and postterm pregnancy. Over the past several years we have completed strategies for each of these conditions (Hobel, Medearis, & Oakes, 1985–1986). Currently, we are developing an extensive network to implement these strategies within a large population in order to test their effectiveness in preventing these problems rather than dealing solely with their effects in terms of impact on morbidity and mortality. The newest component of our network is a prepregnancy planning clinic for high-risk women who are anticipating a pregnancy. Our goal is to begin care early in order to avoid risks and/or provide intervention, thereby reducing risk (Hobel, 1985).

Three of our most effective programs are: the prevention of prematurity, the prevention of genetic disease, and the prevention of complications associated with postterm pregnancy. To illustrate our strategy, the prematurity prevention program is described.

PREVENTION OF PREMATURITY

Etiology

A scientific approach to the prevention of prematurity requires that a hypothesis be set forth prior to developing a program for preventing prematurity. The multiple risk factors causing low birth weight are thought to be similar for both prematurity and intrauterine growth retardation. The preterm infant born too soon and the growth-retarded infant born on time yet small, leads one to ask why the fetus is expelled in the former, but not in the latter? This is indeed an interesting biological question that will require extensive clinical and basic research to answer. Bragonier, Cushner, and Hobel (1984) developed a hypothesis (as outlined in Figure 2). We believe that stress plays the most significant role in increasing the risk of preterm labor. Various forms of maternal behavior and personal characteristics influence the level of stress. We believe catecholamine release (norepinephrine) influences uterine activity and reduces uterine blood flow. The net effect is a reduction in placental function and reduced progesterone production important for the maintenance of pregnancy.

Stages I and II of this hypothesis are considered the silent stages of preterm labor. The conditions listed in Stage I and the biochemical changes occurring in Stage II lead to the more symptomatic Stage IIIA, where uterine

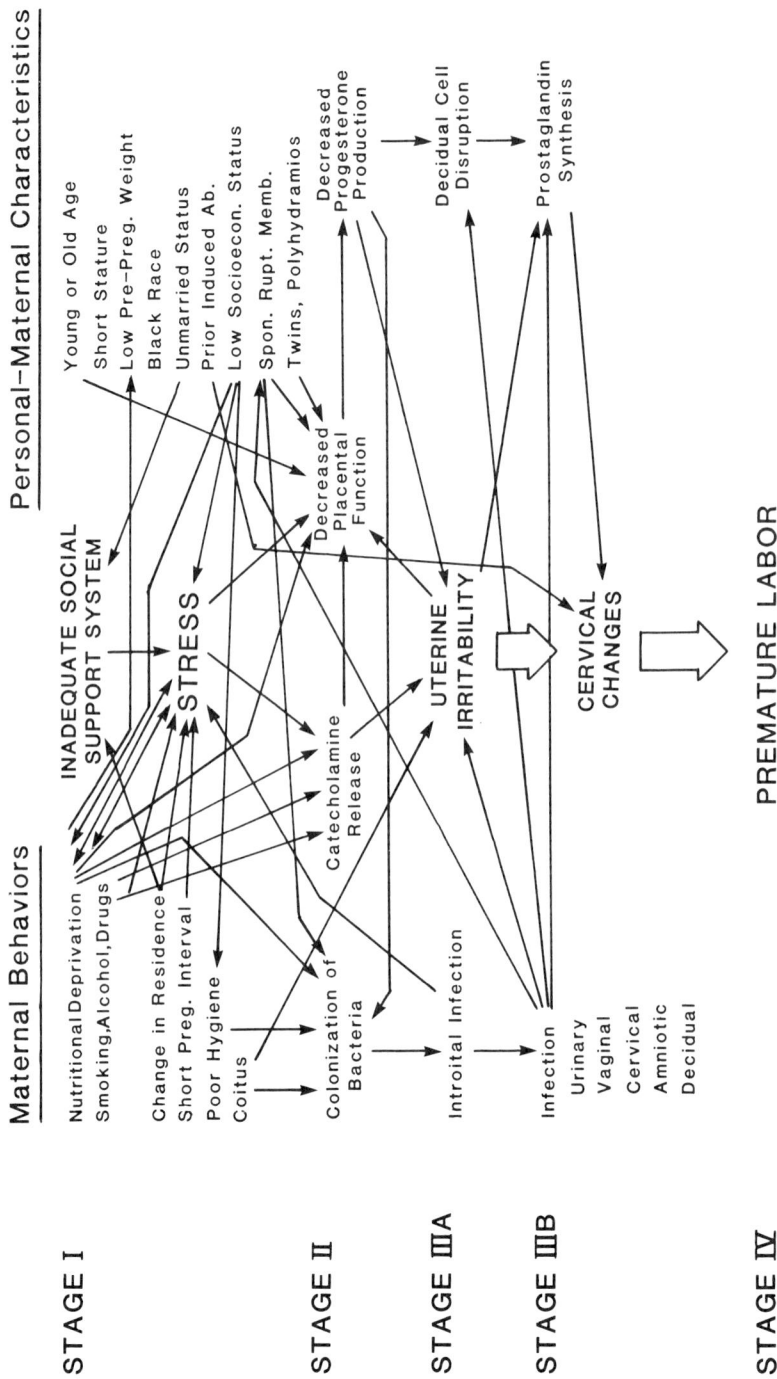

Figure 2. Hypothesis causal diagram for prematurity.

234

contractions cause prostaglandin synthesis in the decidual cells and initiate a cascade of changes (Gustavii, 1975). Cervical effacement and dilatation then allow infection, if present, to ascend into the uterine cavity. Infection is a further stimulus to prostaglandin synthesis and the progression of changes that are described as preterm labor (Stage IV).

The duration of the early stages of preterm labor (I and II) is variable and depends on the occurrence of risk factors and the ability of the patient to cope or alter their effect. Stage III is thought to have a more defined duration, and as it is a symptomatic phase, patients at risk can be identified. Patients are thought to be in this symptomatic phase as briefly as 6–12 hours or as long as 1–2 weeks. It is not uncommon for patients admitted in preterm labor (Stage IV) to relate a history of Stage III symptoms for 1–2 days prior to admission in preterm labor. We believe that this clinically oriented hypothesis of preterm labor is realistic and, as such, provided a basis for designing a program to prevent preterm delivery.

Development of Concept of Prematurity Prevention

Interest in the implementation of programs for the prevention of preterm birth was slow in developing for two reasons. First, even though a risk assessment system was described as early as 1969 (Papiernik-Berkhauer, 1969), a description of the content and methods of this French program was not available in English language journals until 1979 (Papiernik-Berkhauer, 1979). Second, no well-controlled studies were carried out to answer the basic question of "What components of a prevention program are most effective?" Nevertheless, Herron, Katz, and Creasy (1982) published preliminary data describing an educational program thought to significantly reduce the incidence of prematurity by early recognition of preterm labor and intervention with tocolysis (the inhibition of labor with intravenous drugs). These preliminary data generated tremendous interest in the concept of the prevention of prematurity.

The absence of properly designed studies to identify which components of prenatal care influence the incidence of prematurity provided the impetus for the study design of the West Los Angeles Prematurity Prevention Program.

Development of West Los Angeles Prematurity Prevention Program

The West Los Angeles Prematurity Prevention Program (PPP) has three major components:

1. Prenatal Care System   This prenatal care system utilized nurse practitioner teams providing a specific type of prenatal care.

2. Risk Assessment System   This project uses a risk assessment system developed and tested retrospectively on a population of 8,249 women delivering at Harbor-UCLA Medical Center from 1979 to 1983. A patient with any one of the risk factors listed in Table 4 is considered at risk for preterm labor. With a 35% risk rate, the sensitivity of the system was predicted to be 59.8% with a specificity of 64.1%. This risk system is currently being tested in the control clinics of the PPP.

3. Data System The source document for data collection is the Problem Oriented Perinatal Risk Assessment System (POPRAS) (Hobel, 1982) perinatal record. Using the POPRAS record, we have developed an on-line interactive computerized network referred to as PIDS (POPRAS Interactive Data System). This network links the West Los Angeles Area prenatal clinics with the Cedars-Sinai Medical Center's Scientific Data Center (headquarters of the project) and the Harbor-UCLA Medical Center where most patients deliver (Figure 3). This data system provides us with the services listed in Table 6.

Funding

Beginning in 1979, various private organizations, foundations, and state and federal agencies were approached to fund the West Los Angeles PPP. Considerable effort was spent searching available literature to document source material supporting an appropriate intervention strategy. Members of our program visited France to witness and document the French experience. Meetings with Professor Papiernik at the Beclere Hospital in Paris as well as with Philippe Lazar, a statistician at the Research Unit of Epidemiology and

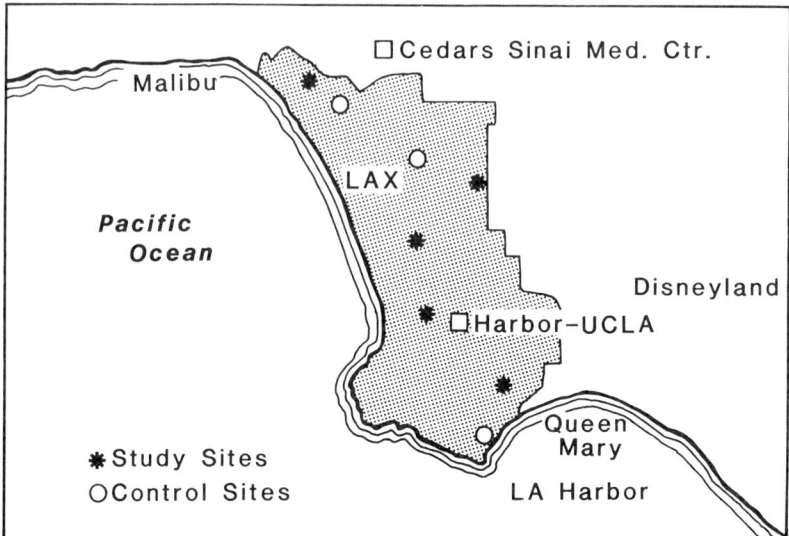

Figure 3.   West Los Angeles Prematurity Prevention Program.

Table 6. Risk assessment list

Variables	Weight
Historical	
Induced abortion	0.267
Habitual abortion	0.773
Previous preterm birth/labor	0.926
Previous neonatal death	0.253
Uterine cervical abnormality	0.480
Previous cesarean section, classical	0.541
Previous myomectomy	3.11
Pregnancy-induced hypertension	0.0433
Chronic hypertension	0.461
Genitourinary infection	0.0801
Renal disease	0.722
Psychiatric	0.379
Tobacco	0.341
Marijuana	0.756
Narcotics	0.592
Developing problems	
Size-date discrepancy	0.325
Severe anemia	0.819
Threatened abortion	1.36
Incompetent cervix	2.47
Surgical	0.632
Multiple pregnancies	1.92
Mild pregnancy-induced hypertension	0.649
Severe pregnancy-induced hypertension	0.853
Bleeding after 20 weeks	1.60
Constant	-3.18

Note. Any variable with a weight greater than 0.225 will place a patient into the group at risk for preterm labor. Any single variable other than history of pregnancy-induced hypertension and history of genitourinary infections will make a patient at risk. Score $> -2.928 =$ high risk; score $< -2.938 =$ low risk.

Statistics at INSERM, were extremely helpful in understanding the complexities of designing a prevention strategy. Armed with an extensive fund of knowledge and a well-conceived study design, we obtained funding from the Maternal and Child Health branch of the state of California in October 1982.

Study Design

Planning sessions for the design of a prematurity prevention program began in the summer of 1980. At the time, a consensus was that the intervention program must be a prospectively randomized trial. How to randomize the patients was the first issue. Retrospective data from four prenatal clinics indicated that each clinic was similar in terms of patient population and demographics. These clinics were randomly assigned to either control or experimental status. We were next confronted with what types of interventions we would test. Our extensive review of the literature suggested that the etiology of prematurity was most likely multifactorial, yet stress appeared to be a central issue (Figure 2). We, therefore, directed our attention toward interventions reducing stress and those prompting the maintenance of pregnancy. This approach was in concert with the interventions used by Papiernik. Thus, our study was to test interventions potentially preventing preterm labor rather than the implementation of an education program for early identification of signs and symptoms of preterm labor and their treatment as proposed by Herron et al. (1982).

In the West Los Angeles Area PPP it was decided that we would test five treatment protocols for high-risk women. The intervention protocols selected were: bed rest, psychosocial support, an oral progestin (Provera), a matched placebo, and a control. All high-risk patients (in the experimental group) received an extensive educational program. The control group in the experimental clinics received only education. In summary, this study design was to determine whether selected interventions would be effective in preventing preterm labor in addition to the effectiveness of education in preventing preterm labor.

Description of Program

In the experimental sites, patients are presented with an invitation to join the PPP. If patients agree to participate, they sign an informed consent before their risk status is determined by the PIDS program. Patients having one or more of the high-risk factors (Table 7) are considered high risk and randomized into one of the five interventions.

In addition to standard risk assessment, a detailed psychosocial history is taken but not used in assessing risk. These data will subsequently be analyzed

Table 7. List of services provided by the POPRAS interactive data system used for data management

1. Computerized system for risk assessment
2. Real-time, computerized randomization scheme for intervention assignment
3. Patient scheduling system
4. Patient tracking
5. Real-time reports for patient visit summary, referral reports, and patient logs and summary statistics on intervention and assignments
6. On-line medical center data entry to provide access to prenatal data

to determine whether or not they could be used to improve our current risk assessment system. All high-risk patients receive education about prevention of preterm labor, signs and symptoms of premature labor, what action to take if symptoms occur, and a class detailing what to expect in the hospital. Patients not having any of the risk factors are considered to be low risk and are randomly assigned to one of two visit protocols (a standard visit schedule or an abbreviated visit schedule) based on certain milestone visits thought to be important during pregnancy. The abbreviated schedule is currently being evaluated to determine if pregnant women with little or no risk can be seen less frequently without an increase in morbidity. In one half of the study clinics, low-risk patients receive a class on the signs and symptoms of premature labor and what to do if they occur; in the other half, they do not receive this information. This tests the value of education for low-risk patients. Patients are followed under these protocols until 37 weeks gestational age. All data for patients who deliver at Harbor-UCLA Medical Center are entered into the data system by a labor and delivery room nurse or data entry clerks.

Preliminary Results

The preliminary results from the 1,135 total deliveries are encouraging, but statistical analysis will not be undertaken until sufficient numbers of patients are studied. From our retrospective study, we had determined a baseline prematurity rate of 7.7% (11.2% in high-risk patients; 5.0% in low-risk patients). Preliminary results show that our control clinics have a prematurity rate of 8.16% (12.5% in high-risk patients; 6.3% in low-risk patients). Study patients, on the other hand, have a prematurity rate of 5.7% (7.4% in high-risk patients; 4.7% in low-risk patients). Preterm births in experimental clinics thus show a reduction of 26% compared to baseline levels and 34% compared to control levels. The rates in high-risk patients are reduced 34% compared to the baseline high-risk patients and 41% compared to the control group high-risk patients. It must be understood that the number of patients delivered is not high enough to draw any specific conclusions.

Cost-Effectiveness of Prevention

Survival and, more importantly, the intact survival of infants with very low birth weight ($<1,500$ g) has improved dramatically over the past 15 years. Initially, improvement came with only modest cost, but further improvement has come at increasingly greater expense. This should not be surprising as the "easiest" infants to save are those requiring the least expense. In 1959, the cost estimate of inpatient hospitalization care (Baumgartner, Jacobziner, & Pakter, 1959) for premature infants was approximately $25 per day. Subsequently, inflation, increasing sophistication of care, cost of equipment, and personnel have multiplied expenditures by a factor of 20 or more. In 1978,

Pomerance, Ukrainski, Ukra, Henderson, Nash, and Meredith reported the average daily cost of care for surviving infants weighing 1,000 g or less at birth to be $450. Recently, the economic aspects (cost and benefits) of neonatal intensive care of very low birth weight infants has been determined by Boyle, Torrance, Sinclair, and Horwood (1983). They concluded that neonatal intensive care increased survival rates as well as cost and, in economic terms, neonatal intensive care suffered a net economic loss. A recent cost benefit analysis (Walker, Feldman, Vohr, & Oh, 1984) suggested that neonatal intensive care for infants weighing less than 1,000 g may not be justifiable. These investigators felt that any judgment concerning the relative economic value of neonatal intensive care of very low birth weight infants would require economic evaluation (using similar methods) of other health programs, such as those for prevention of prematurity.

If the current premature prevention programs are found to be successful, a significant cost savings could be realized. Recently, the Institute of Medicine (IOM) (1985), Committee to Study the Prevention of Low Birth Weight, determined that there would be potential cost saving if a program could reduce the incidence of prematurity by 22%. Since data on the cost of prenatal services are limited, the Committee first carried out an independent survey (Korenbrot, 1985) of prenatal care charges to determine what a prevention program might cost. This survey determined that additional professional services required (beginning in the first trimester) for a woman at high risk of delivery of a low birth weight infant would cost $400. Next, the Committee used this figure in their cost comparison analysis to assess the value of a prenatal care prevention program to a target population in order to demonstrate the potential cost savings resulting from decrease of the low birth weight rate. Using this target population of 110,600 women, the IOM Committee analyzed the costs of prenatal care, initial hospitalization, rehospitalization, and long-term morbidity cost for 12,719 preterm infants. According to the Committee report, a successful program that reduces the incidence of prematurity from 11.5% to 9% would save an estimated $40,912,507 or approximately $369,914 for every 1,000 pregnancies entered into the program.

Table 8. Dollar expenditures for 1983 in Nebraska for crippled children's services, special education, and mental retardation

Crippled children's services:	$ 2,583,445
Special education	$52,704,819
Mental retardation	
Beatrice State Developmental Center	$16,353,305
Community Mental Retardation Aid	$18,252,697
Total	$89,894,266

Table 9. Cost savings estimate for a theoretical Nebraska statewide prematurity prevention program

Assumptions: 1. Reduce incidence of prematurity by 22%
2. Cost savings = $350,000/1,000 pregnancies[a]

Example: State of Nebraska
1983 deliveries = 27,000
Prematurity rate = 5.4% (1,458)
(22% Reduction = 320 preterm infants)

Cost savings: $350,000 × 27 = $9,450,000.00

Note. See text for explanation.
[a]Institute of Medicine (1985).

For the purpose of this book, I obtained vital statistics data from the state of Nebraska and the dollar expenditures for crippled children services, special education, and mental retardation during 1984 in order to assess the potential economic impact of a successful program in the state of Nebraska. As seen in Table 8, in 1983 the state of Nebraska spent approximately 90 million dollars to provide care to persons with disabilities.

Table 9 identifies the potential cost savings for 1983, had a prevention program reduced the incidence of prematurity in Nebraska by 22%. In 1983, the incidence of prematurity in Nebraska was only 5.4%, already low when compared to the national average. There were 27,000 infants born in 1983 and 1,458 were preterm. Using the cost estimate from the Institute of Medicine, the savings for just 1 year would be 9.4 million dollars or approximately 10% of the state's yearly cost for the care of persons with disabilities. Even though these cost savings are attractive and would save the Nebraska taxpayer money, the year-to-year reduction in low birth weight infants would potentially reduce the pool of individuals with disabilities as well as reduce future costs. As attractive as the strategy appears, in my estimation the implementation of a state program of this magnitude would take at least 5 years to accomplish.

Though reducing the incidence of prematurity by 20% is a realistic goal, a prevention program of this magnitude with emphasis on improving the content of prenatal care would effect the incidence of other prenatal and perinatal complications. Therefore, the net effect on reducing costs and morbidity are potentially quite impressive. In summary, obstetrics and the emphasis on perinatal care can provide a significant contribution in the prevention of mental retardation and should serve an important role in accomplishing the goals of this book.

REFERENCES

Baumgartner, L., Jacobziner, H., & Pakter, J. (1959). A critical survey of the New York Program for the care of premature infants. *Journal of Pediatrics, 54,* 725–731.

Boyle, M. H., Torrance, G. W., Sinclair, J. C., & Horwood, S. P. (1983). Economic evaluation of neonatal intensive care of very low birth weight infants. *New England Journal of Medicine, 308,* 1330–1337.

Bragonier, J. R., Cushner, I. M., & Hobel, C. J. (1984). Social and personal factors in the etiology of preterm birth. In F. Fuchs & P. G. Stubblefield (Eds.), *Preterm birth* (pp. 64–85). New York: MacMillan.

Freda, V. J., Gorman, J. G., Pollack, W., & Bowe, E. (1975). Prevention of Rh-hemolytic disease—Ten years clinical experience with Rh-immune globulin. *New England Journal of Medicine, 292,* 1014–1016.

Gustavii, B. (1975). Release of lysosomal acid phosphatase into cytoplasm of decidual cells before the onset of labor in humans. *British Journal of Obstetrics and Gynaecology, 82,* 177–181.

Gustavson, K. H., Hagberg, B., Hagberg, G., & Lewerth, A. (1977). Severe mental retardation in a Swedish County. II. Etiologic and pathogenetic aspects of children born, 1959–1970. *Neuropediatrie, 8,* 293–304.

Hack, M., Merkatz, I. R., Jones, P. K., & Fanaroff, A. A. (1980). Changing trends of neonatal and postneonatal deaths in very low-birth-weight infants. *American Journal of Obstetrics and Gynecology, 137,* 797–800.

Hagberg, G. (1978). The epidemiological panorama of major neuropediatrics handicaps in Sweden. *Clinical Developmental Medicine, 67,* 111–124.

Herron, M. A., Katz, M., & Creasy, R. K. (1982). Evaluation of a pre-term birth prevention program. Preliminary report. *Obstetrics and Gynecology, 59,* 452–456.

Hobel, C. J. (1971). Intrapartum clinical assessment of fetal distress. *American Journal of Obstetrics and Gynecology, 110,* 336–342.

Hobel, C. J. (1979). Assessment of the high risk fetus. *Clinics in Obstetrics and Gynecology, 6,* 367–377.

Hobel, C. J. (1982). Development of POPRAS (Problem Oriented Perinatal Risk Assessment System). In T. R. Harris & J. P. Bahr (Eds.), *Use of computers in perinatal medicine* (pp. 117–139). New York: Praeger.

Hobel, C. J. (1985). Factors before pregnancy that influence brain development. In J. M. Freeman (Ed.), *Prenatal and perinatal factors associated with brain disorders* (pp. 117–195). Bethesda, MD: U.S. Department of Health and Human Services, Public Health Service, National Institute of Health (NIH Publication No. 85-1149).

Hobel, C. J., Hyvarinen, M. A., Okada, D. M., & Oh, W. S. (1973). Prenatal and intrapartum high risk screening. I. Prediction of high risk neonate. *American Journal of Obstetrics and Gynecology, 117,* 1–9.

Hobel, C. J., Medearis, A. L., & Oakes, G. A. (1985–1986). Assessment of fetal health. In N. M. Nelson (Ed.), *Current therapy in neonatal-perinatal medicine* (pp. 1–6). Philadelphia: B. C. Decker.

Hon, E. H. (1959). Observations on "pathologic" fetal bradycardia. *American Journal of Obstetrics and Gynecology, 77,* 1084–1090.

Institute of Medicine. (1985). Committee to Study the Prevention of Low Birth Weight: Division of Health Promotion and Disease Prevention. *Preventing low birth weight.* Washington, DC: National Academy Press.

Korenbrot, C. (1985). *A rapid survey of prenatal care changes in the United States.* Institute of Medicine (Committee to Study the Prevention of Low Birth Weight: Division of Health Promotion and Disease Prevention). Washington, DC: National Academy Press.

Liley, A. W. (1963). Intrauterine transfusion of fetus with hemolytic disease. *British Medical Journal, 2,* 1101–1108.

March of Dimes (Committee on Perinatal Health). (1973). *Toward improving the outcome of pregnancy. Recommendations for the regional development of maternal and perinatal health services.* White Plains, NY: The National Foundation, March of Dimes.

McCormick, M. C., Shapiro, S., & Starfield, B. H. (1985). The regionalization of perinatal services. Summary of the evaluation of a National Demonstration Program. *Journal of the American Medical Association, 253,* 799–804.

Monthly Vital Statistics Report. (1983). *Monthly Vital Statistics Report, 32* (4) (Suppl.), 34–35.

Moser, H. W. (1985). Biologic factors of development. In J. M. Freeman (Ed.), *Prenatal and perinatal factors associated with brain disorders* (pp. 121–161). Bethesda, MD: U.S. Department of Health and Human Services, Public Health Services, National Institutes of Health (NIH Publication No. 85-1149).

Papiernik-Berkhauer, E. (1969). Coefficient de risque d'accouchment premature. *Presses Medical, 77,* 793–794.

Papiernik-Berkhauer, E. (1979). Development of risk during pregnancy. In D. Thalhammer, K. Baumgarten, & A. Polk (Eds.), *Perinatal medicine* (pp. 118–125). Hagerstown, MD: PSG Publishing Co.

Pomerance, J. J., Ukrainski, C. T., Ukra, T., Henderson. D. H., Nash, A. H., & Meredith, J. L. (1978). Cost of living for infants weight 1000 grams or less at birth. *Pediatrics, 61,* 908–910.

Shapiro, S., McCormick, M. C., Starfield, B. H., Krischer, J. P., & Bross, D. (1980). Relevance of correlates of infant deaths for significant morbidity at 1 year of age. *American Journal of Obstetrics and Gynecology, 136,* 363–373.

Susser, M., Hauser, W. A., Kiely, J. L., Paneth, N., & Stein, Z. (1985). Quantitative estimates of prenatal and perinatal risk factors for perinatal mortality, cerebral palsy, mental retardation and epilepsy. In J. M. Freeman (Ed.), *Prenatal and perinatal factors associated with brain disorders* (pp. 359–439). Bethesda, MD: U.S. Department of Health and Human Services, Public Health Services, National Institute of Health (NIH Publication No. 85-1149).

Walker, D. J. B., Feldman, A., Vohr, B. R., & Oh, W. S. (1984). Cost-benefit analysis of neonatal intensive care for infants weighing less than 1000 grams at birth. *Pediatrics, 74,* 20–25.

World Health Organization. (1977). Editorial. Something for all and more for those in greater need. *WHO Chronical, 31,* 150–151.

Chapter 9

Developmental Neurotoxicity

Carol R. Angle and Matilda S. McIntire

This review discusses three areas of developmental neurotoxicity: the status of predictive testing for teratogeneticity and neurological dysfunction, specific factors identified as responsible for the increased susceptibility of the fetus and child to neurotoxins, and the state of knowledge or ignorance concerning the threshold for injury from representative neurotoxins of current concern.

PREDICTION OF HAZARD AND RISK

In an age of chemicals, the prevention and treatment of neurotoxic causes of mental retardation deserves top priority. This would seem a formidable task, given the estimate of 50,000 chemicals in common use with approximately 650 entering the environment every year. There is an urgent need for systematic testing of compounds for neurotoxic and teratogenic hazard—hazard meaning the potential to be dangerous. Simultaneously, there must be well-defined epidemiological evaluations of risk—risk meaning the likelihood for an effect occurring under conditions of exposure (Schardein, 1985; Schardein, Schwetz, & Kenel, 1985).

A time model of neurotoxicity, such as that illustrated in Figure 1, is helpful in the evaluation of both potential hazard and actual risk. The effect of prenatal neurotoxins may be manifested by reproductive failure, fetal loss, teratogenicity, neuroendocrine effects that may not be evident until sexual maturation, or neurobehavioral toxicity manifested as an acute or latent dysfunction or developmental delay. All of these manifestations may be acute or chronic, reversible or irreversible.

Chemicals are considered teratogenic hazards if they disrupt development at doses innocuous to the adult. The births of 10,000 thalidomide victims in 1961 and 1962 roused the scientific community to the need for adequate models of teratogenic potential. As of this date, almost 3,000 chemicals have been tested and at least 1,000 are teratogenic in animals.

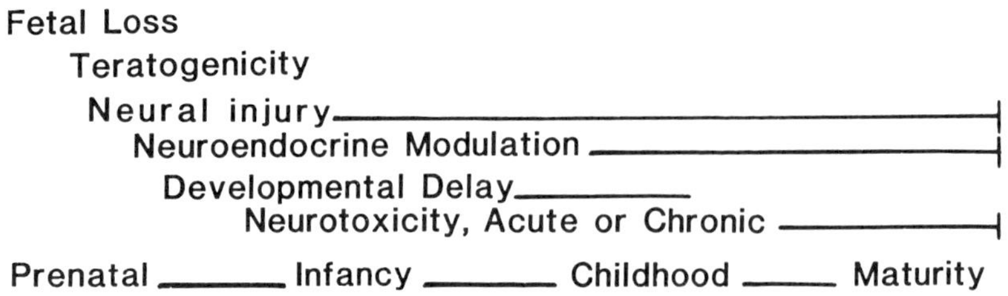

Fetal Loss
    Teratogenicity
        Neural injury————————————————————————————|
            Neuroendocrine Modulation ————————————————|
            Developmental Delay—————————
                Neurotoxicity, Acute or Chronic —————————|
    Prenatal ——————— Infancy ——————— Childhood ——————— Maturity

Figure 1. Time model of neurotoxicity.

Despite this, only the 14 groups of chemicals listed in Table 1 have a documented teratogenic effect in the human fetus. This list does not include chemicals such as aspirin and nicotine, both known to retard fetal growth, and does not consider the potentially large group of chemicals that may affect reproductive capacity, implantation, and fetal survival and growth, or evoke latent neurological sequelae. Of the human teratogens listed in Table 1, 8 of the 14 groups of chemicals were defined as teratogens in humans before they were defined in laboratory animals. This suggests that a potential hazard is indicated by one third (or 1,000 out of 3,000) of teratogenic studies in animals, but that the animal tests have predicted a documented human risk in only 6 of 1,000 or 0.6% (Frankos, 1985). The good intentions of the Kefauver-Harris Amendments of 1962 mandating teratogenic testing have not yet resulted in efficient screening of new drugs.

The productivity of the requirement for testing in at least two mammalian species has been extensively reviewed by Frankos (1985). Of substances identified as human teratogens, positive teratological response was exhibited 85% of the time in the mouse, 80% in the rat, 60% in the rabbit, 45% in the hamster, and 30% in the monkey.

Of 27 compounds suspected of being reproductive or teratogenic hazards (Table 2), only 55% are positive in one or more animal species. These 27 compounds do not include hazardous chemicals, such as the sterilizing gas ethylene oxide, that readily induce chromosomal breaks but that lack sufficiently strong epidemiological correlations with injury.

Concordance is even lower for compounds that do not appear to be human teratogens. Of 165 compounds specifically reported as having absolutely no evidence of human teratogenicity, 41% were positive in more than a single animal species. Concordance for nonteratogenicity was observed 80% of the time in the monkey, 70% in the rabbit, 50% in the rat, 35% in the mouse, and 35% in the hamster.

The variability in the species response and the lack of predictability are only two of the deficiencies of standard teratological testing. More relevant is the lack of systematic testing for reproductive failure, embryonic loss, delayed neuroendocrine dysfunction, and either neonatal or latent neu-

Table 1. Human teratogens

Teratogen	Initial discovery species	Year established as human teratogen	Reference malformation[a]
Alcohol	Rat	1973	CV, craniofacial, limb
Androgens/progestins	Rat	1953	Pseudohermaphroditism, uterine malignancy
Anticancer antimetabolite			
Aminopterin	Human	1956	Skeletal
Fluorouracil	Mouse	1980	Visceral
Methotrexate	Rat	1968	Skeletal
Cytarabine	Rat	1980	Limb, ear
Anticancer alkylating agents			
Busulfan	Rat	1960	Visceral
Chlorambucil	Mouse	1963	Urogenital
Cyclophosphamide	Rat	1964	Digits
Mechlorethamine	Rat	1974	Renal, limb, ear
Anticonvulsants			
Hydantoins	Mouse	1975	Facial, mental
Diones	Human	1975	Facial, mental
Valproate	Rat	1982	CNS
Antithyroid agents	Human	1940s–1950	Hypothyroidism
Methyl mercury	Human	1959	Microcephaly, CNS
Thalidomide	Human	1961	Limb
Lithium	Mouse	1973	CV
D-Penicillamine	Human	1971	Skin
Streptomycin	Human	1960s	Inner ear
Coumarin anticoagulants	Human	1968	Hydrocephalus, chondrodysplasia
Vitamin A analogs	Rat	1983	CV, ear, brain

Modified from Tables 2 and 4 of Schardein, Schwetz, and Kenel (1985).
[a]CV, cardiovascular; CNS, central nervous system.

robehavioral deficits. This has resulted in the request by the FDA for new directions in research concerning drugs and environmental chemicals:

1. Delineation of the fundamental processes in development
2. Fetal pharmacokinetics and metabolism

Table 2. Chemicals with anecdotal effects on human reproduction or development

Agent	Concordant animal lesion	Implicated human finding[a]
Acetone		Birth defects
Benzene	0/3	Birth defects, chromosome aberrations
Boric acid	0/2	Birth defects, sperm abnormalities
Butiphos	0/1	Birth defects, stillbirths
Carbon disulfide	2/2	Decreased fertility, spontaneous abortions
Carbon monoxide	1/3	Stillbirths, birth defects
Chloroprene	1/2	Miscarriages
Dibromochloropropane	0/1	Infertility
2,4-Dichlorophenoxyacetic acid	1/3	CNS, craniofacial
Dimethylformamide	1/3	Miscarriages
Dinitrodipropyl sulfanilamide	0/2	Miscarriages, birth defects
Disulfiram	1/2	Birth defects
Ethylene dibromide	0/2	Decreased fertility
Formaldehyde	2/2	Spontaneous abortions
Hexachlorobenzene	1/3	Stillbirths, neonatal mortality, CNS
Lead	3/4	Infertility, spontaneous abortions, birth defects
Mercuric chloride	1/1	Spontaneous abortions
Methylene chloride	0/2	Birth defects
Methyl ethyl ketone	0/1	Birth defects
Methyl parathion	1/2	Birth defects
Polychlorinated biphenyls	0/1	Low birth weight, midface hypoplasia
Sodium selenite	0/3	Spontaneous abortions, birth defects
Styrene	2/4	Abortions
Toluene	1/2	Birth defects
Trichloroethylene	0/3	Birth defects
Vinyl chloride	0/3	Chromosome abnormalities, miscarriages, stillbirths, sperm abnormalities, birth defects
Xylene	1/2	Birth defects

Modified from Table 7, Schardein, Schwetz, and Kenel (1985).
[a]CNS, central nervous system.

3. Development of sensitive and validated indices of the full range of injury
4. Development of in vitro tests to detect teratological events (Frankos, 1985; Schardein, 1985).

DEVELOPMENTAL SUSCEPTIBILITY

At the present time, drugs and environmental chemicals account for only 2%–3% of teratogenic effects observed in humans, and 65%–70% of all developmental anomalies continue to be of unknown causes (Karrh et al., 1981). The potential magnitude of the role of neurotoxins is proposed as much greater, an inference derived from the relative susceptibility of the developing neurological system as well as the far greater number of chemicals incriminated as neurotoxic but not teratogenic.

Table 3 outlines specific examples of factors in age-related susceptibility. Fetal injury may relate to the adverse effect of a toxin on fetal blood flow and nutrition as well as the induction of toxic metabolities in placental tissue. Not only does nicotine decrease placental and fetal blood flow, but smoking results in covalent DNA adduct formation in the human placenta (Everson et

Table 3. Factors in age-related susceptibility

Organ and effect	Factor
Placenta	
Injury and fetal deprivation	Smoking and DNA adducts placenta
Fetal-placental gradient	Methyl mercury
Gastrointestinal	
High gastrointestinal volume, increased absorption	Lead, endrin
Decreased biliary excretion	Methyl mercury
Decreased gastric acidity	Nitrates
Pulmonary	
High ventilatory volume	Organic solvents
Skin	
Thin stratum corneum	Lindane
Large surface area	Hexachloraphene
Liver	
Microsomal drug metabolism	Phenytoin
Kidney	
Decreased excretion	Methyl mercury
CNS	
Decreased glial storage	Lead
Rapid myelinization	Tetraethyl lead
Neuroendocrine modulation	Chlordecone

al., 1986). Due to the placental barrier, the majority of toxins have a lower concentration in the fetus than in the mother. A notable exception to this is alkyl mercury, which rapidly diffuses across the placenta and results in higher levels of mercury in cord blood than in maternal blood (Skertving, 1973). The fetal pharmacokinetics of predicted neurotoxins deserve more direct investigation.

The relatively large volume of the gastrointestinal tract of children, as well as age-related differences in selective permeability, result in increased absorption. Gastrointestinal absorption of lead in adults is approximately 10% of that ingested, whereas in children absorption is 40%–50%. The amount of toxin ingested per unit of weight is also much greater as is evident from the caloric intake of 100 kcal/kg/d in infants versus 20–30 kcal/kg/d in adults. In epidemic poisonings such as the outbreak of convulsions in Pakistan from the contamination of sugar by endrin (Leads from the MMWR, 1985), it is not surprising that 60% of the cases occurred in children under 9 years of age. Biliary excretion, a major mode of detoxification, has been shown to be grossly deficient in neonates poisoned with organic mercury (Clarkson, Nordberg, & Sager, 1985). Decreased gastric acidity of the neonate accounts for the high risk of nitrate poisoning with methemoglobinemia that may be sufficiently severe to cause hypoxia.

The relatively high ventilatory volume per unit of weight in children contributes to the greater frequency of anesthesia due to inhalation of organic solvents (Garrettson, 1984). Decreased renal excretion of toxin has been shown to be a significant factor in the susceptibility of infants and children to organic and inorganic mercury (Clarkson et al., 1985).

In children, the thin stratum corneum of the skin in association with the large surface area per unit of weight is undoubtedly a critical factor in the hexachloraphene neurotoxicity of neonates (Curley, Kimbrough, Hawk, Nathenson, & Finberg, 1971), as well as for the percutaneous absorption of lindane applied as a topical pediculocide (Ginsburg, Lowry, & Reisch, 1977).

Genetic and developmental differences in microsomal drug metabolism in hepatic and other cells account for different rates of the production and the detoxification of toxic metabolites. A significant breakthrough defining the genetic predisposition to phenytoin-induced birth defects is provided by Strickler et al. (1985), who found a correlation of major birth defects with phenytoin exposure in families with cytotoxic susceptibility of their lymphocytes to microsomal drug-metabolizing systems generating arene oxides. The delineation of genetic differences in the metabolism of xenobiotics is one of the most exciting applications of molecular biology to developmental neurotoxicity.

The enhancement of neurotoxicity by the biochemical characteristics of the developing nervous system is a major concern. Susceptibility to inorganic lead, for example, is attributed to the decreased capacity for glial storage with increased neuronal deposition, whereas the higher toxicity of organic lead for infants than adults is thought to relate to the rapid myelinization process that is more easily interrupted by the tetraethyl lead (Clarkson et al., 1985). Chlordecone (Kepone) in fetal animals has a delayed effect on neuroendocrine modulation of sexual differentiation (Cooper, Vodicnik, & Gordon, 1985). It is proposed that other halogenated hydrocarbons may elicit similar responses, but investigation of neuroendocrine toxicity in the developing organism along with well-defined epidemiological studies of humans are needed to establish this.

The interactions of intrinsic or acquired vulnerability of the nervous system and toxic exposure are important considerations that confound many epidemiological studies. An enhanced effect of a neurotoxin may be seen in a child with a preexisting genetic deficit, such as the susceptibility of children with brain damage to phenothiazines (Angle & McIntire, 1968).

More complex is the interaction of sociocultural deprivation and neurotoxins. Contemporary calculations of the exposure to environmental lead recognize the triple jeopardy of the urban poor: the exposure to lead is highest in low-income areas; in high-lead areas, the amount ingested increases with deficiencies in child care and household cleanliness; the intestinal absorption of lead increases with nutritional deficits (Schwartz, Angle, & Pitcher, 1986). As diagrammed in Figure 2, nutritional and economic deprivation also favor both prenatal neurological deficits and a decrease in the compensatory mechanisms that may override the more subtle neurotoxic effects of lead.

REPRESENTATIVE NEUROTOXINS

Lead

The neurotoxic effect of high exposures with blood lead levels in excess of $80-100$ µg/dl is a well-documented risk for fulminant lead encephalopathy manifested by cerebral edema, seizures, coma, and irreversible brain damage.

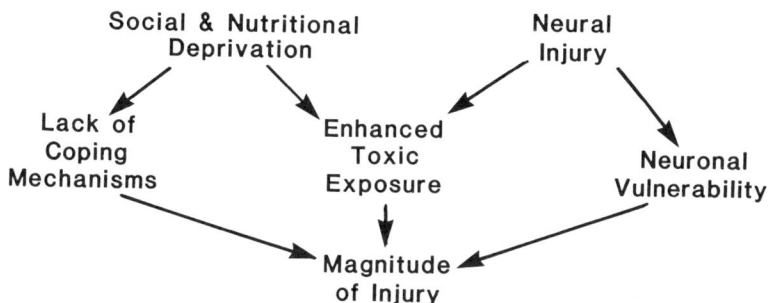

Figure 2.   Interaction of deprivation and neurotoxins.

Much of the research of the past 15 years has focused on the delineation of more subtle disorders of neurological function in children without overt lead encephalopathy. Variables that have emerged in determining the effects of lead on the nervous system include the duration and intensity of exposure and the age of exposure. The quantitative indices of exposure include blood lead, dentine lead, erythrocyte protoporphyrin and erythrocyte pyrimidine 5'-nucleotidase (Angle & McIntire, 1982). Hair lead is now considered an unreliable index subject to the overwhelming effect of exogeneous contamination (Bennett, 1985).

Epidemiological studies of the neurotoxic effects of subclinical lead poisoning have been the subject of intense controversy. Rutter (1983) classified these studies as follows:

1. Clinical studies of children with high blood lead
2. Studies of children drawn from the general urban or suburban pediatric population
3. Children living in close proximity to lead-emitting smelters
4. Studies of mentally retarded or behaviorially deviant children

Clinical studies of children with high lead levels are exemplified by the studies of de la Burde and Choate (1972), which define continuing central nervous system (CNS) impairment in children with initial mean blood leads of 59 μg/dl. Similar studies (Ernhart, Landa, & Schell, 1981; Perino & Ernhart, 1974; Rummo, 1974; Rummo, Routh, Rummo, & Brown, 1979) showed persistent dysfunction at blood lead levels above 40 μg/dl but have been subjected to more intense scrutiny for the possibility that incomplete matching for home effects may have confounded the less striking differences. Despite criticism of virtually all of the studies reported, the high-risk lead exposure groups with blood leads above 40 μg/dl have always performed less well on IQ or other psychometric tests.

The general population studies pioneered by Needleman et al. (1979) involved in-depth neuropsychological testing of children who donated teeth at ages 7 and 8 to provide indices of lead exposure at an earlier age. Despite considerable controversy, it is agreed that average IQ decrements of about 4 points were associated with the higher lead exposure, probably representing blood leads in the range of 30–50 μg/dl. Yule and Lansdown (1983) provide the only similarly structured study to show a greater IQ decrement, in this case estimated as a 6–7 point loss at blood leads above 30 μg/dl. Electrophysiological studies of the effects of blood leads above and below 30 μg/dl (Benignus, Otto, Muller, & Seiple, 1981; Otto, Benignus, Muller, & Barton, 1981; Otto et al., 1982, 1984) utilized relatively experimental electrophysiological measures of the evoked EEG but did provide provocative evidence of alternate CNS functioning of nonovertly lead-intoxicated children with blood lead levels in the 15–30 μg/dl range.

Smelter area studies, primarily those by Winneke, Hrdina, and Brockhaus (1982) and Winneke et al. (1983), have failed to show a significant association between umbilical cord or current blood lead levels below 30 μg/dl and performance on a variety of neuropsychological tests. Studies of mentally retarded or behaviorally abnormal children are extremely difficult to interpret because of the possibility that the increased lead burdens are due to the hyperkinetic disorder or mental retardation rather than the cause of it.

The electrophysiological studies and the consensus that a blood lead of 25–30 μg/dl might be associated with as much as a 4-point decrement in IQ were included in the cost benefit analysis by the Environmental Protection Agency (EPA) that resulted in the phasing down of lead gasoline from 1.10 g/gal to 0.10 g/gal as of January 1986 (EPA 230-05-006). They were also basic to the decision of the CDC Lead Poison Prevention Screening Program that a blood lead above 25 μg/dl is an unacceptable risk.

Mercury

Over the past 20 years, the worldwide epidemics of organic mercury poisoning have repeatedly demonstrated the extreme susceptibility of the fetal and infant brain to the neurotoxic effects of methyl mercury (Clarkson et al., 1985). The Minamata Bay epidemic in Japan involved at least 121 persons with 46 deaths and 21 cases of severe intrauterine brain damage (Kojima & Fugita, 1973). As is now well known, it derived from the discharge into the bay of inorganic mercury, used as a catalyst in the manufacture of acetaldehyde and vinyl chloride. On methylation by the methanogenic bacteria, it entered the food cycle and the methyl mercury levels were as high as 50 ppm in fish and 85 ppm in shellfish. Of the 40 families affected in Minamata, 25 had eaten fish from the bay every day of their lives. Methyl mercury is readily absorbed from the gut, freely crosses the placenta, and also enters the maternal milk with concentrations of 5% of the maternal blood level.

In adults, mercury localizes in the cortex, visual cortex, and cerebellum of the brain, resulting in the classical symptoms of tunnel vision, progressing to visual loss, hearing loss, tremor, and cerebellar dysfunction and mental deterioration. In the fetal brain, however, organic mercury is diffusely deposited, resulting in a syndrome of microcephaly, blindness, hearing loss, spastic cerebral palsy, ataxia, chorea, seizures, and severe retardation. Fetal mercurialism is indistinguishable from multiple other causes of prenatal encephalopathy unless the history is carefully investigated (Koos & Longo, 1976). Since mercury has a half-life of 70 days, levels of mercury in the infant blood and urine may be helpful only in the first 3 months of life—or on assay of dried umbilical cords as was done to establish some of the Japanese cases.

Epidemics in Iraq (Al-Damaluji, 1976; Amin-Zaki et al., 1974; Clarkson, Amin-Zaki, & Al-Tikriti, 1976), Pakistan (Haq, 1963), and Guatemala (Ordonez, Carillo, Miranda, & Gale, 1971) resulted from the use of flour made from grain contaminated by methyl and ethyl mercury fungicides, while the familial epidemic in New Mexico resulted from ingestion of pork from a hog that had been fed grain seed treated with methyl mercury dicyandiamide (Pierce et al., 1972). All established the neurosensitivity of the infant to cumulative body burdens of mercury of less than one half that of adults with neurological symptoms.

Subsequent discovery of the high concentration of mercury in some species of fish throughout the world aroused appropriate concern for the risk to the fetus, with the recommendation that pregnant women should not be exposed to any methyl mercury compounds and should not eat more than 350 g of fish per week (Koos & Longo, 1976).

Halogenated Hydrocarbons

Rogan, Gladen, and Wilcox (1985) provide an excellent review of the reproductive and postnatal morbidity from exposure to the polychlorinated biphenyls, the ubiquitous chemicals employed as lubricants in electrical equipment. The more toxic chlorinated hydrocarbons, such as the insecticides endrin, lindane, and DDT, have long been associated with acute and permanent seizure disorders and residual brain damage from acute intoxications (Angle & McIntire, 1968). The risk for children of epidemic and endemic contamination with the polychlorinated biphenyls (PCBs) is less clear. PCBs are elevated in human milk as well as in cow's milk. The PCBs readily cross the placenta. Clinical toxicity in the pregnant woman is teratogenic, producing a small baby with midface hypoplasia, pigmented skin and gums, conjuntivitis, hypoplastic nails, calcification of the natal teeth and the scalp, comedones and hyperbilirubinemia. In the absence of clinical illness in the mother, less obvious manifestations, such as low birth weight, immunodeficiency, and neurobehavioral dysfunction, have been sought but were not defined in the Michigan data of Weil, Spencer, Benjamin, and Seagull (1981).

Experimental poisoning of the rhesus monkey with PCBs causes delayed cognitive achievement. These findings have not been replicated in humans (Weil et al., 1981) and no follow-up is available of the Japanese children, now 7–9 years old, who had lethargy, apathy, and soft neurological signs at birth (Harada, 1976).

Neurobehavioral dysfunction in association with the other common halogenated hydrocarbons is also difficult to establish. Although 2,3,7,8-tetrachlorodibenzo-p-dioxin (TCDD) is a major contaminant of the common herbicide 2,4-D and is repeatedly defined as a teratogen in animal studies, this has not been established in controlled human studies. Casey and Collie (1984) reported the association of heavy prenatal exposure to 2,4-D with a syndrome of severe mental retardation and multiple congenital anomalies. Other human reports are similarly anecdotal. The large-scale Agent Orange Study reported by the Department of Defense in 1985 failed to define either reproductive failure or anomalies in the offspring of fathers exposed to herbicides contaminated with TCDD. Since this analysis lacked stratification of paternal exposure and incorporated no measures of maternal exposure, additional epidemiological studies are essential.

Organic Phosphorus Insecticides

The neurotoxic and teratogenic effects of the organophosphorus insecticides have been primarily defined in experimental studies in avian models. Embryotoxicity, decreased brain weight, delayed myelinization of the spinal cord, and axial skeletal defects are readily produced in a variety of hatchling birds, and multiple mammalian species have also been affected (Hoffman & Sileo, 1984). Peripheral neurotoxicity due to triorthocresyl phosphate (TOCP) and residual EEG changes after acute poisoning with the organic phosphate insecticides are described in older children and adults but the threshold for neurotoxicity is unknown. Screening tests for neurotoxicity, such as inhibition of the 2-deoxyglucose uptake by mammalian brain (Muller & Martin, 1984), as well as animal testing provide evidence for the hazard of acute and chronic neurotoxicity but do not define the actual risk.

The neuropathy target esterase (NTE) of human lymphocytes has been proposed as a feasible index of population exposure to the neurotoxic effects, since the sensitivity to organic phosphate esters is comparable to NTE of human brain (Bertoncin, Russulo, Caroldi, & Lotti, 1985). Linking population surveys of lymphocyte NTE or other indices to longitudinal studies of neurobehavioral function may provide a clinical barometer of exposure and toxicity. Given the widespread use of these pesticides and preservatives, continued examination is indicated for the effect of organic phosphates and related compounds on fetal survival, teratogenicity, and cognitive, neuroendocrine, and neurobehavioral function.

CONCLUSIONS

Of the 14 groups of teratogenic chemicals, 8 were described in humans before confirmation in animals. In an increasingly contaminated environment, there is still no substitute for skilled clinical observation.

The developing nervous system is uniquely sensitive to neurotoxins. Individuals who are brain damaged are often particularly vulnerable and those who are socioculturally deprived often lack the coping mechanisms to overcome subtle injury. To confound the issue, the relative exposure of children, particularly those who are nutritionally deprived and retarded, exceeds that of adults.

It required several thousand years to define the treacherously low thresholds for developmental neurotoxicity by alcohol, lead, and mercury. The absence of an apparent hazard in the first 20 years of use of any new drug or chemical does not necessarily exonerate it. Biochemical indices that serve as barometers of exposure are essential to well-structured epidemiological studies of neurobehavioral function.

REFERENCES

Al-Damaluji, S. F. (1976). Intoxication due to alkyl mercury-treated seed—1971–72 outbreak in Iraq: Clinical aspects. *Bulletin of the World Health Organization, 53,* 65–81.

Amin-Zaki, L., Elhassani, S., Majeed, M. A., Clarkson, T., Doherty, R. A., & Greenwood, M. (1974). Intra-uterine methyl mercury poisoning. *Pediatrics, 54,* 587–595.

Angle, C. R., & McIntire, M. S. (1968). Persistent dystonia in a brain damaged child after ingestion of phenothiazine. *Journal of Pediatrics, 73,* 124–126.

Angle, C. R., & McIntire, M. S. (1982). Children, the barometer of environmental lead. *Advances in Pediatrics, 29,* 3–31.

Benignus, V. A., Otto, D. A., Muller, K. E., & Seiple, K. J. (1981). Effects of age and body lead burden on CNS function in young children: II. EEG spectra. *Electroencephalography and Clinical Neurophysiology, 52,* 240–248.

Bennett, S. (1985). Commercial hair analysis. Science or scam? *Journal of the American Medical Association, 254,* 1041–1045.

Bertoncin, D., Russulo, A., Caroldi, S., & Lotti, M. (1985). Neuropathy toxic esterase in human lymphocytes. *Archives of Environmental Health, 40,* 139–144.

Casey, P. H., & Collie, W. R. (1984). Severe mental retardation and multiple congenital anomalies of uncertain cause after extreme parental exposure to 2,4-D. *Journal of Pediatrics, 104,* 313–315.

Clarkson, T. W., Amin-Zaki, L., & Al-Tikriti, S. (1976). An outbreak of methylmercury poisoning due to consumption of contaminated grain. *Federation Proceedings, 35*(12), 2395–2399.

Clarkson, T. W., Nordberg, G. F., & Sager, P. R. (1985). Reproductive and developmental toxicity of metals. *Scandinavian Journal of Work and Environmental Health, 11,* 145–154.

Cooper, J. R., Vodicnik, M. J., & Gordon, J. H. (1985). Effects of perinatal Kepone exposure on sexual differentiation of the rat brain. *Neurotoxicology, 6,* 183–190.

Curley, A., Kimbrough, R. D., Hawk, R. E., Nathenson, G., & Finberg, L. (1971). Dermal absorption of hexachlorophene in infants. *Lancet, 2,* 296–297.

de la Burde, B., & Choate, M. S. (1972). Does asymptomatic lead exposure in children have latent sequelae? *Journal of Pediatrics, 81,* 1088–1091.

Ernhart, C. B., Landa, B., & Schell, N. B. (1981). Subclinical levels of lead and developmental deficit—a multivariate follow-up reassessment. *Pediatrics, 67,* 911–919.

Everson, R. B., Randerath, E., Santella, R. M., Cefalo, R. C., Avitts, T. A., & Randerath, K. (1986). Detection of smoking-related covalent DNA adducts in the human placenta. *Science, 231,* 54–57.

Frankos, V. H. (1985). FDA Perspectives on the use of teratology data for human risk assessment. *Fundamental and Applied Toxicology, 5,* 615–625.

Garrettson, L. K. (1984). Direct and indirect chemical exposure in children. *Clinics in Laboratory Medicine, 4,* 469–473.

Ginsburg, C. M., Lowry, W., & Reisch, J. S. (1977). Absorption of lindane (gamma-benzene hexachloride) in infants and children. *Journal of Pediatrics, 91,* 998–1000.

Haq, I. U. (1963). Agrosan poisoning in man. *British Medical Journal, 1,* 1579.

Harada, M. (1976). Intrauterine poisoning. *Bulletin of the Institute of Constitutional Medicine* (Kumamoto University), *25* (Suppl.), 1–60.

Hoffman, D. J., & Sileo, L. (1984). Neurotoxic and teratogenic effects of an organophosphorus insecticide (phenyl phosphonothioic acid-*o*-ethyl-*O*-[4-nitrophenyl] ester) on mallard development. *Toxicology and Applied Pharmacology, 73,* 284–294.

Karrh, B. W., Carmody, T. W., Clyne, R. M., Gould, K. G., PortelaCubria, G., Smith, J. M., & Friedfeld, M. (1981). Guidance for the evaluation, risk assessment and control of chemical embryo-feto-toxins. *Journal of Occupational Medicine, 23,* 397–402.

Kojima, K., & Fugita, M. (1973). Summary of recent studies in Japan on methyl mercury poisoning. *Toxicology, 1,* 43–62.

Koos, B. J., & Longo, L. D. (1976). Mercury toxicity in the pregnant woman, fetus and newborn infant. *American Journal of Obstetrics and Gynecology, 126,* 390–409.

Leads from the MMWR. (1985). Acute convulsions associated with endrin poisoning—Pakistan. *Journal of the American Medical Association, 253,* 334–345.

Needleman, H. L., Gunnoe, C., Leviton, A., Reed, R., Peresie, H., Maher, C., & Barrett, P. (1979). Deficits in psychologic and classroom performance of children with elevated dentine lead levels. *New England Journal of Medicine, 300,* 689–695.

Muller, P., & Martin, L. (1984). The 2-deoxyglucose uptake method as a first screen for neurotoxic compounds. *Canadian Journal of Physiology and Pharmacology, 62,* 998–1009.

Ordonez, J. V., Carillo, J. A., Miranda, C. M., & Gale, J. L. (1971). Epidemiological study of an illness in Guatemala highlands believed to be an encephalitis. *Boletin de la Oficina Sanitaria Panamericana, 172,* 65.

Otto, D. A., Benignus, V. A., Muller, K. E., & Barton, C. N. (1981). Effects of age and body lead burden on CNS function in young children: I. Slow cortical potentials. *Electroencephalography and Clinical Neurophysiology, 52,* 229–239.

Otto, D., Benignus, V., Muller, K., Barton, C., Seiple, K., Prah, J., & Schroeder, S. (1982). Effects of low to moderate lead exposure on slow cortical potentials in young children: Two year follow-up study. *Neurobehavioral Toxicology and Teratology, 4,* 733–737.

Otto, D., Robinson, G., Baumann, S., Schroeder, S., Kleinbaum, D., Barton, C., Mushak, P., & Boone, L. (1984). *Five-year follow-up study of children with low-to-moderate lead absorption: Electrophysiological evaluation.* Presented at the Second International Conference on Prospective Lead Studies, Cincinnati, OH. Available for inspection at U.S. Environmental Protection Agency, Environmental Criteria and Assessment Office, Research Triangle Park, NC.

Perino, J., & Ernhart, C. B. (1974). The relation of subclinical lead level to cognitive and sensorimotor impairment in black preschoolers. *Journal of Learning Disorders, 7,* 616–620.

Pierce, P., Thompson, J., Likosky, W., Nickey, L., Barthel, W., & Hinman, A. (1972). Alkyl mercury poisoning in humans. Report of an outbreak. *Journal of the American Medical Association, 220,* 1439–1443.

Rogan, W. J., Gladen, B. C., & Wilcox, A. J. (1985). Potential reproductive and postnatal morbidity from exposure to polychlorinated biphenyls: Epidemiologic considerations. *Environmental Health Perspectives, 60,* 233–239.

Rummo, J. H. (1974). *Intellectual and behavioral effects of lead poisoning in chil-*

dren. Chapel Hill, NC: University of North Carolina. Available from University Microfilms, Ann Arbor, MI, Publication no. 74-26, 930, Ph.D. thesis.

Rummo, J. H., Routh, D. K., Rummo, N. J., & Brown, J. E. (1979). Behavioral and neurological effects of symptomatic and asymptomatic lead exposure in children. *Archives of Environmental Health, 34,* 120–124.

Rutter, M. (1983). Low level lead exposure: Sources, effects and implications. In M. Rutter, R. Jones, & R. Russell (Eds.), *Lead versus health: Sources and effects of low level lead exposure* (pp. 333–370). New York: Wiley.

Schardein, J. L. (1985). *Symposium: Risk assessment for developmental toxicity.* Part of the 23rd Annual Meeting of the Society of Toxicology, March 12–16, 1984, Atlanta, GA. *Fundamental and Applied Toxicology, 5,* 607–608.

Schardein, J. L., Schwetz, B. A., & Kenel, M. F. (1985). Species sensitivities and prediction of tetratogenic potential. *Environmental Health Perspectives, 61,* 55–67.

Schwartz, J., Angle, C., & Pitcher, H. (1986). The relationship between childhood blood lead and stature. *Pediatrics, 77,* 281–288.

Skertving, S. (1973). Studies in Swedes exposed to methyl mercury through fish consumption. *Proceedings of the Conference on Environmental Effects of Mercury,* Brussels, November 1, 1973.

Strickler, S. M., Miller, M. A., Andermann. E., Danskyu, L. V., Seni, M. H., & Spielberg, S. P. (1985). Genetic predisposition to phenytoin-induced birth defects. *Lancet, 2,* 746–749.

Weil, W. B., Spencer, M., Benjamin, D., & Seagull, E. (1981). The effect of polybrominated biphenyl on infants and young children. *Journal of Pediatrics, 98,* 47–51.

Winneke, G., Hrdina, K-G., & Brockhaus, A. (1982). Neuropsychological studies in children with elevated tooth-lead concentrations. Part I: Pilot study. *International Archives of Occupational and Environmental Health, 51,* 169–183.

Winneke, G., Kramer, U., Brockhaus, A., Ewers, U., Kujanek, G., Lechner H., & Janke, W. (1983). Neuropsychological studies in children with elevated tooth lead concentrations. Part II: Extended study. *International Archives of Occupational and Environmental Health, 51,* 231–252.

Yule, W., & Lansdown, R. (1983). *Lead and children's development: Recent findings.* Presented at the International Conference on Management and Control of Heavy Metals in the Environment, Heidelberg, West Germany. Edinburgh, United Kingdom: CEP Consultants, Ltd.

INTERFACE
BIOMEDICAL/BEHAVIORAL
ASPECTS OF MENTAL RETARDATION

Introduction

Almost 10 years ago, the American Psychological Association conducted an interview with Dr. Michael Rutter and printed it in their monthly newspaper, *The APA Monitor*. In this particular interview they referred to Dr. Rutter as perhaps the finest child psychiatrist in the world. His accomplishments and contributions to the field of child psychiatry are enormous. He is, however, perhaps best recognized for his outstanding contributions to the understanding and treatment of autism. Readers will find that this extremely comprehensive chapter contains a collected summary of all our current knowledge and treatment of autism. This chapter is perhaps symbolic of this book in that the biomedical and behavioral sciences are both utilized in order to understand and thereby treat this complex disorder. Dr. Rutter addresses the major issue of what is known about the biological substrate of autism and what follows from that knowledge in terms of implications for intervention through behavioral approaches.

For a long time, autism was regarded as a serious functional mental disorder (i.e., infantile psychosis). However, it is now classified as a pervasive developmental disorder. This broader definition recognizes the tremendous etiological hetereogeneity of this disorder with both organic and functional components. Dr. Rutter goes on to make a very clear distinction between autism and mental retardation and their similarities and differences. He points out that not all autistic individuals exhibit global intellectual retardation and that 20%–25% have IQs in the normal range. Dr. Rutter presents a concise definition of the four critical criteria for validating this syndrome of autism.

The cognitive and social deficits are carefully detailed by Dr. Rutter as a prelude to analyzing what implications these have for their biological substrates. In his attempt to provide a thorough analysis of autism, Dr. Rutter also reviews our current knowledge as it relates to the biochemical findings, neurophysiological studies, and genetic analyses of this phenomenon. He points out that the new neuroimaging techniques have provided us with a quantum step forward in our ability to study the structure and function of the brain, which will have tremendous implications for better understanding the biological basis of autism.

Dr. Rutter closes his chapter with a lengthy section on treatment implications. He points out that our knowledge of the biological substrate of autism is not at the point where we have direct and specific indicators for effective preventive or curative intervention. Nevertheless, there are important treatment implications that can be quite effective, particularly in tertiary prevention, utilizing the psychological therapies, genetic counseling, and medical treatments (i.e., medication, megavitamin therapy, and other psychopharmacological approaches), all of which focus on the primary and secondary prevention approaches.

Dr. Rutter summarizes his chapter by stating that there is no unequivocal answer available at this time as to the biological basis of autism. However, he indicates that there have been substantial increases in the knowledge and understanding of this phenomenon that make it clear that there is some type of organic brain dysfunction operating in this syndrome. The psychogenic theories that dominated the autistic scene in the 1960s are no longer sufficient to fully explain this complex developmental disability. Dr. Rutter exhorts us to realize that in our treatment approaches, autism requires both a full and systematic medical appraisal and that treatment needs to be planned on the basis that autism is a biologically determined and chronically handicapping condition. Although at present we rely mainly on the behavioral and educational methods of intervention, other biomedical approaches will play a more important role in the future. In short, it would seem that in order to develop a curative approach or reversal of these symptoms of autism, cooperation between the biomedical and behavioral sciences through an interdisciplinary approach is necessary since, as this chapter points out, autism may be the most challenging of all conditions as we search for a cure for mental retardation.

What contribution can behavioral research make in the preventive and curative intervention of mental retardation, particularly as it relates to improving cognition, memory, and learning? "A great deal," according to Dr. Earl Butterfield, a cognitive psychologist, who believes that intelligence training research holds great promise for persons with mental retardation. In his chapter, "To Cure Cognitive Deficits of Mentally Retarded Persons" (Butterfield, 1983), he based his ideas on four trends: 1) behavior modifiers are increasingly teaching "thoughty" behaviors, 2) developmental cognitive psychologists are using instructional methods more often, 3) general experimental psychologists are focusing more on individual differences in cognition, and 4) educational psychologists are focusing more directly on the cognitive processes. A number of subdisciplines in psychology are represented by differential psychology, educational psychology, cross-cultural psychology, psychometrics, developmental psychology, cognitive psychology, and artificial intelligence. Psychologists have been working together on research as it relates to instructional procedures; this represents an alliance that seems to hold great promise to produce progress toward our goal of significantly improving the cognitive deficits of persons with mental retardation. The focus of these subdisciplines is to define and understand the basic processes in functional models of such complex concepts as attention, perception, information processing, memory, learning (including conditioning, reinforcement, and habituation), cognition and metacognition, thinking, concept formation, problem solving, intelligence, and creativity.

As Dr. Brooks and her colleagues point out in Chapter 11, cognitive psychologists studying mental retardation have an enormous task ahead of them—to understand and explain individual differences in cognitive functioning. The field seems to be in the process of developing a theory construction that facilitates our understanding and remediation of such deficiencies of cognitive performance. Although cognitive researchers do not focus on etiology, they nevertheless are seemingly more open to collaborating with individual strategies offered by biomedical researchers. The groundwork for this empirically based theory of mental retardation is addressed via Dr. Brooks's focus on knowledge, language, perception, memory, attention, and problem solving.

This chapter also points out that in the last 14 years the general experimental psychology literature has focused a great deal on memory and its related processes more than any other topic by drawing upon the analogy of a computer and similarities in storage and retrieval of information. Dr. Brooks and her colleagues go on to make specific recommendations for improving cognitive function through our research and knowledge as it relates to short-term and long-term memory approaches. They introduce the concept of meta-cognition (a theory about cognition that is an introspective knowledge about one's own cognitive states), which consists of both knowing about thought processes (academic knowledge) and knowing how to carry them out (practical knowledge). They point out that individuals with mental retardation do not spontaneously use appropriate metamemorial strategies. Researchers have found that when people with retardation are instructed on what strategies to use, they can often use them to recall more efficiently and accurately. However, the major problem that these individuals face is maintaining strategies that are taught and generalizing these strategies or transferring knowledge to new learning situations. Such variables that facilitate the maintenance and transfer of memory strategies are: 1) active participation, 2) overtraining of a strategy, 3) semantic processing of items, 4) feedback concerning the effectiveness of individual strategies, 5) extensive examples concerning the use of each strategy, 6) systematic introduction of components of the strategy, 7) gradual elimination of assistance as training progresses, and 8) the training of such strategies in a variety of contexts.

In probing deeper into the real difficulties with generalization, it may be that people with mental retardation have an extremely difficult time determining similarities between the training task and the generalized task. Dr. Brooks and her colleagues feel that it is this inability to note similarities between problems that is the basis of retarded children's inability to generalize. In short, they point out that children with mental retardation often require more training at metacognitive skills to reach a given criterion and demonstrate less generalization of the strategy to new material. They conclude by pointing out the fundamental similarity in the manner in which retarded and nonretarded individuals learn, despite the fact that there are two major categories of deficiencies in individuals with mental retardation: 1) the general efficiency of the cognitive system and 2) their ability to behave strategically. This is manifested in their performance on learning, memory, and problem-solving tasks. Although we have been very successful in demonstrating that individuals with retardation can be taught specific strategies to be used in specific situations, the struggle continues for an individual with mental retardation to generalize a learned strategy through the enhanced performance in similar but nonidentical situations.

This entire section is directed toward progress in the next 20 years. Past research was directed at analysis of classical conditioning and the study of simple behaviors because that was the limit of our knowledge at the time. The challenge existing before us now is to integrate the behavioral and psychological discoveries with promising new discoveries in biochemical research and all of the neuroscience fields. No longer are we interested in studying just the brain, but knowing how and why the mind functions as well.

REFERENCE

Butterfield, E. C. (1983). To cure cognitive deficits of mentally retarded persons. In F. J. Menolascino, R. Neman, & J. A. Stark (Eds.), *Curative aspects of mental retardation: Biomedical and behavioral advances* (pp. 203–221). Baltimore: Paul H. Brookes Publishing Co.

Chapter 10

Biological Basis of Autism
Implications for Intervention

Michael Rutter

The syndrome of infantile autism has an interesting history in the field of mental retardation. Kanner (1943) showed remarkable clinical acumen in his recognition that children with this disorder differed from those with other forms of mental handicap. Moreover, his now classical description of the characteristics of autism has stood the test of time. Out of the plethora of abnormalities shown, he successfully picked out the few that best represented the core of the condition. Subsequent research has amply demonstrated the wisdom of his decisions in that connection (Rutter, 1985a). In spite of that, concepts of the nature of the disorder have changed radically over the subsequent 4½ decades.

For a long time, autism was regarded as an infantile *psychosis,* a serious functional mental disorder with a particularly early onset. Indeed, it was widely thought that autism might constitute the first manifestation of schizophrenia. It is now clear that this was a mistaken view (Rutter, 1972, 1985a). Autistic children have not withdrawn from reality because of mental illness; rather, they have failed fully to enter reality because of a widespread and serious disturbance in the developmental process. Accordingly, autism is now *not* regarded as a psychosis; instead, it is classified as a pervasive developmental disorder. That means that it is grouped with other abnormalities of development rather than with mental illness as such. Nevertheless, that does not imply that once again, as in pre-Kannerian times, autism should be submerged into an undifferentiated sea of mental handicap. In the first place, knowledge on mental handicap has advanced greatly, as numerous other chapters in this volume document. There is a general recognition that this broad designation, based on the presence of a global deficit in intellectual functioning, contains much heterogeneity. That is so, not only in terms of medical etiologies (which have long been recognized), but also in terms of

This work was supported in part by the John D. and Catherine R. MacArthur Foundation Mental Health Research Network on Risk and Protective Factors in the Major Mental Disorders.

cognitive patterns and behavioral correlates. For example, attention has focused on the unusual compulsive form of self-mutilation associated with the Lesch-Nyhan syndrome (Nyhan, 1976) and on the voracious appetite and subsequent severe obesity that is characteristic of the Prader-Willi syndrome (Ledbetter, Riccardi, Eirhart, Strobel, Keenan, & Crawford, 1981). Questions are being asked about what is special about the neuropathology or neuropsychology of these medical conditions that causes them to be associated with a rather distinctive behavioral syndrome as well as with general mental retardation.

However, autism is not pooled with mental retardation for two other, rather different, reasons. First, the two are conceptually different in that autism is defined in terms of *social deviance,* whereas mental retardation is defined in terms of *intellectual level;* that is, one is social and the other cognitive; also one is a pattern of deviance whereas the other is a degree of deficit. Second, by no means do all people with autism exhibit global intellectual retardation. Probably about a quarter to a fifth have IQs in the normal range (Rutter, 1979).

Nevertheless, empirical findings have been clear-cut in showing that most autistic individuals are mentally retarded to a greater or lesser degree, that their mental handicap is just as "real" as that found in other groups, and that the cognitive deficits are a basic and integral part of autism (see Section "Cognitive and Social Deficits"). IQ level constitutes the single most important prognostic factor (Lotter, 1978). That is, the outlook for independent social functioning is generally very poor when the nonverbal IQ is consistently below 50 when assessed by an experienced skilled clinical psychologist. Conversely, the prognosis is fairly good when the nonverbal IQ is above 70, provided that good language skills were well established by 5 years of age (Lotter, 1978; Rutter, 1970). Attention has now turned to the elucidation of the complex mixture of similarities and dissimilarities between autism and mental retardation.

In this chapter, these are considered as part of the broader question of what is known about the biological substrate of autism and what follows from that knowledge in terms of implications for intervention.

CLINICAL CONSIDERATIONS

Before turning to biological concepts and findings, it is appropriate to consider what sort of condition is to be discussed. To begin with, there is a lot of evidence to show that autism constitutes a meaningful syndrome that differs in a whole series of ways from other psychiatric disorders and from other developmental problems in childhood (Rutter & Schopler, 1987). When defined in terms of the generally agreed four key criteria, the validity of the syndrome is well established. The four criteria are: 1) a general failure to develop interactive social relationships together with various specific abnormalities in inter-personal functioning, particularly a lack of social reciprocity and socioemo-tional responsiveness; 2) language retardation that is associated with a particular form of language deviance involving impaired comprehension, de-layed echolalia, pronominal reversal, and, especially, a relative failure to use language for social communication; 3) ritualistic or compulsive phenomena associated with repetitive stereotyped play patterns; and 4) abnormalities in development that were evident before about 30 months. It should be empha-sized that the condition is defined in terms of *deviance* in these areas of functioning and not just delay or impairment. In other words, diagnosis re-quires a careful assessment of the child's IQ and language development. The diagnosis of autism requires not only that the child's social functioning, language. and play be out of step with his or her general mental development, but also, that they be abnormal in *form* (Rutter, 1984; Rutter & Lord, in press).

If the condition is defined according to these four criteria, we know from well-replicated investigations that: 1) it is not synonymous with mental retar-dation (in spite of the fact that most autistic children are intellectually im-paired), 2) there are many vital differences between autism and schizo-phrenia, and 3) there are many crucial contrasts between infantile autism and the developmental language disorders (Rutter, 1978; Rutter & Schopler, 1987).

An appreciation of these features has led to better agreement throughout the world on the diagnosis of autism, but problems and questions remain. For example, epidemiological studies clearly show that many mentally retarded children display some features of autism but yet not the full syndrome (Wing & Gould, 1979). We do not know whether these constitute varieties of the same condition or rather qualitatively different disorders. In other words, there are many pervasive developmental disorders (especially associated with severe mental handicap) that show some overlap with autism. That area of uncertain diagnostic differentiation concerns the most severely handicapped children.

The second concerns the least handicapped—namely, the question of a possible overlap between mild autism on the one hand and, on the other, so-called Asperger's syndrome or schizoid personality (Wing, 1981). There is not really much problem in differentiating autism from normality, but there are individuals with serious, autistic-like problems in the expression and appreciation of socioemotional cues who are otherwise not significantly re-tarded or impaired in mental development. So far it is not really clear whether these represent mild cases of autism or something quite different. The balance of evidence suggests that most represent mild cases of autism; however, it remains uncertain whether all do so.

A third question is whether autism will ultimately turn out to be a unique medical condition (such as phenylketonuria or Down syndrome), or whether it represents the behavioral manifestations of some more heterogeneous range of organic brain pathology (in the same fashion as occurs with mental retardation or cerebral palsy). Already it is known that *some* cases of autism are due to specific medical conditions of various kinds, but it is not clear whether there will prove to be a homogeneous central core with a single etiology. That remains a possibility, but in the meantime the lesson is that *all* cases of autism require a full medical appraisal (just as required for mental handicap or specific developmental disorders of language).

With these considerations in mind, the question of what might constitute the biological substrate of autism can be tackled. It is appropriate to begin with a discussion of what sort of substrate might be expected on the basis of what is known about the cognitive and social deficits associated with autism.

COGNITIVE AND SOCIAL DEFICITS

Although Kanner (1943), in his initial account of the syndrome, argued that autistic children did not have any basic cognitive impairment, much subsequent research has demonstrated that autism *is* associated with basic cognitive deficits (Rutter, 1979, 1983). Investigations have concentrated on three main issues: the reality or otherwise of the associated mental retardation, the nature of the language disability, and the deficits underlying the social impairments that are characteristic of autism.

Psychometric assessments have indicated that autistic individuals have IQ scores that range from profoundly retarded to superior, but that some three quarters have IQ scores somewhere in the mentally retarded range. At first it was supposed that the low IQ scores might be a secondary consequence of social withdrawal or lack of motivation, but it is now clear that this is not the case. IQ scores show as much temporal stability as those in other populations; they predict educational achievement, they do not vary markedly with changes in psychiatric state, and they predict the onset of seizures in adolescence (the risk being higher in those who are severely retarded). Moreover, although autistic children often have recourse to a stereotyped response following repeated task failure (Koegel & Mentis, 1985), this does not account for their cognitive deficits, as poor task performance has been shown to be a function of task difficulty (Clark & Rutter, 1979) or the nature of task demands (Volkmar & Cohen, 1982).

It may be concluded that the mental retardation shown by the majority of autistic children is just as "real" as in any other group of mentally handicapped individuals.Moreover, it is clear that the cognitive impairment is a very basic feature of the syndrome. The level of IQ is the single most important predictor of outcome. The prognosis is generally poor when the nonverbal IQ is consistently below 50 when tested by an experienced skilled psychologist; conversely, the prognosis is fairly good when the nonverbal IQ is in the normal range *and* when there are good language skills well established by 5 years of age (Lotter, 1978; Rutter, 1970). Also, treatment has little or no effect on IQ in spite of making a substantial impact on other features of the disorder (Howlin et al., in press).

On the other hand, research findings also showed that the *pattern* of cognitive deficit in autism tends to be distinctively different from that usually found in nonautistic mentally retarded groups. Testing on the Wechsler scales (Lockyer & Rutter, 1970) and on the Halstead-Reitan battery (Dawson, 1983) has shown that skills tend to be most evident on visual-spatial and rote memory tasks, with deficits greatest on tasks requiring abstraction, sequencing, or coding. Experimental studies have indicated that autistic children make relatively little use of meaning in their memory and thought processes (Hermelin & O'Connor, 1970), this tendency being most evident in those with generally impaired intellectual functioning (Fyffe & Prior, 1978). They have difficulty reading for meaning with connected prose, in spite of being able to process the meaning of individual words (Frith & Snowling, 1983), and they are more impaired in their ability to process complex temporal sequences than apparently comparable spatial codes (Hermelin, 1976). Even high verbal, nonretarded autistic adults have difficulties in conceptual problem solving (Rumsey, 1985).

The verbal deficits on cognitive testing, together with the numerous language abnormalities, led to more detailed investigations of the nature of linguistic functioning in autistic children. At one time it was suggested that autism might arise on the basis of a particularly severe language handicap. However, the data from studies comparing autism with developmental disorders of receptive language show that this is not likely to be the case. In the first place, autistic children's difficulties do not mainly lie in the area of syntactical skills; rather, their impairment concerns the pragmatics of language (Bartak, Rutter, & Cox, 1975; Cantwell, Baker, & Rutter, 1978; Cromer, in press; De Myer, Hingtgen, & Jackson, 1981; Frith & Snowling, 1983; Tager-Flusberg, 1981a, 1981b). They have little difficulty with the meaning of words as such, but they do have problems with the conceptual and contextual aspects of meaning. Second, their deficit extends beyond spoken language to "verbal" aspects of thought processes. Moreover, within language, the pattern is as much one of language *deviance* as of language *impairment*. A straightforward language hypothesis of deficit is inadequate to account for this pattern. However, even beyond the limitations in language capacity, there is a profound problem in using language for social communication with the reciprocal interchanges and topic development that are characteristic of normal conversation.

For these and other reasons, attention in recent years has shifted to provide a focus on the social deficits associated with autism. Numerous studies have shown that autistic children's play tends to be stereotyped, non-functional, nonsocial, and lacking creativity or imagination (Lord, 1984; Sigman & Ungerer, 1984; Wing, Gould, Yeates, & Brierley, 1977). When young, autistic children do not use people as a source of security or comfort in the ways typical of a normal toddler, they fail to use eye-to-eye gaze as a modulator of vocal interactions (probably the difference lies in the *use*, rather than the amount of gaze), they lack reciprocity and social responsiveness in their interactions with others, and they fail to make personal friendships (Howlin, 1986; Lord, 1984; Rutter, 1978).

The further investigations into the social deficit have taken three main forms. First, there has been an attempt to use observational studies to provide a more fine-grained analysis of social interactions. Thus, van Engeland, Bodnar, and Bolhuis (1985) found that autistic children differed from normal children in both the presence of stereotyped behaviors and the lack of referential social communication. Second, standard tasks have been used to tap specific social behaviors. For example, Sigman and Ungerer (1984) used a variant of Ainsworth's Strange Situation to assess attachment. They interpreted proximity seeking following a reunion as evidence of attachment, but there was little attention to the quality of social behavior. More recently, Rutter et al. (in press) have devised a series of tasks to elicit various forms of interactive behavior that differentiate autistic children from both normal and nonautistic retarded children.

Third, there have been experimental approaches to assess possible deficits in autistic children's ability to make socioemotional discriminations. Several investigations demonstrated that autistic children did *not* differ from mental-age-matched controls in their ability to recognize themselves in the mirror, although they did differ in showing a lack of emotional reaction to their image (Dawson & McKissick, 1984; Ferrari & Matthews, 1983; Spiker & Ricks, 1984). Hobson (1984) also demonstrated that autism was *not* a function of any impairment in the ability to perceive visuospatial perspectives. He went on to demonstrate, using various matching tasks, that autistic individuals *did* differ from both normal and nonautistic mentally retarded individuals in their ability to make socioemotional discriminations (Hobson, 1982, 1983, 1986). Hobson argued that autistic individuals lack the ability to experience empathy because other people's emotions do not make the normal emotional impact. The finding that autistic individuals are also impaired in their discrimination of age and gender cues required that this deficit be extended to the perception of personal meaning.

Baron-Cohen, Leslie, and Frith (1985, 1986), taking a more strictly cognitive perspective, found that autistic individuals were distinctive in their inability to infer other people's intentions or beliefs from sequential/contextual information. The suggestion is that autistic people's social impairment is a consequence of a specific dysfunction in conceiving of mental states.

IMPLICATIONS FOR BIOLOGICAL SUBSTRATE

While a great deal of progress has been made in narrowing down the psychological deficit in autism to its essential features, there is some way to go before that important objective can be reached. In the meanwhile, investigators have interpreted the findings in several very different ways. First, the pattern of verbal deficits has been used to infer a left hemisphere lesion on the grounds that this is what is found with acquired brain lesions in adult life (Dawson, 1983). However, this inference is unwarranted on two separate counts. The cognitive patterns of unilateral brain lesions in early life are not the same as those found in adulthood, and inferences on brain lateralization and localizations cannot be made on the basis of adult findings (Rutter, 1983). But, more importantly, the verbal limitations constitute only one part of the cognitive deficit. As already noted, autistic children also have substantial difficulties in the discrimination of social and emotional cues. The relevance of this finding is that, in adults, this type of deficit tends to be associated with right hemisphere lesions (Borod, Koff, Lorch, & Nicholas, 1985; Heilman, Bowers, Speedie, & Coslett, 1984; Tucker, Watson, & Heilman, 1977). One may conclude that it is unlikely that autism is associated with a unilateral brain lesion on either side of the brain.

Second, Fein, Pennington, Markowitz, Braverman, and Waterhouse (1986) have argued that the basic deficit is social rather than cognitive, mainly on the grounds that there are only modest correlations between cognitive and social impairments and that mentally handicapped children may have cognitive deficits as severe as those found with autism but yet not show autistic-type difficulties in social relationships. There are several problems with this argument. In the first place, it does not explain why many autistic individuals fail completely to gain spoken language, why three quarters show severe mental handicap, why IQ and language are the most powerful predictors of outcome, and why there is the familial association with mental retardation and language disabilities (see next section). If it is supposed that the cognitive retardation is secondary to a social deficit, there is the problem of explaining how this happens; also the low correlation between the two argues against this direction of causation, just as it does against the reverse. Rather, it seems likely that some constellation of linked deficits must be involved. In view of the evidence that there *are* cognitive deficits, it is probable that the constellation as a whole will involve cognition. That poses the question of what sort of cognitive impairment could lead to the serious and lasting lack of emotionally committed, responsive, reciprocal social relationships. The apparent disability in inferring other people's state of mind is a good contender, but further research is required to test adequately the hypothesis.

The third inference is based on the frequency with which autism is associated with global mental retardation and on the well-based observation from epidemiological studies (Wing & Gould, 1979) that many children with severe mental handicap show some autistic feature, albeit not the full syndrome. The assumption that follows is that autism should be conceptualized as a variety of mental handicap in which the severity and extent of the brain damage lead to the pattern of behavioral disorganization that is termed autism. According to that view, autism is simply one of several outcomes of organic brain syndrome. However, that suggestion overlooks the very striking differences between autism and mental handicap.

AUTISM AND MENTAL RETARDATION

As already discussed, a majority of autistic individuals are also mentally retarded. Not surprisingly, therefore, there are many similarities between the two groups of disorders. However, there are also some important differences that are likely to have implications for the nature of the biological substrate. The contrasting pattern of cognitive deficits has already been noted, but, in addition, there are medical disparities. Four main sets of data are particularly relevant. First, there is the finding, initially made a quarter of a century ago in our own follow-up study of autistic children (Rutter, 1970), that about a quarter of those without prior evidence of neurological disorder develop epileptic seizures during the teenage years. The fact that seizures occur, of course, points strongly to some kind of organic brain dysfunction. The development of seizures is also a feature shared with mental handicap. Nevertheless, there is a sharp difference in the pattern of age of onset. Whereas the onset with mentally retarded children is usually in infancy or early childhood, that in autism is typically in adolescence (Deykin & MacMahon, 1979; Richardson, Koller, Katz, & McLaren, 1980). At present, the meaning of the contrast in age of onset of seizures is obscure. but it may be inferred that it is likely to have implications for the nature of the biological substrate.

Second, autism and severe mental handicap are similar in that both may be associated with medical conditions such as infantile spasms (Riikonen & Amnell, 1981; Taft & Cohen, 1971), congenital rubella (Chess, Fernandez, & Korn, 1978; Chess, Korn, & Fernandez, 1971), and the fragile-X anomaly (Blomquist et al., 1985; Blomquist, Gustavson, Holmgren, Nordenson, & Palsson-Strae, 1983; Blomquist, Gustavson, Holmgren, Nordenson, & Sweins, 1982). However, there are also sharp differences in medical correlates. Thus, Down syndrome accounts for about a quarter to a third of cases of severe mental retardation (Hagberg & Kyllerman, 1983), but it is quite rare for it to be associated with autism (Wing & Gould, 1979). Similarly, about a third of children with cerebral palsy show severe mental handicap (Rutter, Graham, & Yule, 1970), but it is decidedly uncommon for cerebral palsy to occur with autism (Wing & Gould, 1979). The implication is that the neuropathology of autism and mental retardation are likely to differ in crucial respects. Of course, no one would suppose that the neuropathology of mental retardation should fit a uniform picture. Nevertheless, it is important to ask what is different between say, Down syndrome, on the one hand, and infantile spasms or the fragile-X anomaly on the other, that accounts for a negligible association with autism in the first case but a relatively strong one in the latter two?

Third, autism and mental retardation have in common an association with complications of pregnancy and the perinatal period. But, once again, the pattern is different. With mental handicap, the strongest association is with the most severe pre- and perinatal abnormalities (Birch, Richardson, Baird, Horobin, & Illsley, 1970), whereas with autism the main link is found with the minor, rather than major, abnormalities (Deykin & MacMahon, 1980; Finegan & Quadrington, 1979; Gillberg & Gillberg, 1983; Torrey, Hersh, & McCabe, 1975). In other words, the complications that are known to carry the greatest risk of overt brain damage are the ones most strongly connected with mental retardation, whereas this is not generally so with autism—except in the special case of twins (Folstein & Rutter, 1977).

Fourth, severe mental retardation is almost always associated with some kind of fairly obvious brain pathology as shown at autopsy (Crome, 1960). In contrast, the few available autopsy studies of autism have either revealed no detectable abnormalities or have shown rather subtle anomalies of a kind that are not easily interpretable (Bauman & Kemper, 1985; Coleman, Romano, Lapham, & Simon, 1985; Darby, 1976; Williams, Hauser, Purpura, Delong, & Swisher, 1980). The mostly negative findings in autism doubtless reflect the inadequacy of our investigative tools, but still they represent a marked difference from the results found in nonautistic mentally handicapped populations. It may be concluded that the biological substrate of autistic and nonautistic varieties of mental handicap are likely to differ. The brain diseases and disorders that give rise to severe mental handicap are, medically and neuropathologically speaking, quite varied. However, most have in common the effect of causing extensive global brain damage. While occasionally that can also be so in autism, it is not the usual picture. There is good reason to suppose that autism is usually due to some form of organic brain dysfunction, but it seems to be of a more subtle nature than generalized damage.

NEUROLOGICAL INVESTIGATIONS

Brain Imaging Studies

The new brain imaging techniques represent a quantum step forward in our ability to study the structure and function of the brain. However, so far they have not advanced our understanding of the biological basis of autism, although they may well do so in the future. Computed axial tomography (CAT) scan studies have shown a mixed bag of abnormalities, but perhaps the main finding has been an increased ventricular volume in some cases (Caparulo et al., 1981; Creasey et al., 1986; Damasio, Maurer, Damasio, & Chui, 1980; Gillberg & Svendsen, 1983; Prior, Tress, Hoffman, & Boldt, 1984; Rosenbloom et al., 1984). It is not yet known whether an increased volume is associated with any differentiating characteristics in clinical features. There are only two studies that have included quantitative assessment of brain density; one with negative findings (Creasey et al., 1986) and one with some significant case-control differences (Jacobson, Le Couteur, Howlin, & Rutter, in press). Such densitometric analyses have their problems, but they carry the potential of showing regional differences that could be of considerable importance (Jacobson, Turner, Baldy, & Lishman, 1985). The reason for the disparity in results between these two studies, both of which concerned adult males with autism, remain obscure and further investigations are needed.

Rumsey and her colleagues at NIMH (Rumsey et al., 1985) reported that glucose metabolism of the brain, as assessed from positron emission tomography (PET), tended to be globally increased in adult autistic men. However, Herold, Frackowiak, Rutter, and Howlin (1985) at Hammersmith did not confirm that finding. Neither study found any right-left difference. Compared with the normal controls, oxygen consumption in the Hammersmith study tended to be lower in the autistic group, but the difference reached statistical significance only in the left anterior temporal and right basal ganglia regions. The finding probably has no localizing value. Sherman, Nass, and Shapiro (1984), using the xenon inhalation technique, found cerebral blood flow to be decreased in autism. In view of these sparse data deriving from different methods of measurement, no firm conclusions can be drawn. So far, the findings concern nonspecific abnormalities that are of little help in understanding the nature of affected brain processes. However, the studies of brain metabolism undertaken to date suffer from two marked limitations. First, they have been concerned with the study of cerebral energy metabolism, rather than with the exploration of specific neurotransmitter pathways. The new generation of PET scan techniques allows such an approach, which could well prove to be more profitable (Herold & Frackowiak, 1986). Second, PET studies of autistic children were designed to evaluate steady state functioning rather than function as tapped by varying specific task demands. The new procedures that can assess brain chemistry under differing cognitive task conditions are likely to prove more informative.

Biochemical Findings

Over the years there have been occasional reports of biochemical abnormalities in sporadic cases of autism (Cohen, Caparulo, & Shaywitz, 1978; Coleman, 1976; Ritvo, Rabin, Yuwiler, Freeman, & Geller, 1978). However, none of these abnormalities has been specific to autism. Moreover, it is notable that several claims have failed to stand the test of replication in independent laboratories, or even of replication by the same laboratory under blind conditions. For example, that has applied to Boullin's report of increased serotonin efflux in platelets (Boullin, Coleman, O'Brien, & Rimland, 1971; Boullin et al., 1982) and possibly to the Scandinavian reports of urinary peptide abnormalities (Gillberg, Trygstad, & Foss, 1982; Le Couteur, Trygstad, Evered, Gillberg, & Rutter, in press). Inevitably, that makes one cautious in the interpretation of new claims such as those on raised levels of homovanillic acid in the cerebrospinal fluid (CSF) (Gillberg, Svennerholm, & Hamilton-Hellberg, 1983) and in the urine (Garnier et al., 1986), or of abnormal endorphin levels in the CSF (Gillberg, Terenuis, & Lonnerholm, 1985). The findings may prove to be significant, but their meaning remains uncertain at the moment.

Serotonin came back into the news 5 years ago with a premature report of an uncontrolled study of three autistic children said to show behavioral and cognitive improvement associated with the reduction of raised serotonin levels through the administration of fenfluramine (Geller, Ritvo, Freeman, & Yuwiler, 1982). It always seemed unlikely that this was a specific therapeutic effect on autistic abnormalities because, although about a third of autistic children show raised serotonin levels, so do a third of nonautistic retarded children as well as patients with a variety of other conditions (Editorial, 1978). Subsequent research has shown much more modest, and inconsistent, benefits following fenfluramine—such improvements as there are being unrelated to changes in serotonin levels (August et al., 1984; Ritvo et al., 1983, 1986).

Most recently of all, Todd and Ciaranello (1985) have reported autoantibodies against serotonin-binding proteins in the blood of 7 out of 13 autistic children. They suggest that a subgroup of autistic individuals may be suffering from an autoimmune disorder (Todd, 1986). The finding requires replication, and the interpretation is necessarily speculative. Nevertheless, it could tie up with Geschwind and Galaburda's (1985) arguments on the possible role of immune mechanisms in the development of the anomalous cerebral dominance thought to play a role in some neurodevelopmental disorders.

Neurophysiological Studies

Although neurophysiological studies of autism have been undertaken over some 2 decades (Fein, Humes, Kaplan, Lucci, & Waterhouse, 1984; James & Barry, 1980), the literature is replete with inconsistent, inconclusive, and nonreplicated findings. Part of the difficulty stems from uncertain comparability between the measures and procedures used in different studies, part from heterogeneity in the sample studies, and part from a failure to use mentally retarded control groups (so that it cannot be determined whether the findings are a function of general developmental retardation or specifically of autism). Several different lines of inquiry have been pursued. First, there have been claims from evoked potential investigations that brain stem information-processing times are prolonged in some autistic children (e.g., Gillberg, Rosenhall, & Johansson, 1983; Skoff, Mirsky, & Turner, 1980), but others have found both prolonged and shortened times (Rumsey, Grimes, Pikus, Duara, & Ismond, 1984; Tanguay, Edwards, Buchwald, Schwafel, & Allen, 1982) or have had more complex differences that are dependent on the nature of the task or stimulus (Courchesne, Lincoln, Kilman, & Galambos, 1985; Novick, Kurtzberg, & Vaughan, 1979). Methodological limitations seem to account for some of the supposedly positive findings that have not been replicated (Rumsey et al., 1984). However, it also appears possible that some autistic individuals do show unusual features in their processing of incoming information; on the other hand, it seems much less likely that this stems from any general depression of brain stem functioning.

Second, investigators have focused on possible impairments in cerebral lateralization. This possibility has been raised by the tendency for some autistic individuals to show less clearly established hand preferences than do normal individuals (Fein et al., 1984; McCann, 1981), and by the evidence, from reaction times (James & Barry, 1983), dichotic listening tasks (Prior & Bradshaw, 1979), and evoked potentials (Dawson, Finley, Phillips, & Galpert, 1986; Dawson, Warrenburg, & Fuller, 1982) that some autistic children show reversed hemispheric asymmetry. Although there have been some failures to find this pattern (Arnold and Schwartz [1983] confirmed it for children with severe developmental language disorders but not for autistic children), there seems to be something in the suggestion of impaired dominance in some autistic individuals. However, it seems that this is most frequently evident in the most mentally retarded persons and it remains uncertain how much the finding reflects general development retardation and how much autism per se.

Third, there have been a variety of clinical EEG studies. Often these have shown an increased rate of abnormalities (e.g., Small, 1975), but the results have been rather uninformative to date. Surprisingly, there have been no systematic attempts to use the EEG to compare autistic individuals who develop seizures from those who do not. However, the routine EEG is an exceedingly crude diagnostic test and it is to be hoped that the future will see greater use of computer analysis and of the study of responses to varying task demands. The limited data available so far from completed EEG analyses (Cantor, Thatcher, Hrybk, & Kaye, 1986) suggest developmental immaturity but no specific features.

Genetic Studies

The last biological approach to consider is that provided by genetic studies. Initially it had been thought that autism was unlikely to involve hereditary factors because it was so unusual to find two autistic members of the same family. However, it is now clear that that was a wrong inference (Folstein & Rutter, 1987). To begin with, although the rate of autism in the siblings is probably only about 2% (Gottesman & Shields, 1982), this rate is many times that of the 1 per 2,500 in the general population. However, Folstein and Rutter's (1977) twin study provided more direct evidence of genetic factors. Twenty-one same-sex twin pairs were investigated, the same comprising the total number obtained from a nationwide search in the United Kingdom. Monozygotic pairs showed a 36% pairwise concordance rate for autism (compared with 10% in dizygotic pairs) and an 82% concordance for cognitive abnormalities (compared with 10% in dizygotic pairs). The findings suggested that, probably, it is not autism as such that is inherited but rather some broader predisposition to language and cognitive abnormalities. The same conclusion regarding a familial association between autism and other cognitive deficits flows from sibling studies. For example, August, Stewart, and Tsai (1981) found that 15% of the sibs of autistic children, compared with 3% of sibs of Down syndrome individuals, showed some form of language disorder, learning disability, or mental retardation. Minton, Campbell, Geen, Jennings, and Samit's (1982) data suggested that there may also be more subtle verbal deficits in sibs. In our own studies (Bartak et al., 1975), it was apparent that the family history of speech delay applied to higher functioning as well as mentally handicapped, autistic children.

Both the twin and family data point to the likelihood that genetic factors are implicated in autism. Also, however, they suggest that what is inherited may not be autism as such but rather some broader set of cognitive disabilities that includes, but is not restricted to, autism. The implication is interesting in its bringing autism back into association with mental retardation and specific developmental disorders of language, an association that had been cast in doubt by the studies of autistic individuals.

The data raise a host of questions that have yet to be answered. Some investigators have wanted to go straight to hypotheses about modes of inheritance. Thus, Ritvo, Spence et al. (1985) and Ritvo, Freeman, Mason-Brothers, Mo, and Ritvo (1985) have argued for an autosomal recessive mode of inheritance. However, this suggestion fails to account for the marked male excess found in autism and the data are open to a variety of other interpretations. But also, their analyses failed to consider the likelihood of genetic heterogeneity.

Such heterogeneity is known to occur because occasional cases of autism have been reported in children with single-gene conditions such as phenylketonuria, but more particularly because of the recent reports that some 5%–15% of cases of autism are associated with the fragile-X anomaly (Folstein & Rutter, 1987). There is no doubt that this rate is far higher than that in the general population because the anomaly is rare in the absence of some sort of handicap. Nevertheless, there is still considerable doubt on whether the association between the fragile X and autism is stronger than that between the anomaly and mental handicap. In the large-scale Scandinavian study by Blomquist et al. (1982, 1983, 1985), some 16% of autistic males showed the fragile X compared with 7% in males with uncomplicated severe and 5% in males with uncomplicated mild mental retardation. On the other hand, Fisch, Cohen, Wolf, Brown, Jenkins, and Gross (1986) found the fragile X in 12.5% of autistic individuals compared with 20.6% of nonautistic mentally retarded subjects; Wright, Young, Edwards, Abramson, and Duncan (1986) reported only one case of fragile X (2.5%) in 40 autistic children studied; Watson et al. (1984) found the fragile X in only 5% of autistic children (and 0% in those not in institutions); and no cases were found in Venter, Hof, Coetzee, Van der Walt, and Retief's (1984) series of 37, in Goldfine et al.'s (1985) series of 37, and in Pueschel, Herman, and Groden's (1985) series of 18 subjects thought to be at high risk because of the presence of dysmorphic features. Moreover, even within a single multi-center study (Blomquist et al., 1985), the variability between centers was great (5%–20%); across studies the range is from 0% to 16% (Brown et al., 1986). Several factors are likely to be important in this variability. First, the fragile-X anomaly is not an unambiguous abnormality like an extra or missing chromosome: it is found in only some, not all, chromosomes; there is uncertainty on the proportion needed to diagnose the phenomenon; it is shown only when cultured under low folate conditions; different laboratories use somewhat different methods; and the extent of inter- and intralaboratory variation has yet to be determined. Second, the frequency of the fragile X may be influenced by the sample characteristics (when it appears to be more frequent in severely handicapped individuals). Third, it seems probable that investigators have varied considerably in the criteria required for the diagnosis of autism. It may be that, among mentally retarded individuals, the fragile X is particularly associated with language and social impairment, but that, nevertheless, this often does not take the form that is characteristic of autism. Finally, claims that a 47% rate of chromosomal abnormalities (only half comprising the fragile X) in autism is a minimum (Gillberg & Wahlstrom, 1985) rest on the inclusion of various abnormalities, of unknown significance, as well as the acceptance of the fragile-X phenomenon on only one abnormal cell out of the 100 examined. Clearly a proportion of autistic children show the fragile-X phenomenon, but it remains unclear quite what the proportion is and whether those cases differ in any systematic way from other cases of autism.

It is unlikely that the fragile X provides the only source of genetic heterogeneity in autism. It has been shown to account for occasional cases of familial aggregation but not for most (August & Lockhart, 1984; Spence et al., 1985). The severity of mental handicap provides another source of heterogeneity. Baird and August (1985) observed that, in their sample, familial aggregation was mainly a feature of autism accompanied by severe mental retardation. Familial loading does occur in cases of autism without severe mental handicap (Bartak et al., 1975; Burgoine & Wing, 1983). Within twin pairs concordant for autism, the IQ differences between the twins have been as great as 50 IQ points (Folstein & Rutter, 1977); the same has been found with multiply affected sibs in the same family (Shell et al., 1984). The possibility that the genetic contribution varies by the degree of intellectual impairment in autism warrants further exploration.

A further issue in genetic research concerns the major question of *what* is inherited. If that extends beyond autism, as clearly it seems to, there is a need to delineate what is distinctive about the varieties of mental handicap and of specific developmental disorders that are associated with autism. Do they differ, for example, in patterns of cognitive functioning or in socioemotional features? Rutter et al. (in press) have devised a variety of socioemotional measures for this purpose, but it remains to be seen what they will show with respect to the disabilities involved in familial loading. Obviously what is required now is a detailed individual study of affected and unaffected family members.

With respect to the pattern(s) of inheritance, it is too early to know whether single-gene effects or a multifactorial threshold of liability effect is more likely, or whether both are involved in different families. The answer might have implications for the further question of the proportion of cases of autism in which genetic factors are implicated in a major way. Are the majority of cases in which no obvious familial loading is evident non-genetically determined? Or is it that we are not looking for the right phenomenon in the families? Obviously, we have to look wider than autism as usually diagnosed, but how widely should we cast the net? The main difficulty here lies in the uncertainty over the phenotype(s) that might be involved. The wide variation in IQ among autistic individuals suggests that etiological diversity is probable; nevertheless, there are well-documented examples of widely varying expression of single disorders (Folstein & Rutter, 1987). The matter cannot be taken further until the detailed family studies now underway have been completed.

A further genetic approach is provided in the recombinant DNA technology that allows a mapping of the genes. This greatly increases the power of pedigree studies to examine co-segregation of the disorder and a set of genetic "markers" in order to reveal genetic linkage (McGuffin, 1987). For example, the marked male excess in autism (Lord & Schopler, 1987), together with the findings on the fragile-X phenomenon, suggest the possibility that some cases of autism may be due to an abnormal gene on the X chromosome (Gurling, 1986). The suggestion is that the fragile-X anomaly may not be a direct cause of autism as such, but rather it develops its association with autism because the fragile site is close to the locus on the chromosome that is directly responsible. Again, it is a possibility that should be followed up.

TREATMENT IMPLICATIONS

It is evident that knowledge on the biological substrate of autism is not yet at the point at which there are direct indicators of generally effective preventive or curative interventions. Nevertheless, already there are important pointers that should have implications for clinical practice.

Genetic Counseling

The most obvious implication is for genetic counseling. This must be preceded by the investigations necessary to provide the data required for genetic guidance. The most obvious requirement is chromosome study, using culture in low folate media to detect the fragile-X phenomenon. As already noted, there are continuing unresolved difficulties with the detection of the fragile X. However, despite these, it is clear from community studies in several countries (Blomquist et al., 1982, 1983, 1985; Bundey, Webb, Thake, & Todd, 1985) that the anomaly is second only to Down syndrome as a cause of mental retardation and that it accounts for a roughly comparable proportion of cases of autism. The procedure to detect the fragile X is time consuming and expensive and it would be helpful if its application could be restricted to subjects known to have a high risk. Apart from restricting it to males (so far there is only one report of fragile-X autistic females [Hagerman et al., 1986]), there are no satisfactory means of screening. The supposedly characteristic physical features (hypotonia, long face, and large ears) are not sufficiently distinctive to be useful, and the characteristic testicular enlargement is not clearly evident until puberty. However, these features, in conjunction with large feet and an above-average head circumference, increase the likelihood of fragile-X phenomenon being found (Thake, Todd, Bundey, & Webb, 1985). Obviously, examination for the fragile X should be a routine in cases of autism in which there is any familial loading for general specific cognitive disabilities. However, a positive family history is an uncertain guide and it is likely that the examination will need to become a routine in all cases of autism and mental handicap in males, and possibly also in females.

The importance of determining whether autistic individuals have the fragile-X anomaly is that often it is transmitted in Mendelian fashion as a sex-linked recessive. This means that, except in sporadic mutations or in cases in which the fragile-X chromosome in a girl comes from the father, the mothers are obligate carriers and there is a substantial risk for mental handicap/autism in subsequent male offspring. Nevertheless, the genetic findings are complex (Fryns, 1984; Hagerman & McBogg, 1983; Sherman et al., 1985; Sherman, Morton, Jacobs, & Turner, 1984) and recurrence rates may be less than the theoretical 50% because not all males with fragile X are retarded; also, there is some risk of mental retardation in the daughters of carriers. If the fragile-X anomaly is detected in a child with autism, similar chromosome studies should be undertaken with all other members of the immediate family, and they should be referred to a medical geneticist for expert advice.

In addition to detection, or exclusion, of the fragile X, clinical appraisal should include systematic family history taking to determine whether any other first or second degree relatives have shown autism, mild or severe mental handicap, delays in language development, reading disabilities, or marked social oddities. It is necessary to extend inquiry to second degree relatives in order to detect recessive transmission. As already noted, there are difficulties in the family inquiry because of the uncertainty regarding the characteristics of the disorders associated with autism. Language retardation is present in 5% of the population (Silva, in press), reading difficulties occur somewhat more commonly (Yule & Rutter, 1985), and mental retardation occurs in 3% (Rutter, Tizard, & Whitmore, 1970)—all estimates varying by the severity cutoff chosen, and with substantial overlap between the disorders.

Also, clinical appraisal and relevant investigations should be undertaken routinely to detect possible medical conditions that may be involved in etiology. Thus, there should be inquiry about perinatal complications and neonatal functioning (with respect to the need for resuscitation and/or intensive care, neonatal convulsions, and poor sucking), checked if possible against contemporaneous medical records. A careful history (with a focus on the possibility of progressive deterioration) and neurodevelopmental examination (with attention to signs of cerebral palsy and loss of purposive movements) should be carried out to detect disorders such as Rett syndrome (Hagberg, Aicardi, Dias, & Ramos, 1983) with which autism may occasionally be confused. The possibility of confusion may also be reduced by a detailed and accurate account and observation of the socioemotional and behavioral characteristics, as they seem to be rather different in Rett syndrome from autism (Kerr & Stephenson, 1985; Olsson & Rett, 1985). In recent years there has been a tendency to rely on standardized questionnaires to diagnose autism; this should be resisted as questionnaires are unlikely to provide the qualitative discriminations needed for accurate diagnosis. Finally, the appropriate blood and urine screening tests for metabolic disorders should be carried out. Their yield is decidedly low, but they do pick out the rare case in which findings reveal conditions that carry a genetic risk or, less often, those that are treatable, such as phenylketonuria, although nowadays this should have been excluded by routine screening in infancy.

These data provide the basis, albeit a most uncertain one, for genetic counseling when no fragile X has been found. There are three main circumstances to be considered. First, there are the rare cases in which autism is associated with a known condition due to a major gene other than fragile X. In this situation, the advice should be based on what is known about the inheritance of the underlying medical condition, rather than on the autism. Second, there are uncommon, but rather more frequent, cases in which autism is associated with a clear and unambiguous history of severe pre-, peri-, or postnatal trauma *giving rise to neurological implications at the time,* and where there is *no family history* of autism or cognitive disabilities. There should be great caution in inferring a nongenetic cause on the basis of low birth weight, or minor/moderate pregnancy complications, or high fever associated with immunization, unless there was contemporary evidence of neurological impairment as well as an absence of any familial aggregation of cognitive disorders. However, when a nongenetic cause can be inferred, the risk of recurrence is probably very low (unless there is reason to suppose that that cause may arise again).

The most common situation, however, is that in which autism is not due to a known single-gene abnormality and in which there is no known nongenetic cause. In these circumstances, the recurrence risk for autism is usually said to be about 1%–3%, and that for cognitive disabilities (including both persistent mental handicap and transient language retardation) about 10%–15% (Folstein & Rutter, 1987). However, these figures are necessarily approximate because they are based on a variety of samples with varying IQ distributions and varying (and often uncertain) diagnostic criteria. As already emphasized, autism that is so far idiopathic is likely to be etiologically heterogeneous. The implication is that a few families will have a high risk of recurrence, whereas in others the risk will be negligible. Unfortunately, at present we have no satisfactory means of telling which is which. As a very rough and ready guide, the risk should be greater than average when there is a heavy family loading for either autism or cognitive disabilities, and less than average if there is no such history, but this commonsense extrapolation is as far as one can go.

Medical Treatments

Two, supposedly specific, treatments for autism based on biological findings have been put forward. First, Ritvo et al. (1983, 1986) administered fenfluramine to autistic children on the rationale that a reduction in serotonin should be beneficial. The drug did reduce blood serotonin levels and claims for therapeutic efficacy (from uncontrolled studies of three patients) were made. Subsequent research (August, Raz, & Baird, 1985; Beisler, Tsai, & Stiefel, 1986; Klykylo, Feldis, O'Grady, Ross, & Halloran, 1985; Ritvo et al., 1983) has shown only quite modest behavioral benefits, which are unconnected with serotonin reduction. Moreover, reports of side effects (irritability, lethargy, anorexia, and one case of regression) have begun to appear (Piggott, Gdowski, Villanueva, Fischhoff, & Frohman, 1986), and in view of its neurotoxicity in animal studies (Pranzatellis & Snodgrass, 1985), this does not seem a worthwhile form of intervention.

Second, on the grounds that the fragile-X anomaly became manifest only when chromosomes were cultured in low-folate media, Lejeune (1982) suggested that folic acid might be used in treatment and reported some cases where this seemed to bring about behavioral improvement. The results of subsequent studies, including blind trials in brothers (Brown et al., 1984) and in identical twins (Rosenblatt et al., 1985), have shown few cognitive or behavioral benefits and no effect on the percentage of cells showing fragile sites. In view of the lack of evidence of any disorder in folate metabolism in fragile-X individuals, this is not a treatment to be recommended at the moment.

Megavitamin therapy has been advocated on general grounds and there is a limited amount of evidence that it may produce slight benefits in some autistic children (LeLord et al., 1981; Rimland, Calloway, & Dreyfus, 1978). However, the rationale has a shaky base and so far there is little indication that it is likely to constitute a generally effective form of treatment in most cases.

The strong implication from clinical and biological studies that autism usually arises on the basis of organic brain dysfunction suggests that neuroleptic drugs might be of benefit. Perhaps rather against expectations, the available data fail to indicate any marked benefits of the kind that are characteristic, for example, of schizophrenia. The major tranquilizers may serve to reduce agitation, anxiety, and overactivity (Campbell, 1978; Winsberg & Yepes, 1978), but in most cases the effects are neither specific nor marked. They are of occasional value in individual cases but they should not be prescribed as a routine. There is a need for further pharmacological studies (particularly as there seems to be marked individual variation in autistic children's responses to drugs), but the biological studies and data provide no specific pointers on which neurochemical effects are most likely to be effective in bringing about behavioral change.

The relatively frequent occurrence of hyperactivity and inattention as symptoms might be thought to suggest the therapeutic use of stimulants (in view of their well-demonstrated short-term efficacy in children of normal intelligence with disorders involving these symptoms). However, such evidence as there is suggests that stimulants are *contraindicated* in autism, at least when it is associated with mental retardation (Aman, 1982). This is not only because they appear ineffective, but also because they can sometimes increase stereotyped behavior. The psychopharmacological findings in autism could carry implications for the better understanding of the biological basis, but the biological studies so far have done little to show which drugs might be more therapeutic.

Psychological Therapies

Finally, there are implications for psychological therapies. During the 1950s and early 1960s, psychoanalytically oriented psychotherapies constituted many clinicians' treatment of choice for autistic children, on the assumption that autism was a psychogenically determined mental illness of early onset. Today, educational and behavioral approaches are the standard (Rutter, 1985b). The demonstration that autism was associated with basic cognitive deficits of presumably organic origin made it less likely that psychodynamic interventions based on assumptions of internal conflict would be appropriate.

In any event, systematic evaluations of special schooling and of developmentally oriented behavioral interventions, combined with family support and counseling, showed them to be of value in both the short- and long-term (Howlin et al., in press; Rutter, 1985b). Equally, however, these evaluations have demonstrated the limitations of psychoeducational methods. They are most successful in reducing the nonspecific problems associated with autism (tantrums, sleep difficulties, fears, and the like), they are of some benefit in increasing the social usage of autistic children's language and play skills, but they make very little difference in the long term to the children's intellectual and language capacities. Probably, too, their impact on the social deficits of autistic children is quite limited. There have been claims that interventions starting in infancy are more successful (Fenske, Zalenski, Krantz, & McClannahan, 1985; Groden, Domingue, Chesnick, Groden, & Brain, 1983), but the evidence on this score is not convincing as yet.

Most of the treatment evaluations concern interventions that were undertaken at a time when our understanding of autistic children's cognitive and social deficits was less than it is today. It remains to be seen whether the current treatment programs will do better.

CONCLUSIONS

It is evident from this brief review of research findings that no unequivocal answer is available as yet on the biological basis of autism. Nevertheless, it is equally apparent that the last few years have seen very substantial advances in several directions. It is now clear that there *is* some type of organic brain dysfunction in autism. The psychogenic theories that dominated the scene in the 1960s no longer require discussion in view of the mass of contrary evidence and the lack of any evidence in support. Equally, however, one can reject the notion of autism as simply one of several nonspecific outcomes following generalized or localized brain damage. There are too many specificities in findings (ranging from the age of onset of seizures to the medical correlates) for that to be plausible. Of course, autistic features *can* result from generalized brain damage but that does not seem to be the usual explanation.

Uncertainty remains on the extent to which autism is etiologically homogeneous or heterogeneous. Clearly there is *some* heterogeneity but there could still be a more uniform core to the syndrome. The point is that modern research neither assumes nor rejects extensive heterogeneity; the matter is subject to empirical study and it requires explicit examination in all biological studies.

In the field of medical genetics, the possibilities of study have been substantially strengthened both by the recognition that there may be "lesser variants" of autism and by the real (albeit still limited) advances in our understanding of the nature of the cognitive deficits associated with autism.

These have led to the development of cognitive and socioemotional measures that, potentially, may be able to detect such "lesser variants." Certainly that possibility warrants careful study. There are many research avenues that warrant exploration. The explosion of knowledge that has greatly extended our investigative approaches in areas extending from brain imaging to molecular biology has rightly reawakened interest in biological studies of autism. It is unclear where the findings will lead, but it will be surprising if the next decade does not contain some real advances in our understanding of the biological basis of autism. Perhaps most of all, there should be a clarification of the role of genetic factors in etiology and a clearer definition of the nature and extent of etiological heterogeneity.

From the viewpoint of the clinician, however, there are two crucially important messages now. The first is that cases of autism require a full and systematic medical appraisal of a kind that would be appropriate for any other complex neurodevelopmental disorder. In this chapter the author has sought to look ahead a little to consider some of the biological aspects of autism that are likely to prove more important as new knowledge accumulates. The second message is that treatment needs to be planned on the basis that autism is a biologically determined chronically handicapping condition. However, that does *not* mean that nothing can be done to help autistic children and their families. On the contrary, there are a variety of ways in which treatment can be planned in order to foster more normal development and to reduce secondary handicaps. These effective treatment strategies at present mainly rely on behavioral and educational methods of intervention, but it is important that they be combined with counseling and social work approaches to deal with the manifold problems faced by the parents of autistic children. Traditional medical treatments, such as the use of drugs, have only a limited ancillary role at the moment. Whether or not that will continue in the future remains to be seen.

REFERENCES

Aman, M. G. (1982). Stimulant drug effects in developmental disorders and hyperactivity: Toward a resolution of disparate findings. *Journal of Autism and Developmental Disorders, 12,* 385–398.

Arnold, G., & Schwartz, S. (1983). Hemispheric lateralization of language in autistic and aphasic children. *Journal of Autism and Developmental Disorders, 13,* 129–139.

August, G. J., & Lockhart, L. H. (1984). Familial autism and the fragile-X chromosome. *Journal of Autism and Developmental Disorders, 14,* 197–204.

August, G. J., Raz, N., & Baird, T. D. (1985). Brief report: Effects of fenfluramine on behavioral, cognitive and affective disturbances in autistic children. *Journal of Autism and Developmental Disorders, 15,* 97–107.

August, G. J., Raz, N., Papanicolaou, A. C., Baird, T. D., Hirsch, S. L., & Hsu, L. L. (1984). Fenfluramine treatment in infantile autism: Neurochemical, elec-

trophysiological, and behavioral effects. *Journal of Nervous and Mental Disease,*
172, 604–612.

August, G. J., Stewart, M. A., & Tsai, L. (1981). The incidence of cognitive disabilities in the siblings of autistic children. *British Journal of Psychiatry, 138,* 416–422.

Baird, T. D., & August. G. J. (1985). Familial heterogeneity in infantile autism.
Journal of Autism and Developmental Disorders, 15, 315–321.

Baron-Cohen, S., Leslie, A. M., & Frith, U. (1985). Does the autistic child have a "theory of mind"? *Cognition, 21,* 37–46.

Baron-Cohen, S., Leslie, A. M., & Frith, U. (1986). Mechanical, behavioral and intentional understanding of picture stories in autistic children. *British Journal of Developmental Psychology, 4,* 113–125.

Bartak, L., Rutter, M., & Cox, A. (1975). A comparative study of infantile autism and specific developmental receptive language disorder: I. The children. *British Journal of Psychiatry, 126,* 127–145.

Bauman, M., & Kemper, T. L. (1985). Histoanatomic observations of the brain in early infantile autism. *Neurology, 35,* 866–874.

Beisler, J. M., Tsai, L. Y., & Stiefel, B. (1986). Brief report: The effects of fenfluramine on communication skills in autistic children. *Journal of Autism and Developmental Disorders. 16,* 227–233.

Birch, H. G., Richardson, S. A., Baird, D., Horobin, G., & Illsley, R. (1970).
Mental subnormality in the community: A clinical and epidemiologic study. Baltimore: Williams & Wilkins Co.

Blomquist, H. K., Bohman, M., Edvinsson, S. O., Gillberg, C., Gustavson, K. H., Holmgren, G., & Wahlstrom, J. (1985). Frequency of the fragile X syndrome in infantile autism: A Swedish multicenter study. *Clinical Genetics, 27,* 113–117.

Blomquist, H. K., Gustavson, K. H., Holmgren, G., Nordenson, I., & Palsson-Strae, U. (1983). Fragile X syndrome in mildly mentally retarded children in a northern Swedish county: A prevalence study. *Clinical Genetics, 24,* 393–399.

Blomquist, H. K., Gustavson, K. H., Holmgren, G., Nordenson, I., & Sweins, A. (1982). Fragile site X-chromosomes and X-linked mental retardation in severely retarded boys in a northern Swedish county: A prevalence study. *Clinical Genetics, 21,* 209–214.

Borod, J. C., Koff, E., Lorch, M. P., & Nicholas, M. (1985). Channels of emotional expression in patients with unilateral brain damage. *Archives of Neurology, 42,* 345–348.

Boullin, D., Coleman, M., O'Brien, R., & Rimland, B. (1971). Laboratory prediction of infantile autism based on 5-hydroxytryptamine efflux from blood platelets and their correlation with the Rimland E-3 score. *Journal of Autism and Childhood Schizophrenia, 1,* 63–71.

Boullin, D., Freeman, B. J., Geller, E., Ritvo, E., Rutter, M., & Yuwiller, A. (1982). Towards the resolution of conflicting findings. *Journal of Autism and Developmental Disorders, 12,* 97–98.

Brown, W. T., Jenkins, E. C., Cohen, I. L., Fisch, G. S., Wolf-Schein, E. G., Gross, A., Waterhouse, L., Fein, D., Mason-Brothers, A., & Ritvo, E. (1986). Fragile X and autism: A multicenter survey. *American Journal of Medical Genetics, 23,* 341–352.

Brown, W. T., Jenkins, E. C., Friedman, E., Brooks, J., Cohen, I. L., Duncan, C., Hill, A. L., Malik, M. N., Morris, V., & Wolf, E. (1984). Folic acid therapy in the fragile X syndrome. *American Journal of Medical Genetics, 17,* 289–297.

Bundey, S., Webb, T. P., Thake, A., & Todd, J. (1985). A community study of severe mental retardation in the West Midlands and the importance of the fragile X chromosome in its aetiology. *Journal of Medical Genetics, 22,* 258–266.

Burgoine, E., & Wing, L. (1983). Identical triplets with Asperger's syndrome. *British Journal of Psychiatry, 143,* 261–265.

Campbell, M. (1978). Pharmacotherapy. In M. Rutter & E. Schopler (Eds.), *Autism: A reappraisal of concepts and treatment* (pp. 337–355). New York: Plenum Press.

Cantor, D. S., Thatcher, R. W., Hrybk, M., & Kaye, H. (1986). Computerized EEG analysis of autistic children. *Journal of Autism and Developmental Disorders, 16,* 169–188.

Cantwell, D., Baker, L., & Rutter, M. (1978). A comparative study of infantile autism and specific receptive developmental language disorders: IV. Syntactical and functional analysis of language. *Journal of Child Psychology and Psychiatry, 19,* 351–362.

Caparulo, B. K., Cohen, D. J., Young, G., Katz, J. D., Shaywitz, S. E., Shaywitz, B. A., & Rothman, S. L. (1981). Computed tomographic brain scanning in children with developmental neuropsychiatric disorders. *Journal of the American Academy of Child Psychiatry, 20,* 338–357.

Chess, S., Fernandez, P. E., & Korn, S. J. (1978). Behavioural consequences of congenital rubella. *Journal of Paediatrics, 93,* 699–703.

Chess, S., Korn, S. J., & Fernandez, P. E. (1971). *Psychiatric disorders of children with congenital rubella.* New York: Brunner/Mazel.

Clark, P., & Rutter, M. (1979). Task difficulty and task performance in autistic children. *Journal of Child Psychology and Psychiatry, 20,* 271–285.

Cohen, D. J., Caparulo, B. K., & Shaywitz, B. (1978). Neurochemical and developmental models in childhood autism. In G. Serban (Ed.), *Cognitive defects in the development of mental illness* (pp. 66–100). New York: Brunner/Mazel.

Coleman, M. (Ed.). (1976). *The autistic syndrome.* Amsterdam: North Holland Publishing.

Coleman, P. D., Romano, J., Lapham, L., & Simon, W. (1985). Cell counts in cerebral cortex of an autistic patient. *Journal of Autism and Developmental Disorders, 15,* 245–256.

Courchesne, E., Lincoln, A. L., Kilman, B. A., & Galambos, R. (1985). Event-related brain potential correlates of the processing of novel visual and auditory information in autism. *Journal of Autism and Developmental Disorders, 15,* 55–76.

Creasey, H., Rumsey, J. M., Schwartz, M., Duara, R., Rapoport, J. L., & Rapoport, S. I. (1986). Brain morphometry in autistic men as measured by volumetric computed tomography. *Archives of Neurology, 43,* 669–672.

Crome, L. (1960). The brain and mental retardation. *British Medical Journal, 1,* 897–904.

Cromer, R. F. (in press). Language acquisition. In W. Yule & M. Rutter, (Eds.), *Language development and disorders (Clinics in Developmental Medicine,* No. 101–102). London: MacKeith Press/Blackwell Scientific.

Damasio, H., Maurer, R. G., Damasio, A. R., & Chui, H. D. (1980). Computerized tomographic scan findings in patients with autistic behaviour. *Archives of Neurology, 37,* 504–510.

Darby, J. K. (1976). Neuropathological aspects of psychosis in children. *Journal of Autism and Childhood Schizophrenia, 6,* 339–352.

Dawson, G. (1983). Lateralized brain function in autism: Evidence from the Halstead-Reitan Neuropsychological Battery. *Journal of Autism and Developmental Disorders, 13,* 369–386.

Dawson, G., Finley, C., Phillips, S., & Galpert, L. (1986). Hemispheric specialization and the language abilities of autistic children. *Child Development 57,* 1440–1453.

Dawson, G., & McKissick, F. C. (1984). Self-recognition in autistic children. *Journal of Autism and Developmental Disorders, 14,* 383–394.

Dawson, G., Warrenburg. W., & Fuller, P. (1982). Cerebral lateralization in individuals diagnosed as autistic in early childhood. *Brain and Language, 15,* 353–368.

De Myer, M. K., Hingtgen, J. N., & Jackson, R. K. (1981). Infantile autism reviewed: A decade of research. *Schizophrenia Bulletin, 7,* 388–451.

Deykin, E. Y., & MacMahon, B. (1979). The incidence of seizures among children with autistic symptoms. *American Journal of Psychiatry, 136,* 1310–1312.

Deykin, E. Y., & MacMahon, B. (1980). Pregnancy, delivery and neonatal complications among autistic children. *American Journal of Diseases of Children, 134,* 860–864.

Editorial. (1978). Serotonin, platelets, and autism. *British Medical Journal, 1,* 1651–1652.

Fein, D., Humes, M., Kaplan, E., Lucci, D., & Waterhouse, L. (1984). The question of left hemisphere dysfunction in autism. *Psychological Bulletin, 95,* 258–281.

Fein, D., Pennington, B., Markowitz, P., Braverman, M., & Waterhouse, L. (1986). Toward a neuropsychological model of infantile autism: Are the social deficits primary? *Journal of the American Academy of Child Psychiatry, 25*(2), 198–212.

Fenske, E. C., Zalenski, S., Krantz, P. J., & McClannahan, L. E. (1985). Age at intervention and treatment outcome for autistic children in a comprehensive intervention program. *Analysis and Intervention in Developmental Disorders, 5,* 49–58.

Ferrari, M., & Matthews, W. S. (1983). Self-recognition deficits in autism: Syndrome-specific or general developmental delay? *Journal of Autism and Developmental Disorders, 13,* 317–324.

Finegan, J., & Quadrington, B. (1979). Pre-, peri-, and neonatal factors and infantile autism. *Journal of Child Psychology and Psychiatry, 20,* 119–128.

Fisch, G. S., Cohen, I. L., Wolf, E. G., Brown, W. T., Jenkins, E. C., & Gross, A. (1986). Autism and the fragile X syndrome. *American Journal of Psychiatry, 143*(1), 71–73.

Folstein, S., & Rutter, M. (1977). Infantile autism: A genetic study of 21 twin pairs. *Journal of Child Psychology and Psychiatry, 18,* 297–321.

Folstein, S., & Rutter, M. (1987). Autism: Familial aggregation and genetic implications. In E. Schopler & G. Mesibov (Eds.), *Neurobiological Issues in Autism* (pp. 83–105). New York: Plenum.

Frith, U., & Snowling, M. (1983). Reading for meaning and reading for sound in autistic and dyslexic children. *British Journal of Developmental Psychology, 1,* 329–342.

Fryns, J. P. (1984). The fragile X syndrome: A study of 83 families. *Clinical Genetics, 26,* 497–528.

Fyffe, C., & Prior, M. R. (1978). Evidence of language recoding in autistic children: A re-examination. *British Journal of Psychiatry, 69,* 393–403.

Garnier, C., Comoy, E., Barthelemy, C., Leddet, I., Garreau, B., Muh, J. P., & Lelord, G. (1986). Dopamine-beta-hydroxylase (DBH) and homovanillic acid (HVA) in autistic children. *Journal of Autism and Developmental Disorders, 16,* 23–29.

Geller, E., Ritvo, E. R., Freeman, B. J., & Yuwiler, A. (1982). Preliminary observations on the effect of fenfluramine on blood serotonin and symptoms in three autistic boys. *New England Journal of Medicine, 307,* 165–169.

Geschwind, N., & Galaburda, A. M. (1985). Cerebral lateralization: Biological mechanisms, associations and pathology. *Archives of Neurology, 42*, 428–459; 521–552, 634–654.

Gillberg, C., & Gillberg, I. C. (1983). Infantile autism: A total population study of reduced optimality in the pre-, peri-, and neonatal period. *Journal of Autism and Developmental Disorders, 13*, 153–155.

Gillberg, C., Rosenhall, U., & Johansson, E. (1983). Auditory brainstem responses in childhood psychosis. *Journal of Autism and Developmental Disorders, 13*, 181–195.

Gillberg, C., & Svendsen, P. (1983). Childhood psychosis and computed tomographic brain scan findings. *Journal of Autism and Developmental Disorders, 13*, 19–32.

Gillberg, C., & Svendsen, P. (1983). Childhood psychosis and computed tomographic brain scan findings. *Journal of Autism and Developmental Disorders, 13*, 19–32.

Gillberg, C., Terenuis, J., & Lonnerholm, G. (1985). Endorphin activity in childhood psychosis: Spinal fluid levels in 24 cases. *Archives of General Psychiatry, 42*, 780–783.

Gillberg, C., Trygstad, O., & Foss, I. (1982). Childhood psychosis and urinary excretion of peptides and protein-associated peptide complexes. *Journal of Autism and Developmental Disorders, 12*, 229–241.

Gillberg, C., & Wahlstrom, J. (1985). Chromosome abnormalities in infantile autism and other childhood psychoses: A population study of 66 cases. *Developmental Medicine and Child Neurology, 27*, 293–304.

Goldfine, P. E., McPherson, P. M., Heath, G. A., Hardesty, V. A., Beauregard, L. J., & Gordon, S. (1985). Association of fragile X syndrome with autism. *American Journal of Psychiatry, 142*, 108–110.

Gottesman, I. I., & Shields, J. (1982). *Schizophrenia: The epigenetic puzzle.* Cambridge, MA: Cambridge University Press.

Groden, G., Domingue, D., Chesnick, M., Groden, J., & Brain, G. (1983). Early intervention with autistic children: A case presentation with pre-program, program and follow up data. *Psychological Reports, 53*, 715–722.

Gurling, H. M. D. (1986). Candidate genes and favoured loci: Strategies for molecular genetic research into schizophrenia, manic depression, autism, alcoholism and Alzheimer's disease. *Psychiatric Developments, 4*, 289–309.

Hagberg, B., Aicardi, J., Dias, K., & Ramos, O. (1983). A progressive syndrome of autism, dementia, ataxia and loss of purposeful hand use in girls: Rett's syndrome: Report of 35 cases. *Annals of Neurology, 14*, 471–479.

Hagberg, B., & Kyllerman, M. (1983). Epidemiology of mental retardation: A Swedish study. *Brain and Development, 5*, 441–449.

Hagerman, R. J., Chudley, A. E., Knull, J. H., Jackson, A. W., Kemper, M., & Ahmed, R. (1986). Autism in fragile X females. *American Journal of Medical Genetics, 23*, 375–380.

Hagerman, R. J., & McBogg, P. A. (1983). *The fragile X syndrome, diagnosis, biochemistry and intervention.* Dillon, CO: Spectra Publishing.

Heilman, K. M., Bowers, D., Speedie, L., & Coslett, H. B. (1984). Comprehension of affective and nonaffective prosody. *Neurology, 34*, 917–921.

Hermelin, B. (1976). Coding and the sense modalities. In L. Wing (Ed.), *Early childhood autism: Clinical, educational and social aspects* (2nd ed., pp. 35–168). Oxford: Pergamon.

Hermelin, B., & O'Connor, N. (1970). *Psychological experiments with autistic children.* Oxford: Pergamon.

Herold, S., & Frackowiak, R. (1986). Editorial: New methods in brain imaging. *Psychological Medicine, 16,* 24–245.

Herold, S., Frackowiak, R., Rutter, M., & Howlin, P. (1985). Regional cerebral blood flow, oxygen and glucose metabolism in young autistic adults. *Journal of Cerebral Blood Flow and Metabolism, 5*(1), S189–S190.

Hobson, R. P. (1982). The autistic child's concept of persons. In D. Park (Ed.), *Proceedings of the 1981 International Conference on Autism, Boston USA.* Washington, DC: National Society for Children and Adults with Autism.

Hobson, R. P. (1983). The autistic child's recognition of age-related features of people, animals and things. *British Journal of Developmental Psychology, 1,* 343–352.

Hobson, R. P. (1984). Early childhood autism and the question of egocentrism. *Journal of Autism and Developmental Disorders, 14,* 85–104.

Hobson, R. P. (1986). The autistic child's appraisal of expressions of emotion: An experimental investigation. *Journal of Child Psychology and Psychiatry, 27,* 321–342.

Howlin, P. (1986). An overview of social behavior in autism. In E. Schopler & G. Mesibov (Eds.), *Social behavior in autism.* New York: Plenum Press.

Howlin, P., & Rutter, M., with Hemsley, R., Berger, M., Hersov, L., & Yule, W. (in press). *Treatment of autistic children.* Chichester: Wiley.

Jacobson, R., Le Couteur, A., Howlin, P., & Rutter, M. (in press). Selective subcortical abnormalities in autism. *Psychological Medicine.*

Jacobson, R. R., Turner. S. W., Baldy, R. E., & Lishman, W. A. (1985). Densitometric analysis of scans: Important sources of artefact. *Psychological Medicine, 15,* 879–889.

James, A. L., & Barry, R. J. (1980). A review of psychophysiology in early onset psychosis. *Schizophrenia Bulletin, 6,* 506–525.

James, A. L., & Barry, R. J. (1983). Developmental effects in the cerebral lateralization of autistic, retarded and normal children. *Journal of Autism and Developmental Disorders, 13,* 43–56.

Kanner, L. (1943). Autistic disturbances of affective contact. *The Nervous Child, 2,* 217–250.

Kerr, A., & Stephenson, J. B. P. (1985). Rett's syndrome in the west of Scotland. *British Medical Journal, 291,* 579–582.

Klykylo, W. M., Feldis, D., O'Grady, D., Ross, D. L., & Halloran, C. (1985). Brief report: Clinical effects of fenfluramine in ten autistic subjects. *Journal of Autism and Developmental Disorders, 15,* 417–423.

Koegel, R. L., & Mentis, M. (1985). Motivation in childhood autism: Can they or won't they? *Journal of Child Psychology and Psychiatry, 26,* 185–191.

Le Couteur, A., Trygstad, O., Evered, C., Gillberg, C., & Rutter, M. (in press). Infantile autism and urinary excretion of peptides and protein-associated peptide complexes. *Journal of Autism and Developmental Disorders.*

Ledbetter, P. H., Riccardi, B. M., Eirhart, S. D., Strobel, R. J., Keenan, B. S., & Crawford, J. B. (1981). Deletions of chromosome 16 as a cause of the Prader-Willi syndrome. *New England Journal of Medicine, 304,* 325–329.

Lejeune, J. (1982). Is the fragile X syndrome amenable to treatment? *Lancet, 1,* 273–274.

LeLord, G., Muh, J. P., Barthelmey, C., Martineau, J., Garreau, B., & Callaway, E. (1981). Effects of pyridoxine and magnesium on autistic symptoms: Initial observations. *Journal of Autism and Developmental Disorders, 11,* 219–229.

Lockyer, L., & Rutter, M. (1970). A five to fifteen year follow up study of infantile psychosis: IV. Patterns of cognitive ability. *British Journal of Social and Clinical Psychology, 9,* 152–163.

Lord, C. (1984). The development of peer relations in children with autism. In F. J. Morrison, C. Lord, & D. P. Keating (Eds.), *Applied developmental psychology* (pp. 166–230). New York: Academic Press.

Lord, C., & Schopler, E. (1987). Neurobiological implications of sex differences in autism. In E. Schopler & G. Mesibov (Eds.), *Neurobiological issues in autism.* (pp. 192–211). New York: Plenum Press.

Lotter, V. (1978). Follow-up studies. In M. Rutter & E. Schopler (Eds.), *Autism: A reappraisal of concepts and treatment* (pp. 475–495). New York: Plenum Press.

McCann, B. S. (1981). Hemispheric asymmetries and early infantile autism. *Journal of Autism and Developmental Disorders, 11,* 401–412.

McGuffin, P. (1987). The new genetics and childhood psychiatric disorder. *Journal of Child Psychology and Psychiatry, 28,* 215–222.

Minton, J., Campbell, M., Geen, W. H., Jennings, S., & Samit, C. (1982). Cognitive assessment of siblings of autistic children. *Journal of the American Academy of Child Psychiatry, 21,* 256–261.

Novick, B., Kurtzberg, D., & Vaughan, H. G. (1979). An electrophysiologic indication of defective information storage in childhood autism. *Psychiatry Research, 1*(1), 101–108.

Nyhan, W. L. (1976). Behavior in the Lesch-Nyhan syndrome. *Journal of Autism and Childhood Schizophrenia, 6,* 235–252.

Olsson, B., & Rett, A. (1985). Behavioral observations concerning differential diagnosis between the Rett syndrome and autism. *Brain Development, 7,* 281–289.

Piggott, L. R., Gdowski, C. L., Villanueva, D., Fischhoff, J., & Frohman, C. F. (1986). Brief communication: Side effects of fenfluramine in autistic children. *Journal of the American Academy of Child Psychiatry, 25*(2), 287–289.

Pranzatellis, M. R., & Snodgrass, S. R. (1985). Fenfluramine therapy for autism. *Journal of Autism and Developmental Disorders, 15,* 439–441.

Prior, M., & Bradshaw, J. L. (1979). Hemisphere functioning in autistic children. *Cortex, 15,* 73–82.

Prior, M. E., Tress, B., Hoffman, W. L., & Boldt, D. (1984). Computed tomographic study of children with classic autism. *Archives of Neurology, 41,* 482–484.

Pueschel, S. M., Herman, R., & Groden, G. (1985). Brief report: Screening children with autism for fragile X syndrome and phenylketonuria. *Journal of Autism and Developmental Disorders, 15,* 335–338.

Richardson, S. A., Koller, H., Katz, M., & McLaren, J. (1980). Seizures and epilepsy in a mentally retarded population over the first 22 years of life. *Applied Research in Mental Retardation,* 123–138.

Riikonen, R., & Amnell, G. (1981). Psychiatric disorders in children with earlier infantile spasms. *Developmental Medicine and Child Neurology, 23,* 747–760.

Rimland, B., Calloway, E., & Dreyfus, P. (1978). The effects of high doses of vitamin B on autistic children: A double blind crossover study. *American Journal of Psychiatry, 135,* 472–475.

Ritvo, E. R., Freeman, B. J., Geller, E., & Yuwiler, A. (1983). Effects of fenfluramine on 14 autistic outpatients. *Journal of the American Academy of Child Psychiatry, 22,* 549–558.

Ritvo, E. R., Freeman, B. J., Mason-Brothers, A., Mo, A., & Ritvo, A. M. (1985). Concordance for the syndrome of autism in 40 pairs of afflicted twins. *American Journal of Psychiatry, 142,* 74–77.

Ritvo, E. R., Freeman, B. J., Yuwiler, A., Geller, E., Schroth, P., Yokota, A.,

Mason-Brothers, A., August, G. J., Klykylo, W., Leventhal, B., Lewis, K., Piggott, L., Realmuto, G., Stubbs, E. G., & Umansky, R. (1986). Fenfluramine therapy for autism: Promise and precaution. *Psychopharmacology Bulletin, 22*, 133–140.

Ritvo, E. R., Rabin, K., Yuwiler, A., Freeman, B. J., & Geller, E. (1978). Biochemical and hematologic studies: A critical review. In M. Rutter & E. Schopler (Eds.), *Autism: A reappraisal of concepts and treatment* (pp. 163–183). New York: Plenum Press.

Ritvo, E. R., Spence, M. A., Freeman, B. J., Mason-Brothers, A., Mo, A. & Marazita, M. L. (1985). Evidence for autosomal recessive inheritance in 46 families with multiple incidence of autism. *American Journal of Psychiatry, 142*, 187–192.

Rosenblatt, D. S., Duschenes, E. A., Hellstrom, F. V., Golick, M. S., Vekemans, M. J. J., Zeesman, S. F., & Andermann, E. (1985). Folic acid blinded trial in identical twins with fragile X syndrome. *American Journal of Human Genetics, 37*, 543–552.

Rosenbloom, S., Campbell, M., George, A. E., Kricheff, I., Taleporos, E., Anderson, L., Reuben, R. N., & Korein, J. (1984). High resolution CT scanning in infantile autism: A quantitative approach. *Journal of the American Academy of Child Psychiatry, 23*, 72–77.

Rumsey, J. M. (1985). Conceptual problem-solving in highly verbal nonretarded autistic men. *Journal of Autism and Developmental Disorders, 15*, 23–36.

Rumsey, J. M., Duara, R., Grady, C., Rapoport, J. L., Margolin, R. A., Rapoport, S. I., & Cutler, N. R. (1985). Brain metabolism in autism: Resting cerebral glucose utilization as measured with positron emission tomography (PET). *Archives of General Psychiatry, 15*, 448–457.

Rumsey, J., Grimes, A. M., Pikus, A. M., Duara, R., & Ismond, D. R. (1984). Auditory brainstem responses in pervasive developmental disorders. *Biological Psychiatry, 19*, 1403–1417.

Rutter, M. (1970). Autistic children: Infancy to adulthood. *Seminars in Psychiatry, 2*, 435–450.

Rutter, M. (1972). Childhood schizophrenia reconsidered. *Journal of Autism and Childhood Schizophrenia, 2*, 315–337.

Rutter, M. (1978). Diagnosis and definition. In M. Rutter & E. Schopler (Eds.), *Autism: A reappraisal of concepts and treatment* (pp. 1–25). New York: Plenum Press.

Rutter, M. (1979). Language, cognition and autism. In R. Katzman (Ed.), *Congenital and acquired cognitive disorders* (pp. 247–264). New York: Raven Press.

Rutter, M. (1983). Cognitive deficits in the pathogenesis of autism. *Journal of Child Psychology and Psychiatry, 24*, 513–531.

Rutter, M. (1984). Infantile autism. In D. Shaffer, A. Erhardt, & L. Greenhill (Eds.), *A clinician's guide to child psychiatry* (pp. 48–78). New York: Free Press.

Rutter, M. (1985a). Infantile autism and other pervasive developmental disorders. In M. Rutter & L. Hersov (Eds.), *Child and adolescent psychiatry: Modern approaches* (2nd ed., pp. 545–566). Oxford: Blackwell Scientific.

Rutter, M. (1985b). The treatment of autistic children. *Journal of Child Psychology and Psychiatry, 26*, 193–214.

Rutter, M., Le Couteur, A., Lord, C., Macdonald, H., Rios, P., & Folstein, S. (in press). Diagnostic and subclassification of autism: Concepts and instrument development. In E. Schopler & G. Mesibov (Eds.), *Diagnosis and assessment of autism*. New York: Plenum Press.

Rutter, M., Graham, P., & Yule, W. (1970). *A neuropsychiatric study of childhood (Clinics in Developmental Medicine, No. 35/36)*. London: Heinemann.

Rutter, M., & Lord, C. (in press). Language disorders associated with psychiatric disturbance. In W. Yule & M. Rutter (Eds.), *Language development and disorders* (*Clinics in Developmental Medicine*, No. 101–102). London: MacKeith/Blackwell Scientific.

Rutter, M., & Schopler, E. (1987). Autism and pervasive developmental disorders: Concepts and diagnostic issues. In M. Rutter, A. H. Tuma, & I. Lann (Eds.), *Assessment, diagnosis and classification in child and adolescent psychopathology.* New York: Guilford Press.

Rutter, M., Tizard, J., & Whitmore, K. (Eds.). (1970). *Education, health and behaviour.* London: Longman.

Shell, J., Campion, J. F., Minton, J., Caplan, R., & Campbell. M. (1984). A study of three brothers with infantile autism: A case report with follow up. *Journal of the American Academy of Child Psychiatry, 23*(4), 498–502.

Sherman, M., Nass, R., & Shapiro, T. (1984). Brief report: Regional cerebral blood flow in autism. *Journal of Autism and Developmental Disorders, 14*(4), 439–446.

Sherman, S. L., Jacobs, P. A., Morton, N. E., Froster-Iskenius, U., Howard-Peebles, P. N., Nielson, K. B., Partington, M. W., Sutherland, G. R., Turner, G., & Watson, M. (1985). Further segregation analysis of the fragile X syndrome with special reference to transmitting males. *Human Genetics, 69,* 289–299.

Sherman, S. L., Morton, N. E., Jacobs, P. A., & Turner, G. (1984). The marker (X) syndrome: A cytogenetic and genetic analysis. *Annals of Human Genetics, 48,* 21–37.

Sigman, M., & Ungerer, J. A. (1984). Attachment behaviors in autistic children. *Journal of Autism and Developmental Disorders, 14,* 31–244.

Silva, P. A. (in press). Epidemiology, longitudinal course, and some associated factors: An update. In W. Yule & M. Rutter, (Eds.), *Language development and disorders* (*Clinics in Developmental Medicine*, No. 101–102). London: MacKeith/Blackwell Scientific.

Skoff, B. J., Mirsky, A. F., & Turner, D. (1980). Prolonged brain-stem transmission time in autism. *Psychiatric Research, 2,* 157–166.

Small, J. G. (1975). EEG and neurophysiological studies of early infantile autism. *Biological Psychiatry, 10,* 385–397.

Spence, M. A., Ritvo, E. R., Marazita, M. L., Funderburk, S. J., Sparkes, R. S., & Freeman, B. J. (1985). Gene mapping studies with the syndrome of autism. *Behavior Genetics, 15,* 1–13.

Spiker, D., & Ricks, M. (1984). Developmental relationships in self-recognition: A study of 52 autistic children. *Child Development, 55,* 214–225.

Taft, L. T., & Cohen, H. J. (1971). Hypsarrhythmia and infantile autism: A clinical report. *Journal of Autism and Childhood Schizophrenia, 1,* 327–336.

Tager-Flusberg, H. (1981a). On the nature of linguistic functioning in early infantile autism. *Journal of Autism and Developmental Disorders, 11,* 45–56.

Tager-Flusberg, H. (1981b). Sentence comprehension in autistic children. *Applied Psycholinguistics, 2,* 2–24.

Tanguay, P. E., Edwards, R., Buchwald, J., Schwafel, J., & Allen, W. (1982). Auditory brainstem evoked responses in autistic children. *Archives of General Psychiatry, 39,* 174–180.

Thake, A., Todd, J., Bundey, S., & Webb, T. (1985). Is it possible to make a clinical diagnosis of the fragile X syndrome in a boy? *Archives of Disease in Childhood, 60,* 1001–1007.

Todd, R. D. (1986). Pervasive development disorders and immunological tolerance. *Psychiatric Developments, 2,* 147–165.

Todd, R. D., & Ciaranello, R. D. (1985). Demonstration of inter- and intraspecies differences in serotonin binding sites by antibodies from an autistic child. *Proceedings of the National Academy of Sciences, 82*, 612–616.

Torrey, E. F., Hersh, S. P., & McCabe, K. D. (1975). Early childhood psychosis and bleeding during pregnancy. *Journal of Autism and Childhood Schizophrenia, 5*, 287–297.

Tucker, D. M., Watson, R. T., & Heilman, K. M. (1977). Discrimination and evocation of affectively intoned speech in parents with right parietal disease. *Neurology, 27*, 947–950.

van Engeland, H., Bodnar, F. A., & Bolhuis, G. (1985). Some qualitative aspects of the social behaviour of autistic children: An ethological approach. *Journal of Child Psychology and Psychiatry, 26*(6), 879–893.

Venter, P. A., Hof, J. O., Coetzee, D. J., Van der Walt, C., and Retief, A. E. (1984). No marker (X) syndrome in autistic children. *Human Genetics, 67*(1), 107.

Volkmar, F. R., & Cohen, D. J. (1982). A hierarchical analysis of patterns of noncompliance in autistic and behavior-disturbed children. *Journal of Autism and Developmental Disorders, 12*, 35–42.

Watson, M. S., Leckman, J. F., Annex, B., Breg, W. R., Boles, D., Volkmar, F. R., Cohen, D. J., & Carter, C. (1984). Fragile X in a survey of 75 autistic males. *New England Journal of Medicine, 310*, 1462.

Williams, R. S., Hauser, S. L., Purpura, D., Delong, R., & Swisher, C. N. (1980). Autism and mental retardation: Neuropathological studies performed in four retarded persons with autistic behaviour. *Archives of Neurology, 37*, 749–753.

Wing, L. (1981). Language, social, and cognitive impairments in autism and severe mental retardation. *Journal of Autism and Developmental Disorders, 11*, 31–44.

Wing, L., & Gould, J. (1979). Severe impairments of social interaction and associated abnormalities in children: Epidemiology and classification. *Journal of Autism and Developmental Disorders, 9*, 11–30.

Wing, L., Gould, J., Yeates, S. R., & Brierley, L. M. (1977). Symbolic play in severely mentally retarded and autistic children. *Journal of Child Psychology and Psychiatry, 18*, 167–178.

Winsberg, B. G., & Yepes, L. E. (1978). Antipsychotics (major tranquilizers, neuroleptics). In J. S. Werry (Ed.), *Pediatric psychopharmacology* (pp. 234–273). New York: Brunner/Mazel.

Wright, H. H., Young, S. R., Edwards, J. G., Abramson, R. K., & Duncan, J. (1986). Fragile X syndrome in a population of autistic children. *Journal of the American Academy of Child Psychiatry, 25*, 641–644.

Yule, W., & Rutter, M. (1985). Reading and other learning difficulties. In M. Rutter & L. Hersov (Eds.), *Child and adolescent psychiatry: Modern approaches* (2nd ed., pp. 444–464). Oxford: Blackwell Scientific.

Chapter 11

Cognition and Mental Retardation

Penelope H. Brooks, Charley M. McCauley, and Edward M. Merrill

The purpose of this chapter is to provide an overview of some of the recent behavioral research in mental retardation that concerns cognition and its facilitation. The discussion necessarily must be limited to only a subgroup of research domains. The ones that have been selected are among those that have been most heavily researched (therefore allowing some rather firm conclusions to be drawn), and/or they are areas of research that offer particular promise for the future.

The group of cognitive psychologists studying mental retardation have a challenging task. While they join other more ''college-sophomore''-oriented researchers in trying to understand cognition in general, their task takes them further into the complicated world of trying to uncover, understand, and explain individual differences in cognitive functioning. The ultimate goal is theory construction that facilitates the understanding and remediation of deficiencies in cognitive performance. Determining which mental processes can be modified and how that can best be accomplished is a central issue that crosscuts the entire field.

It should be noted that cognitive researchers as a rule do not usually recognize etiology as a variable in their research. (Down syndrome is one notable exception.) There seem to be several reasons for this, with the principle one being that many people with mental retardation who function at the relatively higher levels intellectually are unclassifiable with respect to the origins of their mental handicap. Given the penchant of cognitive psychologists for group research designs that include only mildly retarded subjects, and the generally similar performance of so-called cultural-familial retarded persons equated for age and IQ, etiology does not seem to be a relevant variable in most cognitive studies.

The research that is reviewed in this chapter includes studies on the representation of knowledge. language, perception, memory, attention, and problem solving. While there are no major breakthroughs to report, it can be said with certainty that progress is clearly being made in laying the groundwork for an empirically based theory of mental retardation.

REPRESENTATION AND LANGUAGE

Representation refers to the stored knowledge that we have about the world. This knowledge concerns objects, events/actions, and causal, spatial, and temporal relationships. As scientists, we infer the existence of representation from the way an individual uses certain symbol systems, particularly language—either spoken, written, signed, or otherwise coded—as in pictures, models, photos, cartoons, and stick figures. Thus, if children speak about giraffes, we assume that they have some concept of giraffes. Similarly, if a giraffe is drawn, recognized, or used in a sentence that is comprehended by children, we infer that they have some conceptual representation of the object giraffe. The manner in which individuals access these representations and how representations are organized in memory has been the subject of considerable research. The specific questions most pertinent to mental retardation are:

1. Does representation differ with intellectual level?
2. If so, can representation be influenced by modification techniques?

While representation is best reflected in an individual's linguistic output, the semantic content of that output is seen as the purest display of cognitive representation. Semantic knowledge refers to the meaning associated with words, phrases, sentences, and other units of language. This meaning is involved not only in the comprehension and expression of language, but also in the process of thinking. Because of the important role of semantics in intellectual ability, the relationship of semantic knowledge to mental retardation is a critical theoretical and practical link.

Research on Semantic Knowledge

If we assume that what children can say and comprehend is a reflection of what they know and how their knowledge is organized, then descriptions of children's spontaneous speech acts can contribute significantly to our understanding of the development of semantic knowledge. This approach was taken by Coggins (1979). He has collected two-word utterances from 3- to 6-year-old children with Down syndrome and classified these utterances on the basis of their relational meanings (e.g., agent-action, agent-object, action-object, possessor-possession, etc.). He found that the spontaneous speech of Down syndrome children did indeed contain the same categories of relational meanings as did the speech of nonretarded children matched on developmental level. He concluded that children with Down syndrome are able to "identify underlying regularities in experience; discriminate and identify attributes of objects and people; distinguish action from the recipient of that action; discriminate self from persons and objects; and, recognize and identify change in spatial position orientation. The findings also suggest the possibility that processes and structures by which meaning is known, represented, and created in the sensorimotor period may be quite similar to that of normal children" (p. 178).

An alternative approach for studying semantic knowledge focuses on the way in which people use meaning to identify objects and events. One way to conceptualize the meaning of a linguistic event is to think of it as a node in a giant network that has a node for each word, concept, or idea that a person knows. The links in the network between the particular linguistic unit and other units specify the "meaning" of the given unit. For example, if there are links established in the network between "giraffe" and "animal" and "zoo," then, the two latter terms likely are part of the meaning of "giraffe." The organizational networks that comprise a word's meaning are not easy to study, yet such research is necessary in order to identify differences between the semantic knowledge of mentally retarded and nonretarded individuals. McCauley and Sperber and their students (McCauley, Sperber, & Roaden, 1978; Sperber, Ragain, & McCauley, 1976) have conducted a series of studies on the ability of retarded and nonretarded children and adults to categorize objects into their superordinate categories (giraffe-animal) and to identify characteristics of objects (airplane—wings, fly). The major dependent variable in many of their studies was speed (reaction time). The tasks were varied and included picture naming and sentence verification as well as other tasks prominent in the information processing literature. Their findings support the general conclusions drawn from Coggins's study. Individuals with retardation appear to form categories (e.g., dogs, cats) and to establish hierarchical relationships among categories (e.g., the categories of "dog" and "cat" are both viewed as instances of the "animal" category) in a manner similar to that of nonretarded individuals. Retarded adults are, however, consistently slower in making a superordinate judgment (i.e., that a cat is an animal) than nonretarded adults (Davies, Sperber, & McCauley, 1981). Thus, while both groups apparently have the requisite knowledge and have it stored in the same way qualitatively, persons with retardation appear to have a relatively greater difficulty in retrieving the knowledge as indexed by retrieval speed.

If asked to judge whether a particular property is associated with an object (e.g., whether a carrot is orange, whether birds can fly, whether money can be spent), retarded adults are faster at recognizing statements about what can be done to an object (e.g., "an airplane can be flown") than statements about the physical characteristics (e.g., "an airplane has wings"). This latter finding, the authors conclude, is consistent with the view that action properties are central in early concept formation. Children are known to form concepts in terms of their own action on them; retarded adults apparently organize information according to the same rules. The investigators found no evidence for qualitative differences in semantic organization between retarded and nonretarded children, other than the finding that retarded adolescents and adults appear to be more like mental age-matched nonretarded children than chronological age-matched adolescents (see Sperber & McCauley, 1984, for a comprehensive review of this work).

Modifiability

Since issues of semantic development significantly overlap with those of language development in general, the facilitation of semantic development in individuals with mental retardation is often synonymous with the more general issue of facilitating language acquisition. Actually, the question of whether language can be modified is a complex one with two answers. If the question is paraphrased as a query about whether children can be influenced to output more, or to use more and different words or small syntactic units, the answer is "yes." Behavioral techniques have repeatedly demonstrated that babies (including babies with Down syndrome) can be conditioned to make more sounds (Poulson, 1983) and children and adults can be conditioned to talk more. Furthermore, new words and constructions can be taught in a manner that enables their generalization to new contexts (Baer & Guess, 1971; Stephens, Pear, Wray, & Jackson, 1975; Welch & Pear, 1980; Wheeler & Sulzer, 1970—to name only a few). This type of facilitation certainly has an important role. Many theorists believe that increasing the single-word vocabulary is essentially teaching children to say the names of categories that they already have. Thus, increasing vocabulary at least increases communication. If, as it has been persuasively argued by Vygotsky (1978), Feuerstein, Rand, Hoffman, and Miller (1980), and their followers, much of cognition is socially mediated, a great deal of information is transmitted via parents, siblings, and other significant people in children's lives. The greater the children's understanding of the topics and relationships (vocabulary) conveyed by these educators, the more comprehensive will be their cognition.

A second interpretation of the question could be, "Can training increase the rate of language development in retarded children?" To date, there have been no successful demonstrations of enhanced progression through the stages of development. However, differences in maternal interaction style do appear to be reliably associated with differences in children's linguistic ability (Hamilton & Sherrod, in preparation; Peterson & Sherrod, 1982; Sherrod, Siewert, & Cavallaro, 1984) and differences in scores obtained on the Bayley Scales of Infant Development (Mahoney, Finger, & Powell, 1985). According to Sherrod and colleagues, mothers whose conversational style includes a high incidence of descriptions of their child's ongoing activities (activity-relevant language) provide a richer linguistic environment than do mothers whose conversational style is not relevant to their child's activities. Similarly, Mahoney et al. have reported a positive relationship between maternal responsiveness (relative to a controlling or directive style) and scores obtained on the Bayley. These results suggest that it may be possible to teach parents to interact with their infants in such a way as to facilitate language development.

We have mentioned two lines of research that suggest that the language difficulties of individuals with mental retardation are at least partially remediable: (1) behavioral techniques that seek to teach or increase the output of specific linguistic constructions, and (2) observational techniques that seek to identify aspects of the linguistic environment that facilitate language acquisition. S. Warren and A. Kaiser (personal communication, September 1986) are currently examining the efficacy of a language training technique that draws upon the general results of both areas of research. In this new approach, they make use of well-established behavior techniques for teaching linguistic skills while providing an enriched linguistic environment in which retarded children may learn. This approach is designed to take advantage of children's propensity to acquire language in a natural meaningful context. While it is still too early to draw firm conclusions about the effectiveness of this approach, we believe that it is an effort in the right direction.

PERCEPTION

Perception can be functionally defined as the process of extracting information emanating from the objects, places, and events encountered in the world around us (Gibson & Levin, 1975). Clearly, perceptual processing involves all of the senses, taken both individually and in combination. However, since the visual system has been the subject of the greatest number of experiments, the discussion here is limited to the processing of visual information. Only a selected set of experiments are reviewed that are relevant to two aspects of perceptual processing that make an important contribution to the understanding of retarded-nonretarded differences in cognitive performance: perceptual learning and perceptual processing speed.

Perceptual Learning

Higher order cognitive processing is not conducted on all information that impinges on the senses. In the early stages of perceptual processing, there is a considerable filtering of stimulus information, with some aspects of the information being selected for additional processing and other aspects of the information being ignored. The selected features are then transformed using processes that combine and organize information contained in individual features into a smaller number of larger perceptual units. A straightforward example of perceptual processing can be found in the way people distinguish constellations in the night sky. From a random collection of stars, stars irrelevant to the constellation of interest are ignored, while relevant stars are given continued processing and are organized into a single higher order precept—for example, the "Big Dipper." The organization of features at this perceptual stage of processing serves to reduce the number of units that receive continued processing, and hence, allows the processing of the meaning of a pattern to occur more readily. It is generally believed that the efficient filtering of relevant features and the appropriate organization of features into larger units are strongly dependent upon learning experiences. The learning that takes place in establishing these aspects of perceptual processing is considered to be unlike other forms of learning (Gibson, 1969) and is thus afforded special status by researchers concerned with the cognitive development of the human organism.

One research program that addresses differences in perceptual learning between mentally retarded and nonretarded individuals is the one being conducted by Joseph Fagan at Case Western Reserve University. In his research, Fagan uses an infant visual recognition memory paradigm. The general procedure is quite straightforward and is based on the observation that an infant prefers to look at a novel visual stimulus rather than one that was previously seen. A visual stimulus is presented and after the infant has viewed the stimulus for a specified period of time it is removed and two more are presented, one that is new and one that is identical to the stimulus previously shown. To the extent that the infant looks at the new stimulus more than the previously viewed stimulus, it is inferred that the infant has abstracted and retained some information about the original stimulus. Fagan's own interest in this procedure is in the development of tests of infant recognition memory as valid predictors of later intelligence (see Fagan & Singer, 1983). However, it is also clear that the recognition memory paradigm requires the infant to use processes that are very similar to those involved in perceptual learning. That is, the infant must be able to discriminate relevant from irrelevant features of stimuli, filter out the irrelevant information, retain the newly acquired information, and identify the similarities across the stimuli. Hence, studies of infant visual recognition memory contribute to an understanding of many of the processes involved in perceptual learning.

In a series of studies, Fagan and his colleagues (Fagan, 1981; Fagan & McGrath, 1981) have assessed the relationship between infant visual recognition memory, or as we have suggested, perceptual learning and intelligence. For example, Fagan and McGrath (1981) examined the relationship between preference for novel stimuli at 4–7 months and performance on vocabulary tests at 4–7 years. The participants in the Fagan and McGrath study had previously participated in experiments on infant recognition memory conducted by Fagan (1971, 1973, 1976, 1977). The predictive validity coefficients between the infant's performance on the vocabulary tests at 4–7 years of age ranged from 0.37 to 0.57, and were statistically significant. The strength of these correlations provides some support for the contention that early differences in perceptual learning capabilities may contribute to later differences between mentally retarded and nonretarded individuals in the performance of more molar cognitive tasks. An important goal of future research will be to delineate the particular aspects of the perceptual learning process that are deficient in individuals with mental retardation and to determine the manner and extent to which perceptual learning can be enhanced.

Perceptual Processing Speed

A second avenue of research that we believe has been and will continue to be fruitful examines differences between mentally retarded and nonretarded individuals in perceptual processing speed. While cognitive theory has not progressed to the point where it is possible to establish a direct relationship between perceptual processing speed and performance on more complex cognitive tasks, it seems logical that such a link exists. To the extent that many complex cognitive activities involve the parallel, or overlapping, operation of component processes (McClelland, 1979), then differences in processing speed at the perceptual level may result in subsequent processing that is based on incomplete or inaccurate data, resulting in a failure to complete the sequence of processing, or possibly qualitative differences in the final behavior (Sperber & McCauley, 1984).

McCauley and Merrill have completed a series of studies that investigate retarded-nonretarded differences in perceptual processing speed (Merrill et al., 1985; Sperber, Merrill, McCauley, & Shapiro, 1983). Their data indicate that mentally retarded individuals are significantly slower than nonretarded individuals at perceptually encoding picture stimuli for the purpose of making either a physical identity match (e.g., determining that two identical pictures of a dog match) or making a name identity match (e.g., determining that pictures of different dogs are the same because they have identical labels). The encoding process that precedes determining whether two stimuli physically match takes about 400 msec for mentally retarded and 300 msec for nonretarded adults. A same name identity match involves encoding times of 500 msec for retarded individuals and 400 msec for nonretarded individuals. Of major importance, the speed of perceptual processing exhibited by mentally retarded individuals is slower than that exhibited by both their equal chronological age (CA) and equal mental age (MA) counterparts. This latter finding suggests that perceptual processing speed may be related in some fundamental way to differences in IQ independent of differences in MA. This conclusion is supported by the results of other investigators (Lally & Nettlebeck, 1977; Nettlebeck & Lally, 1979) who have obtained similar results using visual masking procedures. The research currently being conducted by Merrill and McCauley is designed to determine what factors may account for retarded-nonretarded differences in perceptual processing speed and how differences in perceptual processing speed impact upon the performance of more molar cognitive tasks.

MEMORY

In the last 15 years, probably more research has been reported in the general experimental psychology literature on memory and memory-related processes than on any other topic. To a somewhat lesser degree, that has also been the case in mental retardation research. Memory research more than any area of cognitive psychology has made use of the computer metaphor. The metaphor includes such concepts as the storage and retrieval of information, and it specifies the structures (e.g., memory stores) and processes (e.g., memory search processes) that form the bases of thought. The next sections briefly discuss what this line of research has revealed in regards to mental retardation.

Sensory Memory

Each sensory system seems to have a holding mechanism associated with it, the properties of which are dictated primarily by the physiology of the system. Sensory memory is generally thought to be a relatively brief holding station where incoming information is registered, sorted out, and, via pattern recognition and attention processes, some information is sent to short-term memory for further processing. While some have questioned the centrality of the sensory memory's role in everyday cognition (e.g., Haber, 1983), it still seems important to determine the extent to which those structures are intact in persons with mental retardation. The data on that question are mixed, probably as the result of some methodological anomalies in some of the early studies. Recent work (e.g., Hornstein & Mosley, 1979) suggests that the sensory stores for vision and audition are structurally sound in retarded persons with respect to the amount of information that can be stored and how long that information can be retained (Stanovich, 1978). The mental retardation-related difficulties noted in earlier experiments (e.g., Spitz & Thor, 1968; Welsandt & Meyer, 1974) are probably the result of more general deficiencies in attentional processing skill, such as those involved in selecting and extracting information from a stimulus (Nettlebeck & Brewer, 1981).

Short-Term Memory

Much more is known about short-term memory (STM) in individuals with retardation than is known about sensory memory. Early theoretical formulations (e.g., Ellis, 1963) suggested that STM was an important locus of severe mental retardation-related deficiencies. While Ellis subsequently modified his theory (Ellis, 1970), his original formulation generated a great deal of research.

Because there has been so much research, the discussion of STM can be divided into issues about potential structural differences and issues about process differences. On the structure side, there is at this time only limited research suggesting a mental retardation-related deficiency. Clark and Detterman (1981) reported differences between retarded and nonretarded persons on memory for lifted weight, a task that minimizes the use of strategies. Laine and Baumeister (1985), however, found no evidence for structural deficiencies in STM in a task possibly even more nonstrategic than that used by Clark and Detterman. Laine and Baumeister asked retarded and nonretarded persons to discriminate intensity differences between pure tones. The critical interaction of delay interval between tones by subject group was not significant. In general, the ability of determined experimenters to eliminate the possibility of strategy use by intelligent subjects can have only limited success, and the question of structural defects in STM remains viable. Several important characteristics of STM that may be of the structural variety do seem to be IQ-related and thus relevant to the discussion of mental retardation. One is memory span (the number of digits, letters, etc. that can be repeated back to the experimenter verbatim) as has been thoroughly documented (e.g., Bachelder & Denny, 1977a, 1977b). The second is memory retrieval speed or search rate. Numerous studies indicate that information is retrieved from STM more slowly in lower than in higher IQ persons (e.g., Maisto & Baumeister, 1984). This difference may possibly be remediable or due to characteristics of the research paradigm, but that has yet to be demonstrated. Thus, the finding of retarded-nonretarded differences in STM search rate must be added to the growing data suggesting differences in the efficiency or speed with which basic mental processes can be executed by retarded and nonretarded persons (see Jensen, 1982; Sperber & McCauley, 1984, for reviews of this literature).

Rehearsal/organizational/attentional strategies are important to the discussion here given their central role in facilitating information storage in a relatively permanent form. Ellis concluded by 1970 that the failure of retarded persons to spontaneously rehearse information in STM was a major factor in their memory difficulties. Recent experiments have indeed shown this to be the case. The situation appears to be analogous to the situation with young nonretarded children that Flavell (1970) termed a "production deficiency." A production deficiency simply means that under appropriate circumstances retarded persons and young children fail to initiate and execute a strategy that would facilitate their information processing. What followed from the initial experiments were a series of training studies aimed at encouraging developmentally immature and retarded subjects in strategy use and then evaluating their performance relative to subjects who used the strategies spontaneously. Results were encouraging. For example, Belmont and Butterfield (1969, 1971) conducted an extensive series of training studies using a subject-paced free recall task (i.e., subjects could study materials as long as they wanted). They developed a training procedure that impacted both on rehearsal activities during learning and on retrieval activities during recall. Their training procedure proved to be quite successful. Other investigators have been successful in inducing the use of other types of rehearsal strategies, like grouping items by category before rehearsing them.

In summarizing the recent literature on rehearsal processes in persons with mental retardation, Borkowski, Peck, and Damberg (1983) have reached conclusions similar to those of these authors:

> Mentally retarded individuals typically exhibit a deficit in rehearsal and in STM. However, the growing number of successful training studies in which attention is paid to both rehearsal (or acquisition) strategies and retrieval techniques, and, more importantly, to explicit methods for generalizing these strategies to transfer tasks suggest that deficits in STM may be reduced by providing the mentally retarded with adequate cognitive instructions. The extent of improvement, however, seems limited. (p. 490)

One of the most frustrating and long-standing problems in mental retardation research is that even when mentally retarded persons can be shown to have retained a strategy for some time, they still are often unable to transfer and/or generalize the strategy to novel situations. Quoting Blackman and Lin (1984):

> There is firm and ample evidence that people classified as EMR can demonstrate the acquisition and maintenance of task-specific cognitive strategies. The generalizability of these strategies, however, is largely restricted to other laboratory tasks that differ minimally from the original training context in both stimuli and task demands. The generalization of these strategies to more meaningful academic or social problem solving has not been demonstrated. (p. 257)

It should be noted here that there are projects currently underway that may allow us to better understand the strategy transfer and generalization problems of persons with mental retardation. Those projects are based on sound theoretical models of the learning process and they extend far beyond the simple laboratory context. We refer to the work of Campione and Brown (1977, 1978, 1984) and Feuerstein, Haywood, and others on instrumental enrichment (Arbitman-Smith, Haywood, & Bransford, 1984; Feuerstein et al., 1980). This work shows promise but is still in its infancy.

Long-Term Memory

The first question that comes to many people's minds when long-term memory (LTM) and mental retardation are discussed is "Are there anatomically based structural deficits in the LTM of retarded individuals that cause them to forget information more rapidly than do nonretarded individuals?" This seemingly complex question can be answered quite simply—at the present time, the analysis of forgetting done in 1969 by Belmont and Butterfield still seems adequate: *if* the degree of initial learning is equal for retarded and nonretarded persons, then the forgetting rate is also equal. The problem is in getting retarded and nonretarded individuals to exhibit equivalent degrees of initial acquisition, and that is why the focus on strategies, subroutines, and even more molar information acquisition processes is so prominent in behavioral research on mental retardation.

The discussion of LTM can profitably be divided into two sections (cf. Tulving, 1972). Most research on LTM has to do with the retention of autobiographical, temporarily based information of the sort encountered in list-learning experiments. This kind of episodic information is eventually forgotten, at least in part, and is usually recalled by trying to reconstruct the original acquisition situation. Common examples of reconstruction from long-term (episodic) memory are trying to remember the name of your fourth-grade teacher or what your parents gave you for high school graduation. Reconstruction in this case usually involves a search of LTM followed by an attempt to reconstruct or "put yourself back in" the context of the fourth-grade classroom or high school graduation party. It is research on this episodic type of LTM that has dominated mental retardation research. Unfortunately, much of this research is of questionable ecological validity. Of what importance is it in one's life to retain for long periods of time, lists of words, pictures, or anything else encountered in a laboratory experiment? What is needed to complete the picture of long-term episodic memory is experiments on the ability of retarded individuals to retain events, episodes, and so forth that happen in and are significant to their daily lives. We should note, however, that this problem is not unique to mental retardation research, as Neisser (1976), among others, have made this plea in the general experimental psychology literature.

The other, less researched, type of LTM involves the learning, retention, and organization of semantic/conceptual knowledge. This type of knowledge is extracted from our experience. It includes such things as word meanings, concepts, and rules relating them. From a series of studies that began in the mid 1970s and that is continuing, McCauley and Sperber and now McCauley and Merrill have reported data that suggest some rather clear conclusions about LTM for semantic knowledge in persons with mental retardation (see Sperber & McCauley, 1984). First, as noted above, there is reason to believe that once knowledge is acquired, it is stored in memory in a manner qualitatively the same for retarded and nonretarded persons. Second, and again as previously noted, there are clear quantitative differences in the rate with which semantic knowledge can be retrieved; that is, there are clear efficiency differences between retarded and nonretarded persons when retrieval speed is the dependent measure and both groups of subjects are highly familiar with the to-be-retrieved information. Third, under conditions in which semantic knowledge could be useful, mentally retarded persons often don't spontaneously retrieve it. This is a production deficiency of sorts just as was discussed for the spontaneous use of strategies. The failure of retarded persons to use the semantic knowledge that they have often results in their scoring poorly on certain sections of achievement and IQ tests, like the similarities subtest of the Wechsler Intelligence Scale for Children (WISC) (e.g., how are a plum, banana, orange, and apple alike?).

ATTENTION

Attentional capabilities have long been assumed to play a potentially significant role in determining overall intellectual ability, and current empirical and theoretical approaches to understanding the cognitive aspects of mental retardation suggest that this belief is still widely held. The rationale underlying this conviction is quite straightforward. Because mentally retarded individuals exhibit performance deficits relative to nonretarded individuals across a wide range of cognitive tasks, it seems reasonable to consider the possibility that the performance deficits result, at least in part, from differences in the execution of fundamental cognitive abilities that are common to many of these tasks. Attentional processes are assumed to mediate virtually all cognitive activities, and thus are candidates for strong consideration.

It is important to recognize that "attention is not a single concept, but the name given to a complex field of study" (Posner, 1975, p. 441). It encompasses a variety of processes. We have divided these processes into two major categories. First, attention can be a selective process, whereby some information from external or internal stimulation is perceived and subsequently analyzed and other information is ignored (Pick, Frankel, & Hess, 1975). Second, attention can be viewed as a limited supply of central processing resources (Kahneman, 1973; Norman & Bobrow, 1975). This supply can be flexibly allocated to different cognitive activities or components of a single activity. Cognitive processes that are activated concurrently are assumed to compete for the available resources. Deficits in cognitive performance result when the resource demands of particular processes leave little capacity for other activities.

Selective Attending

The majority of theoretical and empirical work on attentional capabilities of persons with mental retardation has contrasted the performance of retarded and nonretarded individuals on discrimination learning tasks (Fisher & Zeaman, 1973; Zeaman & House, 1963). Since this literature and the resulting theory have been reviewed and evaluated elsewhere (Borkowski et al., 1983; Zeaman & House, 1979), we will not do so here. The fundamental results of this research suggest that mentally retarded individuals are deficient, relative to nonretarded individuals, at selecting the targeted dimension—color, shape, size necessary to discover the correct stimulus. Still in question, however, is the extent to which these differences represent, as

Zeaman and House (1979) contend, unmodifiable structural characteristics of the human processing system.

Attention as Processing Capacity

When attention is viewed as a limited amount of processing resources that can be allocated to cognitive processing in a flexible manner, two critical determinants of task performance emerge. First, individuals may differ in the efficiency with which they flexibly allocate capacity across component processes involved in complex cognitive tasks. Second, the amount of capacity required by each component process may differ for different individuals. It is generally regarded that with practice and experience, certain basic processes that initially require a considerable portion of an individual's supply of processing capacity become increasingly automated until they require minimal resources to be executed (Posner, 1978). The notion here is that as the basic processes of cognitive activities, for example perceptual encoding, come to require less of an individual's available resources, more is left over for the execution of more complex and higher order activities such as problem solving and inference making.

To the extent that mentally retarded individuals, relative to nonretarded individuals, inefficiently allocate their available processing resources or the basic processes of cognitive activities require more of the available resources of retarded relative to nonretarded individuals, then one would expect to find the performance deficiencies in persons with mental retardation across a wide range of cognitive tasks (Carr, 1984; Sperber & McCauley, 1984). The available literature, however, has not involved a comparison of mentally retarded and nonretarded individuals in these domains. Nonetheless, it has been reported that the ability to allocate efficiently processing capacity in accordance with task demands varies with developmental level (Lane, 1979) as does the attention requirements of basic component processes (Manis, Keating, & Morrison, 1980). These results are at least suggestive that this domain of research has the potential to be extremely illuminating.

PROBLEM SOLVING

The area of cognitive research in mental retardation in which the need for more research is self-evident is certainly that of problem solving. Virtually every activity in life involves, or at one time involved, a problem to be solved—how to get dressed in the morning, how to get to the dentist, how to get to work, how to do laundry. Even being a subject in a research study presents a problem to be solved; for example, a subject often asks, "What am I supposed to do here?" The quantity of theory and research conducted on problem solving, however, does not reflect the importance of understanding problem-solving difficulties, particularly when retarded people are involved.

Almost all of the theory and much of the research has been conducted with nonretarded people.

A ''problem'' is informally defined as the state of wanting something but not being able to obtain it directly. That is, a gap separates problem solvers from where they want to be. To solve the problem, the individual must: 1) understand the nature of the gap, and 2) find and employ procedures (operators, moves) to bridge the gap (Hayes, 1978).

Many theorists think of the second stage—finding and employing procedures to bridge the gap—as a search through alternative paths to find the correct (or an appropriate) path. Hayes (1978) distinguishes two basic search procedures: the random search and the heuristic search. Random search is essentially guessing and is a developmentally primitive strategy (i.e., an extremely inefficient study used by younger children). Heuristic searches, however, are much more efficient and consist of three major methods: proximity methods; pattern matching; and planning by modeling, analogy, and abstraction. The proximity method consists of getting closer and closer to the goal—frequently comparing where one is with where the goal is. Pattern matching consists of recognizing good moves or operations or situations because one has prototypes stored in memory. Thus recognizing a puzzle piece, a chess layout, or a familiar street corner can give one information about progress and directions toward the goal. Abstraction consists of finding a similar but simpler problem, solving it, and trying the solution strategies on the more complex problem.

The task of assessing intelligence-related differences in the various processes involved in problem solving has been undertaken by Herman Spitz and his colleagues. Spitz and Borys (1984) recognized that the first stage of problem solving is representing (understanding) the problem correctly. They subdivided the second stage of problem solving—that of finding and employing procedures for solving a problem—into three separate components: devising a solution plan, executing the solution plan, and deriving a general principle. In their research they have assessed the problem-solving abilities of mentally retarded individuals of differing levels of intellectual functioning. Their data indicated that the lower IQ subjects exhibited a tendency to guess at the solution (i.e., used a random search strategy), suggesting deficiency in the ability to understand the problem situation. The higher IQ subjects were able to understand the problems and devise solutions but could not execute these solutions when confronted with complex problems. Spitz and Borys suggest that this difficulty results from insufficient capacity available in working memory. More complex problems require more memory for past moves and actions than do less complex problems.

Based on his work with nonretarded children, Siegler (1981) has argued persuasively that age-related changes in problem-solving ability follow a consistent developmental or stage-like sequence. Mastery of the problem reflects only the final stage. Premastery level cognitive behavior reveals several discrete stages in which incomplete solution strategies are consistently applied. For example, on problems that involve the consideration of two or more dimensions in order to be solved (e.g., conservation [height, width of container], balance beam [weight and distance from fulcrum]), very young children tend to reason by focusing on only the most salient dimension. In the next stage, subordinate dimensions come to be used, but only when the dominant ones are the same (e.g., if liquid in two glasses is the same height, then the width of the glass must be considered). In the third stage, both dimensions are considered but children exhibit an inability to resolve conflicts between the dimensions; that is, they cannot solve the problem if the two dimensions suggest opposite solutions. Finally, the fourth stage involves considering and appropriately weighing the contribution of all dimensions, thus resulting in the accurate resolution of the problem.

Butterfield and Ferretti (1985; Ferretti & Butterfield, 1983, 1985) have applied this rule-assessment approach to the study of retarded children. They reasoned that training problem-solving strategies to children should be most effective when one attempts to train only one rule level above the child's current cognitive status. In other words, children following Level I rules can be trained to solve a problem using Level II rules but not Level III rules, and so forth. Their results confirmed this hypothesis. However, compared to nonretarded children, the mentally retarded children needed a great deal of extra training and prompting to transfer the strategy to other structurally similar problems (1983). In a subsequent report (1985) these investigators proposed that a more effective approach would be to teach retarded individuals self-management procedures (e.g., selection, revision, and monitoring their strategies in addition to training them to solve specific problems). In an experiment to assess the efficacy of such an approach, three groups of gifted and three groups of retarded children were compared: those who were not instructed, those who were taught specific task strategies only, and those who were taught specific strategies *and* self-management procedures. The investigators found *no* evidence that teaching self-management procedures helped retarded children perform better on related transfer problems. They tentatively concluded that it may *not* be possible to minimize individual differences in problem solving by teaching these more general problem-solving strategies. Such strategies evolve or emerge in intellectually gifted people as a by-product of hundreds of encounters with environmental challenges. Ferretti and Butterfield suggest that a better understanding of the conditions of the emergence of strategies in nonretarded children may be a prerequisite to arranging for their appearance in retarded people.

METACOGNITION

Some people are efficient at solving problems and remembering names, lists, addresses, and so forth. In part, this efficiency is attributable to their knowledge about their own cognitive states and processes (e.g., they know about their memory and their own strengths and weaknesses in remembering). They can thus plan and apply appropriate strategies to facilitate their learning and remembering. This kind of introspective knowledge about one's cognitive states and processes is called "metacognition" or "cognition about cognition" (Borkowski, Reid, & Kurtz, 1984; Flavell, 1976, 1978). Metacognition consists of both knowing *about* thought processes (academic knowledge) and knowing *how to carry them out* (practical knowledge). The two forms of knowledge do not necessarily coexist. The academic knowledge of cognitive processes is relatively easy to measure once the concepts are theoretically delineated; practical knowledge must be inferred from performance.

Metacognition in Act of Remembering

Most of the research on metacognitive processing has focused on memory processes and metamemorial knowledge. Remembering requires the organization of several metamemorial skills: One must be able to ask and answer the question, "Am I going to remember some particular material?" The answer depends on two aspects of knowledge: 1) knowledge about memory processes and 2) awareness of memory states.

Knowledge about Memory Processes   Most of what we know about retarded people's knowledge of memory processes has come from interviews with them. These interviews generally consist of describing different memory contexts and either asking which context would make remembering the material easier or asking how they would make sure they remembered the information. Justice (1985) summarizes this work and lists five skills that appear to be MA related:

1. Understanding that memory is fallible (Brown, 1978; Eyde & Altman, 1978
2. Being aware that events intervening before recall can interfere with memory (Brown, 1978)
3. Knowing that immediate recall is more accurate than delayed recall (Eyde & Altman, 1978)
4. Choosing a longer study time as more effective in producing better recall (Brown, 1978; Friedman, Krupski, Dawson, & Rosenberg, 1977)
5. Generating appropriate strategies for accurate memory (e.g., rehearsal) (Eyde & Altman, 1978)

There are several dimensions of metamemorial knowledge that do not appear to be related to MA:

1. Knowing that relearning material should be easier than original learning (Eyde & Altman, 1978)
2. Knowing that learning material in isolation is more difficult than learning material in a context

3. Knowing that learning related pairs of words (e.g., dog-cat) is easier than pairs of unrelated words (Brown, 1978)

Awareness of Memory States   The ability to assess accurately the current state of one's memory system is another aspect of metamemory. According to Justice (1985), three tasks have been used to assess this awareness:

1. A *Feeling of Knowing Task* asks children whether they think they would be able to recognize items that they couldn't recall earlier. Performance on this task appears to be MA related (Brown, 1978).
2. A *Recall Readiness Task* asks children to study material until they think they can recall it perfectly. Brown and Barclay (1976) found that mentally retarded children, even at MA-8, were quite poor at this task. With training, retarded people with higher MAs (8) became more proficient.
3. A *Study Time Apportionment Task* asks children to study a list of items that they have previously learned. Efficient use of time would be to spend the most time studying items that they had previously missed. Brown and Campione (1977) found that retarded children with MAs of 6 and 8 did not spontaneously apportion study time in this manner. However, it was possible to train the older MA children to use this strategy effectively.

While there is some evidence that metamemorial knowledge is related to memory performance (Kendall, Borkowski, & Cavanaugh, 1980), there are also research reports in which no relationship between the two variables was found (Kramer & Engle, 1981). Justice (1985) argues that conclusions about the metamemorial knowledge-performance relationship (or lack thereof) should await the production of a reliable test of metamemorial knowledge. Present tests either rely too heavily on verbal comprehension skills or are too procedurally complex to be a pure measure.

Generalization and Selection of Strategies

There is rather general agreement that people with mental retardation do not spontaneously use appropriate metamemorial strategies (Brown, 1974; Campione & Brown, 1977, 1978). Recent research has sought to discover whether experimenter-constructed strategies can be used by retarded people to facilitate learning. The results of this research are clear. When retarded people are instructed on what strategies to use, they can often use them to recall more efficiently and accurately (Campione & Brown, 1977; Glidden, 1979). The biggest problems come when such strategies are tested for longevity (maintenance) and generalizability (transfer to new learning tasks). Several variables have been isolated that facilitate the maintenance and transfer of memory strategies in educable mentally retarded children: 1) active (versus passive) participation by the children, 2) extensive (over)training of the strategy, 3) semantic processing of the items, 4) feedback concerning the effectiveness of the strategy, 5) extensive examples provided by the experimenter concerning the use of the strategy, 6) systematic introduction of the components of the strategy, 7) gradual elimination of the experimenter's active role as training progresses, and 8) training of the strategy in a variety of contexts (Kendall et al., 1980).

Generalization of strategies to very new material (far generalization) is not often observed with retarded people. Burger, Blackman, Clark, and Reis (1982) believe that the problem in generalizing strategies lies in the ability of subjects to detect similarities between the training tasks and generalization tasks, regardless of whether the tasks are memory, verbal extraction, or so forth. It may be this ability to note similarities between problems that is the basis of retarded children's inability to generalize.

Not only are subjects required to generalize strategies, but they often must select from among a set of available strategies and sequence the application of those strategies. Training in these areas is possible with both mentally retarded and normally developing children. As is the case with most of these skills, there is no qualitative difference between mentally retarded and non-retarded children. The mentally retarded children often require more training at metacognitive skills to reach a given criterion, and demonstrate less generalization of the strategy to new material.

CONCLUSIONS

There is one domain of research in which investigators have not found compelling differences between mentally retarded and nonretarded individuals. It appears that the knowledge that mildly and moderately retarded individuals have about objects and relationships in the world is organized in a manner that is very similar to that of nonretarded individuals. This is an important conclusion because it suggests a fundamental similarity in the manner in which retarded and nonretarded individuals learn, at least when that learning occurs incidentally.

Despite this basic similarity, however, it is obvious from this review that mental retardation is characterized by deficiencies in a number of different cognitive abilities. The majority of the deficiencies can be grouped into two major categories. First, there are deficiencies that have to do with the general efficiency of the cognitive system. Mentally retarded individuals have been found to be less efficient, as indexed by processing speed, than nonretarded individuals at executing such processes as perceptual encoding, searching short-term memory, and retrieving well-learned information from long-term memory. Second, there are deficiencies that are associated with the ability to behave strategically. These deficiencies are manifest in the generally inferior performance exhibited by mentally retarded individuals, in tasks of learning/memory and tasks that involve problem solving.

Whether or not it is possible to remediate the cognitive deficiencies exhibited by mentally retarded individuals appears to depend in some measure on the nature of the deficiency. To date, there is no convincing evidence that indicates that retarded-nonretarded differences in basic cognitive processing speed can be minimized through training. In many instances, data relevant to issues of cognitive processing efficiency are obtained from individual subjects over the course of several days. Despite such extensive practice, large differences between retarded and nonretarded individuals are still obtained. Of course, it may be that practice alone is not sufficient to significantly alter the magnitude of the obtained differences. What is needed before firm conclusions can be drawn is a greater specification of the factors that underlie individual differences in processing efficiency, thereby enabling attempts at remediation to be focused more directly on those aspects of the cognitive system that are deficient in retarded individuals.

Researchers have, in general, achieved greater success with their attempts to modify the strategic functioning of mentally retarded individuals. It has been repeatedly demonstrated that persons with retardation can be taught specific strategies to be used in specific situations. However, there is little evidence to indicate that once a strategy is learned retarded individuals will generalize the trained strategy for use in similar but nonidentical situations in which the use of the strategy would enhance performance. Training persons with retardation to use more general self-management strategies has not proven to be effective in eliciting the spontaneous use and generalization of task-specific strategies. Perhaps an additional step in which an emphasis is placed on teaching retarded individuals to recognize similarities among different problem situations would make training procedures more effective. Still, there is a great deal yet to be learned about generalization before one can hope to achieve any major successes in the attempts at training. We therefore expect that these topics will receive considerable research attention in the next several years.

REFERENCES

Arbitman-Smith, R., Haywood, H. C., & Bransford, J. D. (1984). Assessing cognitive change. In P. H. Brooks, R. Sperber, & C. McCauley (Eds.), *Learning and cognition in the mentally retarded* (pp. 433–471). Hillsdale, NJ: Lawrence Erlbaum Associates.

Bachelder, B. L., & Denny, M. R. (1977a). A theory of intelligence: I. Span and the complexity of stimulus control. *Intelligence, 1,* 127–150.

Bachelder, B. L., & Denny, M. R. (1977b). A theory of intelligence: II. The role of span in a variety of intellectual tasks. *Intelligence, 1,* 237–256.

Baer, D. M., & Guess, D. (1971). Receptive training of adjectival inflections in mental retardates. *Journal of Applied Behavioral Analysis, 4,* 129–139.

Belmont, J. M., & Butterfield, E. C. (1969). The relations of short-term memory to development and intelligence. In L. P. Lipsitt & H. W. Reese (Eds.), *Advances in child development and behavior* (Vol. 4, pp. 29–82). New York: Academic Press.

Belmont, J. M., & Butterfield, E. C. (1971). Learning strategies as determinants of memory deficiencies. *Cognitive Psychology, 2,* 411–420.

Blackman, L. S., & Lin, A. (1984). Generalization training in the educable mentally retarded: Intelligence and its educability revisited. In P. H. Brooks, R. Sperber, & C. McCauley (Eds.), *Learning and cognition in the mentally retarded* (pp. 237–263). Hillsdale, NJ: Lawrence Erlbaum Associates.

Borkowski, J. G., Peck, V. A., & Damberg, P. R. (1983). Attention, memory, and cognition. In J. L. Matson & J. A. Mulick (Eds.), *Handbook of mental retardation* (pp. 479–497). New York: Pergamon Press.

Borkowski, J. G., Reid, M. K., & Kurtz. B. E. (1984). Metacognition and retardation: Paradigmatic, theoretical, and applied perspectives. In P. Brooks, R. Sperber, & C. McCauley (Eds.), *Learning and cognition in the mentally retarded* (pp. 141–164). Hillsdale, NJ: Lawrence Erlbaum Associates.

Brown, A. L. (1974). The role of strategic behavior in retardate memory. In N. R. Ellis (Ed.), *International review of research in mental retardation* (Vol. 7, pp. 55–111). New York: Academic Press.

Brown, A. L. (1978). Knowing when, where, and how to remember: A problem of metacognition. In R. Glaser (Ed.), *Advances in instructional psychology.* Hillsdale, NJ: Lawrence Erlbaum Associates.

Brown, A. L., & Barclay, C. R. (1976). The effect of training specific mnemonics of the metamnemonic efficiency of retarded children. *Child Development, 47,* 71–80.

Brown, A. L., & Campione, J. C. (1977). Training strategic study time apportionment in educable mentally retarded children. *Intelligence, 1,* 94–107.

Burger, A. L., Blackman, L. S., Clark, H. T., & Reis, E. (1982). The effects of hypothesis testing and variable format training on the generalization of a verbal abstraction strategy in EMR learners. *American Journal of Mental Deficiency, 86,* 405–413.

Butterfield, E. C., & Ferretti, R. P. (1985). Toward a theoretical cognitive hypothesis about intellectual differences among children. In J. B. Borkowski & J. D. Day (Eds.), *Memory and cognition in special children.* Norwood, NJ: Ablex.

Campione, J. C., & Brown, A. L. (1977). Memory and metamemory development in educable retarded children. In R. V. Kail & J. W. Hagen (Eds.), *Perspective on the development of memory and cognition.* Hillsdale, NJ: Lawrence Erlbaum Associates.

Campione, J. C., & Brown, A. L. (1978). Toward a theory of intelligence: Contributions from research with retarded children. *Intelligence, 2,* 279–304.

Campione, J. C., & Brown, A. L. (1984). Learning ability and transfer propensity as sources of individual differences in intelligence. In P. H. Brooks, R. Sperber, & C. McCauley (Eds.), *Learning and cognition in the mentally retarded* (pp. 265–294). Hillsdale, NJ: Lawrence Erlbaum Associates.

Carr, T. H. (1984). Attention, skill, and intelligence: Some speculations on extreme individual differences in human performance. In P. H. Brooks, R. Sperber, & C. McCauley (Eds.), *Learning and cognition in the mentally retarded* (pp. 189–215). Hillsdale, NJ: Lawrence Erlbaum Associates.

Clark, P. A., & Detterman, D. K. (1981). Performance of mentally retarded and nonretarded persons on a lifted-weight task with strategies reduced or eliminated. *American Journal of Mental Deficiency, 85,* 530–538.

Coggins, T. E. (1979, March). Relational meaning encoded in the two-word utterances of stage 1 Down's Syndrome children. *Journal of Speech and Hearing Research,* 166–178.

Davies, D., Sperber, R. D., & McCauley, C. (1981). Intelligence-related differences in semantic processing speed. *Journal of Experimental Child Psychology, 31*, 387–402.

Ellis, N. R. (1963). The stimulus trace and behavioral inadequacy. In N. R. Ellis (Ed.), *Handbook of mental deficiency*. New York: McGraw-Hill.

Ellis, N. R. (1970). Memory processes in retardates and normals. In N. R. Ellis (Ed.), *International review of research in mental retardation* (Vol. 4, pp. 1–32). New York: Academic Press.

Eyde, D. R., & Altman, R. (1978). *An explanation of metamemory processes in mildly and moderately retarded children*. Final report of project sponsored by the Bureau of Education for the Handicapped, ERIC Document Reproduction Service No. ED 162 455.

Fagan, J. F. (1971). Infants' recognition memory for a series of visual stimuli. *Journal of Experimental Child Psychology, 11*, 244–250.

Fagan, J. F. (1973). Infants' delayed recognition memory and forgetting. *Journal of Experimental Child Psychology. 16*, 424–450.

Fagan, J. F. (1976). Infants' recognition memory of invariant features of faces. *Child Development, 47*, 627–638.

Fagan, J. F. (1977). Infant recognition memory: Studies in forgetting. *Child Development, 48*, 68–78.

Fagan, J. F. (1981). *Infant memory and the prediction of intelligence*. Paper presented at the meeting of the Society for Research on Child Development, Boston.

Fagan, J. F., & McGrath, S. K. (1981). Infant recognition memory and later intelligence. *Intelligence, 5*, 121–130.

Fagan, J. F., & Singer, L. T. (1983). Infant recognition memory as a measure of intelligence. In L. P. Lipsitt (Ed.), *Advances in infancy research* (Vol. 2, pp. 31–78). Norwood, NJ: Ablex.

Ferretti, R. P., & Butterfield, E. C. (1983). *Testing the logic of instructional studies*. Paper presented at the Gatlinburg Conference on Mental Retardation and Developmental Disabilities, Gatlinburg, TN.

Ferretti, R. P., & Butterfield, E. C. (1985). *The effects of self-management training on the efficiency and generalizability of problem-solving of gifted children and mentally retarded children*. Paper presented at the Gatlinburg Conference on Mental Retardation and Developmental Disabilities, Gatlinburg, TN.

Feuerstein, R., Rand, Y., Hoffman, M., & Miller, R. (1980). *Instrumental enrichment*. Baltimore: University Park Press.

Fisher, M. A., & Zeaman, D. (1973). An attention-retention theory of retardate discrimination learning. In N. R. Ellis (Ed.). *International review of research in mental retardation* (Vol. 6, pp. 169–256). New York: Academic Press.

Flavell, J. H. (1970). Developmental studies of mediated memory. In H. W. Reese & L. P. Lipsitt (Eds.), *Advances in child development and behavior* (Vol. 5, pp. 181–211). New York: Academic Press.

Flavell, J. H. (1976). Metacognitive aspects of problem solving. In L. B. Resnick (Ed.), *The nature of intelligence*. Hillsdale, NJ: Lawrence Erlbaum Associates.

Flavell, J. H. (1978). Metacognitive development. In J. M. Scandura & C. J. Brainerd (Eds.), *Structural/process theories of complex human behavior*. Alphen a. d. Rijn, The Netherlands: Sijtoff & Noordhoff.

Friedman, M. Krupski, A., Dawson, E. T., & Rosenberg, P. (1977). Metamemory and mental retardation: Implications for research and practice. In P. Mittler (Ed.), *Research to practice in mental retardation*. Hillsdale, NJ: Lawrence Erlbaum Associates.

Gibson, E. J. (1969). *Principles of perceptual learning*. New York: Appleton-Century-Crofts.

Gibson, E. J., & Levin, H. (1975). *The psychology of reading*. Cambridge, MA: MIT Press.

Glidden, L. M. (1979). Training of learning and memory in retarded persons: Strategies, techniques, and teaching tools. In N. R. Ellis (Ed.), *Handbook of mental deficiency, psychological theory and research* (2nd ed.). Hillsdale, NJ: Lawrence Erlbaum Associates.

Haber, R. N. (1983). The impending demise of the icon: A critique of the concept of iconic storage in visual information processing. *The Behavioral and Brain Sciences, 6*, 1–54.

Hayes, J. R. (1978). *Cognitive psychology: Thinking and creating*. Chicago: Dorsey Press.

Hornstein, H. A., & Mosley, J. L. (1979). Iconic-memory processing of unfamiliar stimuli by retarded and nonretarded individuals. *American Journal of Mental Deficiency, 84*, 40–48.

Jensen, A. R. (1982). The chronometry of intelligence. In R. J. Sternberg (Ed.), *Advances in the psychology of human intelligence* (Vol. 1, pp. 255–310). Hillsdale, NJ: Lawrence Erlbaum Associates.

Justice, E. M. (1985). Metamemory: An aspect of metacognition. In N. R. Ellis & N. W. Bray (Eds.), *International review of research in mental retardation* (Vol. 13, pp. 79–143). New York: Academic Press.

Kahneman, D. (1973). *Attention and effort*. Englewood Cliffs, NJ: Prentice-Hall.

Kendall, C. R., Borkowski, J. G., & Cavanaugh, J. C. (1980). Metamemory and the transfer of an interrogative strategy by EMR children. *Intelligence, 4*, 255–270.

Kramer, J. J., & Engle, R. W. (1981). Teaching awareness of strategic behavior in combination with strategy training: Effects on children's memory performance. *Journal of Experimental Child Psychology, 32*, 513–530.

Laine, R. A., & Baumeister, A. A. (1985). Short-term memory for a pure-tone stimulus among mentally retarded and nonretarded persons. *Intelligence, 9*, 237–257.

Lally, M., & Nettelbeck, T. (1977). Intelligence, reaction time, and inspection time. *American Journal of Mental Deficiency, 82*, 273–281.

Lane, D. M. (1979). Developmental change in attention-deployment skills. *Journal of Experimental Child Psychology, 38*, 16–29.

Mahoney, G., Finger, I., & Powell, A. (1985). Relationship of maternal behavioral style to the developmental status of organically impaired mentally retarded infants. *American Journal of Mental Deficiency, 90*, 296–302.

Maisto, A. A., & Baumeister, A. A. (1984). Dissection of component processes in rapid information processing tasks: Comparison of retarded and nonretarded people. In P. H. Brooks, R. Sperber, & C. McCauley (Eds.), *Learning and cognition in the mentally retarded* (pp. 165–188). Hillsdale, NJ: Lawrence Erlbaum Associates.

Manis, F. R., Keating, D. P., & Morrison, F. J. (1980). Developmental differences in the allocation of processing capacity. *Journal of Experimental Child Psychology, 29*, 156–169.

McCauley, C., Sperber, R. D., & Roaden, S. K. (1978). Verification of property statements by retarded and nonretarded adolescents. *American Journal of Mental Deficiency, 83*, 276–282.

McClelland, J. L. (1979). On the time relations of mental processes: An examination of systems of processes in cascade. *Psychological Review, 86*, 287–307.

Merrill, E. C., McCauley, C., Sperber, R., Littlefield, J., Rider, E., & Shapiro, D. (1985). *Age- and intelligence-related differences in semantic encoding speed*. Paper presented at the meeting of the Society for Research on Child Development, Toronto, Canada.

Neisser, U. (1976). *Cognition and reality*. San Francisco: W. H. Freeman.

Nettelbeck, T., & Brewer, N. (1981). Studies of mild mental retardation and timed performance. In N. R. Ellis (Ed.), *International review of research in mental retardation* (Vol. 10, pp. 61–106). New York: Academic Press.

Nettlebeck, T., & Lally, M. (1979). Age, intelligence, and inspection time. *American Journal of Mental Deficiency, 83,* 398–401.

Norman, D. A., & Bobrow, D. G. (1975). On data-limited and resource-limited processes. *Cognitive Psychology, 7,* 44–64.

Peterson, G. A., & Sherrod, K. B. (1982). Relationship of maternal language to language development. In R. L. Schiefelbusch (Ed.), *Bases of language intervention* (Vol. 1, pp. 191–268). Baltimore: University Park Press.

Pick, A. D., Frankel, D. G., & Hess, V. L. (1975). Children's attention: The development of selectivity. In E. M. Hetherington (Ed.), *Review of child development research* (Vol. 5, pp. 325–383). Chicago: University of Chicago Press.

Posner, M. I. (1975). Psychobiology of attention. In M. S. Gazzaniga & C. Blakemore (Eds.), *Handbook of psychobiology* (pp. 441–480). New York: Academic Press.

Posner, M. I. (1978). *Chronometric explanations of mind*. Hillsdale, NJ: Lawrence Erlbaum Associates.

Poulson, C. (1983). DRO as a control procedure in the conditioning of infant vocalization rate. *Journal of Experimental Child Psychology, 363,* 471–489.

Sherrod, K. B., Siewert, L. A., & Cavallaro, S. A. (1984). Language and play maturity in preschool children. *Early Child Development and Care, 14,* 147–160.

Siegler, R. S. (1981). Developmental sequences within and between concepts. *Monograph of Society for Research on Child Development, 46,* 1–74.

Sperber, R., & McCauley, C. (1984). Semantic processing efficiency in the mentally retarded. In P. H. Brooks, R. Sperber, & C. McCauley (Eds.), *Learning and cognition in the mentally retarded* (pp. 141–163). Hillsdale, NJ: Lawrence Erlbaum Associates.

Sperber, R., Merrill, E. C., McCauley, C., & Shapiro, D. (1983). *Intelligence-related differences in the efficiency of semantic encoding*. Paper presented at the annual meeting of the Society for Research on Child Development, Detroit.

Sperber, R. D., Ragain, R. D., & McCauley, C. (1976). Reassessment of category knowledge in retarded individuals. *American Journal of Mental Deficiency, 81,* 227–234.

Spitz, H. H., & Borys, S. V. (1984). Depth of search: How far can the retarded search through an internally represented problem space? In P. Brooks, R. Sperber, & C. McCauley (Eds.), *Learning and cognition in the mentally retarded*. Hillsdale, NJ: Lawrence Erlbaum Associates.

Spitz, H. H., & Thor, D. H. (1968). Visual backward masking in retardates and normals. *Perception and Psychophysics, 4,* 245–246.

Stanovich, K. E. (1978). Information processing in mentally retarded individuals. In N. R. Ellis (Ed.), *International review of research in mental retardation* (Vol. 9, pp. 29–60). New York: Academic Press.

Stephens, C. E., Pear, J. J., Wray, L. D., & Jackson, G. S. (1975). Some effects of reinforcement schedules in teaching picture names to retarded children. *Journal of Applied Behavior Analysis, 8(4),* 435–447.

Tulving, E. (1972). Episodic and semantic memory. In E. Tulving & W. Donaldson (Eds.), *Organization and memory* (pp. 381–403). New York: Academic Press.

Vygotsky, L. S. (1978). *Mind in society.* Edited by M. Cole, V. John-Steiner, S. Scribner, & E. Souberman. Cambridge, MA: Harvard University Press.

Welch, S. J., & Pear, J. J. (1980). Generalization of naming responses to objects in the natural environment as a function of stimulus modality with retarded children. *Journal of Applied Behavior Analysis, 13,* 629–643.

Welsandt, R. F., Jr., & Meyer, P. A. (1974). Visual masking, mental age, and retardation. *Journal of Experimental Child Psychology, 18,* 512–519.

Wheeler, A., & Sulzer, B. (1970). Operant training and generalization of a verbal response form in a speech deficient child. *Journal of Applied Behavioral Analysis, 3,* 139–147.

Zeaman, D., & House, B. J. (1963). The role of attention in retardate discrimination learning. In N. R. Ellis (Ed.), *Handbook of mental deficiency* (pp. 159–223). Hillsdale, NJ: Lawrence Erlbaum Associates.

Zeaman, D., & House, B. J. (1979). A review of attention theory. In N. R. Ellis (Ed.), *Handbook of mental deficiency, psychological theory and research* (2nd ed., pp. 63–120). Hillsdale, NJ: Lawrence Erlbaum Associates.

BEHAVIORAL ASPECTS OF MENTAL RETARDATION

Introduction

It would appear to some that the researchers in the behavioral sciences often question the seeming overemphasis by biomedical researchers on a "medical model" in the discussion about the symptoms of mental retardation and the excitement we show toward new technology in the biomedical field, particularly the neurosciences. We fully understand their views and often have to remind ourselves not to be swept up in the more dramatic achievements in biomedical sciences. The advances in the behavioral sciences can be just as dramatic. Although these advances appear to occur in a time-released manner, the overall results are just as significant. We have been chastised at times because of our overemphasis on the biomedical aspects, since 75%–90% of all mental retardation is in the mild range, which is often the arena of the sociocultural research—the major focus of the behavioral sciences.

The name synonymous with the field of the sociocultural aspects of mental retardation is Robert Edgerton. Dr. Edgerton is one of the, if not *the,* leading exponents of research in this area and has been so recognized for his contributions by the American Association on Mental Deficiency and the Association for Retarded Citizens. His numerous contributions and over 26 years of research in the field have focused primarily on mildly mentally retarded adults. He points out that there is enormous skepticism present as to our ability to reduce by half this large group of individuals by the year 2000, and rightly so.

Many of the authors in this book are very optimistic and upbeat about the chances for the prevention and curative intervention in mental retardation. Dr. Edgerton provides us with some much needed sobering analyses in our efforts to significantly reduce mild mental retardation. As we look at some of the data from the U.S. Bureau of the Census, it seems that this may be the first time in our society where children are much worse off than adults. We seem to be going through a significant social change in this country. Factors that are creating this situation are shown in statistics from a variety of government and private social agencies:

321

1. Approximately 13.8 million (or 22%) of Americans under the age of 18 live in poverty, up from 14.3% in 1969–1970; some 48% of all black children live in poverty, up from 39.6% in 1969. The federal government defines the poverty level for a family of four as an income of approximately $11,000.
2. Poor white children outnumber poor black children 2 to 1 but while blacks constitute only 15% of all children, they equal 32% of all poor children.
3. Children living with the mother in a single-parent home are four times more likely to be poor than those in two-parent homes. Of the 800,000 families who fell into poverty in 1981–1983, more than half of them were in households with two parents.
4. Twenty-two percent of all American children live in families headed by women, but more than half of all poor children live in such households, which is up twice that of the 1959 rate. This is graphically illustrated by Figure 1, which shows the number of persons living below the poverty level.

Despite these alarming statistics, Dr. Edgerton presents three potentially effective approaches toward secondary prevention with the mildly mentally retarded individual. The first approach focuses on identifying and augmenting alternative cognitive strategies and skills; the second encourages the forma-

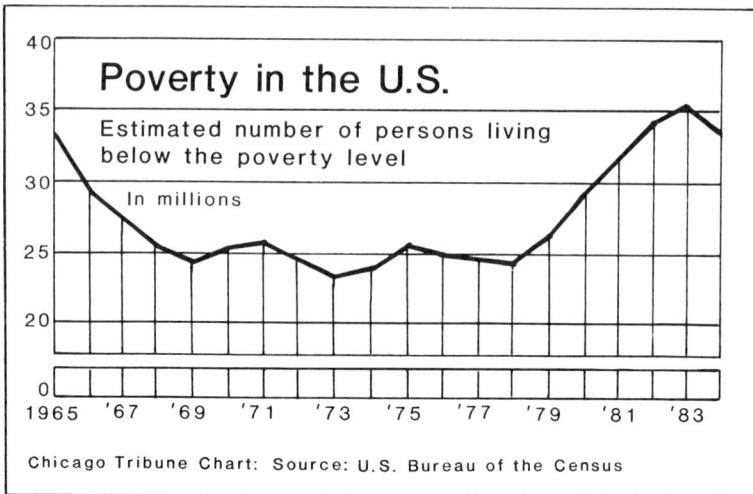

Figure 1. Estimated number of persons in the United States who live below the poverty level. The number of Americans living in poverty dipped in 1984 after a 5-year increase.

tion of symbiotic support groups; and the third provides more positive social roles in this group of individuals. Dr. Edgerton's own research has pointed out these approaches may be very effective since we have found that mildly mentally retarded adults have been able to "cure" themselves of the mental retardation in that they no longer seek or receive services as mentally retarded persons, no longer think of themselves as retarded, and are not thought of as retarded by others with whom they interact. In essence, developmental research indicates that the prevalence of mild mental retardation has tended to decrease with age and could be accelerated utilizing the approaches that he has suggested. Finally, Dr. Edgerton points out that even if we are not able to accomplish this task totally, we must not overlook the fact that adults with mild mental retardation are quite capable of living with minimal help from others and can make significant contributions in return.

Dr. Lou Rowitz is uniquely qualified to write a chapter on the multidimensional approaches to reversing mild mental retardation labels. As a long-time editor of the journal, *Mental Retardation,* his editorial responsibilities have required his direct involvement in almost all areas of research in mental retardation. He provides us with a unique insight into the different perspectives that one can have in developing curative approaches to mental retardation.

Dr. Rowitz aptly points out that individuals trained in different conceptual and professional disciplines will have their own viewpoint regarding prevention and cure based upon their disciplinary perspectives. The editors recall very vividly the first national conference on curative approaches to mental retardation in the early 1980s. After 3½ days of presentations by renowned experts in various disciplines from around the country, it became quite obvious how very little we knew about each other's disciplines because of our highly specialized areas of research, which oftentimes is a prerequisite for publishing in the elite journals. We also recall a conversation between a developmental neuropathologist, who was talking about "abnormal brain development," and Dr. Sidney Bijou (the grandfather of behavior modification with mentally retarded children). Dr. Bijou is known as a very gentle, patient, and understanding individual, but he became so exasperated that he finally challenged the neuropathologist by saying, "These are not brains— these are kids we are talking about." Dr. Rowitz seems to capture this alarming problem that serves as an explanation of the very essence of this book—which is, if we really could accomplish a 50% reduction in the incidence of mental retardation, we would need a more interdisciplinary cooperative mechanism for achieving this task.

Dr. Rowitz presents a new conceptual approach to cure that dispels the old linear approach to prevention. This new conceptual approach is based upon a circular process with feedback between primary, secondary, and tertiary areas based upon input from the biomedical, psychological, educational, and sociological dimensions. This interdisciplinary perspective on cure is supported by the analysis of three case studies. Rowitz believes that this interdisciplinary perspective can increase our curative endeavors and have important policy implications for persons with mental retardation.

Chapter 12

Perspectives on The Prevention of Mild Mental Retardation

Robert B. Edgerton

My 26 years of research in the field of mental retardation have been concentrated on the lives of mildly retarded adults (Edgerton, 1984). It is only with considerable trepidation that I have accepted the challenge of discussing issues of preventing mental retardation in this population because, as virtually every serious investigator has noted, mild mental retardation has proven to be very difficult to prevent.

Although the goal set by the President's Committee on Mental Retardation in 1972 for reducing the incidence of mental retardation "by half" has not been reached, there have been impressive advances in both the primary and secondary prevention of many kinds of more severe, "organic" forms of mental retardation (Clarke & Clarke, 1977; Zigler, 1978), and as Menolascino, Neman, and Stark (1983) have recently shown at the first national conference devoted to "The Search for Cures," there is great promise for still further advances. Mild mental retardation has proven to be more difficult to "cure." As Clarke and Clarke wrote in their guest editorial in the *American Journal of Mental Deficiency* (May 1977), "Mild retardation poses seemingly intractable problems, exhibiting in extreme form the major social problems with which industrial societies are beset" (p. 531).

Because between 75% and 90% of all mental retardation is in the mild range (Ramey & Finkelstein, 1981), and because mild retardation is overwhelmingly associated with poverty, the 50% reduction in the incidence of mental retardation called for by the President's Committee on Mental Retardation in 1972 required a concentrated attack against those conditions that are thought to cause mild retardation among the poor, as well as major interven-

I gratefully acknowledge support for this research from NICHD Grant No. HD 04612, the Mental Retardation Research Center, UCLA, and NICHD Program Project Grant No. HD 11944-02, the Community Adaptation of Mildly Retarded Persons.

tion programs to enable afflicted children to overcome their intellectual limitations.

Although many commentators have written that it is overstating matters to say that we have the knowledge to reduce mild mental retardation by half if we would only use it, an assertion repeated by Rosalynn Carter in 1977, we do in fact possess considerable knowledge about prevention. We know, for example, that the cognitive abilities of mildly retarded children can be improved by a variety of interventions. In general, the earlier, the more comprehensive, and the longer lasting these interventions are, the greater the resulting cognitive gains (Ramey, Campbell, & Finkelstein, 1984). We also know what many of the conditions are that put a developing fetus at risk for mild mental retardation: teenage pregnancy; poor pre- and neonatal care; malnutrition; poor obstetrical care; maternal infections and toxins; physical traumata of all sorts; a host of environmental hazards such as radioactivity, alcohol, and lead; and many others.

But this knowledge, however incomplete, tells us what might be done to reduce the incidence of mildly retarded infants, or what steps may be effective in improving the learning abilities of such children if they are born. But even if all our knowledge were to be applied—it never has been in the past—many mildly retarded children would still be born (for polygenic reasons of low parental intelligence, if no other), and no program of early remediation would be totally effective. And so, we must anticipate that the future would witness a good many mildly retarded children becoming mildly retarded adults, joining the several millions of Americans who currently occupy that status.

In general, these mildly retarded adults, like their counterparts in the past years, would have experienced a lifetime of failure at home and in school; in most cases, they would have had only limited opportunity for normal experience; in many cases, this pattern of socialization would exacerbate any cognitive difficulties that child might have experienced earlier in life. As we have seen in our own ethnographic research, and just as Zigler (1984) found in laboratory research, these persons would enter their adult years handicapped by overdependency, wariness of adults, and an unwillingness to risk failure (Edgerton, 1984; Zigler, 1984). Preadapted for failure in normal adult life, and beyond the age when rapid improvement in cognitive or social competence could reasonably be expected, these mildly retarded adults have historically begun their postschool lives expecting little of themselves. Others in their worlds have typically expected less of them, and allowed them even less.

And yet, there is a paradoxical finding: as years pass, most of these adults improve their social competence, so much so that many appear to become indistinguishable from many nonretarded persons. This pattern of improving social competence over time has been reported for many years (Cobb, 1972), suggesting to many, as it did to Clarke and Clarke (1977, p. 531), that time may somehow "compensate" for both cognitive limitations and experiential deprivation: "It is fortunate that many mildly retarded persons tend to show a shift towards 'normality' with increasing age; it seems that life experiences and the passage of time may be compensatory." Although this pattern of improving social competence over time is both more complex and ephemeral than is commonly understood (Edgerton, 1983; Jackson, 1977), it nevertheless does suggest that there is reason to hope that some mildly retarded adults can be "cured."

I suggest that the numbers of adults who could be "cured" (i.e., who could live without special services and would no longer see themselves or been seen by others as mentally retarded) could be increased if we were to terminate certain practices that are now commonplace, and if we were to institute other practices that are now all too uncommon.

RELATIVITY OF CLASSIFICATION

But first, we must remind ourselves that mild mental retardation is an administrative category, it does not derive from a scientific nosology. Who is admitted to the category or excluded from it can be arbitrary, depending on an IQ criterion that slides up or down in response to changing social, economic, and political considerations. In 1959, when the Heber committee of the American Association on Mental Deficiency (AAMD) set the upper limit for mental retardation at IQ ≤ 85—or 1 SD below the mean—they defined almost 16% of the U.S. population as mentally retarded. In 1973, when the Grossman committee of the AAMD, lowered the IQ criterion from 85 to 70, they reduced the numbers of mentally retarded persons in the United States from about 32 million to less than 6 million (Zigler, Balla, & Hodapp, 1984). When the 1983 Grossman committee called for greater flexibility in determining whether someone with an IQ a few points over or under 70 was to be classified as mentally retarded by allowing clinical judgment to enter into the diagnostic process, they once again affected the numbers of persons eligible to become mentally retarded (Grossman, 1983) (see Table 1).

Table 1. Definitional evolution of mental retardation

Date of passage	Source	IQ upper limit	Results
1959	Heber Committee of AAMD	≤ 85	16% of the U.S. population defined as M.R.
1973	Grossman Committee of AAMD	≤ 70	Number of persons classified as M.R. dropped
1983	Grossman Committee of AAMD	≤ 70 + Clinical judgment	Number of persons classified as M.R. once again affected

These committee decisions were not frivolous. They reflected beliefs about the normal distribution of intelligence, the relationship of IQ to academic achievement and social adjustment, as well as assessments of the availability and efficacy of services for mentally retarded persons. While it must stretch anyone's credulity to claim that Americans today, or in 1973, could succeed in school or in life with *lower* IQs than were necessary for success in 1959, we can easily understand why social and economic factors made 70 a more feasible cutoff than 85. Medical services, hospital care, educational programs, SSI, vocational training, and residential facilities, among other essential needs, are expensive and even when mental retardation is defined by a lower IQ such as 70, these services have never been available to all the persons who have been eligible for them. At the risk of laboring the obvious, we could "cure" a great many persons of mild mental retardation by lowering the upper IQ criterion to, say, 65. And on scientific grounds alone, it would be very difficult, indeed, to demonstrate that persons excluded from the category "mental retardation" by such an act (i.e., those with IQs between 66 and 70) have appreciably lower cognitive or social skills that persons with IQs between 71 and 75, and these persons are *now* excluded from the category.

I am emphasizing these kinds of definitional issues because the challenge of preventing mild mental retardation cannot be divorced from social, economic, and, therefore, political considerations. We need only recall that when Yerkes tested close to 2 million recruits during World War I, he found that the average mental age of White American adults was only 13—well below the expected average of 16, and barely above the mental age of 12 then used as the upper limit of "feeblemindedness" (Gould, 1981). The absurdity of an intelligence testing procedure that identified half of the population as feebleminded was not lost on the U.S. Army, which inducted these men despite their low "intelligence." These men could fill needed roles as soldiers. Others, such as proponents of eugenics and restricted immigration, chose to ignore this absurdity, but it is a fair bet that if tax-funded services had been available to persons defined as "feebleminded," the numbers of people defined as eligible would have been reduced, and without delay.

The changes in the criteria for classifying persons as mentally retarded are not *simply* arbitrary, not *simply* economic, not *simply* founded on a belief in the normal distribution of intelligence (Wortis, 1970). Since the 1920s, changes in classification have also been influenced by two empirical findings: first, that some persons with low IQs can nevertheless make good social adjustments once they leave school, and second, that some low IQ persons who display poor social adjustment early in their adult lives may improve that adjustment as they grow older (Lakin, Bruininks, & Sigford, 1981; McCarver & Craig, 1974). These related findings led to efforts to develop measures of adaptive behavior (AB) in order to supplement the IQ criterion, and they led to the conclusion, now accepted as part of our scientific knowledge, that the prevalence of mental retardation decreases after the age of 15 (Gruenberg, 1964).

This is not the place to discuss the history of attempts to develop tests of AB that would achieve parity with IQ as criteria for the classification of mental retardation (cf. Meyers, Nihira, & Zetlin, 1979), except to note that tests of AB have not yet achieved widespread acceptance as diagnostic criteria for mild retardation (Zigler, 1984), and may, in fact, be losing ground to "clinical judgment." But the finding that AB can change over time has important implications for the prevention of mental retardation.

Before we explore the significance of this phenomenon further, we should point out that while some mildly retarded persons undeniably improve their social adjustment, including their cognitive competence, as they grow older, others do not. In fact, the percentage of persons who improve over time varies from time to time and place to place in response to a host of changing social, economic, and cultural considerations (Edgerton, 1981). There are always some who fail, and sometimes, most do. This is true even in Sweden, where extensive social services are committed for furthering the normalization of its mentally retarded citizens. For example, all 19-year-old Swedish men not identified as mentally retarded in school are given an IQ test during their preinduction examination for military service. Those who are found to have IQs below 70 (1.5% of all men tested) are rejected for military service (Granat & Granat, 1973); when the social adjustment of these low IQ men was subsequently examined, half were judged to have made a good social adjustment, but half were poorly adjusted (Granat & Granat, 1978). It should be sobering to realize that half of these young men who escaped classification as mentally retarded persons in school were nevertheless poorly adjusted in their postschool lives. However, this is consistent with research findings in the United States that have consistently reported failure in attempts to specify variables capable of predicting differential success in postschool or postinstitutional adjustment (Cobb, 1972; Edgerton & Bercovici, 1976). Within the range of mild retardation, IQ is a poor prognostic variable (Lakin et al., 1981; McCarver & Craig, 1974); success in social adjustment seems to result not from a few more IQ points but from fitting attributes of the person—especially aspects of personality, self-esteem, and motivation—to features of the environment to which he or she is attempting to adapt.

I shall return to this issue in a moment, but the point I want to emphasize here is that the success that mildly retarded persons have in fitting themselves to certain environments takes time to develop, and until years of adaptive trial and error have passed, most individuals experience many periods of frustration and failure in social adjustment. So it was for 50% of those young men in Sweden, and so it has been for the hundreds of mildly retarded adults whose lives my colleagues and I have studied intensely for many years.

The lives of the mentally retarded people whom we have studied in community settings are marked by dramatic changes. These changes are often abrupt and have dramatic consequences. An individual or a couple, living in a group home or their own apartment, may have a highly stable pattern of life activities for a year or even longer before any significant change occurs, although it is common for changes to be more frequent than this. When change in a life pattern does take place, it is often sudden and traumatic, followed by a period of turbulent readjustment. Jobs are lost, but usually regained. Friends or lovers leave, often to reappear or be replaced. Happiness is replaced by despair, and in time, there is happiness again. The process is one of oscillation, from a positive social adjustment, to a troubled one, then back and forth.

None of this should be very surprising. Patterns of life in our urban centers today are anything but static. For example, Lillian Rubin graphically documented the unstable life patterns of working class families who had little job security during poor economic conditions. She called her book, *World of Pain* (Rubin, 1976). Unless they are closely supported by their parents or other devoted benefactors, most mildly retarded adults in community settings also live markedly unstable—and sometimes painful—lives. They face the ordinary vicissitudes of life in poverty plus some not-so-ordinary ones. They usually come to community life with little experience in managing everyday life and seldom have available resources that would permit them to stabilize themselves in times of stress. They lack job security, credit, union support, insurance, savings; they often lack friends or relatives who will support them (see Figure 1). If personnel from the service delivery system do not intervene effectively, the result can be turmoil, and in our research experience, that support is often slow in coming or is absent altogether. Moreover, when agencies do intervene, the result is frequently a return of the troubled person to a more restricted group home, or some other more closely supervised setting. In 1920, the superintendent of Rome Asylum in New York observed that many young adults who failed on their first trial at community living succeeded if given a second chance in another environment. He added this:

> Most of us normal individuals have at one time or another been at the point of
> failure, and probably would have failed had indulgent parents and friends not
> given us a chance to try again and yet again until we actually found ourselves.
> (p. 28)

Alas, Bernstein's lesson of 67 years ago must be relearned, again and yet again.[1]

The first implication, then, is obvious. To define unwanted behavior as "social failure" is to deprive a mildly retarded adult of the time, and the experience, needed to achieve a more stable and positive adaptation. We can

---

[1] I first came across this passage in an excellent essay by Lakin et al. (1981).

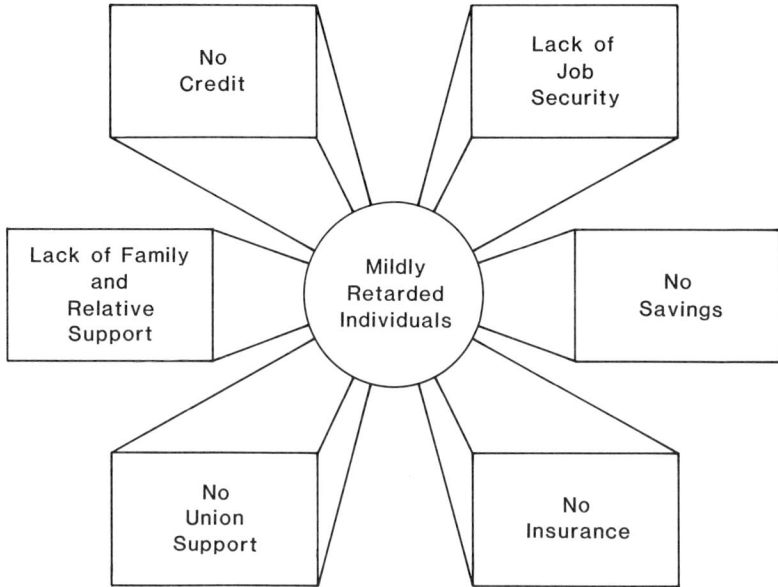

Figure 1. Obstacles to daily living for mildly retarded individuals.

lower the prevalence of mild mental retardation if we resist the temptation to intervene in the lives of these people, moving them into more restricted environments simply because they have problems in social living.

There is also a second point. In order to fail, they must first have the opportunity. Many do not. Instead, their lives are restricted in parental homes, group homes, or larger institutions where they are protected against failure in the trials of life by being denied the opportunity to experience life without supervision or protection. Those who supervise and protect often have the best of intentions, and they can also point to a good bit of social reality. Not all young adults outgrow their turbulent early lives to achieve a more stable, positive social adjustment. Many have severe problems, endangering themselves and others (Edgerton, 1981). There *are* risks, and for some the risks are great. Nevertheless, without the chance to experience less-restricted, more independent social lives, there can be no success. Even persons with normal intelligence can be socialized into social incompetence if they are denied the opportunity to live as ordinary people. When a person with normal intelligence is incorrectly diagnosed as being mentally retarded early in life, and thereafter socialized as a highly protected, "retarded," person, this effect can be seen clearly (Edgerton, 1986). Allowing persons with low IQs to try their hand at living more normal lives is risky. Many will fail, bringing suffering to themselves and those who care about them. Yet many will endure, will draw greater happiness from life, and will give more to others than would otherwise be possible. They will, that is, cure themselves.

Down syndrome persons are a case in point. Today, many such persons live full lives. They work competitively, engage in many leisure activities, travel by themselves, marry, and become good friends with others. Thirty years ago, Down syndrome children were routinely institutionalized; from today's perspective, they seem to have been the victims of extraordinary ignorance. For example, when George Tarjan was Medical Director of what was then Pacific State Hospital in the 1950s, he found that many of the "higher functioning" patients who had helped to feed bedfast patients were being released to community settings. When Dr. Tarjan suggested that Down syndrome patients could take over this task, it was pointed out to him that this was contrary to the then prevailing medical guidelines that decreed that Down syndrome patients were not competent to feed bedfast patients. These guidelines were based on the conventional "unwisdom" of that time, which had it that a Down syndrome person could not learn to feed another patient properly, with the resulting danger that food would be aspirated, endangering the lives of the bedfast patients. To make a long story short, Tarjan ignored this advice and Down syndrome patients fed other patients perfectly well. From our vantage point, the fears of 30 years earlier seem preposterous. How will our current practices of restricting the lives of mildly retarded persons seem 30 years hence?

The natural process by which some persons eventually leave the ranks of the mentally retarded cannot take place unless these people are given the opportunity to succeed. But we can and should do more than allow a process of community adaptation to take its natural course. There are affirmative steps that we could take in order to accelerate the processes by which some persons naturally develop greater social and cognitive competence.

ROUTES TOWARD SECONDARY PREVENTION

Among the many potentially effective approaches that could be instituted, I shall mention three that have emerged from my own research: 1) identifying and augmenting alternative cognitive strategies and skills, 2) encouraging the formation of symbiotic support groups, and 3) providing more positive social roles (see Figure 2).

Augmenting Alternative Cognitive Skills

There is growing evidence that certain kinds of interventions can improve cognitive abilities, including those required for IQ test performance (Haywood & Wachs, 1981; Zigler, 1978). As Butterfield (1983) has indicated, there are promising developments in training cognitive skills, including memory and generalization, by separating complex intellectual operations into

SECONDARY PREVENTION FOR MENTAL RETARDATION

Identify and augment alternative cognitive strategies and skills.

Encourage the formation of symbiotic support groups.

Provide more positive social roles.

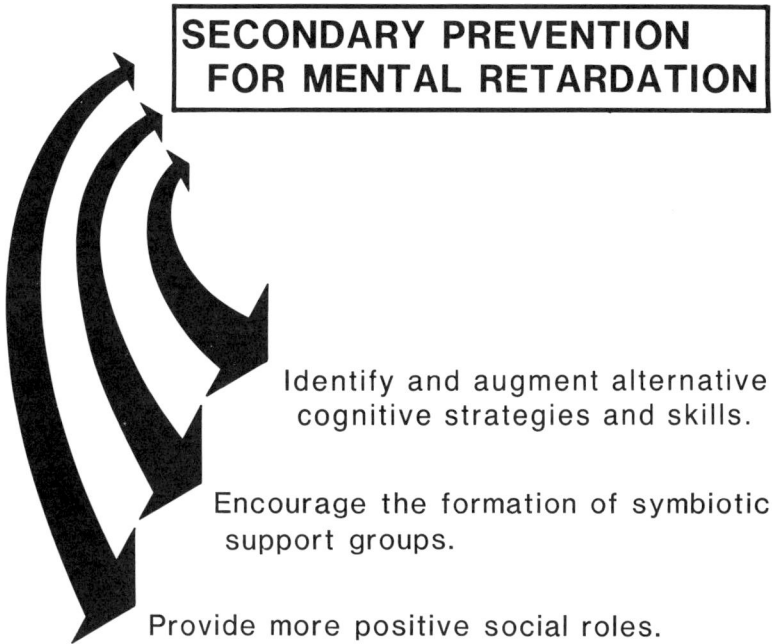

Figure 2.   Routes toward secondary prevention.

their component parts. Others have noted the importance of "mediated" learning (Arbitman-Smith, Haywood, & Bransford, 1984), including meta-cognitive processes that include self-conscious strategies for problem solving (Baumeister, 1984; Haywood, Meyers, & Switzky, 1982). In the practical world of community living, most mildly retarded adults receive no training in cognitive skills, and the minority that do receive services usually do so in the context of an independent living skills or adult education program. The content of these programs varies, but as these programs are taught to the persons whom we have studied, that is, when cognitive skills are implicated in the training, these are taught more or less as they would be in an ordinary academic setting (Bercovici, 1983). There are not enough individuals in our various research samples who have received cognitive skills training as adults for us to assess the efficacy of this training, but our data suggest that even if this training does sometimes improve cognitive skills, there is a more effective approach that could be taken.

Most of the adults in our samples have reported that they disliked cognitive skills training (e.g., reading, writing, mathematics, money management, telling time, etc.) whether these skills were taught in school or in training programs later in life. They have also said that they cannot remember what they were taught, an assertion that is supported by their poor mastery of these skills in their everyday lives. In questioning these people about their school or adult training experiences, and in observing some of these classes and programs, it is apparent that the typical metacommunication from teacher to students is this: "There is a correct way to perform this task (e.g., multiplication or telling time); I know that correct way, and I'll now teach it to you." In more formal language, this approach is "response limiting," assuming a closed system of appropriate knowledge. The students have a profound fear and expectancy of failure in tasks like these and they are little motivated to try again, only to suffer the pain of yet another failure, as Zigler, his colleagues, and many others have shown (Zigler, 1984).

Yet at the same time that mildly retarded adults resist the efforts of others to teach them cognitive skills, they often develop their own strategies for problem solving. For example, a man who could not read, but enjoyed watching TV, developed his own mnemonic for memorizing relevant portions of the TV schedule; another had a metamemory strategy for remembering telephone numbers; still another man could not perform any of the mathematical skills taught in school (e.g., multiplication, subtraction, division), but he could manage to fit his income to his expenses by means of a complex, cumbersome, but effective pictorial system for visualizing amounts of money (sometimes represented by piles of bills and coins). These strategies were alternatives to the standard skills taught in schools; they were time consuming but they *worked,* and for these individuals, school skills did *not* work.

This should not be surprising. Ordinary middle-class people with normal intelligence sometimes use alternative cognitive strategies in preference to the skills they were taught in school. For example, Jean Lave and her colleagues (Lave, Murtaugh, & de la Rocha, 1984) have demonstrated that ordinary grocery shoppers estimate the value of an item not by a mathematical calculation of price to volume, but alternative strategies. Moreover, these strategies are reasonably accurate, which is fortunate because when these shoppers were later asked to calculate the value of grocery items in terms of price-volume relationships, they lacked the mathematical skills to do so.

Mentally retarded adults often have trouble exhibiting the skills necessary to shop well (Williams & Ewing, 1981), yet they are sometimes taught to shop using the same mathematical operations that are so foreign to ordinary shoppers. In fact, as Levine and Langness (1985) have reported, some mentally retarded persons shop quite effectively in supermarkets by employing alternative strategies of item and quantity selection, as well as payment at the cash register. Levine and Langness (1985) believe that mildly retarded adults are in general quite adept at developing alternative metacognitive strategies, including ways to plan, monitor, and evaluate their problem-solving performance. Not all of these alternative strategies are strictly cognitive, but then problem solving is not purely cognitive; it also involves motivation and emotion. Metastrategies often include ways of avoiding cognitive overload and subsequent feelings of confusion, as well as ways of embarrassment. For example, some persons always pay the cashier with a large denomination bill, putting the burden of making change on the cashier (we sometimes do the same when traveling in a foreign country).

If we recognize that mentally retarded persons can sometimes be more successful in solving their problems of everyday life by adopting alternative metacognitive strategies that differ from those taught in schools, then it may be possible to augment and enhance those strategies by a form of "mediated learning" (Feuerstein, Rand, Hoffman, & Miller, 1980) in which someone in the role of teacher or friend can help a retarded person who has not yet developed his or her own alternative metacognitive strategies to find ones that are congenial and effective for that particular person in solving particular problems. It may also be possible to enhance the generalization of these strategies (Campione & Brown, 1977).

Symbiotic Support Groups

Just as some adults develop alternative strategies for problem solving, some adults are able to locate or construct environments to which they can adapt successfully. In many instances, these environments differ markedly from the values and expectations of their parents or case managers. Often, these adults drift toward lower income neighborhoods, where they live in more deteriorated housing, eat junk food, clean house indifferently if at all, live on SSI, watch TV, and establish friendships with others who do the same (Edgerton, 1982). Parents and case managers may be appalled by these lifestyles and may attempt to change them. A particularly telling example has been provided by a mother who eventually understood that the lifestyle she and her husband desired for their mildly retarded 24-year-old daughter was not the lifestyle the daughter valued and that their efforts to impose their success-oriented values on her would have to be modified (Kaufman, 1980):

> There are many kinds of success: the one that is most meaningful for her may turn out to be centered around all-night sessions with friends, a baby or two, and SSI for income. Ten months ago I would have shuddered at the scenario. Today I would be a good deal more accepting if it occurred. (p. 22)

Conflicts of this sort are as painful as they are counterproductive. Instead of imposing our "quality of life" standards on mentally retarded persons who cannot reasonably be expected to maintain them, it would be better to offer a range of options. One option is to allow these persons to choose their own lifestyles, as Kaufman did. But not every parent or case manager can see this option from their child's or client's perspective. It might be helpful, therefore, if there were programs in place that could provide options combining the skills and competencies of mentally retarded persons in ways that would be symbiotic. Important as matching roommates clearly is, few programs today offer residents an informed choice of co-residents (Halpern, Close, & Nelson,

1985). Attempts to provide vocational training to "composite workers," two or three persons who as a unit could work more effectively than they could as individuals, are now underway in many parts of the country.

The same concept could be applied to community residential care. Once again, the principle can be drawn from the natural occurrence of cooperative living arrangements among some of the young adults whose community adaptation we have studied. Although there is a continuum of residential options available to mentally retarded persons in southern California ranging from group facilities, through "family care homes," to "semi-independent" apartment complexes, in all of these options the primary decision-making authority for the conduct of the residents lies with a nonretarded supervisor or caregiver. Unless the retarded resident is capable of living independently, he or she has no residential options but one of these, or returning to the parental home where "adult" supervision would continue and perhaps intensify.

Fully independent living is unattainable for many mildly retarded persons, and has been throughout our history. Yet it remains a cruelly tantalizing goal, one that sets unreasonably high expectations for too many mentally retarded persons, their parents, and service providers. We should remind ourselves that for most Americans, independent living is far more a symbolic expression of our American value on self-reliance than it is an empirical reality. Most Americans receive all manner of support and assistance from parents and kin throughout much of their lives. Many do not leave their parental homes to "live independently" until they marry. Even then, they live *with* a spouse, and they usually continue to receive support from their parents and kin—now from two sets rather than only one. This pattern is more common in some parts of the United States than others, among some religious and ethnic groups than others, and at some income levels more than others, but according to U.S. Census data, in 1983 only 8% of the total U.S. household population actually lived alone—that is, truly independently; 88% lived in a family household, and 73% lived as a married couple household.[2]

There are no data on the numbers of mentally retarded persons who marry, but it is commonly estimated that they do so much less frequently than nonretarded persons (Gendel, 1975). As a result, the most common and desired U.S. residential arrangement is often unattainable to mentally retarded persons. As Lakin et al. (1981) observed in their perceptive review of the early history of community adaptation in the United States, mentally retarded people not only need time to adapt well, they need the help of others. Because the majority of these people have only limited members of kinsmen who will support them, and because they have limited access to marital partners, the

[2]See *Current Population Reports: Population Characteristics,* Series P-20, No. 388; Household and Family Characteristics, March 1983, U.S. Department of Commerce, Bureau of the Census; and *Current Population Reports: Population Characteristics,* Series P-20, No. 389; Mental Status and Living Arrangements, March 1983, U.S. Department of Commerce, Bureau of the Census.

majority must content themselves with living alone or in a supervised residential facility.

Cooperative living arrangements have been overlooked as an option. In the course of our years of field research we have discovered a few instances of cooperative living arrangements in which three or more mentally retarded adults established their own group living patterns. For example, one young woman shared an apartment with a couple who subsequently married. This co-residing unit has survived the marriage (they all went on the honeymoon together); with the exception of sexual relations, which are exclusive to the married couple, these three people share virtually everything including all of the housekeeping chores and their incomes. In another example, a married couple and a young man rented a house together. They too shared their income and the housekeeping duties; this cooperative arrangement, too, lasted for several years until the single man moved out (Ward, 1983). There are two important points here. Cooperative living arrangements like these offer considerable autonomy in living because there is not direct supervision by a "nonretarded adult." As a result, living skills, including responsibility, may be learned in a more natural (i.e., less supervised) and more lasting fashion. Proof of this assertion, of course, would require a larger sample, and controlled, longitudinal research.

But there is a second, even more intriguing, possibility that derives from the symbiotic character of these living arrangements. Like "composite jobs," there can be composite residences in which the various skills, talents, and preferences of co-residing persons can be combined in a symbiotic way that allows people to live satisfactorily as a unit, even though they might lack the skills, attitudes, or motivation to do so as independent individuals. If this supposition is correct (and recall that we have studied only a few such arrangements), then communal living may be a long-term option and not just an "odd-couple" transitional or "learning" stage, preliminary to marriage or greater independence. Although there is now some resistance to communal living on the part of parents and service providers (sometimes based on uneasiness about the lack of supervision, the potential for "personality conflict," and the fear of sexual impropriety if the residence is coeducational), it might nevertheless be a worthwhile innovation for some agencies to promote communal living arrangements as an option within the currently available continuum of care. Some supervision would be required, especially in the initial "settling-in" stages, and shifts of residences from one home or apartment to another would surely occur. But whenever this kind of arrangement "works"—that is, becomes symbiotic—it could help mentally retarded adults to live more fully, on their own resources.

Positive Social Roles

The need to provide mentally retarded persons with more socially valued roles in life has been discussed for many years, but as Wolf Wolfensberger (1984) has recently reminded us once again, all too little has been accomplished in this regard. Since the ability to support oneself through work is so central to our value system, efforts to help mentally retarded persons toward more positively valued roles has focused on vocational training and placement, especially in competitive employment. Some progress has been made and hopefully still more progress lies ahead, because anyone who can become self-supporting is, by definition, no longer mentally retarded; more jobs equals lower prevalence.

I would like to suggest that we who are concerned about mentally retarded people, as well as society in general, are missing an opportunity to do much better in providing opportunities for more positive social roles. First, it is not true that all mildly retarded adults regard "having a job" as essential to their self-esteem, or even to their success in community living; for many, SSI is a perfectly acceptable alternative (Edgerton & Bercovici, 1976). Jobs are hard to find, generally involve unpleasant work activities, and are easily lost. If lost, SSI payments can be very difficult to reinstitute (Koegel & Kernan, 1983).

Nevertheless, the majority of mentally retarded adults with whom we have done research over the last two decades say that they want to help other people. After a lifetime of being dependent—of being the recipients of help from others—it is not surprising that these people would like to reciprocate. Many say that nothing would raise their self-esteem more than being able to help others, nothing, that is, unless it was being *paid* to help others. In my opinion, there are many important "helping" roles in our society that are now undermanned and could be filled by many mildly retarded adults. I'll mention only a few that have come to my attention because mildly retarded individuals in our research samples have volunteered for these jobs, have enjoyed the helping role, and have been successful at them in the judgment of their supervisors. That a few highly motivated persons were able to succeed in these roles does not prove that these roles could be filled by most mildly retarded persons. but it is my conviction that many mildly retarded persons would like to try these roles and that many could do so successfully.

First, there is an obvious need for expanded day care facilities for the children of working parents. I can see no reason why many mildly retarded adults, women more so than men, would not be willing and able to make a helpful contribution to day care centers. There are many roles to be filled in such centers; most would entail rewarding contact with children, and most would require little supervision by existing staff. Second, nursing homes throughout the country are understaffed; retarded persons could push wheelchairs, serve meals, help with various aspects of patient care, and perhaps most important, they could provide human contact and conversation to infirm and aging patients who are now so often alone. These roles could be filled by men as well as women. Third, retarded persons could help to serve meals to infirm persons who live at home; they could also provide other helpful services and could offer companionship. In southern California, several religious organizations offer these kinds of services and are in need of volunteer staff. Fourth, they could help with many jobs in what are now all-too-often moribund social and recreational programs designed for handicapped children or adults; mildly retarded patients used to fill roles like these in large state institutions. They could surely do so today in community-based programs.

Roles like these are available in every community; they do not have to be created, they already exist, but go unfilled. Most mentally retarded persons could find public transportation to jobs like these, although in some instances a shuttle-bus service might be required. I do not know how many mentally retarded persons would volunteer for "human service" jobs like these, but if the jobs were presented positively, and transportation were available, I believe that many would. With good supervision and a positive attitude by co-workers, they could make a contribution. But what if they were paid? I assume that these programs and facilities do not have the funds to hire more staff, but what if the jobs like these were tied to SSI? I realize that there are serious issues in tying SSI payments to work requirements, and I am no expert on the political or legal complications that such a proposal entails, but if SSI payments to mildly mentally retarded persons involved assignment to a work requirement like those I have mentioned, positive social roles would become positive jobs, good for the retarded adults' self-esteem and good for the recipients of their helping services. It need not cost any more to have socially useful jobs like these done than it costs now to pay mentally retarded persons to stay home where they fill no socially useful role of any kind.

CONCLUSION

I have called attention to a natural process in the course of which some mildly retarded adults, in time and with the support of others, "cure" themselves of mental retardation. That is, they no longer seek or receive services as mentally retarded persons, no longer think of themselves as retarded, and are not thought of as retarded by others with whom they interact. In the natural world, then, the prevalence of mild mental retardation tends to decrease with age. I have discussed some steps that I believe could reduce prevalence further. Obviously, my suggestions are speculative and without empirical testing will remain yet another set of programmatic urgings, the wisdom of which can legitimately be questioned.

But whether my specific recommendations are the best ones is less important than my basic point. That point is that even if we assume that mildly retarded persons have some as yet unidentifiable central nervous system impairment that limits their abilities to learn or to solve problems as rapidly or as well as most people, it is clearly possible for many of these people to live with a minimum of help from others, and, as is too often overlooked, for them to make contributions to others in return. It is also obvious that we can define everyone in this population as intellectually incompetent and we can easily restrict their opportunities to socially disvalued roles.

Without for a moment suggesting that we as a society should not intensify our efforts to reduce the *incidence* of mild mental retardation by eliminating those conditions that are known to put a developing fetus or a young child at risk, we must also realize that the *prevalence* of mild mental retardation can and does vary as a direct function of social circumstances and cultural beliefs, and it is to these social circumstances and beliefs that we must look if we also wish to prevent or reverse the prevalence rate of mental retardation.

REFERENCES

Arbitman-Smith, R., Haywood, H. C., & Bransford, J. D. (1984). Assessing cognitive change. In P. H. Brooks, R. Sperber, & C. McCauley (Eds.), *Learning and cognition in the mentally retarded* (pp. 433–471). Hillsdale, NJ: Lawrence Erlbaum Associates.

Baumeister, A. A. (1984). Some methodological and conceptual issues in the study of cognitive processes with retarded people. In P. H. Brooks, R. Sperber, & C. McCauley (Eds.), *Learning and cognition in the mentally retarded* (pp. 1–38). Hillsdale, NJ: Lawrence Erlbaum Associates.

Bercovici, S. M. (1983). *Barriers to normalization: The restrictive management of retarded persons.* Baltimore: University Park Press.

Butterfield, E. C. (1983). To cure cognitive deficits of mentally retarded persons. In F. J. Menolascino, R. Neman, & J. A. Stark (Eds.), *Curative aspects of mental retardation: Biomedical and behavioral advances* (pp. 203–221). Baltimore: Paul H. Brookes Publishing Co.

Campione, J. C., & Brown, A. L. (1977). Memory and metamemory development in educable retarded children. In R. V. Kail, Jr., & J. W. Hagan (Eds.), *Perspectives on the development of memory and cognition* (pp. 367–406). Hillsdale, NJ: Lawrence Erlbaum Associates.

Clarke, A. D. B., & Clarke, A. M. (1977). Prospects for prevention and amelioration of mental retardation: A guest editorial. *American Journal of Mental Deficiency, 81,* 523–533.

Cobb, H. (1972). *The forecast of fulfillment: A review of research on predictive assessment of the adult retarded for social and vocational adjustment.* New York: Teacher's College Press.

Edgerton, R. B. (1981). Crime, deviance and normalization: Reconsidered. In R. H. Bruininks, C. Meyers, B. Sigford, & K. Lakin (Eds.), *Deinstitutionalization and community adjustment of mentally retarded people* (pp. 145–166). Washington, DC: Monograph of the American Association on Mental Deficiency, No. 4.

Edgerton, R. B. (1982). Deinstitutionalizing the mentally retarded: An example of values in conflict. In A. Johnson, O. Grusky, & B. Raven (Eds.), *Contemporary health services: A social science perspective* (pp. 221–235). Boston: Auburn House.

Edgerton, R. B. (1983). Failure in community adaptation: The relativity of assessment. In K. Kernan, M. Begab, & R. Edgerton (Eds.), *Environments and behavior:*

The adaptation of mentally retarded persons (pp. 123–143). Baltimore: University Park Press.

Edgerton, R. B. (1984). Mental retardation: An anthropologists's changing view. In B. Blatt & R. Morris (Eds.), *Perspectives in special education: Personal orientations* (pp. 125–156). Glenview, IL: Scott-Foresman.

Edgerton, R. B. (1986). A case of delabeling: Some practical and theoretical implications. In L. Langness & H. Levine (Eds.), *Culture and retardation: Life histories of mildly retarded persons in American society* (pp. 101–126). The Netherlands: Reidel.

Edgerton, R. B., & Bercovici, S. (1976). The cloak of competence—years later. *American Journal of Mental Deficiency, 80,* 485–497.

Feuerstein, R., Rand, Y., Hoffman, M., & Miller, R. (1980). *Instrumental enrichment: An intervention program for cognitive modifiability.* Baltimore: University Park Press.

Gendel, E. S. (1975). *Sex education of the mentally retarded child in the home.* Arlington, TX: National Association for Retarded Citizens.

Gould, S. J. (1981). *The mismeasure of man.* New York: W. W. Norton.

Granat, K., & Granat, S. (1973). Below-average intelligence and mental retardation. *American Journal of Mental Retardation, 78,* 27–32.

Granat, K., & Granat, S. (1978). Adjustment of intellectually below-average men not identified as mentally retarded. *Scandinavian Journal of Psychology, 19,* 41–51.

Grossman, H. J. (Ed.). (1983). *Classification in mental retardation.* Washington, DC: American Association on Mental Deficiency.

Gruenberg, E. M. (1964). Epidemiology. In H. A. Stevens & R. Reber (Eds.), *Mental retardation* (pp. 259–306). Chicago: The University of Chicago Press.

Halpern, A. S., Close, D. W., & Nelson, D. J. (1985). *On my own: The impact of semi-independent living programs for adults with mental retardation.* Unpublished manuscript.

Haywood, H. C., Meyers, E., & Switzky, H. N. (1982). Mental retardation. *Annual Review of Psychology, 33,* 309–342.

Haywood, H. C., & Wachs, T. D. (1981). Intelligence, cognition, and individual differences. In M. Begab, H. Haywood & H. Garber (Eds.), *Psychosocial influences in retarded performance: Vol. I. Issues and theories in development* (pp. 95–126). Baltimore: University Park Press.

Jackson, R. (1977). Post school adjustment of the mentally retarded: A critical note on the Nebraskan longitudinal survey of Baller, Charles and Miller. *Journal of Mental Deficiency, 21,* 273–281.

Kaufman, S. Z. (1980). A mentally retarded daughter educates her mother. *Exceptional Parent, 10,* 17–22.

Koegel, P. K., & Kernan, K. T. (1983). Issues affecting the involvement of mildly retarded individuals in competitive employment. In K. T. Kernan, M. Begab, & R. Edgerton (Eds.), *Environments and behavior: The adaptation of mentally retarded persons* (pp. 173–192). Baltimore: University Park Press.

Lakin, K. C., Bruininks, R. H., & Sigford, B. H. (1981). Early perspectives on the community adjustment of mentally retarded people. In R. H. Bruininks, M. Begab, & R. Edgerton (Eds.), *Deinstitutionalization and community adjustment of mentally retarded people.* Washington, DC: Monograph of the American Association on Mental Deficiency, No. 4.

Lave, J., Murtaugh, M., & de la Rocha, O. (1984). The dialectical constitution of arithmetic practice. In B. Rogoff & J. Lave (Eds.), *Everyday cognition: Its development in social context.* Cambridge, MA: Harvard University Press.

Levine, H. G., & Langness, L. L. (1985). Everyday cognition among mildly mentally retarded adults: An ethnographic approach. *American Journal of Mental Deficiency, 90,* 18–26.

McCarver, R. B., & Craig, E. M. (1974). Placement of the retarded in the community: Prognosis and outcome. In N. R. Ellis (Ed.), *International review of research in mental retardation* (Vol. 7, pp. 146–207). New York: Academic Press.

Menolascino, F. J., Neman, R., & Stark. J. A. (1983). *Curative aspects of mental retardation: Biomedical and behavioral advances.* Baltimore: Paul H. Brookes Publishing Co.

Meyers, C. E., Nihira, K., & Zetlin, A. (1979). The measurement of adaptive behavior. In N. Ellis (Ed.), *Handbook of mental deficiency* (2nd ed., pp. 431–481). Hillsdale, NJ: Lawrence Erlbaum Associates.

Ramey, C. T., Campbell, F. A., & Finkelstein, N. W. (1984). Course and structure of intellectual development in children at high risk for developmental retardation. In P. H. Brooks, R. Sperber, and C. McCauley (Eds.), *Learning and cognition in the mentally retarded* (pp. 419–432). Hillsdale, NJ: Lawrence Erlbaum Associates.

Ramey, C. T., & Finkelstein, N. W. (1981). Psychosocial mental retardation: A biological and social coalescence. In M. Begab, H. Haywood, & H. Garber (Eds.), *Psychosocial influences in retarded performance: Vol. I. Issues and theories in development* (pp. 65–92). Baltimore: University Park Press.

Rubin, L. B. (1976). *World of pain: Life in the working-class family.* New York: Basic Books.

Ward, T. W. (1983). *Living together alone: Symbiosis as an adaptive strategy among mildly retarded adults.* Unpublished M.A. paper. Department of Anthropology, University of California, Los Angeles.

Williams, R. D., & Ewing, S. (1981). Consumer roulette: The shopping patterns of mentally retarded persons. *Mental Retardation, 19,* 145–149.

Wolfensberger, W. (1984). Social role valorization: A proposed new term for the principle of normalization. *Mental Retardation, 21,* 234–239.

Wortis, J. (1970). Poverty and retardation. In J. Wortis (Ed.), *Mental retardation: An annual review* (Vol. 1). New York: Brunner/Mazel.

Zigler, E. (1978). National crisis in mental retardation research: An editorial. *American Journal of Mental Deficiency, 83,* 1–8.

Zigler, E. (1984). A developmental theory on mental retardation. In B. Blatt & R. J. Morris (Eds.), *Perspectives in special education: Personal orientations* (pp. 173–209). Glenview, IL: Scott, Foresman.

Zigler, E., Balla, D., & Hodapp, R. (1984) On the definition and classification of mental retardation. *American Journal of Mental Deficiency, 89,* 215–230.

Chapter 13

Multidimensional Approaches to Reversing Mild Mental Retardation Labels

Louis Rowitz

The issue of "cure" is a complex one. In a preceding volume, Stark (1983) defined cure as "significantly increasing the current level of intellectual functioning and the concomitant level of social adaptation" (p. 2). Stark also tied the concept of cure to efforts related to secondary prevention. In this chapter, it is my intention to expand the meaning of cure and to show that "cure" can be seen from a number of different perspectives.

The idea of cure is strongly dependent upon the definition of the problem. The definition of the problem is dependent not only on the physical and behavioral manifestations of the problem, but also on the interpretation of these manifestations by individuals trained in different conceptual and professional orientations. For example, a physician will view an individual in one way because his or her orientation is toward certain physical signs and symptoms of a problem, whereas a psychologist will look at behavior that deviates from a defined norm. The nonclinician will look beyond the individual to observe sociological, economic, cultural, and other global effects of individual behavior.

With regard to mental retardation, each professional group views prevention and cure from its own disciplinary perspective. There is rarely a crossover between these perspectives as each group attempts to dominate a discipline-oriented field with its own theoretical and conceptual perspective. Thus, each professional group incorporates its narrow definition of the problem and thus biases its discussions of cure and its ramifications. This is not to imply that major breakthroughs do not occur within a field, but rather that additional major breakthroughs cannot occur unless interdisciplinary activities develop.

In a recent paper on prevention (Rowitz, 1986), some of these arguments were discussed. To begin with, prevention must entail more than medical intervention if prevention is really going to be a viable goal of professionals working in the field of mental retardation. Second, a multiprofessional approach should be taken if prevention activities are to succeed. Thus, no one professional group should dominate in the areas of mental retardation prevention. Professionals from all human service disciplines must work together on the development and implementation of prevention policies and programs. The ultimate goals are to lessen the incidence and thus the total prevalence of mental retardation and also to improve the quality of life of those people who have already been labeled mentally retarded. If we are to improve our cure rates for people with mental retardation, multiprofessional efforts are essential.

In this chapter I conceptually expand the approaches to studying the curative aspects of mental retardation. Also, I look at the general question of reversal of diagnosis as a type of cure. Case history information from a small group of people and their families as they relate their experiences over a 25-year period is reviewed. The discussion concludes with a brief summary.

CONCEPTUAL APPROACHES TO CURE

Most discussion of the three levels of prevention present these concepts in a linear fashion. Primary prevention refers to actions that take place prior to the onset of a disease or a social problem in order to stop the problem from occurring or to modify its course (Goldston, 1977). Primary prevention is prevention in the true sense of the word. It may be undertaken by physicians to prevent biological problems from occurring, teachers to prevent educational problems from occurring, social scientists to prevent psychosocial or societal problems from occurring, and so on in many other fields (Rowitz, 1986). Price, Bader, and Ketterer (1980) defined secondary prevention as activities directed at individuals who show early signs or symptoms of a medical or social problem. Stark (1983) has argued that intervention and treatment at the secondary level may lead to cure. Lastly, tertiary programs refer to rehabilitation programs that may improve the ability of individuals to survive in the community and also may prevent some disabilities from becoming worse (Price et al., 1980; Rowitz, 1986).

Even the previous discussion gives the impression that the three levels of prevention are separate and occur at three different locations. If curative activities are to increase, then prevention activities need to be reviewed in a more integrated fashion. Figure 1 shows the relationship between prevention and cure. Here, the relationship is shown in a circular manner in order to demonstrate that prevention activities are interactive. All primary prevention activities, with either a positive or negative effect, will impact on the entire

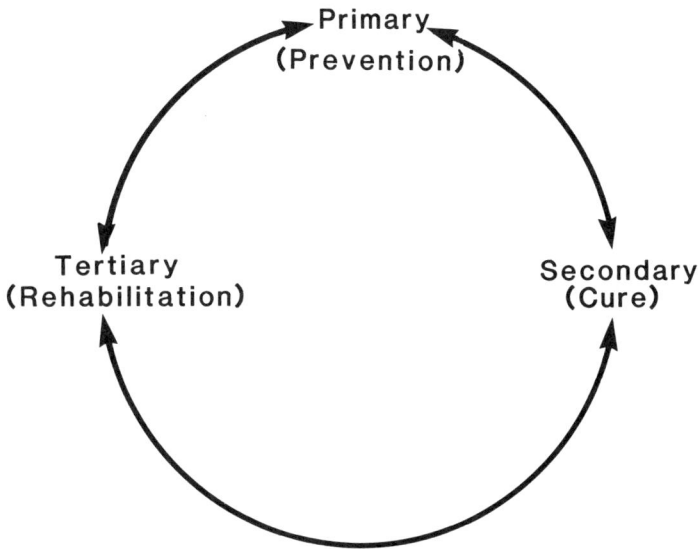

Figure 1. Relationship between prevention and cure.

social fabric of society. For instance, if we were to have a breakthrough on the prevention of some type of mental retardation, no new cases of that disorder would be referred to the professionals at the secondary or tertiary level. These professionals would continue to serve existing cases but would need to re-define or designate a new population to serve in the future. The primary prevention breakthrough would also give clues to secondary prevention re-search and service, possibly leading to cures for people with the specific disorder.

Secondary prevention services are aimed at improving the quality of life of people with a disorder or disability. They want either to halt the problems that they treat or to increase the adaptational capacity of people with the problem. For example, some early intervention programs are directed at in-creasing the cognitive ability and the socioenvironmental adjustment of the individual with mental retardation through the experiences with the educa-tional system. This, it is hoped, will eventually lead to success in living in the community over time. If early intervention programs are successful, the im-pact on the primary prevention level will occur, which in turn will lead to information that will help the primary prevention professionals in their at-tempts to prevent the problems in the first place.

Tertiary prevention workers are also concerned with improving the quali-ty of life of their clients. With the improvement in rehabilitation strategies and methods in recent years, we have learned much about the skills of individuals with handicaps. This information should aid both the work on prevention and on cure. Thus, the process of care from prevention to early treatment and rehabilitation must be seen as part of an integrated process that gives feedback to workers at various points of the cycle.

Prevention activities must be seen as a multiprofessional process. This is true for primary, secondary, and tertiary forms of activity. Also, in the specific arena of "cure," an interdisciplinary perspective is needed to understand as well as to advance our work on mental retardation. This interdisciplinary process is demonstrated in the diagram presented in Figure 2. Problems and solutions are defined differently in the biomedical, psychological, sociological, and educational area. In addition, each sphere is also governed by separate operating theories and methodologies. For example, the biomedical sphere is governed by the medical model and the psychological sphere generally follows a behavioral model. The sociological model follows a perspective

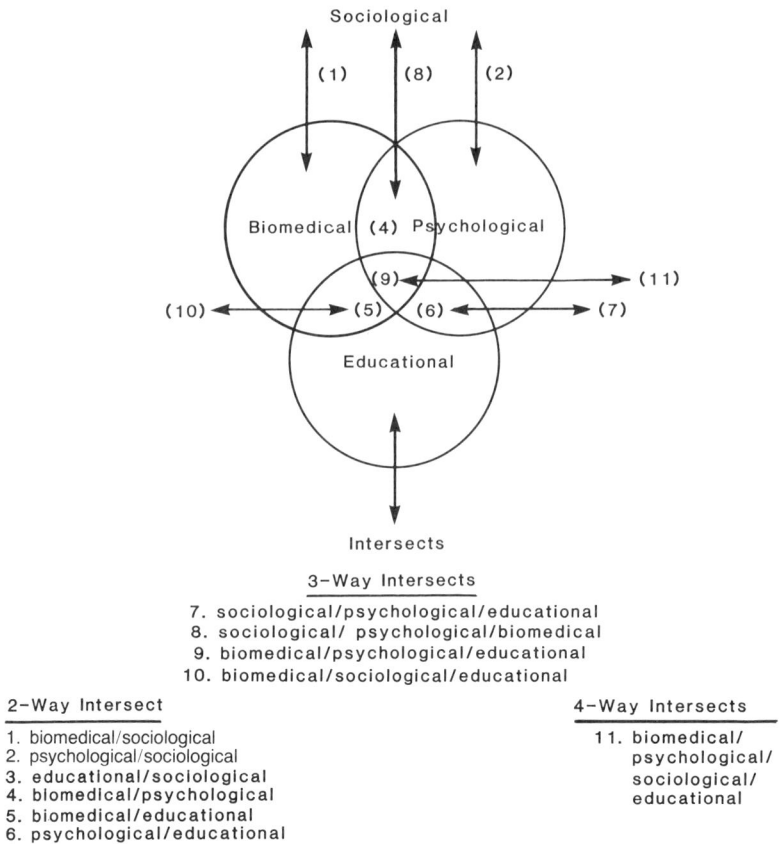

3-Way Intersects

7. sociological/psychological/educational
8. sociological/ psychological/biomedical
9. biomedical/psychological/educational
10. biomedical/sociological/educational

2-Way Intersect

1. biomedical/sociological
2. psychological/sociological
3. educational/sociological
4. biomedical/psychological
5. biomedical/educational
6. psychological/educational

4-Way Intersects

11. biomedical/
    psychological/
    sociological/
    educational

Figure 2.   Interdisciplinary perspectives on cure.

that looks at the mechanisms of social organizations. This is a somewhat simplistic explanation in that each sphere also includes a number of competing theories of explanation. Each sphere is also concerned with cure. This has been successfully presented previously (Menolascino, Neman, & Stark, 1983). Thus, we are able to review much literature on the biomedical issues related to cure, psychological issues related to cure, and so on.

Figure 2 demonstrates that curative issues also intersect spheres. There can be curative breakthroughs at the intersects of: 1) biomedical/sociological, 2) psychological/sociological, 3) educational/sociological, 4) biomedical/psychological, 5) biomedical/educational, and 6) psychological/educational spheres. In addition, 7) early intervention programs operate in the psychological/educational area and may impact on the sociological/psychological area (sociological/psychological/educational intersect). Other three-area intersects include: 8) sociological/psychological/biomedical, 9) biomedical/psychological/educational, and 10) biomedical/sociological/educational. As can be seen with this figure, each new intersect offers new opportunities for collaboration as well as new perspectives on definition of problems and their potential cures. Finally, cures are possible at the intersect of all four areas. This is the multiprofessional interdisciplinary approach to cure. In addition, it is synergistic in that the end result of the collaboration of all areas is more comprehensive in effect than the sum of the parts. This level of collaboration is the foundation for concerns with ethics and public policy. It is in reality a systems level approach to cure.

Curative efforts lead not only to improvements in primary, secondary, and tertiary prevention activities, but these efforts also lead to possible reversals in labels of mild mental retardation that have already been applied. Moreover, it is possible to have a label of mild mental retardation in the educational sector but to be considered normal in the sociological (community) sector (Rowitz, 1981). This phenomenon has been called "the 6-hour retarded person." When the labeled individual leaves school, he or she often loses the mild mental retardation label. However, these people may still have failures in community adaptation in adulthood as a result of prior experiences within the school and the community. Thus, at the same time that a label reversal of mild mental retardation occurs, other labels become attached to this individual because of difficulties in community living. These problems can be viewed at the intersect of sociological/psychological/educational (7) functioning. At this intersect, curative activities will need to be concerned with training that increases the chances for successful life course community living.

In the remainder of this chapter, case histories are presented that document label reversals in order to show the complexities of cure at the intersect of the four sectors discussed in this section.

DOCUMENTATION OF REVERSALS
IN LABELS OF MENTAL RETARDATION

Although it is possible to document that a label reversal of mental retardation has occurred and to categorize the reversal as a "cure," it may be that the reversal is due to a mistake in initial diagnosis. Placing responsibility for diagnostic mistakes is an exceedingly difficult process. However, a diagnostic mistake may lead to further testing, which might clarify problems in such a way that cures may occur when these cures might not have been possible without the early diagnostic mistakes. Moreover, changes in the American Association on Mental Deficiency Diagnostic Code in 1973, which dropped borderline mental retardation as a form of mental retardation, affected a large number of people who were labeled mentally retarded prior to 1973, but not afterward (Grossman, 1973). It is hard to argue that this is cure, but it becomes a form of cure in actual practice. Leaving school may also lead to dropping a label of mild mental retardation, which contributes to the fuzzy definition of "cure." If the school-labeled individuals succeed in community living and adaptation, then the school programs have trained these people well for community living and thus have brought about a "social cure."

In 1959, Farber undertook a study of retarded children and their families (Farber & Jenne, 1963), and Farber and I restudied these families in 1985–1986. In the restudy we found a few cases of children who had experienced a reversal in their mental retardation label between 1959 and 1986. These cases are presented in part below to demonstrate the principles presented in this chapter. Names and places in the cases are changed to protect the identity of families who agreed to participate in the study. It is clear from the following cases that mental retardation is a family affair.

Barbara is 40 years old and was labeled mildly mentally retarded early in life. Barbara had trouble with her eye-and-hand coordination and had difficulty in being tested. She had trouble through school academically. It became clear later that Barbara was not mentally retarded. Her sister and mother report in the following vignette on some of the ramifications of Barbara's problems.

> Mary (a sibling): "My sister is not retarded but was misdiagnosed in the old days. At age 40, Barbara wants to be retested. I have shied away from learning disabilities in my own career because I feel that psychologists can do a tremendous amount of damage when they misdiagnose. Barbara has had a tough life. I worry about what will happen to her when my mother dies and I will be solely responsible for her because I don't know how she will manage financially."
>
> Barbara's mother gives another side of the story. She points out that Barbara has been working at a state mental health facility for over 20 years. She began work as an institutional worker and has managed to move up in the system to a mental health technician position. Her mother says she is self-sufficient and has traveled extensively.
>
> Although Barbara has been hurt by her learning problems, she has been able to live successfully in the community. Whereas she started school in special educable mentally handicapped classes, she left high school at age 16 from a regular class. She did not feel

that school was for her. Thus, Barbara has been able to give up the mental retardation label and function normally, although with problems, in the community. In looking at Barbara's life, cure must be viewed from the perspective of her physical problem, the educational reevaluation and placement into regular classes, psychological issues of adjustment, and her ability to adjust to the community living as an adult (No. 11 intersect).

Another parent's testimony came in the form of a letter.

The mother said, ". . . (I) must state that my son now functions at a high level. His problem is hearing loss, visually handicapped and aphasia. He has difficulty in communicating.

When his father, who died in 1963, and I took part in the [1959] research, our son attended a school for retarded children because there was no other school that would accept him due to his multiple handicaps. Yet he was noticeably different than the other students.

I later remarried when my son was 24 and attending a special workshop. Later he had special training for his handicaps. [After the special training] my son was given a job with a state agency that mans cafeterias in public buildings. My son lived in an apartment with a young man of similar handicap over a period of ten years. They did a tremendous job.

My son is now moving to a special building for hearing impaired people. He is on his own, he travels alone, and has held a job for over twelve years. He has worked hard and made it."

In the above case, the man was labeled retarded as well as handicapped. The retarded label was eventually reversed although his visual and hearing problems remained. He learned how to function in the community. He received special training that aided him in his community adaptation (No. 10 intersect).

The final case to be discussed is a special one in which the individual whom I call David wrote an autobiographic response in which he describes what happened to him. What appears to be the situation in David's case, as well as in the one just discussed, is that some children with hearing defects and also learning problems were labeled mentally retarded in the late 1950s. This was prior to the major redefinition of problems to include a new category of problems called learning disabilities. Now David's comments:

"After birth, I constantly cried (no tears) just an irritating, screaming, uncontrollable gesture, moving head and arms about, seemingly without reason.

I had ear and throat infections constantly. I was on all sorts of medication . . . I couldn't sit up until I was seven months old.

My parents took me to a general practitioner. His diagnosis was that there was nothing physically wrong, but I was slow in development.

When I was three, I had a complete physical at a special child clinic by a neurologist. In his opinion, I was pretty alert and showed an I.Q. range of about 70 to 80.

In September of 1958 I was enrolled in a regular kindergarten class where the teachers thought I might be having a hearing loss."

In the succeeding pages of his autobiography David reports that he was falling behind in his academic work. It was not until he was 9 years old that he was placed in an ungraded class for the hearing impaired. He attended private parochial schools and began to perform at average levels. He had some academic problems in high school. His overall performance was average to below average. He became extremely active in athletics. He started dating. He graduated from high school. He eventually also graduated from a community college at age 23 and won the All-American Junior College Marathon. He eventually received his college degree in 1980 at the age 27. He has since gone back for advanced training for a teaching certificate in physical education.

David's work experiences are limited. He has done seasonal work and has worked summers. He was harassed on the job because of his hearing problems. In his early 30s David is just finishing school. He appears to have overcome his early diagnosis of mental retardation. He has proved his ability to handle academic work and has also been quite active in sports. In fact, he has even qualified for the Boston Marathon. David was a slow starter, but appears to be moving toward independent living. He is still self-conscious about his hearing aid and he has difficulty in communication. Yet, there is evidence of positive growth in spite of biomedical problems. His cure has occurred at the intersect of sociological (community)/psychological/educational sectors. The biomedical sector can be added if one counts the positive medical service experiences that have aided David in his adjustment to society.

CONCLUSIONS

In this chapter, a new model for the study of cure is presented. The model is based on viewing "cure" from an interdisciplinary perspective integrating information and findings from the biomedical, psychological, educational, and sociological dimensions. The chapter further looks at prevention as a circular rather than linear process with feedback between the prevention, cure, and rehabilitation areas. One aspect of cure that utilizes information from a multidimensional perspective relates to reversals in labels of mental retardation. Three cases are presented to show the beginnings of qualitative analysis of the conceptual model presented in this chapter. Refinements in the model are necessary, but I believe that an interdisciplinary perspective will increase our curative endeavors and have important public policy implications for people with mental retardation in the future.

REFERENCES

Farber, B., & Jenne, W. C. (1963). Family organization and parent-child communication: Parents and siblings of a retarded child. *Monographs of the Society for Research in Child Development, 28,* 1–78.

Goldston, S. E. (1977). Defining primary prevention. In G. W. Albee & J. M. Joffee (Eds.), *The issues: An overview of primary prevention* (pp. 7–17). Hanover, NH: University Park of New England.

Grossman, H. J. (Ed.). (1973). *Manual on terminology and classification in mental retardation.* Washington, DC: American Association on Mental Deficiency.

Menolascino, F. J., Neman, R., & Stark, J. A. (Eds.). (1983). *Curative aspects of mental retardation: Biomedical and behavioral advances.* Baltimore: Paul H. Brookes Publishing Co.

Price, R. K., Bader, B. C., & Ketterer, R. F. (1980). Prevention in community mental health: The state of the art. In R. K. Price, R. F. Ketterer, B. C. Bader, & J. Monahan (Eds.), *Prevention in mental health* (pp. 9–20). Beverly Hills, CA: Sage Publications.

Rowitz, L. (1981). A sociological perspective on labeling in mental retardation. *Mental Retardation, 19,* 47–51.

Rowitz, L. (1986). Multiprofessional perspectives on prevention. *Mental Retardation, 24*, 1–3.

Stark, J. (1983). The search for cures of mental retardation. In F. J. Menolascino, R. Neman, & J. A. Stark (Eds.), *Curative aspects of mental retardation: Biomedical and behavioral advances* (pp. 1–6). Baltimore: Paul H. Brookes Publishing Co.

APPLICATIONS AND FUTURE DIRECTIONS

Introduction

This book would not be complete without a chapter written by Dr. Allan Crocker. Few people are more respected for the dedication and genuine concern for individuals with mental retardation and their families than Dr. Crocker. As a pediatrician, he has been associated for over 30 years with one of the finest pediatric hospitals in the world, Boston's Children's Hospital, at which he is the Director of the Developmental Evaluation Clinic. His chapter on the "Dilemmas of the Mental Retardation Clinician: An Assignment for the Researcher" points out the clinician's difficulty in being concerned with the future while consumed with overwhelming responsibilities each day in clinical teaching or research. In essence, Dr. Crocker provides a blueprint for researchers to focus their attention in order to answer the applied questions that can directly help clinicians on a day-to-day basis. Most assuredly, this is what we must accomplish if we are to make any significant reduction in the prevalence of mental retardation.

Dr. Crocker provides a "slice" of his life in which he kept a log of his professional activities and responsibilities over a 2-week period. It is truly impressive what Dr. Crocker accomplished in this period of time and it serves as a reminder of our responsibility as researchers to provide research findings that can be easily utilized and acted upon. Finally, Dr. Crocker closes with an exhortation to researchers that lists 11 priority areas that he feels will make substantial contributions to preventing mental retardation at the primary, secondary, and tertiary levels.

The final chapter on the "Future Prospects for Curing Mental Retardation" by the coeditors is not so much a conclusion as it is a call for a beginning of a new trend in research in the prevention and curative intervention of mental retardation. The editors first discuss research prospects for the next 20 years by analyzing the contributions of both basic and applied research findings as they relate to this overall field. This heuristic and interdisciplinary process is exemplified by reviewing the individual contributions of all the various disciplines through their diagnostic and treatment approaches, with the end result being curative goals. It is hoped that the authors have shown how any one discipline could either by itself or in combination with other disciplines so significantly reverse the symptoms of mental retardation that an individual would no longer fit the criteria for mental retardation. It is also hoped that this chapter will help to spark this call for a national effort to achieve these goals and objectives through such a comprehensive approach so necessary for the future.

Chapter 14

Dilemmas of the Mental Retardation Clinician
An Assignment for The Researcher

Allen C. Crocker

Curative Aspects of Mental Retardation: Biomedical and Behavioral Advances, a preceding volume by Menolascino, Neman, and Stark (1983), was clearly dedicated to change. Speaking as it did of advances and amelioration, it served as a forum for research. The remarks of this chapter approach the process from the other direction; it is an entreaty directed to the researcher from the clinician. Perhaps it would be more appropriate to say that a ''challenge'' rather than an ''assignment'' is being extended to the researcher, as the word ''challenge'' was used by Menolascino (1977) with its implications also of sharing, joining, and understanding.

The concept of a clinician, as utilized here, is that of a worker who is busy with service. In the field of mental retardation, such a person is often salaried, and not uncommonly is worried about the stability of such support. By and large, clinicians in the 1980s have left behind the philosophy of nihilism that characterized the scene 20 years ago. Most clinicians get some in-service educational opportunities, but still retain a healthy bewilderment on many issues. The clinician is expected to face directly the concerns of the client and of the family, and so is obliged to have feelings of accountability for the state of the art. Clinicians are in a key position to perceive that the field has many knowledge gaps.

For a credible analysis of the dilemmas experienced by the mental retardation clinician, there was a requirement to be specific and timely. An efficiency in this regard would be to use myself as the clinician of reference. The format of scientific reports discourages the use of first-person pronouns, but at least one could in this way assure authenticity and clearance. Furthermore, I

This work was supported in part by Project 928, Division of Maternal and Child Health, and Project 03DD0135/13, Administration on Developmental Disabilities, Department of Health and Human Services.

357

qualify as a clinician in that I am busy with service, salaried, worried, hopeful, bewildered, in direct contact with families, and well aware of the gaps. So I ask the reader's pardon for my reporting in such a personal fashion.

I work in the Developmental Evaluation Clinic (DEC), a study unit for persons with developmental disabilities, located in the Children's Hospital in Boston. The DEC is one of the 52 University Affiliated Facilities (UAFs) for mental retardation and developmental disabilities, a network of academically oriented training and service units, most of which are partially supported by federal funds (Division of Maternal and Child Health and/or the Administration on Developmental Disabilities). The DEC provides diagnostic, program-planning, and specialty program services for children and adults, as well as pre- and in-service training and technical assistance in this field.

The factor of timeliness in the tabulation of clinician concerns was secured by employing the 2-week period of April 22 to May 5, 1985, ending 1 week before the Nebraska conference, for review. In that interval I kept a log of my professional activities. Those that related to administration, personnel issues, and housekeeping for the UAF, as well as those involved with clinical issues not in the mental retardation area, were separated. The remainder constitutes an inventory of pursuits in the retardation field. These will be analyzed for material relevant to the assignment (or challenge) for the researcher. May I state again that this sample is personal and limited, not universal, but it can be defended as truly representative.

Actually, this dialogue with researchers is in concurrence with the legislative description of the required activities of a UAF. In Section 102(10) of P.L. 95-602 (the Rehabilitation, Comprehensive Services, and Developmental Disabilities Amendments of 1978), it advocates "providing researchers and government agencies sponsoring service-related research with information on the needs for further research."

TWO WEEKS OF A MENTAL RETARDATION CLINICIAN'S ACTIVITIES

The topical areas that came into consideration in this period, in discussions or in patient service, are presented in five categories. Material covered is on-site (the DEC), elsewhere in the medical center or in the city, and at the Down Syndrome State-of-the-Art Conference.

Meetings/Discussions with UAF Colleagues

Design of a Prader-Willi Syndrome Clinic   A group of professionals in the DEC (psychology, nutrition, medicine, physical therapy, and vocational rehabilitation) is in the process of establishing a formal interdisciplinary clinical service for these young people and their families. About 40 such patients have come to our attention recently, and their needs are very broad. Beyond the direct clinical assignment, there is a hope to establish a better understanding of the intrinsic elements—such as genetic factors, pathophysiology of the hyperphagia, nutritional management of obesity, motor function problems inherent in the syndrome, cognitive and emotional development, and educational and vocational needs (Mitchell, Howard, Wharton, Osborne, & Van Gelder, 1985). Regrettably, third-party reimbursements will not cover all of the associated personnel and other costs, and grant support has not yet become available.

Growth of Children with Down Syndrome An earlier study from the DEC (Cronk, 1978) provided the first systematic normative charts on the growth of children with Down syndrome, covering from birth to 3 years of age. A plan is now underway to obtain interim and current information on that early population and others, to complete the graphs of growth into the teen years.

Education of the Public A meeting of the DEC Advisory Committee reviewed the facility's current activities and potential in the area of educational outreach to the general public. It was agreed that every center has an obligation to extend accurate information on topics such as an understanding of exceptionality, resources for services, programs for prevention, and new techniques for diagnosis and treatment. The possible modes include the print media, television, school curricula, hotlines, publications, and legislator education. A quandary arises because of the need for expert help if this work is to be done effectively.

Down Syndrome Early Language Study Plans are being discussed to join with Dr. Jon Miller of the UAF in Madison, Wisconsin, to learn more about language acquisition, utilizing the children and families in our Down Syndrome Early Consultation Program.

Data Systems for the Clinic A DEC staff meeting addressed our continuing perplexity about the extent of demographic and clinical data that is appropriate to collect on our service population, and the techniques by which this is best done. There are database requirements for the funding agencies, for the medical center, and for potential use in clinical investigation. This will cover over 2,000 active clients per year. Another committee was appointed.

New England Regional Genetics Group (NERGG) Plans NERGG, as it is called, is a coalition of genetics service providers, public health planners, and consumer groups from the six New England states, founded by and based in our UAF (Crocker, 1984a). A Steering Committee meeting agreed on the advisability of devoting a major session at the next annual meeting to the regional applications of the ''new genetics'' (DNA probes, etc.) (see Latt, Kurnit, Bruns, Schreck, Morton, Kunkel, Lalande, Aldridge, Neve, Tantravahi, Kanda, Lindner, & Meryash, 1985; and Woo, Lidsky, Guttler, Chandra, & Robson, 1983).

Adoption of Handicapped Children A discussion was held to plan an upcoming presentation at the American Association on Mental Deficiency annual meeting on the experiences of the DEC's ''Adoption Collaborative.''

This program, carried out jointly with Project IMPACT, a special needs adoption agency in Boston, has been bringing particular supports to families adopting children with developmental disabilities, training related state agency personnel, and systematically reviewing the factors in 100 previous successful adoptions of this type.

Down Syndrome Early Intervention Program Reunion In 1970 the DEC had begun one of the first specific programs for early guidance of families who had children with Down syndrome from birth to 3 years of age. Originally started as an evaluation of the effects of 5-hydroxytryptophan and pyridoxine on motor development, it grew to encompass all aspects of "The Young Child with Down Syndrome." When the book of that title (Pueschel, 1984) finally became available, a reunion was held so that the involved families could have access to the book. This took place on Sunday, May 5, 1985, and proved to be a heartening social occasion (young people included).

Meetings/Discussions with Hospital Colleagues

Sexual Abuse of Children Consideration was given to the relevance of a project on sexual abuse (Newberger & Newberger, 1984; Watson, 1985). The DEC has been concerned for several years with the special vulnerability of children with developmental disabilities and with the difficulties of limited parents.

Planning for Ambulatory Services There was a meeting among several of the diverse programs in the hospital that have issues of child development in their purview, regarding closer collaboration for service and training. The developmental field is so broad that it is sometimes a large assignment to bring together, for example, work on mental retardation with that on the effects of divorce, but there are common interests.

Home Health Care for Children with Chronic Illness A planning group met to discuss the increasing hospital commitment to supports in the home for the care of children who have disabilities or chronic illness. The DEC feels a particular interest in this important service area (see Kohrman, 1984; Mackta, 1984), particularly for households where there are children with serious multiple handicaps or progressive central nervous system disorders.

Home Visit Plans for NICU Graduates The Children's Hospital is one of the eight sites for the Robert Wood Johnson Foundation's "Infant Health and Development Program." As a member of the local group's Advisory Committee, I established plans to join with their staff during some of the follow-up home visits for preterm infants.

Possible Outside Donation for Treatment Program In this period I had a delightful surprise when a visitor indicated contact with a philanthropist who might be willing to provide funding for a new program, perhaps in the area of early intervention. This lead will be thoughtfully followed through.

Design of Birth Defects Service An alliance is being formed between the hospital's Genetics Division and the DEC for the creation of a coordinated developmental, clinical, and scientific service for the study and support of children with multiple congenital anomaly syndromes and certain genetic disorders. This is designed to bring previously fragmented services together, particularly incorporating key surgical specialties as needed.

Cognitive Styles in Underachieving Children A discussion was held with an educator in another clinic who is interested in the problem-solving methods of young people with perceptual handicaps but normal intelligence.

Research Center Executive Committee A meeting was held on May 2 of the Core Executive Committee, of which I am a member, for the hospital's Mental Retardation Research Center (one of the 13 NICHD-supported units of this type). Consideration was given to the sharing of resources, computer services, acceptance of a new investigator, and preparation of a renewal application.

Adaptive Environments Services Plans were discussed for a possible office and demonstration area within the new hospital building for the Adaptive Environments Center, Inc., an allied facility that could provide assistance to families of disabled children in development of adaptive equipment, modifications of the home, and enhancement of the environment.

Studies in Ambulatory Services Area A planning session occurred for the Department of Pediatrics on potential supports for investigations in the various outpatient programs, including studies in toxicology, maternal PKU, SIDS, school placements, rehabilitation engineering, and the rhythmic behavior of small infants.

Meetings/Discussions with Outside Colleagues

Self-Advocacy Conference I agreed with plans to lead a workshop on marriage and sexuality at an upcoming conference for adults with mental retardation, sponsored by the Massachusetts Association for Retarded Citizens. The "Yes, we can . ." theme of these conferences represents an important new force.

Prevention Coalition A discussion was held on the formation of a "National Coalition for the Prevention of Mental Retardation," with joining by the American Academy of Pediatrics, the American Association on Mental Deficiency, the American Association of University Affiliated Programs, the Association for Retarded Citizens of the United States, and the President's Committee on Mental Retardation. This group plans to present a common voice on concerns for the prevention of developmental disabilities in the country as a whole, with projects on information sharing, marketing of innovative prevention strategies, preparation of joint resolutions and policy papers, and assistance to states in the preparation of state prevention plans.

Network of Genetics Networks There was also a discussion of forming a National Genetics Public Health Consortium, which would bring together the interests and activities of the New England Regional Genetics Group and the seven other regional genetics projects.

Maternal and Child Health Training Programs The feasibility was considered of the DEC joining with the UAF at the University of Rochester in the building of in-service training programs in maternal and child health for Title V program people in the various state health departments of Regions I and II.

The Center for Creative Arts Therapies (CCAT) The Program Development Committee of the CCAT met to plan establishment of scholarships for various clients (young people, old people, disabled people) in art, music, and dance therapy in Boston.

Iron-Deficiency Anemia A pediatrician from Australia, who has been carrying out a project on the effects of iron deficiency on infant behavior and learning, stopped by for a visit and discussion on this topic.

Interdisciplinary Teams I participated in the videotaping of a discussion on the strengths and weaknesses of interdisciplinary clinical teams in developmental centers, for Project BRIDGE of the American Academy of Pediatrics.

Contacts with the Press Articles related to the DEC appeared in the *Boston Magazine* on a court settlement against an obstetrician in the circumstances of a child with multiple anomalies and in the *Boston Globe* on Alzheimer disease complicating Down syndrome.

Student Meeting on Prevention Programs A teaching session with medical students on the subject of prevention of mental retardation inevitably came around to inquiry about accountability in prevention programs. These considerations are limited by the many unknowns in our understanding of the causation of retardation and by the difficulty in accurate determination of incidence and prevalence figures (Crocker, 1982, 1984b).

Massachusetts Down Syndrome Congress On April 27, I gave a talk at the annual meeting of this parents group on "An Overview of the State of the Art with Respect to Down Syndrome," reporting on the recent national conference. Parents are gratified by some gains in knowledge, but restless about areas where our comprehension is incomplete.

Patient-Related Activities

The following examples of my direct patient and family contacts in this period are given to illustrate the functions and interests of a mental retardation clinician in a tertiary center.

Clinic Visits J., 6 months, GMl-gangliosidosis, discussion of bone marrow transplant; R., 14 months, Canavan disease, procurement of home health care; J., 18 months, ? Mucolipidosis IV, diagnostic concern; A., 2 years, Sandhoff disease, gastrostomy tube, seizures; J., 5 years, ? autism, behavioral training program concerns; S., 7 years, leukodystrophy of unknown origin, ? hereditary syndrome; H., 35 years, mild M.R., arrangement of transportation services; plus four children in the Down Syndrome Early Consultation Program (concerns with heart disease, early intervention, parent adjustments).

Phone Calls A., 2 years, Hurler syndrome, discussion of goals in early intervention program; C., 3 years, microcephaly, litigation in progress; F., 16 years, Hunter syndrome, ? congestive heart failure; L., 22 years, Hunter syndrome, day program plans; J., 25 years, Hunter syndrome, risk of dental repair with anesthesia.

Postmortem Review Y., 6 months, Down syndrome, unexpected death 3 weeks after surgical repair of AV canal.

Quandaries in Diagnostic Coding (Difficult decisions while processing DEC primary assessment patients' records, using ICD-9-DM, particularly in relation to probable causation of developmental disability.) D., 4 years, possible Prader-Willi syndrome, normal chromosomes, unusual behavior; J., 5 years, possible cerebral dysgenesis, in picture of cerebral palsy, hearing impairment, high myopia, failure to thrive; E., 8 years, learning disabilities of unknown origin, with emotional disturbance; S., 10 years, placenta previa with vaginal bleeding, prematurity; R., 13 years, erythroblastosis but no evidence of true kernicterus; M., 17 years, first called autism, but now with spasticity and scoliosis.

Down Syndrome State-of-the-Art Conference

During this same interval, on April 23–25, 1985, an international conference was held in Boston, during which I was a planner and moderator. This was organized by the National Down Syndrome Congress and sponsored by the National Institute of Handicapped Research. It was designed (and titled) to be a "state-of-the-art" listing of knowledge regarding Down syndrome, in the areas of biomedicine, education, psychosocial aspects, and community living. Hence, the participating clinicians (and investigators) documented, with much vigor, where the effort must now come from in future research. The proceedings have now been published (Pueschel, Tingey, Rynders, Crocker, & Crutcher, 1987). Some representative dilemmas can be mentioned here.

The etiology of nondisjunction (leading to trisomy 21) remains unsolved. Thuline mentioned Warkany's earlier list of 30 hypotheses; Jagiello described the five "most durable theories" (production line, persistent nucleoli, hormonal imbalance, delayed fertization, and relaxed selection) plus 16 others to consider, many built on the observation of the role of maternal age. Regarding gene effects from the trisomy, Patterson and Epstein listed those known to date on receptors, growth factors, enzymes, and transport (see Chapter 2 also). Kurnit speculated on pathogenesis by changes in cell-cell recognition and adhesiveness, affecting cell migration and causing hypoplasia. The uniformity around the world of the birth incidence was discussed by Holmes, who noted the possibility of securing more accurate prenatal risk measurement from analysis of maternal serum alpha-fetoprotein.

In the area of early intervention programs (Hanson, Bricker), more information is needed on the learning style in Down syndrome and on the most pertinent outcome measures for early intervention. The paucity of studies was deplored on the educational potential (including reading) for these children and on the effects of integration in school (Fredericks, Zadig). Miller commented on incomplete understanding of the patterns of language development and of the best language-learning environment. Appropriate goals in secondary education (productivity, integration, independence) can be visualized (Bellamy), but limited and segregated plans prevail nationally. Incomplete access to medical insight and support was noted by Perske and Dybwad. The pathological model commonly used in studies on family dynamics prompted Turnbull (educator and mother of a disabled child) to ask "Who are these researchers and why are they saying all these awful things about us?" Moses wondered about our knowledge on the maintenance and reinforcement of dreams. New studies on supported employment are changing the scene for work opportunity (Karan), and must continue. Gilhool and Nerney spoke of the importance of community-based residence programs. Research is needed in the health area (thyroid disease, resistance to infection, nutrition, aging, etc.), said Pueschel.

This special conference underlined the changing status of understanding and support for persons with Down syndrome; new information is at hand, but many critical elements are unfinished.

PATIENT POPULATION

A listing of the backgrounds of the patients seen in the Developmental Evaluation Clinic provides a profile of the cumulative experiences of the clinicians who work there. Table 1 presents the diagnostic classification of the primary referral patients (all ages, but principally children), who come for comprehensive interdisciplinary assessment, from schools, physicians, community agencies, residential programs, and so forth. Not included are those who are seen in special projects (PKU, Infant Follow-up, Down Syndrome Program, lipidoses and mucopolysaccharidoses, Prader-Willi, Work Experience Program, etc.).

The incidence figures (numbers and percent) reflect the encounters of a specialty service in a tertiary hospital; different numbers would pertain in a community clinic, a pediatrician's office, or a school district (Crocker & Nelson, 1983). It will be noted that the largest components are the prenatal influence syndromes, the environmental and behavioral problems, and those disabilities listed as of unknown origin. There is a moderate occurrence of

Table 1. Diagnostic classification of DEC patients referred for comprehensive assessment

		Number	Percent
I.	Hereditary issues	125	5
	Inborn errors of metabolism (aminoacidopathies, 16; mucopolysaccharidoses, 12; lipidoses, 6; galactosemia, 1)	36	
	Other hereditary syndromes (muscular dystrophy, neurofibromatosis, tuberous sclerosis, Laurence-Moon-Biedl syndrome, ichthyosis, fragile-X syndrome, other familial chromosomal abnormalities, etc.)	60	
	Familial retardation of probable polygenic origin	29	
II.	Early influences on embryonic development	860	32
	Sporadic chromosomal changes (Down syndrome, 219; other chromosomal anomalies, 34)	253	
	Multiple congenital anomalies "Prenatal influence" syndromes (includes congenital rubella, 36; C.I.D., 4; toxoplasmosis, 1; herpes, 2; congenital hypothyroidism, 6; and other syndromes—Williams, 11; Prader-Willi, 10; Rubinstein, 5; fetal alcohol, 5; Apert, 4; de Lange, 4; and Goldenhar, 2)	607	
III.	Other pregnancy problems and perinatal morbidity	291	11
	Fetal malnutrition (placental insufficiency, toxemia, drug addiction, maternal uterine cancer, multiple pregnancy)	31	
	Prematurity, neonatal asphyxia, hyperbilirubinenia, hypoglycemia, trauma	260	
IV.	Acquired childhood diseases	115	4
	Complications of infection (meningitis, 25; encephalitis, 25; pertussis, 1; varicella, 1)	63	
	Lead poisoning	1	
	Cranial trauma	27	
	Cerebral tumors	5	
	Cardiac arrest, asphyxiation	9	
V.	Environmental and behavioral problems	477	18
	Psychosocial deprivation	171	
	Parental neurosis, psychosis, character disorder	67	
	Emotional and behavioral disorders	90	
	Childhood psychosis, autism	149	
VI.	Unknown causes	823	30
	(Borderline to mild mental retardation, 434; moderate to profound, or unspecified, 389)		

Note. 1967–1984; $n = 3,756$ (2,691 shown to be retarded).

perinatal difficulties, but surprisingly few children had hereditary syndromes or postnatally acquired medical problems.

The situation that is coded as "unknown" has a number of possible backgrounds. The most common is that of multiple minor misfortunes (mildly preterm, young single parent, repeated infections, etc.), none of which can be considered ascendant, with additive effects likely. Another group has some neurological signs suggesting specific cortical involvement (seizures, muscle tone abnormalities, upgoing toes) but no events in the anamnesis with which this can be correlated. A final group has no clues at all, and is referred to locally as the "unknown unknowns."

Actually, the various assignments in Table 1 (regarding causation) are in part merely those of settings or timing. In practice the vast majority of those in Category II are also of unknown etiology. As assuredly as nondisjunction has obscure genesis, so do 90% or more of the congenital anomaly syndromes. Furthermore, the determinants of most of the behavioral syndromes, psychoses, and autism are not understood. These are indeed areas where the mental retardation clinician is poorly accommodated for responsibility in family counseling or planning for prevention.

COMPONENTS OF RELEVANCE TO RESEARCH

Two weeks of a mental retardation clinician's activities have thus been recorded, with some information about the background setting. From that experience, an enumeration can be made of issues that call for a continuing research approach. If a longer period of notation had been used, the list of issues would be longer. A general classification is provided first, and then particular priorities are indicated.

Etiology

Prenatal Influence　Improved understanding in the field of teratology, or disordered embryological development, can be said to be one of our largest areas of scientific deficiency. The children appear with microcephaly or with multiple congenital anomalies at a steady rate, commonly with important developmental handicap, and our explanations are lacking. One can conjecture about the possibility for greater roles than have been appreciated to date for environmental teratogens and subtle intrauterine infections.

Chromosomal Aberrations　Studies of the route to trisomy must view the event in its broader context, beyond the factors in maternal aging. As the National Down Syndrome Congress states, "Down syndrome is the leading clinical cause of mental retardation."

Origins of Prematurity　Important reductions have occurred in the infant mortality rate; much of this represents improved techniques in care for the small baby. However, the incidence of premature onset of labor remains high (approaching 7%) and is poorly understood. The most critical elements of support in prenatal care, which may impact on prematurity, must be identified (see Chapter 7 also).

Nosology

Pervasive Developmental Disorders   The 299 series in the *Diagnostic and Statistical Manual of Mental Disorders (DSM-III)* remains a troubled area. A structure has been created for Infantile Autism (299.0), but the exclusions are often uncertain. The category of 299.9 (Childhood Onset Pervasive Developmental Disorder) is now used, uneasily, for many clinical presentations formerly called "autistic-like" or the "atypical child," while 299.8 is somewhat vaguely listed as Atypical P.D.D., or none of the above. The more generic manual, *ICD-9-CM*, assigns early childhood psychoses to 299.8 and 299.9. In current clinical experience these unusual young people are being seen at a considerable rate (? increased). There is an appropriate concern when these diagnoses are used that there may on occasion be a discrete organic cause, as in fragile-X syndrome (Meryash, Szymanski, & Gerald, 1982).

Mucolipidoses   Confusion remains in the group of hereditary disorders of oligosaccharide and glycoprotein metabolism, formerly called mucolipidoses, where the elucidation of specific enzymopathies has proven arduous and the range of clinical expression uncertain.

Leukodystrophy   The finding of a major deficiency in white matter (e.g., by CAT scan) can have a multiplicity of possible origins that are difficult to differentiate and have widely varying implications.

Clinical Management

Alzheimer Disease in Down Syndrome   In current times the most pressing concern for families in which a member has Down syndrome is the accumulating alarm about premature senescence. The uncertainty regarding long-term preservation of function has been extremely defeating, and the inability of scientific workers to provide basic information on prevalence has fueled this.

Bone Marrow Transplant   The potential remains indeterminate for significant amelioration of the major inborn errors of metabolism by transplant of enzyme-producing bone marrow. Some evidence for suggestively useful assistance (Krivit et al., 1984; Rappeport & Ginns, 1984) keeps this prospect in the active consideration of clinicians and families.

Prader-Willi Syndrome   An era has begun of comprehensive efforts in the effective management of Prader-Willi syndrome, but this large task is hindered by limitations in understanding of the pathophysiology.

Maternal Serum Alpha-Fetoprotein Screening in Pregnancy   The promise of more accurate determination of risk for fetal involvement with

Down syndrome by the use of measurement of maternal serum alpha-fetopro-tein (AFP), has added greatly to the latter's value as a screen. Large-scale studies are needed now to determine the relevance of reduced AFP results. It has been suggested (Cuckle, Wald, & Lindenbaum, 1984; Merkatz, Nitowsky, Macri, & Johnson, 1984) that up to 40% of pregnancies with Down syndrome could be detected.

Immunological Characteristics of Persons with Down Syndrome Debate continues about idiosyncratic immune responses in Down syndrome, of potential relevance to infections, viral carrier states, and endocrinopathies.

Airway Problems in the Mucopolysaccharidoses Narrowing of the upper airway in young persons with Hurler, Hunter, and related mucopolysac-charide disorders, is a problem that is receiving increasing documentation (Shapiro, Strome, & Crocker, 1985). Difficulties that result include obstruc-tive sleep apnea and complications of anesthesia.

Supports to Individuals and Families

Thoughtful investigations are needed regarding: outcomes of home health care, positive components of family coping, successful adoption of children with disabilities, the role of self-advocacy, prevention of child abuse, differ-ent styles of early intervention programs, effects of integrated education, adapting the environment for better quality of life, use of creative art therapies, and supported work programs.

Ethical Core

Deployment of Resources Among the numerous areas where reflec-tion and study are appropriate regarding best use of available societal re-sources, one must list the use of expensive and hazardous experimental therapies. The accomplishment of bone marrow transplantation is estimated to cost $200,000 for a small child and have a mortality up to 40%. In the instance of the 6-month-old girl with GMl-gangliosidosis, already develop-mentally compromised, who was mentioned before, the dilemma was a major one. The family was seeking a facility that would perform the transplant; one assumes they will find such a facility.

Intervention in a Serious Phase of Terminal Illness A troubling aspect of the "right to treatment" discussion was at hand during postopera-tive complications of the 25-year-old man with Hunter syndrome. An analysis is needed of the dynamics of care providers, families, and our culture, for situations of this sort.

Community and Family Living Amendments The controversy en-gendered by Senate bills 2053 and 873 demonstrates the importance of having data from continuing research on the personal effects of family and small group living arrangements versus institutional residence for persons with mental retardation. Involved as well is our society's apparent lack of conviction regarding integration of exceptional citizens.

Systems

To complete the listing of areas where research could be productive, one could list as well: education of the public, techniques of clinical data collection, applications of new genetics methods, interdisciplinary team functioning, and interorganizational coalitions for enhancing prevention activities.

AN EXHORTATION TO THE RESEARCHER

This is a personal paper from the beginning, though with a broader motivation. I have shared with you a time-limited sample of this mental retardation clinician's endeavors, and then extracted from those some major lines of pertinence to research. I close, then, with a statement of my own convictions regarding which research directions should be considered preeminent. I pass these on as an entreaty to my colleagues in the research world. Furthermore, I pledge to be active in such studies as well, and to expedite the work of others.

Topics of Priority for the Researcher

1. Improved understanding of teratogenesis
2. The routes of chromosomal nondisjunction
3. Prevention of prematurity
4. The bases of autistic phenomena
5. Alzheimer-like changes in Down syndrome
6. Use of maternal serum alpha-fetoprotein in prenatal screening for Down syndrome
7. Gene cloning, recombinant DNA studies
8. The styles of early intervention programs
9. The educational outlook for persons with Down syndrome
10. The potential for supported work programs
11. Societal viewpoints on the deployment of human service resources

I urge others to look at 2 weeks of their own, keep a journal, and then consider what the implications of their individual dilemmas may be for the studies in which we all should join. I would welcome hearing from you.

REFERENCES

Crocker, A. C. (1982). Current strategies in prevention of mental retardation. *Pediatric Annals, 11,* 450–457.

Crocker, A. C. (1984a). Regionalization of health service systems. In E. M. Eklund (Ed.), *Developmental handicaps: Prevention and treatment II* (pp. 80–97). Silver Spring, MD: American Association of University Affiliated Programs for Persons with Developmental Disabilities.

Crocker, A. C. (1984b). Prevention of developmental disabilities: Fundamental considerations for public policy. In *Action for prevention* (pp. 52–63). Williamsburg, VA: Virginia Mental Retardation/Developmental Disabilities Prevention Conference.

Crocker, A. C., & Nelson, R. P. (1983). Mental retardation. In M. D. Levine, W. B. Carey, A. C. Crocker, & R. T. Gross (Eds.), *Developmental-behavioral pediatrics* (pp. 756–770). Philadelphia: W. B. Saunders.

Cronk, C. E. (1978). Growth of children with Down's syndrome: Birth to age 3 years. *Pediatrics, 61,* 564–568.

Cuckle, H. S., Wald, N. J., & Lindenbaum, R. H. (1984). Maternal serum alpha-fetoprotein measurement: A screening test for Down syndrome. *Lancet, i,* 926–929.

Kohrman, A. (1984). Pediatric home care: A ten-point agenda for the future. In *Home care for children with serious handicapping conditions* (pp. 98–105). Washington, DC: Association for the Care of Children's Health.

Krivit, W., Pierpont, M. E., Ayaz, K., Tsai, M., Ramsay, N. K. C., Kersey, J. H., Weisdorf, S., Sibley, R., Snover, D., McGovern, M. M., Schwartz, M. F., & Desnick, R. J. (1984). Bone-marrow transplantation in the Maroteaux-Lamy syndrome (Mucopolysaccharidosis Type VI). *New England Journal of Medicine, 311,* 1601–1611.

Latt, S. A., Kurnit, D. M., & Bruns, G. P., Schreck, R. R., Morton, C. C., Kunkel, L. M., Lalande, M., Aldridge, J., Neve, R., Tantravahi, U., Kanda, N., Lindner, G., & Meryash, D. (1985). Molecular genetic approaches to human diseases involving mental retardation. *American Journal of Mental Deficiency, 89,* 420–430.

Mackta, J. (Ed.). (1984). *One day at a time.* Cedarhurst, NY: National Tay-Sachs and Allied Diseases Association.

Menolascino, F. J. (1977). *Challenges in mental retardation.* New York: Human Sciences Press.

Menolascino, F. J., Neman, R., & Stark, J. A. (1983). *Curative aspects of mental retardation: Biomedical and behavioral advances.* Baltimore: Paul H. Brookes Publishing Co.

Merkatz, I. R., Nitowsky, H. M., Macri, J. N., & Johnson, W. E. (1984). An association between low maternal serum alpha-fetoprotein and fetal chromosomal abnormalities. *American Journal of Obstetrics and Gynecology, 148,* 886–894.

Meryash, D. L., Szymanski, L. S., & Gerald, P. S. (1982). Infantile autism associated with the fragile-X syndrome. *Journal of Autism and Developmental Disorders, 12,* 295–301.

Mitchell, W., Howard, R. B., Wharton, R., Osborne, P. S., & Van Gelder, M. (1985). Personal communication.

Newberger, E. H., & Newberger, C. M. (1984). *Sex with children: A moral analysis.* Presented at International Congress on Child Abuse and Neglect, Montreal, September 1984.

Pueschel, S. M. (Ed.). (1984). *The young child with Down syndrome.* New York: Human Sciences Press.

Pueschel, S. M., Tingey, C., Rynders, J. E., Crocker, A. C., & Crutcher, D. M. (1987). *New perspectives on Down syndrome.* Baltimore: Paul H. Brookes Publishing Co.

Rappeport, J. M., & Ginns, E. I. (1984). Bone-marrow transplantation in severe Gaucher's disease. *New England Journal of Medicine, 311,* 84–88.

Shapiro, J., Strome, M., & Crocker, A. C. (1985). Airway obstruction and sleep apnea in Hurler and Hunter syndromes. *Annals of Otology, Rhinology, and Laryngology, 94,* 458–461.

Watson. J. D. (1985). Talking about the best kept secret: Sexual abuse and children with disabilities. In M. J. Schliefer & S. D. Kelin (Eds.), *The disabled child and the family: An exceptional parent reader*. Boston: Exceptional Parent Press.

Woo, S. L. C., Lidsky, A. S., Guttler, F., Chandra, T., & Robson, K. J. H. (1983). Cloned human phenylalanine hydroxylase gene allows prenatal diagnosis and carrier detection of classical phenylketonuria. *Nature, 306,* 151–155.

Chapter 15

Future Prospects for Curing Mental Retardation

*Frank J. Menolascino
and Jack A. Stark*

In the 4 years since *Curative Aspects of Mental Retardation* was published, (Menolascino, Neman, & Stark, 1983) we have been genuinely touched by the compliments of our colleagues who have commented on the major theme of the book—the removal of the long-accepted concept of the "irreversibility" of mental retardation. Although we expected a more controversial response, the acceptance of the word "cure" in the context of primary, secondary, and tertiary prevention (particularly with the emphasis on the reversibility process of early secondary prevention) has been truly gratifying. It has been interesting to note the increasing use of the word "cure" with other syndromes in fund-raising efforts for research into the prevention and reversal of multiple sclerosis, muscular dystrophy, and spinal cord injury or paralysis.

As we attempt to understand what the very essence of mental retardation is and what are some of the fundamental aspects or common bases for mental retardation, we realize that we must develop a comprehensive multidisciplinary and interdisciplinary approach involving both the biomedical and behavioral sciences if we are to reduce significantly the different causes of mental retardation. In this chapter, we briefly address the future prospects for the preventive and curative intervention of this complex phenomenon.

Figure 1 is a visual representation of the growth and development of research toward the prevention and reversal of mental retardation. If we focus on Phases 3 and 4, it is clear that the biomedical and behavioral sciences are converging as a result of significant new breakthroughs in the neurosciences enhanced by such diagnostic techniques as the neuroimaging tools discussed in Section III. If one also accepts the previously mentioned statement that the growth and development of scientific achievements follow an exponential growth of doubling every 10–15 years, we would, therefore, have a 25%–40% increase in new research since the previous book was published. In short, based upon this formula, at least on a quantitative basis, over one half

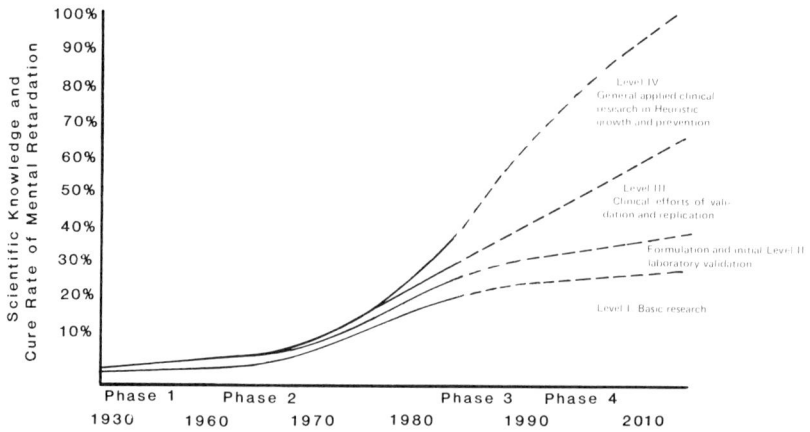

Figure 1. Growth and development of research on curative aspects of mental retardation as a function of scientific knowledge. (From Menolascino, F. J., Neman, R., & Stark, J. A. *Curative Aspects of Mental Retardation.* Baltimore: Paul H. Brookes Publishing Co., 1983; reprinted with permission.)

of our total accumulated knowledge of mental retardation research findings is the result of research done in the last 10–15 years. Although many of us who are researchers in the field have been tremendously frustrated by the lack of funding for research projects in these areas, we can at least be comforted to see the growing peripheral body of knowledge in both the biomedical and behavioral sciences that could have great implications for mental retardation. We continue to observe that national efforts to prevent mental retardation are fragmented with no coordinated system intact to bring together the findings of various disciplines. This state of affairs does not bode well if we are to accomplish the goal of reducing by 50% the prevalence of mental retardation by the end of the century as stated in the 1972 President's Committee on Mental Retardation. This is especially true for 75% of the mentally retarded population who are functioning in the mild range. The economic and sociocultural conditions that are contributory to this larger group of persons with mental retardation will make it quite difficult for us to accomplish this goal by the year 2000.

Also, in the previous text we presented analogies of the concept of cure based upon prevention and intervention analogies in agriculture, medicine, sociocultural retardation, and genetic disorders. In the agricultural analogy cited previously, we demonstrated that we can essentially produce a corn crop on an acre of land by using incremental and production technology that can bring about extremely rare results, such as 300 bushels of corn per acre. The same type of concept can be applied to persons with mental retardation in that a heuristic or cumulative building approach can boost up the mentally retarded

Table 1. Interdependence of research efforts in the diagnosis, treatment, and cure of mental retardation

Basic processes	Diagnosis	Treatment	Cure
1. Genetics	Cell sorter assessment of gene, enzyme-chromosome constellation	A. Cyto-genetic treatment B. In utero alteration via gene therapy	In utero correction of defective genes
2. Neurobiology	Cell, dendrite and axon analyses; understanding of underlying causes of cellular development	A. Cell stimulation B. Normalization of cell misfunctioning	A. Enhanced cell redevelopment B. Thickening of dendritic replacement
3. Neurophysiology	Specific physiological and metabolic analyses	A. Psychopharmacology B. Replacement diets	A. Normal biochemical functioning B. Absence of abnormal metabolic functioning
4. Neuroanatomy	Synaptic and neurotransmitter analyses	A. Selective medications for synaptic modulation B. Stabilization of remaining functions	Normal synaptic functioning via reestablishment of functional pathways
5. Neuropathology, neurosurgery	Brain tissue analysis	Tissue transplant	Tissue regeneration
6. Neuroendocrinology	Peptide and hormonal analyses	Peptide infusion or alteration	Enhancement of attention, memory, learning—attainment of higher cognitive state
7. Obstetrics/perinatology	Evaluation of fetal status and environment via ultrasound and amniocentesis	Intrauterine surgery, dietary procedures, and stress reduction	Prevention of prematurity, hypoxia, and high-risk entities

(continued)

Table 1. (continued)

Basic processes	Diagnosis	Treatment	Cure
8. Developmental neurotoxicology	Blood, organ, and tissue analyses and monitoring	Chellation and/or replacement therapy in newborn and early childhood	Prevention of teratogenesis, fetal alcohol syndrome, lead intoxication, etc.
9. Nutritional therapy	Blood, tissue, physiological, and behavioral analyses	Selective vitamin and mineral therapy with or without special diets	Increased cognitive, social adaptive, and physiological functioning
10. Behavior/learning	Standardized tests on biological intelligence, past functions and general intelligence: adaptation to external world	A. Infant stimulation— neuropsychological dimensions B. Very specialized education and training in childhood C. Support of family structure for the child	A. Enhanced levels of intellectual functioning B. Enhanced social adaptive learning C. Able to function independently in society (e.g., work)
11. Ecobehavioral analysis	Observation of behavior and physiological parameters	In vivo cognitive enhancement and prosthetic environmental settings	Enhanced adaptability leading to independent functioning

person's level of functioning to a higher level or even to a level in which they would no longer meet the criteria of cognitive, social, adaptive, and skill deficits. Table 1 illustrates this cumulative building process in which interdependence of research efforts in the diagnosis, treatment, and cure of mental retardation improves at each advanced level. It is representative of the roles that various biomedical and behavioral disciplines can play in alleviating all of the criteria that define mental retardation.

If we select as an example of this process a Down syndrome individual and trace through these steps, we realize that at any one stage we might be able to significantly or totally reverse the syndrome of mental retardation or at least significantly enhance one's level of functioning if only parts of each of the following biomedical/behavioral intervention strategies are utilized. For instance, if we are able to develop a prenatal diagnosis in the early embryonic phase of pregnancy, then we may be able to achieve genetic cures by the use of technological sampling and subsequent treatment of a few embryonic cells (i.e., the zygote) shortly after the onset of pregnancy. The effects of this curative intervention would be manifest throughout intrauterine life and early on throughout the extrauterine periods of life. Gene therapy could be successful then on an ongoing developmental basis in preventing mental retardation. If such a process is not possible, then we may be able to minimize brain dysfunction through enhanced cell redevelopment, enzyme and protein replacement, tissue regeneration, memory enhancers, pharmacological enhancement, and neurotransmitter functioning through the use of dietary procedures as well as "cognitive boosting" by environmental and behavioral intervention strategies.

Finally, we hope that people will remember this book as our second and renewed effort in achieving the goal of significantly reducing the prevalence of mental retardation. We also hope that those who question the reality of our goals will keep Merton's (1972) words in mind:

> If a writer is so cautious that he never writes anything that cannot be criticized, he will never write anything that can be read. If you want to help other people you have got to make up your mind to write things that some men will condemn. (p. 105)

REFERENCES

Menolascino, F. J., Neman, R., & Stark, J. A. (Eds.). (1983). *Curative aspects of mental retardation: Biomedical and behavioral advances.* Baltimore: Paul H. Brookes Publishing Co.

Merton, T. (1972). *New seeds of contemplation.* New York: New Directions Publishing Corporation.

Index

A-68 protein, 7
AAMD (American Association on Mental Deficiency), mental retardation definition of, 327
Absence seizure, 137
Abstraction, problem solving and, 308
Acetazolamide, 135
Acetone, 248
Achievement
  PKU and, 69, 71–73
  see also School performance
Acquired immunodeficiency syndrome, see AIDS virus
Adoption, 359–360
AFP (alpha-fetoprotein), 367–368
Agent Orange, neurotoxicity of, 254–255
Aging, cognitive function and, 24
AIDS virus, 16–17
Airway problems, mucopolysaccharidoses and, 368
Alcohol, fetal effects of, 20, 191–193, 247
Alobar holoprosencephaly, CT scan of, 127
Alpha-fetoprotein screening, 367–368
Alzheimer disease
  Down syndrome and, 367
  genetic marker for, 8–9
  proteins and, 7
American Association on Mental Deficiency (AAMD), mental retardation definition of, 327
Aminopterin, teratogenicity of, 247
Anatomical malformations, see Fetal abnormalities
Androgens, teratogenicity of, 247
Anencephaly, nutrition and, 187–189
Aneuploidy

secondary effects of, mechanisms in, 41
  see also Trisomy 21
Animal model(s)
  diet and, 161–173
    see also Diet, animal models and
  hemispherectomy, 105–107
  plasticity, 107–110
  trisomy 21, 46–55
    see also Trisomy 21, animal model of
Anticancer agents, teratogenicity of, 247
Anticoagulants, teratogenicity of, 247
Anticonvulsant treatment, 138–142
  magnesium as, eclampsia and, 185
  nutrition and, 190–191
  sedative drugs in, 141
  teratogenicity of, 247
Antithyroid agents, teratogenicity of, 247
Apolipoprotein E (Apo-E), nerve repair and, 14, 15
Asperger's syndrome, autism versus, 267
Asphyxia, perinatal, 120
Atonic seizure, 137
Attention, 306–307
Atypical absence seizure, 137
Autism, 261–262, 265–285
  biochemical findings in, 274–275
  biological substrate implications of, 271–272
  brain imaging in, 273–274
  clinical considerations in, 266–268
  deficits associated with, 268–270
  definition of, criteria for, 266–267
  genetic counseling and, 280–282
  genetic studies in, 276–279

379